Basrah, Baghdad, and Beyond

BASRAH, BAGHDAD, and BEYOND

The U.S. Marine Corps in the Second Iraq War

Col. Nicholas E. Reynolds, USMCR (Ret.)

Naval Institute Press
Annapolis, Maryland

Naval Institute Press
291 Wood Road
Annapolis, MD 21402

Library of Congress Cataloging-in-Publication Data

Reynolds, Nicholas E.
  Basrah, Baghdad, and beyond : the U.S. Marine Corps in the second Iraq
War / Nicholas E. Reynolds
       p.   cm.
    Includes bibliographical references and index.
    ISBN 1-59114-717-4 (alk. paper)
    1. Iraq War, 2003—Campaigns. 2. United States. Marine Corps—History—
21st century. I. Title.
    DS79.764.U6R493 2005
    956.7044'345—dc22

                                                              2005008537

Printed in the United States of America on acid-free paper ∞
12 11 10 09 08 07 06 05   9 8 7 6 5 4 3 2
First printing

CONTENTS

DIRECTOR'S FOREWORD

This book is about Marines in the first phase of Operation Iraqi Freedom. It spans the period from September 11, 2001, a clearly visible signpost on the road to war in Iraq, to March and April 2003, when the coalition removed Saddam Hussein from power, to November 2003, when the last few Marines and their equipment left Kuwait to return to their bases in the United States. For many Marines and sailors it turned out to be a relatively short respite from Iraq, but November saw a clear end to their participation in what has also been called the Iraq War and the Second Gulf War. When Marines returned to Iraq in 2004, they would be fighting a war that was very different from the one they had fought in the spring of 2003, and from the uneasy peace that followed in late spring and summer 2003.

The primary focus of the book is I Marine Expeditionary Force (MEF): the run-up to the war in 2002 and early 2003, especially the development of "the plan," with its many changes; the exhaustive rehearsals and other preparations; and then the conduct of Phases III and IV, decisive combat operations and the immediate postwar period, mostly under the control of the U.S. Central Command's Coalition Forces Land Component Command (CFLCC). That is not to say that the text neglects other organizations, such as the MarCent headquarters in Bahrain, or Combined/Joint Task Force–Consequence Management, or the Military Coordination and Liaison Command in northern Iraq, only that the primary focus is on the MEF and the interactions of its constituent elements. Other History and Museums Division texts will soon offer detailed narratives on Marines in Operation Enduring Freedom, Combat Service Support in Operation Iraqi Freedom, Task Force Tarawa, and the 3d Marine Air Wing.

This is not intended to be finished history, one of the big green volumes that tells the official story. It is too early for that. But it is not too early for a first draft of that history, necessarily imperfect, incomplete, and subjective. These are the first salvoes, intended to bracket the target and start the process of adjusting fire. My view is that it is important to get rounds down range early on, at a time when memories are still relatively fresh and a reasonable number of official sources have become available. My hope is that this book will prove to be a useful overview and introduction to the subject, especially for its Marine students who want to understand the prologue to the continuing war; that it will stimulate further research and healthy debate; and that readers will come forward with comments and corrections.

The author, Col. Nicholas E. Reynolds, USMCR, is an infantry officer who has served as a field historian and writer with the division since 1992. He is the author of two other histories, one on Marines in Operation Just Cause and another on Marines in the Caribbean during the 1990s. In January 2000 he became officer in charge of our Field History Branch. In January and February 2003 he directed the mobilization and deployment of all of our field historians and our one combat artist. Colonel Reynolds himself deployed to the theater to serve with the Military History Group at CFLCC. From that base he supervised Marine history operations during the combat phase of Operation Iraqi Freedom and helped to record combined and joint history. After the war he remained on active duty to write this text and is now a civilian on the faculty at the Naval War College in Newport, Rhode Island. He holds a D.Phil. in history from the University of Oxford.

This narrative is published as a work in the public domain. While I consider the sources and information presented to be authoritative, the opinions it contains are those of the author, not of the United States Marine Corps. It is my hope that making this work available to the widest audience in the near term will help to recognize the achievements—and the sacrifices—of the Marines and sailors who deployed to Iraq and Kuwait in 2003.

John W. Ripley
Colonel, USMC (Ret.)
Director, History and Museums Division

PREFACE

As Colonel Ripley points out, this is not a finished official history but an operational history from one official historian's point of view. It is not intended to be a desktop guide for future operators but rather a framework for understanding Marine participation in the Iraq War by describing how Marines coped with the set of challenges they faced in 2002 and 2003. Some of the implied lessons may turn out to be universal, such as the ways Marine staff officers worked in the joint arena. But some of the issues that were pressing in Iraq in March and April 2003 may turn out to be irrelevant in other times and places, except in the sense that the past is prologue, that we need to understand where we have been if we want to understand where we are.

Two-thousand-four was not a bad time to write this history. I had access to an array of sources that flowed into the History and Museums Division between the summer of 2003 and the spring of 2004. The efficiencies of the computer age played an important role. It has probably never been easier to track down sources and conduct follow-on interviews or ask participants to expand on the record. Above all, I tried to rely on primary sources: oral history interviews, command chronologies, personal journals, and various contemporary documents. Some of the material is based on personal observation from my time in Kuwait and Iraq in the spring of 2003. I found one or two published accounts particularly useful, especially those that clearly laid out how the author knew what he was reporting. (A personal favorite is *In the Company of Soldiers* by Rick Atkinson, a journalist who is also a respected military historian.) I have written extensive endnotes in the hope that future students of the war will be able to continue where I leave off. Occasionally, I have purposely omitted a name or a source because of the sensitivity of what someone told me. But that is rare. While I am not as free with my opinions as a journalist or an academic might be—I was, after all, writing on government time as a member of a disciplined service—I have tried to report both the good and the not so good.

This book would not have been possible without the assistance of a lot of people. I want to begin by acknowledging my brother Marines—and one sister Marine—in the Field History Branch, who, in 2003, did an amazing job of collecting the raw material of history before it was lost. They served in various billets, both Marine and joint, from the Horn of Africa to northern Iraq, enduring austere and sometimes dangerous conditions to get the job done. Their examples often inspired me. Lt. Col. Dave Watters, my successor as officer in charge, was the first to volunteer for mobilization in the fall of 2002, when the war clouds were still forming. Maj. Melissa Kuo, who served with 1st Force Service Support Group (FSSG), was nearly struck by the first missile the Iraqis fired at the Marine Expeditionary Force on 20 March 2003. CWO Bill Hutson, who drew a difficult assignment in the early days of the war, wrote to me a few days later to thank me for giving him the opportunity to serve instead of complaining about his luck. Col. Reed Bonadonna, a talented journal writer, was with Task Force Tarawa during the heavy fighting at An Nasiriyah. Lt. Col. Mike Visconage and Maj. Carroll Harris were at neighboring commands during the war, and we formed a kind of historical wolf pack when we flew into Iraq in late April to conduct a series of interviews in Ad Diwaniyah. It was a week I will not soon forget. Maj. Ted McKeldin, Army Lt. Col. Tommy Ryan, and I visited with the British division a few days later, collecting data in and around Basrah. Our British colleagues were wonderful hosts, and I cannot say enough good things about their hospitality and their openness. My hosts at CFLCC in the Military History Group under Col. Neil Rogers were equally generous with their resources, especially Maj. Shane Story, who stayed in touch after the war while he was writing the official CFLCC history.

After returning to Washington, I read every one of our historians' personal journals, as well as many of the documents and oral histories they collected—great sources for putting some flesh on the dry bones of official records. For the same reason, I looked at a lot of great combat art created by Staff Sgt. Michael D. Fay, who is not only one hell of a field Marine but also the only other member of the branch who was over fifty when the war broke out. It was good to have at least one other Marine in the group who could remember what it was like to be in the Corps in 1975. All of the field historians' materials ultimately found their way into the unit's finding aid, ably compiled by Lt. Col. Nate Lowrey in order to provide a guide to the vast amounts of data that we collected. Then–Lt. Col. Jeffrey Acosta, who served at MarCent headquarters in Bahrain during the war, added many useful documents he collected at that command, as well as a short history of MarCent in the operation. Col. Jon Hoffman, Maj. Chris Warnke, and Capt. Chris Kennedy did the same after their trips to Iraq in the late spring and summer of 2003. Staff Sgt. Dennis Shannon, with whom I went to Haiti on a memorable deployment many years ago, did an excellent job of cataloguing and selecting photographs for the book.

I also want to express my appreciation to all of the Marines who received our field historians in March and April 2003. The 3d Marine Air Wing and the FSSG went out of their way to make us feel welcome. So too did virtually all of the Marines who sat for interviews, before and after the war. They interrupted busy schedules to meet, in some cases for many hours. One commander even sat for a video teleconference interview a few hours before his Marine Expeditionary Unit mounted out for the Middle East. Another commander met with me for half a day in Quantico during his pack-out to return to the MEF and ultimately to Iraq. Talk about dedication to the historical record!

The staff of the Historical Division was uniformly helpful, from the director, Colonel Ripley, and the deputy director, Colonel Hoffman, to the Marine on the quarterdeck. I want to express my thanks to all and to single out a few people for special thanks. The chief historian of the Marine Corps, Chuck Melson, was there for us whenever we needed him. During the writing stage, he shared the remarkable trove of data that he collected, and he was good enough to read the manuscript in draft. The Field History Branch partnered with the Oral History and Archives Sections to conduct and acquire some thirteen hundred interviews. Dr. Gary Solis, friend and colleague, was instrumental in the process, as were Dr. Fred Allison, not to mention Fred Graboske and his staff, Christine Laba and Robert Piehel. Danny Crawford, Chief of Reference, remains one of the linch-pins of the division. Annette Amerman, also of Reference, did great work cor-recting and editing the troop list (the devil is always in the details when it comes to troop lists). I would be remiss if I omitted Charles Grow, the curator of the art collection, always imaginative, helpful, and cheerful; graphic designer Steve Hill, who produced wonderful maps; librarian Evelyn Englander, always willing to chase down one more source for a writer; and Carol Beaupre, the director's exec-utive assistant, ever responsive to calls for help of many kinds.

Jay Hines, the CentCom command historian, was good enough to read and comment on the text, as was my neighbor at the War College, Col. Bill Hartig, late of the I MEF staff. The manuscript finally got into decent shape thanks to the world-class word processing skills of Tina Offerjost of Stafford, Virginia, not to mention the editing skills of Jill Hughes.

Last but far from least is my wife, Becky, fondly known as "the Boss" to the branch, who not only agreed to let me interrupt my civilian career one more time and go to war for a few months but was also as loving and supportive as any man could want while I was away. I promised her that this would be my last big adventure. I'll try to keep that promise. But I will always cherish the camaraderie of the field historians, an unusual band of brothers, and keep a uniform on hand—just in case.

Semper Fidelis!

Nicholas Reynolds
Colonel, USMCR (Ret.)

Basrah, Baghdad, and Beyond

1

Tampastan and Afghanistan

Prelude to War in Iraq

Before September 11, 2001, the Marines at United States Central Command (CentCom) were housed in a tan building that looked something like a double-wide trailer on cinder blocks. It stood almost literally in the shadow of the imposing, and very permanent looking, CentCom headquarters at the north end of MacDill Air Force Base near the shores of Tampa Bay in Florida. Up until then it was forgivable for visitors to think that the Marine Forces Central Command, known as MarCent Tampa, was an afterthought, one of CentCom's many appendixes. That was not quite the case, although the situation was as complicated as an infernal machine designed by Rube Goldberg.

MarCent Tampa was a liaison element run by a chief of staff, a colonel by the name of John A. Tempone, who was stationed at MacDill and charged with representing the Marine Corps before CentCom. Colonel Tempone did not command any fighting forces, and there was no commanding general on the books, although there was an informal arrangement whereby the senior Marine on the CentCom staff could step into that role. When there was a formal requirement for Marine forces, or for a Marine general officer, the Commanding General, Marine Forces Pacific (MarForPac), who had two corps-size Marine expeditionary forces at his disposal, would engage; curiously, MarCent Tampa was an outpost of that command, whose headquarters was thousands of miles away in Hawaii at Camp H. M. Smith on the island of Oahu. MacDill and Smith had few things in common, aside from the palm trees. With forces spread from California to Korea and Okinawa, MarForPac was, by name and location, part of Pacific Command, well placed for engagement in Indonesia, Korea, or the

Philippines, while CentCom was responsible for the Middle East, on the other side of the world. It was the joint command that had fought the Gulf War of 1990–91 against Iraq and maintained steady pressure on Iraq throughout the 1990s and into 2001, mostly by orchestrating an international coalition of forces to enforce the no-fly zones in the northern and southern thirds of the country, which were known as Operations Northern Watch and Southern Watch.[1]

CentCom was now very much in the limelight again. The day after the attacks on New York and Washington on September 11, Secretary of Defense Donald H. Rumsfeld directed CentCom to prepare "credible military options" to neutralize the terrorist threat to the United States. This spanned contingency plans against a variety of potential targets, including Iraq and Afghanistan. The Bush administration initially believed these two countries had played a role in supporting or sponsoring the attacks. However, it soon became clear that it was Afghanistan, not Iraq, that harbored the terrorist organization that had planned the attacks. By 21 September the CentCom commander, Gen. Tommy R. Franks, USA, had briefed President George W. Bush on a plan to take the war to that organization, the Moslem fundamentalist Al Qaeda, and to the equally fundamentalist Taliban government of Afghanistan. It would not be an exaggeration to say that Al Qaeda, run by the Saudi millionaire Osama bin Laden, had purchased a share of the government, and that he could more or less do as he pleased in the remote, mountainous country wedged in between Pakistan and the other "stans," the small successor states to the Soviet Union north of Afghanistan.[2]

General Franks's plan to destroy the Taliban and to eradicate Al Qaeda relied heavily on indigenous opposition forces within Afghanistan, especially those known as the Northern Alliance, with heavy support from U.S. airpower, Special Forces, and other government agencies. A broad range of coalition partners, especially NATO allies, offered various kinds of support. The operation ultimately known as Enduring Freedom would consist of several simultaneous lines of operation ranging from reconnaissance and information operations to unconventional warfare and deep air attacks on enemy lines of communication. American forces would not be heavily committed on the ground. It was, like Goldilocks's porridge, neither too much nor too little but "just right," an imaginative mix of traditional and "transformational" approaches. No one on the United States side wanted to follow the Russian example, set during years of bloody and ultimately futile fighting, mostly by conventional forces against guerrilla bands, that ended in Russian defeat in 1989. Nor did they want to follow earlier American examples of simply firing a few missiles at an elusive enemy.[3]

Exactly what the Marine Corps could or would contribute to a fight in a landlocked country was not clear at first, but the MarForPac staff in Hawaii began to focus far more on CentCom than it normally did, eventually splitting itself more or less in two, with one group for the Pacific and another for the Middle East. The first challenge was to gain and maintain "situational awareness"—jargon in this war for knowing what was going on—and then to develop and weigh potential courses of action. For example, could any of the battalion-sized Marine Expeditionary Units (Special Operations Capable) (MEUs[SOC]), which were loaded on ships, spread throughout the world, and combat ready, be brought to bear? Two suggestions came from then–Lt. Gen. Michael W. Hagee, who was serving as the commander of I Marine Expeditionary Force (I MEF). He passed the word up the chain of command to CentCom that the Marine Corps could contribute Special Operations Capable MEUs to a fight in Afghanistan and that it could stand up a task force for a mission known as "consequence management."[4]

This was certainly in line with the thinking of the commandant of the Marine Corps, Gen. James L. Jones Jr., who wanted it known that the Marine Corps was willing and able to commit a Marine Expeditionary Brigade (MEB) to the new contingency. General Jones was a proponent of the view that a MEB (which could be made up of two MEUs) was the kind of organization that worked well in joint and coalition operations; a brigade of any kind was a relatively familiar concept to a planner from another service.[5]

The first suggestion set in motion a chain of events that led to the creation, under MarCent's operational control, of the Combined/Joint Task Force–Consequence Management (C/JTF-CM), which came to be based at Camp Doha, Kuwait. Commanded and staffed largely by Marines from I MEF augmented by Reserve Marines from I MEF Augmentation Command Element (I MACE), C/JTF-CM's unusual mission was to assist local governments in coping with the effects of a nuclear, biological, or chemical (NBC) attack by, for example, Al Qaeda or Iraq. Its table of organization was equally unusual, eventually coming to include contingents from a number of allied nations, especially NBC units from Germany, Slovakia, and the Czech Republic. Although it was never called to manage the consequences of an NBC attack during the eighteen months of its formal existence, from October 2001 to May 2003, it could have made an enormous difference had Kuwait or another Arab ally been attacked and was a notable experiment.[6]

Thousands of miles away from Kuwait, Afghanistan, or Hawaii, the small MarCent office building in Tampa began to hum with operational intensity—the increasingly more organized and purposeful chaos that characterizes a successful wartime staff. The deputy commander of MarForPac, Brig. Gen. John G. Castellaw, came to spend time on scene, helping with the interface between that command and CentCom. Other augmentees of various sorts, including recently retired officers and the categories of Reservists known as Individual Mobilization Augmentees (IMAs) and Individual Ready Reservists (IRRs), flowed in.[7]

Only half in jest, some began to refer to MacDill as "Tampastan." The work-day there was now as long as the workday for Americans in or near Afghanistan, but it was more complicated in some ways, and there were still the peacetime responsibilities of home and family after hours. It wasn't dangerous like combat, but it was very stressful, and a few CentCom officers suffered heart attacks or other forms of burnout. For Marines there was the additional twist of a compli-cated "battle rhythm" that spanned numerous time zones. They often had to repeat the same evolution many times over. For example, if an event happened in the Middle East during the day, which was nighttime in Tampa, MarCent offi-cers faced it when they came to work in the morning, which was still nighttime in Hawaii. They would then have to recap the facts, and their discussions, for Mar-ForPac a few hours later, near the end of their workday but at the beginning of MarForPac's. On many issues, they also had to engage I MEF, which was a con-stituent part of MarForPac. Built around 1st Marine Division, 3d Marine Air Wing, and 1st Force Service Support Group, it was the Marine Air-Ground Task Force (MAGTF) that was most likely to send Marines to fight in the Middle East. Being located at Camp Pendleton near San Diego, California, it was in yet another time zone.

There was another small staff at work on contingency plans for Marine opera-tions against the enemy in Afghanistan—the MarCent Coordination Element (MCE), commanded by the redoubtable Col. John B. Kiser and based at the Naval Support Activity (NSA), Bahrain, a compact facility where the Comman-der, U.S. Naval Forces, Central Command (NavCent) flew his flag. To bolster the handful of officers at MCE, the Marine Corps created the designation "Com-manding General, MarCent-Forward" for an officer who was already in theater for the multinational CentCom exercise in Egypt known as "Bright Star" and who was able to assume some of the responsibilities of a service component com-mander.[8] That officer was Brig. Gen. James N. Mattis, the commanding general of the 1st Marine Expeditionary Brigade (1st MEB, the smaller MAGTF embed-ded in I MEF), who was tasked briefly with commanding C/JTF-CM but soon shifted his focus to Bahrain and Afghanistan.[9]

A historian could follow the course of Marines in Operations Enduring Free-dom and Iraqi Freedom by answering the question, Where is General Mattis? Born in Richmond, Washington, and educated at Central Washington State College, Mattis was commissioned on 1 January 1972. In 2001 he was a trim fifty-one years old. Especially when wearing his reading glasses, he looked like a military intellectual, which would not have been far from the mark. But he was also a field Marine par excellence. Even in a Corps of energetic men and women with a bias for action, to say nothing of their single-minded devotion to their pro-fession, he stood almost in a class by himself. General Mattis's official biography on the World Wide Web was characteristically brief; it did not contain any personal data, only a list of the military schools he had attended and the commands he had held, along with the obligatory official photo (without the glasses). He had been a lifelong student of war, known for his voracious but discriminating appetite for the printed word. He believed "we face NOTHING new under the sun" (emphasis in original). It followed that to understand a problem, the approach he recommended was to study its history. For example, during Desert Shield/Desert Storm, when he had commanded an infantry battalion, he had read Bruce Catton's *Grant Takes Command,* studying the need for commanders to get along, as well as books by Erwin Rommel and Bernard Law Montgomery, presumably to learn about desert warfare.[10] On one occasion, General Mattis described himself as a student of "Sun Zinni," a tongue-in-cheek reference to another "one of them field Marines that reads," the iconoclastic Gen. Anthony C. Zinni, who had retired in 2000 after serving as the commander in chief at Cent-Com and had always stressed the need to understand the cultural dimension of war. General Mattis could relate well to enlisted Marines and to senior Pentagon officials, equally comfortable in the roles of salty platoon commander and—less salty—policy maker. Some have described General Mattis as more demanding than most commanders and slow to warm to officers who were not on his team, but also as willing to "go to hell and back" for his Marines.[11] He liked to say that the secret of success was "brilliance in the basics." There can be no question that that is what he demanded of his Marines, but there was nothing basic about his ability to think outside the box.

Within days of his arrival in Bahrain on 27 October, General Mattis was shaping plans for amphibious raids into Afghanistan, in effect following up on General Hagee and General Jones's readiness to use a MEU or, better yet, a MEB in that country. Mattis reported to Vice Adm. Charles W. Moore, the commander of NavCent, which included the Marines then afloat in theater. Admiral Moore was charged with responsibilities ranging from deployment and sustainment to warfighting, which meant he was able to send forces into combat. Moore has been described as an unusually aggressive officer, interested in finding ways to take the fight to the enemy; he and General Mattis had no trouble understanding each other. A fellow innovator, Admiral Moore took the unusual step of designating Mattis as the sole commander for the ad hoc Task Force 58 (TF 58), which made him "the first Marine to command a naval task force in wartime."[12] General Mattis was now serving both as ComMarCent-Forward and as commander of a task force preparing for combat. In accordance with his request, it would be designated Task Force "Chaos" after the effect he wanted to have on the enemy, and he himself would use the call sign "Chaos" for the next two years.[13]

Under the control of NavCent were the two amphibious ready groups (ARGs) in theater. Each carried a MEU(SOC) built around a battalion landing team of infantry, a helicopter squadron, and a combat service support element. The two units were the 15th MEU(SOC), in the ARG built around the USS *Peleliu* (LHA 5), and the 26th MEU(SOC), in the ARG built around the USS *Bataan* (LHD 5). Together they formed TF 58. Admiral Moore made it clear he did not want TF 58 to have a large staff, like some MEBs that had literally hundreds of Marines and sailors on their books. This was fine with Mattis, who liked to work with a very small staff of trusted individuals. The upshot was that the staff stayed small, never exceeding forty officers and men. It focused on broad-brush planning, while the MEUs relied on their own staffs for the detailed planning and conduct of operations. A sensible corollary was the decision not to "composite" the two MEUs—that is, to meld them into one force under one staff—but to keep them intact and to create a supported/supporting relationship between them whereby one MEU would take the lead for a time, and then the other. In the words of the TF 58 command chronology: "While one MEU executed a mission, the second MEU . . . could conduct detailed planning for the follow-on mission."[14]

By 3 November, General Mattis had briefed Admiral Moore on his concept of operations. The admiral provided additional guidance, telling the Marines he wanted them to defeat Taliban and Al Qaeda forces. Moore thought the Marines would make a difference, that a "squad of Marines running through Kandahar would turn the tide."[15] But soon the mission changed from conducting raids to seizing a forward operating base in order to attack lines of communication and generally support coalition operations.[16]

By the middle of November, the coalition's Afghan allies had driven the Taliban's ragtag forces from most of the country's larger cities, including the capital, Kabul, and TF 58 was ready to launch. On 25 November, traveling some four hundred nautical miles from the beachhead, 15th MEU(SOC) flew in to seize a landing strip in Afghanistan that became known as Forward Operating Base (FOB) Rhino. This was the start of roughly two months of Marine operations in country, first in and around Rhino, and later from Kandahar Airfield, which 26th MEU(SOC) was to seize on 14 December.

Repeating a phrase attributed to war correspondent Richard Harding Davis in 1885 and used many times since, General Mattis wrote in a 26 November message, "the Marines have landed and the situation is well in hand."[17] It was, in the words of the Naval Institute's annual review of the Marine Corps, a display of "flexibility and operational reach . . . [that] stunned many outsiders."[18] The task force's movement from ship to shore was right out of the Marine Corps doctrine known as "Expeditionary Maneuver Warfare," which called for fast and deep movements, directly from the sea to objectives inland. But this was still something relatively new and largely untried. General Mattis was not exaggerating when he commented that if he had proposed this kind of operation at Quantico or Newport, Rhode Island, the home of the Naval War College, he would have been told it could not be done.[19]

In the meantime, back in Hawaii there were changes afoot that would shift some of the burden from the small liaison elements in Tampa and Bahrain, and from General Mattis himself. On 24 October, the Commander, MarForPac, Lt. Gen. Earl B. Hailston, had formally taken on the additional duty of Commander, U.S. MarCent, and begun to play a much more prominent role in the CentCom arena.[20] By January 2002 Hailston was in the process of moving his flag to Bahrain "to establish [the] MARCENT HQ in theater in support of CINCCENT [Commander in Chief, CentCom] and Operation Enduring Freedom."[21] Even though he occasionally shuttled back to Hawaii, Bahrain became his home for much of the next year and a half.[22] Hailston's move, made with some two hundred of his Marines, signaled the Marine Corps' intent to build a strong infrastructure in theater to support Marine commanders on the ground. It was as much a matter of Iraq as it was of Afghanistan; by early 2002 the administration had directed the military to plan for a possible war with Iraq while consolidating its gains in Afghanistan.

The new MarCent headquarters in the Gulf were not even up to the standard of MarCent Tampa's building; like virtually all Marine headquarters in and around the Persian Gulf through the summer of 2003, it was never much to look at, let alone to work in. At first MarCent even had trouble finding a home in theater. When they landed at Sheikh Issa Air Base in Bahrain, the Marines from Hawaii and Tampa started to build an expeditionary headquarters on a part of the base. But the initiative had not been fully cleared with the Bahrainis—there had been some kind of cross-cultural misunderstanding—and they "requested" that MarCent find somewhere else to go. The MCE commander, Colonel Kiser, who was familiar with Arab ways and with the Navy establishment, came up with a quick solution. He crafted an arrangement with NavCent for MarCent to come onto the Naval Support Activity itself, even though there was little room to spare on that small base. NavCent agreed to allow MarCent to set up on a baseball field that was, by turns, the source of fine dust and, when it rained, some very sticky mud.[23]

The result was an unusual overlay of temporary structures on a base with some amenities. Some of the MarCent Marines worked in the general-purpose tents on the baseball field. They had some air-conditioning—as much for the computers as for the Marines—but were often hot and uncomfortable. Other Marines worked in only slightly more comfortable expeditionary buildings. Like most Marines on major staffs after September 11, the MarCent Marines worked incredible hours, under great pressure, with little time off. But there was a small upside: less than one hundred yards away was a well-stocked food court, as well as a gym, exchange, and swimming pool. Sometimes, when the force protection condition was high, one might witness the anomalous sight of half-camouflaged U.S. Navy personnel with loaded rifles sitting or lying among the palm trees and brush outside the food court, on the lookout for any terrorists who might have made it through the perimeter, which was an elaborate affair with concrete barriers, barbed wire, and sentries. (This was not quite as farfetched as it sounds; not only was there a continuing terrorist threat, but, especially in early 2003, there were also anti-American demonstrations and occasional terrorist attacks throughout the region.) If there had been a firefight, the personnel on base could have watched it while sipping cappuccinos. It was an unusual way to go to war.

MarCent now became the only purely "service component command" in theater, with the enormous responsibility of providing and sustaining thousands, and potentially tens of thousands, of Marines and sailors. Like his counterparts at NavCent; Army Forces, Central Command (ArCent); and Air Forces, Central

Componency

The first time outsiders tried to understand the relationship between Central Command's "service components" and "functional components," their heads spun and they had to reach for their favorite painkiller. Each service had a "service component," with a headquarters and a staff, commanded by its senior officer in theater. These components were MarCent, NavCent, ArCent, and CentAF. Their purpose was to provide and sustain their forces. NavCent and CentAF were commands that could easily transform themselves into functional commands—that is, commands responsible for combat at sea and in the air. It seemed natural for the naval commander to take on the additional duty of the Coalition Forces Maritime Component Commander (CFMCC) for naval warfare, while the CentAF commander could become the Coalition Forces Air Component Commander (CFACC) for the fight in the air. There was even a commander for special operations, Coalition Forces Special Operations Command (CFSOC). It also seemed natural for the ArCent commander to become dual-hatted as the Coalition Forces Land Component Commander (CFLCC), but what about MarCent? There were no provisions for an Expeditionary Forces Component Command. In the Gulf War of 1990–91, there had been nothing even remotely like a functional component command for the war on land; the CentCom commander, Army Gen. H. Norman Schwartzkopf, had decided to take on the additional duties of being his own land component commander, not unlike the Confederate general Braxton Bragg, who had been his own supply officer. After he became the CentCom commander in the late 1990s, General Zinni had wrestled with the problem. His view was that the United States had fought two ground wars in Desert Storm. General Schwartzkopf had taken on more than any one man could handle, and the efforts of the Army and the Marine Corps had not been fully coordinated. Zinni decided that he wanted the Army and the Marine Corps to establish a standing joint land forces component command in the region. This became Joint Task Force–Kuwait (JTF-Ku), with its headquarters at Camp Doha, Kuwait.* Marines—and Marine units—rotated through the command, whose staff was largely identical with that of ArCent. In the fall of 2001, for example, then–Brig. Gen. Emerson Gardner Jr., USMC, was in command of JTF-Ku. ArCent and JTF-Ku morphed into CFLCC in late 2001, under the command of a three-star Army general, Lt. Gen. Paul T. Mikolashek, who moved his flag to Kuwait in December. Like his predecessor Zinni, General Franks wanted a strong CFLCC, with its own staff, to focus on the ground war while he focused on his own responsibilities for the war at the next higher level. The officer who was to command CFLCC in 2003, Lt. Gen. David D. McKiernan, found that there was "huge goodness in that arrangement."**

*Tom Clancy with Gen. Tony Zinni (Ret.) and Tony Koltz, *Battle Ready* (G. P. Putnam's Sons: New York, 2004), p. 315. See also Zinni interview. In 2003, while serving at CFLCC, Marine Brig. Gen. Christian M. Cowdrey made much the same point, commenting that the combined/joint land headquarters CFLCC fulfilled a function that would have been difficult for any other organization to fulfill—that of orchestrating the plan. Cowdrey interview.
**Kevin Peraino, "Low-Key Leader; Lt. Gen. David McKiernan Is the Soft-spoken Soldier with the Hard Job of Commanding U.S. Ground Forces in Iraq," *Newsweek* Web Exclusive, 19 March 2003.

Command (CentAF), General Hailston reported to the Commander in Chief, Central Command, General Franks, who held sway over all U.S. forces in the region, whatever their purpose. Unlike his counterparts, General Hailston was not a warfighter. He would get the Marines to the war, make sure they had what they needed for the fight, and generally offer advice to General Franks on how best to employ them. It was Hailston's job to look forty-five to sixty days into the future, anticipate Marine requirements, and then fulfill them, all in all an enormous undertaking. But when Marines went into combat, they would fight under one of the "functional components" like the Coalition Forces Maritime Component Command (CFMCC), which was NavCent's warfighting guise. For example, Admiral Moore became both the NavCent commander and the CFMCC commander. There were similar arrangements for CentAF and ArCent to become, respectively, the Coalition Forces Air Component Command (CFACC) and the Coalition Forces Land Component Command (CFLCC). This was a radical departure from the organization for Desert Storm some ten years earlier, which had been fought without a unified land command.[24]

This created a dilemma for the Marine Corps, naval infantry with an air arm that did not fit neatly into any of these categories. In 2001 the result was another set of complications. Task Force 58 initially reported to NavCent/CFMCC. This was a natural relationship, especially while the task force remained afloat. Once it was ashore, and after CFLCC had stood up in mid-November, it had to develop a relationship with that headquarters, which had assumed responsibility for all operations on land in Afghanistan. Accordingly, on 30 November, CFMCC assigned tactical control (TaCon) of TF 58 to CFLCC—without giving up operational control (OpCon). Especially at first there was some friction between TF 58 and CFLCC; the CFLCC culture was "Big Army," the world of large staffs and detailed reporting, certainly a change for the Marines on TF 58. But over time everyone made it work: the "TF 58 staff was able to adapt to the new information requirements while continuing to develop a solid working relationship with the CFLCC staff. The positive relationship would last throughout the operation as CFLCC buttressed and represented CTF 58's interests."[25]

Most Marine staff officers in the Persian Gulf became well versed in the intricacies of operational control and tactical control. By and large, what General Hailston exercised was operational control—organizing and employing forces, sustaining them, and assigning general tasks—but not tactical control, which was the specific direction and control of forces, especially in combat. (The two exceptions were C/JTF-CM and an organization known as the Marine Logistics Command [MLC], which would play a prominent role in the Iraq War in 2003.) Like the organization for the land war, this, too, was different from Desert Storm. Then the senior Marine in theater, Lt. Gen. Walter E. Boomer, had commanded I MEF and MarCent, a heavy burden for one commander, who in both capacities reported directly to General Schwarzkopf.[26]

General Zinni has argued that especially in a major contingency, each function requires a separate staff, with a different focus.[27] General Hailston's chief of staff, Col. Stephen W. Baird, believed the arrangement in Desert Storm had stressed the I MEF staff and forced General Boomer to divide his time between warfighting and service component issues.[28] Having one commander responsible for "shaping, providing, and sustaining" Marine forces and another commander for warfighting would free the warfighter to focus on combat. The service component commander, who would be senior, could forge a relationship with the commander in chief and protect the sanctity of the Marine Air-Ground Task Forces (MAGTFs)—that is, resisting the understandable propensities of non-Marines to break MAGTFs into their building blocks, splitting ground and air components apart and sending them to fight with their counterparts in the Army and the Air Force.[29] The MET commander in Iraq, General Conway, later added the commonsense point that it would have been difficult for him to command both

MarCent and MEF, since in one capacity he would be the equal of the CFLCC commander, and in the other, his subordinate.[30]

Even with the improved organization of the force, there was some service rivalry. One notable point of contention was the "force cap" placed on the Marines while TF 58 was ashore—CentCom decreed that initially there could not be more than one thousand Marines and sailors in Afghanistan in late 2001. Some Marines interpreted this as a gratuitous slap in the face, "Big Army" making sure the Marines did not steal the show—and, by extension, making it easier for the Army to assume the Marine mission in Afghanistan, a process that was well under way by mid-January 2002.[31] But the Marines complied and were still able to carry on with their mission.

TF 58 was released from CFLCC control on 3 February 2002.[32] Although small numbers of Marines stayed in country, either as individuals or as units, for quite some time, the 26th MEU(SOC) left Afghanistan on 13 February. This spelled the end of TF 58's engagement in that country. Now the nature of TF 58's achievement was even clearer. Apart from validating some of the tenets of expeditionary maneuver warfare, it showed Marines, literally and figuratively, how far they had come from the traditional "two up and one back" mind-set that had characterized the war in Vietnam and, to a certain extent, Desert Storm, which had had some of the characteristics of an old-fashioned linear battlefield.[33]

Task Force 58's experience also showed Marines how far they had come since Desert Storm in another way. Despite the friction over matters like the force cap (some friction was inevitable), there had been nothing like the bad blood and the temper tantrums that are discernable beneath the surface of the memoirs of the Gulf War; in Afghanistan, and then in Iraq, senior participants almost uniformly reported that the level of cooperation was unparalleled, both among the services as institutions and among their chiefs as individuals. To cite just one example, CFLCC's General McKiernan stated categorically "there were no rifts" between the various commanders.[34]

There are a number of possible explanations for the "era of (relative) good feeling"—the general atmosphere of trust—among the services after September 2001. These range from the maturing of joint routines at the combatant commands, to the exigencies of the situation—that is, the unifying effect of the events of September 11—to the backgrounds and the personalities of the commanders. A number of controversial issues, such as the employment of Marine Air in the joint environment, which had been a serious point of contention during Desert Shield/Desert Storm, had more or less been resolved during the decade since the Gulf War. CentCom commanders like General Zinni—first and always a Marine but also something of an iconoclast and nothing if not a "joint" visionary—had created and exercised joint structures such as Joint Task Force–Kuwait, with its provisions for alternating Marine and Army commanders. Similarly, Operations Northern Watch and Southern Watch, run for years by U.S. and allied air forces to enforce the no-fly zones in the top and bottom one-thirds of Iraq, were successful combined and joint operations.[35]

Analyzing the backgrounds of the participants in the Iraq War, historians Williamson Murray and Maj. Gen. Robert Scales, USA (Ret.), have made the comment that the officer corps was far better trained and educated in 2003 than it had been during the Gulf War, let alone Vietnam. The key here is the word "educated"; beginning in the 1980s, officers were not only well trained, able to perform battlefield tasks, but they could also think in "operational terms." "The new emphasis," Murray and Scales wrote in their excellent overview of the period, "was on maneuver, deception, exploitation, and decentralized leadership."[36] In the Marine Corps the reform movement had started informally with meetings after hours at Quantico—sometimes over beer, but just as likely over coffee or Diet Coke—and spread little by little to other bases. Many of the ideas that emerged were eventually enshrined in doctrine, particularly *FMFM 1: Warfighting,* during the commandancy of Gen. Alfred M. Gray in the late 1980s. Not everyone became a maneuverist, but it is fair to say that by the end of the 1990s, virtually everyone was familiar with the term and had been influenced by it in some way.[37]

The personalities of the commanders, and how they meshed, were also part of the picture. General McKiernan commented that "the big strength in this campaign was the personalities of the various component commanders. . . . You can say a lot of that [inter-service cooperation was possible] because of developments in joint doctrine and training . . . but a lot of it [was] . . . also in the chemistry between . . . the leaders."[38] General Franks, with his down-to-earth style, was known as an officer who listened to his subordinates. A strong proponent of military transformation, he was a commander who identified the desired "effects . . . and tasks and purpose, but [left] . . . the planning to the component commanders."[39] He had a long-standing "joint" reputation, having been the ArCent commander under Zinni. It had been a natural progression for him to take the commander's chair and continue the joint tradition. Even after becoming the commander, General Franks had stayed in touch with General Zinni, using him as an unofficial mentor and even trying, in late 2002, to use him as an official mentor for a CentCom exercise. (Zinni did not come to theater, because by then his blunt pronouncements against the coming war had made him persona non grata with the Pentagon.)[40] At MarCent, General Hailston had an unusually varied background, having served as an enlisted infantryman officer, an aviator (whose call sign was "Titan"), and an FSSG commander. He had relationships with other senior commanders, especially Coalition Forces Air Component

Command's (CFACC) Lt. Gen. T. Michael Moseley, that went back many years. He also had a reputation for not suffering colonels gladly and for taking good care of his younger Marines—not necessarily bad traits to have in 2002 and 2003 (at least so long as you weren't a colonel). The journals of the field historian assigned to his headquarters, Lt. Col. Jeffrey Acosta, attested to the general's ability to ask penetrating questions across a broad range of subjects, and to keep supplies and equipment flowing to theater.[41]

Murray and Scales assert that General McKiernan, who was to become CFLCC commander in September 2002, "proved to be an inspired choice."[42] An armor officer who was quiet but compelling, McKiernan's background included joint and combined experience, in addition to senior Army commands. He, too, was not afraid of new ideas and wanted to find the best organization for the fight—as opposed to doing things the way they always had been done. He had what *Newsweek* was to call "a temperament as . . . even as the desert," which also made it easy for him to work with other services.[43]

For virtually all Marines in theater the officer who set the tone was Lt. Gen. James T. Conway. A graduate of Southeast Missouri State University, he was commissioned in 1970 and had had a successful career in the infantry. When away from the fleet, he served as the commanding officer of the Basic School and then as president of the Marine Corps University. He also served two tours on the joint staff in Washington. From 2000 to 2002 he was the commanding general of the 1st Marine Division, and then from August to November 2002 he served as the deputy commanding general at MarCent, which gave him an opportunity to work closely with General Hailston on CentCom issues while he waited to take command of I MEF. This was the commandant's initiative. General Jones wanted to maintain continuity on the West Coast and to make General Conway even better prepared for his next job—to command the MEF and to balance its equities against MarCent and CFLCC requirements.[44]

Murray and Scales described General Conway as "big"—he was well over six feet tall—"bluff, well-read, and well educated," and concluded that he "represented all that was best about the new United States Marine Corps, which General Al Gray as the commandant had built up."[45] He was a popular commander, described as an officer and a gentleman who was good to work for and who took care of his troops.[46] He was nothing if not involved in what his subordinates were doing. For example, he had a policy of wanting to be briefed in person on unusual, high-risk evolutions, as a young British reconnaissance officer was to discover during the war when he was whisked from his position in the desert in order to brief the MEF commander, in person, on an upcoming operation. It was typical of General Conway to focus on the extraction plan; he wanted to be sure there was a plan to take care of the soldiers and Marines in the worst case.[47] Even months after the war, he remained acutely conscious of the casualties that had occurred during the campaign—able to recite numbers and remember individual cases.[48] He has described his own command style as "democratic," which meant he preferred to command by first listening to his subordinates and then outlining his intent. He knew when to give his subordinates free rein and when to intervene. A review of the journals kept by the field historian at I MEF headquarters during the Iraq War reveals that, like General Hailston, General Conway spent much of the time asking questions and gathering information. They also show that he was typically optimistic, slow to anger, and virtually unflappable—equal to any challenge, whether contemplating the possibility of a chemical attack or dealing with a difficult counterpart or subordinate. These were all traits that he would need in Operation Iraqi Freedom.[49]

2

Inside Our Own OODA Loop

Joint Planning for War in Iraq

Operation Enduring Freedom set the stage for Operation Iraqi Freedom. The second operation was not a clear-cut sequel to the first; for military planners, there was no straight line from success in Afghanistan in the winter of 2001–2 to a war in Iraq in 2003 to remove the dictator Saddam Hussein from power. But Enduring Freedom was in many ways the starting point for Iraqi Freedom.

Coalition Forces Land Component Command (CFLCC) and Coalition Forces Maritime Component Command (CFMCC) were still very much in existence when the focus shifted from Afghanistan to Iraq early in 2002. The Marines in Task Force 58 who fought in Afghanistan between November 2001 and January 2002 had operated under both of these commands and had developed good relationships with them. If anything, General Franks was more convinced of the need for an organization like CFLCC in a war with Iraq. In Afghanistan there were few U.S. troops on the ground, but a war with Iraq could be a larger, more complex undertaking by far and most likely would be won or lost on the ground. Alongside CFLCC and CFMCC, CFACC and CFSOC also remained very active commands that the Marines would engage.

Both for the individuals who went to Afghanistan and for the organizations that sent them, the experiences of TF 58 in Enduring Freedom set some of the specific conditions for war in Iraq. Integrated into a combined, joint operation that fused airpower, special operations, and information operations, the Marines had operated hundreds of miles from the beachhead, relying heavily on Marine airlift, especially by CH-53E Sea Stallion helicopters followed by KC-130 Hercules cargo carriers. They had succeeded without a large staff, or a plan that was hundreds of pages long, relying instead on common sense, good liaison officers, and "hand con" (not a formal relationship like TaCon or OpCon but one sealed with a handshake).

The focus began to shift to Iraq even before TF 58 left Afghanistan. In the wake of September 11, the administration had looked to see if Iraq was behind the attacks on the World Trade Center and the Pentagon before deciding to fight in Afghanistan. But it seems that Iraq was never far from the administration's mind and that while overthrowing the Taliban and uprooting Al Qaeda were short-term objectives, Iraq—more specifically, removing the regime of Saddam Hussein—had always been a long-term objective. Military planners followed the administration's lead on both Iraq and Afghanistan.[1] In the fall of 2001, staff officers from Headquarters Marine Corps (HQMC) to CentCom to CFLCC were considering the possibility that U.S. forces could be called upon to invade Iraq. There were some preliminary planning directives, but even without them many Marines and Army officers simply assumed that Iraq would come after Afghanistan. CFLCC's Maj. Gen. Henry W. Stratman, USA, spoke for many when he said that after September 11 the assumption was not whether, but when, the United States would go to war with Iraq.[2]

In January 2002, General Hailston, in his capacity as the Commanding General, Marine Forces Pacific, directed I MEF to focus its efforts on preparing for "contingencies" in the CentCom theater: "CG, MARFORPAC . . . decided to focus I MEF efforts on preparation for contingencies in the CENTCOM theater. I MEF's role in PACOM activities was minimized or assumed by III MEF and MARFORPAC" to the virtual exclusion of other activities.[3]

This was when the MEF's "iron majors and lieutenant colonels" (along with a few colonels) who make any large staff run earned their pay. They entered into what was for many of them the most intense period of their careers in the Marine Corps, one that would not let up for some eighteen months. Even before they deployed from the United States, they came close to spending every waking minute working on the plan, often in windowless secure spaces. When they weren't working in a vault, they might be traveling from one drab base to another for a conference or a war game. They no longer had any time for themselves—let alone their families or their "honey do" lists.

For the I MEF G-2, the focus on CentCom meant embarking on "a wide variety of activities, including presentation of many staff orientation and mission analysis briefings, . . . supporting estimates and plans, . . . development [of requirements], . . . hosting visits from national and theater intelligence organizations (CIA, DIA, MCIA, CentCom, ArCent, and V Corps) and [making] liaison trips." For its part, the MEF's G-3 Current Operations section became involved in various exercises in the CentCom area of operations (AO). In April, for example, it participated in the exercise "Lucky Sentinel," a combined/joint computer-assisted command post exercise designed to train and sustain the battle staff of Joint Task Force–Kuwait. It was conducted "in conjunction with ARCENT; CENTAF; and the Kuwaiti military"—good practice for the events that were about to unfold. Similarly, the MEF G-3's Future Operations section used exercises like "Desert Scimitar" and "Lucky Sentinel" to prepare for war in the Middle East, while the MEF G-5 was involved in longer-range, high-level operational planning. In the subdued words of the I MEF command chronology, "G-5 directed most of its efforts . . . [to] . . . details [of] I MEF's slice of the USCINC-CENT's plan in concert with the nation's strategic objectives."[4]

This was a dramatic understatement. For a few months, G-5 took the lead in the intense and exhausting task of laying the groundwork for Marines to participate in a war for Iraq. In January 2002, General Hagee sent one of his lead planners for Korea, Lt. Col. George W. Smith Jr., to Tampa with Col. Jonathan G. Miclot, the G-5 officer at 3d MAW. Their mission was to represent MarCent, not just the MEF, on CentCom's Long-Range Planning Element (LRPE).[5] This was a happy consequence of Marine staffing practices. In his MarCent capacity as a component commander, General Hailston made the decision to let I MEF, the warfighting command subordinate to him, play the leading role in operational planning.

The LRPE was small and run mostly by Army ground officers, who had been working in the same directorate as Maj. Gen. Keith J. Stalder, an even-tempered Marine aviator who was the deputy J-3 at CentCom and would become the deputy commanding general of the MEF later in the year. Since late 2001, the focus of the LRPE's very compartmented work had been Iraq, and the timeline was short—this was not theoretical planning for some unlikely contingency in the distant future. The word was that CentCom might need to be ready to fight as early as the spring of 2002; this could be a "come as you are" war. In that regard it would not be unlike the campaign in Afghanistan, which had been a relatively quick success.

The vision that guided the planning was to win by creating "shock and awe" through multiple lines of operation putting simultaneous pressure on the enemy—from the air, from conventional ground operations, and from various kinds of special operations, to include "non-kinetic" operations and operations by proxies like the Kurds. (There were three main groups in Iraq: the Shia majority, the ruling Sunni minority, and the Kurds. The Kurds lived a more or less autonomous existence in the northeast corner of the country and had large, well-armed militias. Neither the Kurds nor the Shia had much love for Saddam Hussein, who had suppressed them in unimaginably brutal ways.) For Marines, "shock and awe" was something like the "combined arms effect," on a grand scale, of forcing the enemy into a series of dilemmas he could not resolve; if he turned to face one threat, he would make himself vulnerable to another threat. It was something like facing mortars and machine guns at the same time: was the infantry better off staying in fixed positions during a mortar attack, or getting out of its holes into a field of machine gun fire?

While often associated with the air offensive in what was not yet officially known as Operation Iraqi Freedom, "shock and awe" was more than a theory of air warfare. The concept has both a recent and a more distant past. In the recent past it can be traced to a book published by the National Defense University (NDU) in Washington in December 1966 by Harlan K. Ullman and James P. Wade titled *Shock and Awe: Achieving Rapid Dominance,* with contributions by retired generals Charles Horner, USAF, and Frederick Franks, USA, both of Desert Shield/Desert Storm fame, and retired Adm. Leon A. Edney, who had been commander in chief at Atlantic Command. The authors' purpose was to offer an alternative to the strategy of overwhelming force—sometimes called the Powell Doctrine, on display in Desert Storm—by pointing to the potential of the many new technologies to achieve "rapid dominance" that would paralyze the enemy's will to resist, ideally but not necessarily before any ground forces were committed. It is easy to see why this doctrine is especially attractive to the Air Force, as it suggests that air power alone could be decisive.

The authors of the NDU book readily conceded that their theory was not entirely new, with antecedents in the World War II concept of "Blitzkrieg" and various operations since. Iraq War historians Williamson Murray and Maj. Gen. Robert Scales discuss how General Zinni and his Army counterparts used ideas like "rapid dominance" and "overmatching power" when they considered joint contingency plans against Saddam Hussein.[6] Zinni himself has commented that after Desert Storm, a more or less traditional war, he was convinced that the Marine Corps needed to learn to think along multiple lines of operation. Marines would also have to work better in the joint arena. These were, he said, the lessons he tried to inculcate in I MEF after he became its commanding general in 1994. He added the sage comment that, like many, he imagined at the time that he was on the cutting edge, but realized later that the winds of change were blowing in other places in the Marine Corps around the same time. Transformation is not a straightforward, top-down process.[7]

Looking back to 1989, Murray and Scales found an interesting precedent—a small war before Desert Storm that was almost like a laboratory experiment of the ideas that dominated planning in 2001 and 2002. This was Operation Just Cause in Panama in 1989: "Maneuver in Panama was nonlinear and focused on control of the whole operational area rather than on the sequential capture of key terrain and high ground characteristic of more traditional forms of maneuver."[8] Just

Cause was complemented by new forms of technology, such as laser-guided bombs that enabled pinpoint targeting, that were to improve markedly over the next ten years, in turn enabling further strides in doctrine. Murray and Scales concluded that Just Cause had little effect on Desert Storm, which did not incorporate much of this kind of "shock and awe," and added that the U.S. military's lack of preparation for the postwar period in Panama had contributed to widespread looting and lawlessness after the fighting had stopped.[9]

Throughout 2002 and into 2003, the basic concept for a war of "shock and awe" against Saddam Hussein did not change. General Franks made sure of that. Nor did other threshold concepts change once they had been established. These had to do with the basic organization for combat—how the Marines would organize for the fight, to whom they would report—and with basing the 3d Marine Air Wing (3d MAW) in theater. Smith and Miclot found that their counterparts in the Long Range Planning Element were working from a scenario that had two Marine expeditionary brigades (MEBs) performing various missions, mostly to do with security, in southeast Iraq while the Army's V Corps carried the fight to the enemy in the north. Over the next forty days, the two Marine planners worked patiently to lay down the MEF "marker"—that is, the argument that the Marines should fight as one MEF in Iraq, the whole MEF being greater than the sum of its parts, let alone two independent MEBs.[10]

This took some doing. Although it was something they had always known and heard, Smith and Miclot learned again, firsthand, just how peculiar the concept of the Marine Air-Ground Task Force (MAGTF) is to non-Marines; no other service has anything quite like it. Many Marine and Army units of apparently comparable size are not in fact comparable; the Marine unit typically has more organic power, because it comes with its own air support. This is one of the factors that led to disconnects when joint planners were placing Army and Marine units on the board. As Lieutenant Colonel Smith put it, it was difficult to get into the Army's "comfort zone"—to make his Army counterparts comfortable with the "MEF single battle" concept, but he felt that after forty days of hard work, he and Miclot had succeeded.[11]

The other threshold issue they took on was bed-down for the MAW—essentially a matter of forward basing. This may not sound like a particularly dramatic issue, but with the U.S. Air Force occupying ever more space on the air bases in Kuwait, it was important for the Marine Corps to stake claims to space for its aircraft near the front. Otherwise the MAW would have had to look for bases farther afield, which would degrade its ability to get into the fight and especially to provide responsive close air support. Miclot worked hard and succeeded; Smith considers him one of the unsung heroes of the war for identifying, and resolving, the bed-down issue early on.[12]

On 12 February 2002, in Washington, Smith and Miclot back-briefed the trio of officers who held the key positions for shaping basic Marine Corps policy and "major muscle movements" in 2002 and 2003: Lieutenant Generals Hailston (in his MarCent capacity), Hagee (in his I MEF capacity), and Emil R. Bedard (the deputy commandant of the Marine Corps for Plans, Policies, and Operations [PP&O], basically the commandant's G-3). Smith and Miclot were gratified to find that the generals wholeheartedly supported their work on both the "unity of the MAGTF" and the bed-down issues, something that did not change for the life of the operation. Within a few months, General Hagee would become commandant and General Conway would take his place at MEF; but at the top of the Marine Corps, the MEF-MarCent-PP&O nexus remained the central forum for consultations and decisions about Iraq and certainly played a prominent role in the sourcing conference that took place later in February to come up with a preliminary troop list for Iraq. (The levels of involvement shifted somewhat over time. Initially, PP&O played the most prominent role. As the lay-down for Iraq started to gel, MarCent and MEF played more prominent roles, while PP&O tended to monitor developments. Although under CentCom's operational control, MarCent also reported to Headquarters Marine Corps, generally to PP&O, on strictly Marine Corps business, such as deciding which Marine units to deploy to CentCom or how to outfit them.)[13] Thanks to the state of technology for secure communications, the commanders and the planners were able to stay in very close touch throughout the process, and the senior officers who were read in on Iraq could develop and maintain arguably the best situational awareness in the history of warfare: they could find out almost anything they wanted to know about the preparations for war.[14]

It was Marine Corps doctrine that the MEF should not only fight as a MAGTF but that it should also plan as a MAGTF: planners for the constituent parts of the MAGTF should integrate their work. They should not work as stovepipes—waiting to interface at senior levels after plans were well advanced. Instead they needed to function as a network, at all levels, from the start.[15]

MEF officers used the same approach in their work with other services. In the interests of coordinated planning, Lieutenant Colonel Smith and Col. Joseph D. Dowdy, who was the MEF G-5 officer at the time, reached out to their counterparts during the many planning conferences that took place over the next few months. These included sessions at Transportation Command (TransCom) at Scott Air Force Base in Illinois; V Corps headquarters at Heidelberg, Germany; and CFLCC headquarters at Camp Doha, Kuwait, not to mention the commanders' conferences chaired by CentCom on a regular basis. The Marines were generally able to establish and maintain good relationships with their counterparts, especially at the working level. Sometimes it even reached the point where planners identified more with one another than with their parent commands—a sure sign that relationships had gelled.[16]

It was always assumed that MEF would fight under CFLCC. When CFLCC had taken control of land operations in Afghanistan in November 2001, CentCom had charged it with the traditional JTF-Ku missions of defending Kuwait and generally being prepared for war with Iraq. That had not changed in 2002, and from the start CFLCC had played the central role in planning for the ground war against Iraq and for I MEF's role in it.[17] The arrangement was that, exercising operational control, MarCent would flow the MEF to theater and provide for its sustainment, relying mostly on the Marine Logistics Command (MLC) drawn largely from the 2d Force Service Support Group for that purpose. But then MarCent would assign MEF to CFLCC's tactical control for combat operations alongside the Army's V Corps. The result, General McKiernan commented later, would be the first time since the Korean War that there would be a combined "operational-level, land component command/warfighting headquarters."[18]

Like planning, educating other services about the MAGTF and safeguarding its equities was a continuous process. It went on long after the initial lessons in Tampa in January and February 2002. Marines at many levels engaged their counterparts at CFLCC and other commands, finding ways to make the lessons stick without being resented by their "students." The process started at the top. From the highest levels on down, Marine commanders and planners stayed on message. General Hailston continued to defend the MEF's identity as a MAGTF. While still MEF commander, General Hagee did the same when meeting with General Mikolashek, who remained in command at CFLCC through the summer of 2002. Then, when General Conway was preparing to replace General Hagee as the MEF commander and General McKiernan became the new general on this particular block, Conway hosted McKiernan and his subordinates at Camp Pendleton. First the Marines presented the MEF capabilities brief. Among other "lessons" about the MAGTF, General Conway wanted to make sure his new boss understood that "our air" was also "his air"—a concept General McKiernan came to embrace.[19] He also wanted to give his subordinates—now–Major General Mattis, who had become commanding general of the 1st Marine Division, and Maj. Gen. James F. Amos, the 3d MAW commander—a chance to talk through issues with CFLCC planners. The specific issues were perhaps not as important as opening channels of communication among general officers at CFLCC and MEF; the participants remember feeling that the meeting cleared the air. General McKiernan's view—that CFLCC was there to "shape" the fight by its subordinates, not to plan it—must have gone over well with the Marines.[20]

The generals set the tone for their respective commands, and much the same process happened at lower levels as subordinates worked their way through the many practical issues involved in joint operations. General McKiernan character-ized the prevailing attitude throughout CentCom as: "Let us coordinate, and let us cross talk, and then come . . . together at a series of . . . conferences. . . . I would say that that was always done very well."[21] In addition to the exchanges between counterparts, most commands also made a point of exchanging competent liai-son officers, just as General Mattis had done in Afghanistan. One of the impor-tant lessons learned in Afghanistan and Iraq seemed to be that commands under-stood the importance of finding strong officers to serve as liaison officers (LNOs); LNO was no longer a suitable billet for an underachiever whom a commander wanted out of sight and mind.[22]

Once again, technology helped the process along. Counterparts and liaison officers may have held personal meetings whenever they could, but they also could and did look each other in the eye almost every day over secure video-teleconferencing links—this happened before, during, and after combat. Virtu-ally all of the senior officers in theater were regular and, it seemed, enthusiastic users of this technology. At the same time, there was a robust exchange of e-mails and discussions in chat rooms on the SIPRnet (the secure military Internet sys-tem, Secret Internet Protocol Router Network), where officers could also consult the drafts of one another's plans and work through revisions. In short, there were unparalleled opportunities for the secure coordination of operations, especially in peacetime; OpSec—operational security—did not have to be the obstacle to effi-cient planning it had been in virtually every other major war before Operation Iraqi Freedom. It was no longer as true that senior headquarters imposed opera-tion plans and orders on subordinate commands. Looking at the process of plan-ning for Iraq, a Fort Leavenworth study concluded that since networks in "the information-age . . . enable, . . . distributed, parallel planning, V Corps, I MEF, and the subordinate divisions were near-equal architects for the final plan."[23]

In retrospect, integrating with CFLCC appears to have been relatively easy com-pared to working with CFACC. Groups of Army officers, especially at CFLCC and in parts of V Corps, came to accept and even embrace the concept of the MAGTF as an organization with integrated ground, air, and support assets. Although there were nuances in the picture that make it difficult to generalize, it is safe to say that the same was never true to the same degree of CFACC, the coalition air forces com-manded by Lieutenant General Moseley, who was not only a functional and a com-ponent commander but also one whose forces had been conducting operations in theater for quite some time, especially Operation Southern Watch. They were fly-ing combat missions under his command while his counterparts were still thinking about what they would bring to the fight if and when it occurred.

Before leaving CentCom, General Zinni had laid some of the groundwork for cooperation between CFACC and the MEF by instituting a Standard Operating

Procedure for Joint Fires, which addressed "battlefield coordination, direction, and procedures for . . . air and ground-based fires systems" and was ratified by all of the service chiefs.[24] He had his Army and Marine Corps subordinates work out an arrangement for the employment of Marine air under JTF-Ku, and established the general principle that Marine air would support Marine ground forces, offering any "excess" sorties to CFACC.[25] In 2002, while he was still at the MEF, General Hagee and General Moseley renewed the same general agreement about the employment of Marine air with General Moseley:

> LtGen Moseley, . . . LtGen Hagee, . . . and LtGen Hailston . . . met in June . . . and agreed to make CFACC the airspace control authority, with I MEF MACCS [Marine Air Command and Control System] controlling air in support of I MEF. I MEF would publish its own Direct Support Air Tasking Order (DS ATO) to task I MEF aircraft, which was to be included in CFACC's theater ATO. When LtGen Conway took command of I MEF from LtGen Hagee, the arrangements and relationships did not change; LtGen Moseley continued to endorse the principle of I MEF MACCS controlling air assets supporting the MAGTF [on the] ground.[26]

When interviewed in the spring of 2003 about cooperation with CFACC, Generals Hailston and Amos were upbeat about the subject. They reported general agreement with General Moseley on the role of Marine air in the looming conflict—one that was different from that in Desert Shield/Desert Storm when a fair chunk of Marine air had been split off from the MEF and worked for the equivalent of the CFACC.[27] As General Amos put it, he found General Moseley to be a commander who readily understood the utility of the MAW as a part of the MAGTF while asserting his own rights to the airspace over the battlefield.[28]

The problem, once again, was finding a way to get into the joint comfort zone—to get things right at the working level, to focus not on general agreements but on specific details that would apply in 2003. The default setting at CFACC was to control all of the air space in the area of operations. The Air Force liked to control air space through the Air Tasking Order (ATO), described as "the daily master plan . . . [which] listed all of the strikes, CAPs [combat air patrols], tanker missions, and other supporting functions for a 24-hour period."[29] ATOs were prepared about ninety-six hours before their time of execution. Accustomed to decentralized planning, and interested primarily in supporting the MEF's scheme of maneuver, the Marine aviators had not changed overmuch from Desert Shield/Desert Storm, when they had been "deeply suspicious" of what they saw as an inflexible system that might not be able to respond to last-minute requests for support—that is, the Air Force system seemed to be better suited for strategic or operational offensives than for the kind of tactical uses that were the bread and butter of Marine air. In the end, in this new war the agreement among the generals was to "nest" Marine command and control under CFACC. There would be a Marine ATO within the CFACC ATO; the primary mission for Marine air would be to support the MEF scheme of maneuver; excess sorties would be made available to CFACC—and there would be provisions for the reverse to occur as well.[30]

A related and very complex issue was the separation of what came to be known as "Air Day," the day the air offensive would begin, and "Ground Day," the day the ground offensive would begin. (These terms were commonly abbreviated as "A-Day" and "G-Day." In this war, there was an often-confusing mix of civilian and military acronyms whose meanings were not entirely clear to everyone.) To summarize what was a lengthy and sometimes hard-fought set of transactions: CFACC thought the war should start with its house brand of "shock and awe"— attacking carefully selected targets with precision munitions, some simultaneously, others in a particular sequence. The main targets were the air defense capabilities that had survived Operations Northern and Southern Watch, as well as leadership and command-and-control nodes. With their coverage of nearly two-thirds of Iraq, Northern and Southern Watch represented an early, ongoing, and effective suppression of enemy air defense (SEAD) campaign.

At times it seemed that CFACC thought the air offensive could win the war by itself; there was a precedent of sorts in Serbia when NATO air attacks in 1999 had, by themselves, brought about the desired result: "in every way that mattered, air power won the fighting in Kosovo, while ground units served to consolidate that victory."[31] This fit with the view, held by many in Washington, that Saddam's regime was held together largely by the threat of force, and for that reason his support was weak and shallow. This was a variant on the "kick in the door and the house will collapse" train of thought, assiduously promoted by people like Iraqi exile Ahmed Chalabi, that seemed to guide a lot of the planning for this war.[32]

It followed, for those who held this belief, that CFACC planning did not have to be as integrated as planning by other CentCom components and that Cent-Com should allow CFACC enough time to create its war-winning effects. That would be something on the order of thirty days—not too different from the thirty-eight days in Desert Storm that had preceded the ground war; in that war, the two campaigns had not been integrated but sequential. Now, in 2002, CFACC wanted a boundary that put Baghdad under its control for those thirty days, as well as the use of Marine fixed-wing assets that, presumably, the Marine Corps would not need until the ground war started. This was not only an argument against synchronicity; it also undermined the "MEF single battle" doctrine. Simply put, the Marines did not want to break up the MAGTF, even temporarily.

Unwilling to give up the benefits of synchronizing the air and ground campaigns, many Army and Marine officers consistently argued for a much shorter air offensive. Lieutenant Colonel Smith remembered that as early as late February 2002, the prevailing view at CentCom was that the offensive should last no more than forty-eight hours.[33] Within MEF, General Amos continuously repeated that his first and most important priority was supporting the Marines on the ground. General Mattis was one of the leading proponents of synchronicity, making his arguments forcefully throughout the planning phase. He wanted almost no preliminary air attacks before the ground attack and for the air and ground offensives to start very close to the same time. One of the planners at Division, Lt. Col. Paul J. Kennedy, came to the conclusion that it was Mattis who won the MEF over to his way of thinking by "socializing" (that is, effectively promoting) his concept, which stood the CFACC concept on its head. If the air and ground campaigns were synchronous, or nearly synchronous, the MAW would have few airframes to spare for CFACC, because it would be busy supporting the MEF.[34]

No matter who originated the idea, MEF consistently argued for a much briefer air offensive in its dealings with CFLCC, which adopted much the same position, and made its arguments to other elements in the CentCom chain. These arguments became more compelling in late 2002 as CentCom focused more and more on the southern oil fields after concern for their preservation turned into a strategic imperative. In the end, one of the most telling arguments against a lengthy preliminary air offensive was that it would put Saddam Hussein on notice that the ground offensive was coming and would give him time to sabotage his own oil fields, as he had in the Kuwaiti oil fields during the Desert Storm air offensive. It was largely for that reason that in December 2002 and January 2003 MEF and CFLCC joined forces to argue for no preliminary shaping whatsoever, which did not resonate with CFACC. The final prewar consensus was that the air offensive should be relatively short and that the two phases should be as closely integrated as possible.[35]

The commander of the British air component in Iraq, Air Vice Marshall Glenn L. Torpy offered a good summary of the factors at play in the final stages of the debate in early 2003, which suggests how difficult it was to close the gap between CFACC and the other components:

As we developed our thinking . . . there was a shortening of that phase [the air phase] and it came down in the early part of . . . [2003] from approximately 16 days . . . to a matter of five days. . . . That was driven even closer together, as we got closer to the likelihood of the operation's being executed, for three factors. . . . First of all, there was a growing realization that we needed to secure the southern oil fields as swiftly as possible to prevent any subsequent damage. . . . There was a nervousness by the American land component and by General Franks over the vulnerability of having a very large land contingent in a fairly small area in Kuwait [waiting for the air campaign to end]. . . . General Franks felt that if he had the ability to synchronize the components together as comprehensively as possible then he would have the [best] chance of . . . getting the campaign over and done with as quickly as possible.[36]

In the days just before the war, the commanders appear to have agreed to shorten the air campaign even further. According to the Fort Leavenworth study, the final plan was for the gap between A-Day and G-Day to be fifteen hours. This happened after "Colonel Kevin Benson, the CFLCC C-5 [with whom Marine planners had an excellent relationship] developed and forwarded to the CentCom staff a series of position papers advocating adjust[ments in] . . . the G-A day sequence."[37]

The dispute over the separation of A-Day and G-Day went hand in hand with a painful set of disputes over the Time Phased Force and Deployment Data (commonly known as TPFDD, closely related to the TPFDL, with the "L" standing for "List"), the computerized system for getting U.S. forces to a fight in good order. It could phase forces to match a plan—and make sure the support they needed would arrive at the right time. Especially in a small, single-service contingency, this was the kind of rational process everyone was comfortable with. In large deployments the process was trickier; there was a finite amount of lift—especially airlift—that the services had to share. Most of these assets belong to Transportation Command. When the debate over the sequence of the campaign has not been settled, and when no one knows when the war will start, the result can be a three- or four-sided scramble for scarce resources. This is generally what happened between January and July 2002. No one had enough forces in theater at that point; there was not even a firm date by which everyone had to be ready to cross the line of departure. But there was strong and continuing pressure to be ready to flow forces to theater, which lent some urgency to the discussions about the TPFDD. Believing they would start the fight, and having their own plan for that phase (which they had developed more or less on their own), CFACC planners argued that they should be first in line. But if CFACC won the TPFDD argument, then it mattered less who won the argument about the separation of A-Day and G-Day, because the ground forces could not be in theater and ready to fight until CFACC had finished moving its forces. In other words, the danger was that the TPFDD could drive the war plan, which was the reverse of what the typical staff officer envisioned: the TPFDD was designed to be a tool for planners. We had, Lieutenant Colonel Smith concluded wryly, gotten inside our own OODA loop.[38]

There were additional complications to do with the relative priorities for moving Army and Marine Corps assets, with the Army generally wanting to lift more than the Marine Corps. Various forms of these disputes continued for some time—leading one wag (who has chosen anonymity) to comment, "War is simply the continuation of service politics by other means." In the end the core dispute was not resolved as much as sidestepped. In the diplomatic words of Fort Leavenworth's detailed look at the Army in Operation Iraqi Freedom, the TPFDD "lacked the flexibility and responsiveness required by senior leaders," which meant the Pentagon decided not to use it.[39] In early 2003, CentCom would use another process to flow troops to theater. Whatever CentCom or the Pentagon decided, the Marine Corps always had the advantage of being able to fall back on its habitual relationship with the Navy and the maritime prepositioning ships ([MPS], preloaded with heavy equipment) in order to get to a fight—not to mention the fact that the MAGTF was by its very nature designed for deployment even before the first planner sharpened the first pencil.

Yet another important part of the planning process was intertwined with the disputes about the timing of the offensive and the use of the TPFDD. This was perhaps the most important piece of the interlocking puzzle for the Marines—the base plan for the ground war. Throughout 2002 the plan went through a number of major and minor changes, approximately five of the former and some two dozen of the latter.[40] There are a number of complementary explanations for this. One is relatively simple—so simple that it seems almost trivial. It falls into the "for want of a nail" school of historical writing, meaning that some small details can matter a great deal. (It was Benjamin Franklin who said, "for want of a nail, the shoe was lost; for want of a shoe, the horse was lost; for want of a horse, the rider was lost.") This explanation has to do with the U.S. military's near-obsession with "bulletized" PowerPoint briefings, which are easy to prepare on a computer and then transmit over the Internet. The "bullets" in a briefing may summarize months of careful work, or they may stand alone with nothing to back them up. What often happened in 2002 was that one PowerPoint briefing led to another—a planner would come up with a carefully reasoned course of action and summarize it in a brief. Then a commander, perhaps two or three echelons higher, or even in another service, would ask a question or order a change. The result could be a course of action that looked good on a PowerPoint slide but had not been thoroughly staffed. That part of the plan would be "one PowerPoint brief" deep, and would either collapse of its own weight or have to be rescued by planners scrambling to do the staff work to back up the change.[41]

The Marines often thought the other services pressed for too much detail too early, which they resisted on the grounds that once something was on a PowerPoint slide it could look more final than it was. The bottom line is that the SIPRnet was sometimes a double-edged sword. It usually made concurrent planning easier, but it also made it easier to circulate half-formed ideas, which could—and did—lead to extra work for planners who were already so busy that they were close to forgetting the names of their children.

Another explanation for the nature of the process is that Secretary Rumsfeld had a particular vision he wanted to implement. He was nothing if not an advocate of transformation, and he often made it clear that the military establishment was moving too slowly in the direction that he—and many military thinkers—wanted to go. He certainly did not want to approve a plan anything like Desert Storm. There was simply no need for it, especially after the Afghan operation had demonstrated the potential for the new way of war, with its innovative and very joint lines of operation. There was also the use of "smart" munitions that were both efficient and effective; five bombs from one aircraft could now achieve the same effects that all the bombs from five aircraft had tried to achieve in 1991. Complementing the transformational argument was the military-political argument identified with the neoconservative movement, which had a long-standing policy on Iraq. Bolstered by inside information from Iraqi exiles around Ahmed Chalabi, senior Pentagon officials focused on the fact that the Iraqi army was a shadow of its former self; it was about one-third the size it had been when Saddam invaded Kuwait and would crumble under an American assault. In addition, the Iraqi people were said to be dissatisfied with the regime and ready to welcome the invaders as liberators. After the invasion, the United States and its coalition partners could soon draw their forces down, and the Iraqi opposition could step in to run the country. The bottom line for the Pentagon was that the United States did not need to send five hundred thousand troops across the line of departure to do the job.[42]

Secretary Rumsfeld and General Franks worked closely on the development of the plan, which stemmed in part from the fact that the combatant commanders reported to the secretary of defense (and certainly not to any of the service chiefs, as General Franks made very clear in his memoirs, with its colorful, "aw, shucks, I'm just a country boy" language.) It was also a function of Rumsfeld's hands-on style and his determination to implement his vision. In his memoirs, General Franks described frequent personal meetings—and almost daily telephone contact—between the two men. Franks would propose a course of action. The secretary would react to the proposal and ask him to come up with a new course of action in a few days—at most a week or two—or to provide additional details. This set a grueling pace. Although General Franks concluded that the final product was all the more robust on account of the process, the short-term effect of the secretary's input was to place additional burdens on the planning staffs at Cent-Com and its subordinate commands like MarCent and MEF.[43]

Even without PowerPoint or the secretary's input, planning the ground war would have not have been easy. Joint planning on a large scale is just plain hard, and it is not something that happens often, especially for Marines. Most Marine deployments and exercises (with the notable exception of Ulchi Focus Lens in Korea) were on a much smaller scale, which was fine with the Marine leaders who believed that the Corps should focus its efforts on preparing for real-world, MEB-size commitments while the MEF performed the Title X functions (of organizing, equipping, and training the force).[44] Not that it was much easier for Army officers. They were certainly more used to operating on a large scale—the Army was still preparing its officers to staff and fight at the corps level, as it had since before World War II—but as General McKiernan pointed out, this was the first time in decades that a CFLCC would plan and fight a combined/joint operation above the corps level.

The starting point for understanding the plan for the ground war was Desert Storm in early 1991, when General Schwarzkopf had painstakingly assembled a coalition of over five hundred thousand troops in and around Saudi Arabia to expel the Iraq invaders from Kuwait. No one moved north until all of the troops were in theater, equipped and ready to attack. After the air campaign that lasted over a month, more than fifteen U.S. and allied divisions advanced into Kuwait and Iraq. The ground war lasted only some one hundred hours before the United States announced a cease-fire—Kuwait having been liberated. With the exception of the Kurds in northern Iraq, who came under the protection of a combined/joint task force in Operation Provide Comfort in the spring of 1991, the Iraqis were more or less left to their own devices. This had devastating consequences for the Shi'ite rebels, especially those in the South, who had dared to rise up against Saddam in the confusing days that followed the ground war.[45] It was Saddam's suppression of the Kurds and the Shia that had led to Operations Southern Watch and, later, Northern Watch, to enforce the no-fly zones in the southern and northern thirds of Iraq through 2003 and that helped to keep the Iraqi military in check.

The planners of Desert Storm would have been comfortable with the Cent-Com plan that was on the shelf for war with Iraq: Operation Plan (OPlan) 1003-98. The premise of the plan was that Iraq had once again attacked Kuwait, that CentCom had come to its defense and counterattacked, its objective being the removal of Saddam Hussein and his regime. It was a relatively heavy plan, with five divisions crossing the line of departure—and with I MEF supplying the command element.[46] In late 2001, before focusing on Afghanistan, CFLCC planners had considered a limited objective plan—an attack to seize the oil fields in southern Iraq—which did not take as its starting point OPlan 1003. After they were tasked in early 2002 to come up with a more ambitious plan, they still did not use 1003 as the starting point but developed new courses of action. The course of action favored by General Mikolashek, the CFLCC commander at the time, was in line with CentCom's concept of "shock and awe," emphasizing speed and surprise. It was an audacious plan calling for the force to avoid the lengthy build-up that would announce U.S. intentions and, using prepositioned equipment, launch one division deep into Iraq with a view to reaching Baghdad within ten days.[47]

CFLCC took this plan on the road, and through all of the various personal and impersonal contacts—including the planning conferences of various sorts—it evolved into something not more but less audacious that came to be known by the rather nonmilitary phrase "generated start." This was a throwback to Desert Storm and 1003 in that it called for a deliberate build-up of decisive strength before anyone crossed the line of departure. The build-up would take approximately ninety days, and the simultaneous attack by two corps would take up to ninety more days to get to Baghdad.[48] The results of the first MEF Operational Planning Team (OPT), which ran from 13–19 March at Camp Pendleton, further illustrate both the plan's general outlines and the MEF's role in it. The OPT assumed that MEF would be a supporting effort, with the Army's V Corps (usually based in Germany) as the main effort. The MEF would deploy 1st Marine Division, 3d Marine Air Wing, 1st Force Service Support Group, and a regimental combat team out of II MEF to serve as "Task Force South." The OPT came up with a concept that called for the division to attack northwest from Kuwait to seize the airfield at Jalibah, which would become a support area, including a forward arming and refueling point (FARP), before proceeding to seize the airfields in the vicinity of Qalat Sikar and Al Kut to the northeast, much closer to Baghdad. At this point the OPT expected CFLCC to order a significant pause to allow the Army to flow additional forces and supplies before continuing the attack toward Baghdad. (The pause was an idea that never sat well with the Marines.) In the meantime, Task Force South would resume responsibility for southern Iraq, addressing any threats the division had bypassed and in general securing support areas and lines of communication.[49]

This did not play well in Washington. Considering the possible scenarios that could lead to war with Iraq, few at the Pentagon were willing to accept a plan that took ninety days to launch. The word came down that Secretary of Defense Rumsfeld was unhappy with the ponderous nature of the "generated start," which would not only be logistics intensive but would also sacrifice any hopes of surprising the enemy. The result was that CentCom felt pressure to develop ever lighter, more creative scenarios.[50]

The warfighters moved the plan in the direction that Rumsfeld indicated. By early summer, the pendulum had swung so far to the "light" that there was a plan under consideration for something like two brigades—perhaps one Army and one Marine—to cross the line of departure soon after a *casus belli* had occurred. To be sure, this would be a "running start"—this small force would be reinforced by heavier forces from the Army and Marine Corps as soon as they could get to the fight. The running start seemed to mean starting early but finishing late, since the force would once again have to wait for reinforcements before moving north for the decisive battle of Baghdad. Marine planners pointed out that there was no need for two corps headquarters to control the running start, and argued that the MEF could provide command and control for the initial phase of the operation. It would be better suited for the task, because, unlike V Corps, it not only had organic subordinate commands, but it was also experienced in running and controlling air operations, which V Corps was not. At least initially, the Army was reluctant to accept this argument.[51]

East Coast Marines in a West Coast Plan

What became Task Force Tarawa started as Task Force South. The concept for a task force to follow in trace of Division, to be charged with neutralizing any threats that Division had bypassed and then securing the MEF's lines of communication, was certainly on the table by March 2002. At a time when the Pentagon wanted to keep the force light and HQMC was thinking in terms of "global sourcing"—that is, pulling assets from all over the world to meet the potential need for Marines in CentCom—it made sense for PP&O, "the Commandant's G-3" at Headquarters Marine Corps, to look to II MEF in Camp Lejeune, North Carolina, to supply something like a MEB-size force to float to theater on the amphibious task force (ATF) that was based on the East Coast. The location and capacity of amphibious shipping helped to determine where the forces would come from and how big they would be. Since there was another ATF on the West Coast, the Marine Corps could use the ATFs to get two separate elements to the fight quickly and securely. The East Coast Marines could mount out of Morehead City, North Carolina, onto their own ATF without adding to the long list of units for deployment from the West Coast, and the two forces could travel by different routes. Another reason to look to Camp Lejeune was that the only other remaining MEB-size force was in Okinawa. That force needed to stay there in case it was needed in Korea. At this point the planners were looking at a MEB-size unit that would not fight as a MAGTF. It might deploy without the MEB command element. If that happened, all of its parts could be parceled out after arrival in theater. Whether to include a command element with the East Coast contingent was a matter mostly for the I MEF commander to decide. This would happen only after General Conway took the helm in the fall of 2002.*

*G. W. Smith interview no. 2; Reynolds journal, entry for 1 July 2004 (reporting the comments of Col. Ronald J. Johnson, PP&O Current Ops officer and Task Force Tarawa G-3).

The pendulum started to arc back toward the middle in the second half of 2002, toward the ultimate, or "hybrid," version of the plan—a mix of elements from the "generated start" and the "running start." One of the problems with the running start turned out to be that it was very difficult to come up with an optimal time to attack, considering the trade-offs between strength and surprise. When would the mix be right—early enough for surprise but late enough to allow CFLCC to build up the strength that it needed to do the job? Over the summer, some of the planners considered deploying a stronger initial force—perhaps two Army brigades and two Marine regimental combat teams that could attack thirty days after the force flow started. An attractive feature of the stronger force was that with it CFLCC could attack simultaneously in two directions— with the Army attacking to the northwest, toward the city of An Nasiriyah, and the Marines attacking to the northeast, toward Basrah, Iraq's second city, and the nearby southern oil fields.[52] (The Marines had mixed feelings about Basrah, especially the suggestion that they seize and run Basrah International Airport, no doubt an important symbolic target but one that could become a "force sump," because to run the airport they would have to protect it from portable antiaircraft rockets, and that would mean controlling the city, which could take a Regimental Combat Team [RCT] a long time.[53]) By late July, the Army had accepted the proposition that MEF would control the initial phase of the war, roughly the first seventy-five days, and that the 3d Infantry Division (ID) would be under MEF control at least for that period. There was further discussion of a lengthy (30–45-day) pause in the middle of the campaign to build up supplies for the final assault, a proposition that had not become any more attractive to the Marines. Finally, there was discussion about another large city—Baghdad—but there would not be anything like a final decision about how to tackle the capital until much later.[54]

September saw a declaration by General Franks that President Bush wanted CentCom to be prepared for war within sixty to ninety days and that CFLCC needed to be prepared to execute across the continuum of force—that is, with either a heavy or a light plan. During the same month, the MEF began to work with British Royal Marine planners on their potential role in an offensive; initial plans called for one Royal Marine commando (the rough equivalent of a Marine Corps battalion) to fight under the MEF. The Royal Marines appeared ideally suited for an amphibious assault against targets on the Al Faw peninsula in southeastern Iraq.[55]

The American Marines took an immediate liking to their British counterparts—as individuals and as warriors—and welcomed them as reinforcements. This was eventually to lead Col. Christopher J. Gunther, who became MEF G-5 in the second half of 2002, to take advantage of a brief to the British high command to ask for a second Royal Marine commando, tossing in as a sweetener the possibility that a U.S. Marine MEU might work under British command.[56]

Most versions of the plan included a healthy dose of "deep" and special operations against carefully selected targets, like those seen in Afghanistan, which had impressed General Franks favorably. There would be two Joint Special Operations Task Forces (JSOTFs): JSOTF-N and JSOTF-W, the first to work with the anti-Saddam militias in Iraqi Kurdistan in the northeast part of the country, and the second to secure any potential launch sites for Scud missiles in the western desert between Baghdad and the Jordanian border (which had been used by the Iraqis in Desert Storm to attack Israel). But that was not to be the extent of special operations; there would be Special Operations Forces (SOF) elements at work throughout the country, adding their capabilities to the force mix in all areas of operation. MEF planners took the initiative to coordinate with SOF, for example, by traveling to Fort Campbell, Kentucky, for an unexpectedly cordial and productive session. Once again, the Marines found that they continued to get good results when they reached out to other communities.[57]

In October, MEF held a general officer symposium to develop "a common understanding of the . . . operation plan." It would have been more accurate to say the state of "operational planning," since "the" plan did not yet exist—even though it was now beginning to be known as Operation Plan 1003V. During the same month, there was a MEF exercise based on an invasion of Iraq, and advance parties from the MEF began to deploy to Kuwait to stand up a MEF command post (CP), soon followed by the I MEF Command Element, which deployed to Camp Commando, a few miles west and north of Kuwait City, and prepared to participate in CFLCC exercises. By late November there were approximately 850 members of the MEF staff in Kuwait, along with approximately 100 members of the 1st Marine Division staff.[58]

As the commanders and their staffs began to settle in—or at least try to settle in—during December, they realized they could be living in the desert for quite some time. Despite the pronouncements from CentCom, there was still nothing like a timeline—no one knew for sure when the war would start, or even if it would start. On 9 December, General Conway spoke to his officers at Commando and told them they might be in Kuwait for the long haul. He wanted to dispel rumors that the Marines were going home after the current round of exercises. He did not know if there would be a war but ventured the guess that it might come "as late as February," which was still during the "cool" season, the "right" time to go to war. But he concluded that if the Marines had to fight in the heat, they would fight in the heat.[59]

Around the same time, senior Marine officers debated whether they should push for a large-scale deployment. The issue was this: if the MEF arrived early, in force, a large number of Marines might spend a number of months in Kuwait waiting for a war that might never come. On the other hand, if the troops stayed home until the situation gelled, they might not be able to get to theater in time if the pace of events were to speed up and the war started on short notice. General Mattis—supported by Colonel Gunther—is said to have pleaded the case for flowing the forces in the near future. Colonel Gunther pointed out that at worst the Marines would get some good training; it would be like going to a very big series of combined arms exercises in a desert other than the Mojave at 29 Palms, California.[60]

In the meantime, General McKiernan, who had replaced General Mikolashek in September, was working to turn CFLCC into a more joint command. McKiernan liked to say that CFLCC was made up of a number of "tribes" and "subtribes"— that is, members of different services, American and allied, as well as members of different branches of the Army. (Many Marines forget the extent to which Army officers often identify with their military occupational specialty.) His method was to do "a lot of training and tribal team building." One McKiernan initiative was to reorganize the staff along functional lines in order to break down the old-fashioned "G-1, G-2, G-3, G-4" stovepipes and encourage cross talk among the various disciplines. Virtually every day in late 2002 and early 2003 the CFLCC staff held some sort of exercise, in addition to participating in CentCom exercises and various rehearsals. (This may turn out to have been one of the most extensively rehearsed wars in U.S. history.) In short, the point was to change the original tribal identity, to make CFLCC into a joint tribe, a headquarters with a joint outlook.[61]

General McKiernan didn't just want to change the tribe's way of thinking; he also wanted to change its makeup. In the fall of 2002 there was also a push to get the other services, especially the Marine Corps, to send more officers to CFLCC. The long-standing joint manning document called for a complement of some ninety Marines; in the early fall there was only a handful of Marines at Camp Doha, ordered to CFLCC by MarCent. One or two had even been at Doha since the fall of 2001 and were filling key billets. Two of these officers were Col. Gregory J. Plush, USMCR, whose title was MarCent liaison but who functioned for months more or less as the senior Marine on the staff, and Col. Marc A. Workman, USMCR, chief of the Deep Operations Coordination Cell in the C-3. General McKiernan relied heavily on Workman to plan what was known as the "deep fight"—operational fire support well beyond the front lines, which at CFLCC in 2002 and 2003 was about "creating (desired) effects," not just destroying targets.[62]

What Marines Do for Christmas

25 December at Camp Commando

Commando sat at the base of Mutla Ridge, one of the few parcels of distinguishable terrain in an otherwise flat and largely treeless country. In August 1990 the Iraqis had used the ridge to shell the camp below; shell holes and shattered buildings were still here and there within its confines. For a Christmas treat, MEF Headquarters Group gave its members a rare opportunity to venture outside Camp Commando on a ten-kilometer run to the ridge and back (and to find out that they were not in the same shape that they had been in at Camp Pendleton). Armed guards were posted along the route to defend against possible terrorist attacks. Even with the terrorist threat, and the sand that offered little traction, it was an enjoyable outing. Back at Camp Commando, Generals Amos and Mattis spent their time talking about Baghdad with a handful of MEF officers. General Mattis said he wanted to get north of the Tigris as quickly as possible to minimize the time his division would be susceptible to weapons of mass destruction (WMD); General Amos said he wanted to put the Wing on a "JDAM [or "smart" bomb] diet" so that he would have enough precision munitions for the big fight in the city. Then they ranged over a variety of issues—from where to place boundaries between Army and Marines; how to coordinate fires and control air space; the integration of information and covert operations on the one hand and conventional operations on the other; and general techniques, tactics, and procedures for fighting in urban terrain. One of the participants, Lt. Col. George Smith, remembered thinking that this "pure warfighting" talk was the ultimate professional military education session.*

*Reynolds Journal, entry for 19 July 2004; Interview with Lt. Col. George W. Smith, 8 June 2004 (MCHC, Washington, D.C.)

McKiernan was so pleased with Workman—in particular his experience as a MAGTF planner able to coordinate a range of effects—that he resisted any moves to replace Workman, who wound up serving at CFLCC for the duration, working up to eighteen hours a day for months on end. (It was only after they had been working together for some time that Workman mentioned he was a rancher by profession, and not a regular officer, which McKiernan at first refused to believe—a backhanded compliment to the professionalism of this Reserve artilleryman who literally had to sell the farm in order to stay on active duty.)[63] In October, reinforcements for Plush and Workman began to trickle in. General McKiernan asked for the best Marine general that Headquarters Marine Corps could find, and Maj. Gen. Robert L. Blackman soon received orders to serve as the chief of staff at CFLCC. General Blackman, who had commanded the 2d Marine Division and most recently served at CentCom headquarters in Tampa, was respected both as a Marine and as a team player in the joint arena.[64] After his arrival in country, General Blackman repeatedly urged HQMC to provide more officers for the staff. In late November, Col. Patrick J. Burger, USMCR, arrived at Doha to serve as the senior MEF liaison officer and began to coordinate the activities of the growing number of Marines liaison officers who were not technically part of the CFLCC staff but who in most cases might as well have been.[65] In January, during a trip to Washington, D.C., General McKiernan himself again requested Marine augmentation for the CFLCC staff. It is hard to escape the conclusion that if CFLCC was short of Marines, it was a reflection of Marine manpower constraints and certainly not of a desire by "Big Army" to limit the number of Marines at CFLCC or the influence of Marine doctrine.[66] In the end there were some seventy Marines at CFLCC, still short of the number in the joint manning document that the Army and the Marine Corps had long since agreed to, but certainly at a level where the liaison officers could effectively represent the Marine point of view. More importantly, the staff became even more joint in the interests of putting the common interest ahead of any one service or nationality.[67]

By November both the CFLCC and the MEF staffs were ready to exercise the most recent version of the CFLCC portion of the CentCom plan, which now bore the name "Cobra II" and still called for a relatively small force to advance from Kuwait into southern Iraq. Maj. Evan A. Huelfer, CFLCC's lead planner, commented that although there were some changes, the outlines of the "four brigade" initial attack had not changed markedly over the intervening months.[68]

What was somewhat different in the fall was the hope that the U.S. Army's 4th Infantry Division—augmented by a British division—would advance from Turkey into northern Iraq, toward Baghdad, at roughly the same time.[69] Generals Franks, Mikolashek, and McKiernan all wanted near-simultaneous attacks into Iraq from north and south—the main attack coming from Kuwait, with a supporting attack by coalition forces from Turkey. This was an idea that certainly sat well with the outgoing commandant of the Marine Corps and incoming head of European Command, Gen. James L. Jones Jr., who wanted to do what he could to make it happen, and was willing to commit Marine units if it made sense to do so.[70] The attack from the north would be able to secure important targets in the north such as the oil fields around Kirkuk and Saddam's "hometown," Tikrit, which was considered to be one of his bases of power.[71]

"Lucky Warrior 03-1" was a CFLCC exercise testing command and control, including the links between CFLCC and MEF, and focusing on the initial phases of war. It began on 24 November, just in time for Thanksgiving, and was a precursor to the CentCom exercise "Internal Look 03," which tested three scenarios from OPlan 1003V at the next higher level and occurred in early December with MEF participation. General Blackman remembered later that the scenario at the time was for CFLCC elements to cross the line of departure with two brigade combat teams (BCTs) from 3d Infantry Division and one MEU, all under the MEF. The MEU would take the southern city of Umm Qasr, while the two BCTs would take the oil fields. There would of course be follow-on forces under this "running start" scenario.[72]

After these exercises, General McKiernan decided he needed a stronger force that could move fast; unless CFLCC were stronger from the outset, he would not be able to accomplish all of the set tasks at the same time. It seemed, for example, that CFLCC would have to choose between maintaining security on the southern oil fields and moving north. As McKiernan put it on 19 December 2002: "We do not have enough combat power to simultaneously penetrate [Iraq] and move straightaway . . . to Baghdad and do all the other tasks we have to do in southern Iraq . . . secure the oilfields, keep Basrah out of the fight, develop our logistic support areas, deal with displaced civilians, deal with enemy prisoners of war, cross the Euphrates."[73]

After the war, on 1 May 2003 General McKiernan made the comment that this was "probably the most critical decision I made [during Operation Iraqi Freedom] . . . I made a case for additional forces . . . that were ready to conduct ground operations . . . [for a] two-corps operation, with a penetration as a form of maneuver by the main effort, and a [simultaneous] supporting attack by the MEF to fix everything over on the east side."[74]

Next there was a series of video teleconferences (VTCs) between General McKiernan and CentCom so that General McKiernan could make his case. In Major Huelfer's words, it went something like this:

> Lieutenant General McKiernan made a plea to General Franks, and said, "Hey, look, you're asking to attack at C + 15 [fifteen days after starting the force flow], but we won't have enough forces on the ground to do both of those operations simultaneously. We cannot go out to Nasiriyah and toward Basrah at the same time." . . . So . . . I think the light went on, he [General Franks] said, "Okay." . . . The very next day, General Hailston [the MarCent commander] came up . . . to Kuwait, and the next thing you know . . . [Marine] regiments were flowing into Kuwait.[75]

In fact, there was an intermediate step. The talks between McKiernan and Franks led to talks between theater and the Pentagon—a sometimes painful process described by McKiernan's assistant, Terry Moran (no doubt with tongue in cheek), as a "tug-of-war": "We had a series of VTCs where we were asking to move the force posture from X to X plus Y. We were in a tug-of-war with CentCom and with OSD [the Office of the Secretary of Defense] on how big Y could be." It seemed that whatever increase CFLCC requested, "they would try to skinny [it] . . . down."[76] Nevertheless, the end result was that CFLCC came to develop the heavier, two-corps plan, under which the 3d ID reverted to V Corps.[77]

This plan was truly a hybrid—a good combination of the "generated start" and the "running start." The force was by far smaller—and more agile—than the force with which General Schwarzkopf crossed the line of departure in 1991, but it was developing a respectable amount of combat power. Where Schwarzkopf had had two Marine divisions at his disposal, it was now fairly official that if and when the order was given, the MEF would bring its entire division–wing–FSSG team along with some 7,100 Marines from Camp Lejeune. General Conway decided he wanted them to come with the 2d MEB command element;[78] he wanted a second Marine command element in country to take on the distinct security and stability missions in southern Iraq that had originally been foreseen for Task Force South a few months earlier.[79] The MEF's subordinate elements, then, were to be 1st Mar Div, 3d MAW, 1st FSSG, Task Force Tarawa, and the MEF Engineer Group (MEG), an MEF-level engineering asset. The last was a concept that was unfamiliar to many Marines. Made up of Marine engineers and Navy SeaBees under the command of a rear admiral, the MEG was an initiative that dated back to the days when General Zinni was the MEF commander. The point was for the MEF to be able to do "one-stop shopping" for its engineering needs, especially in major deployments.[80]

In December 2002 and January 2003, the rough outline of the "hybrid" plan was for the Army's V Corps to move north through the western desert of Iraq with at least one full division, with the ultimate goal of capturing Baghdad. Meanwhile, the MEF would move north on a more central axis, the "obvious" route to Baghdad, which leads into and through the heart of Iraq, the Fertile Crescent between the Tigris and Euphrates Rivers. The Army remained the main effort, the Marines were the supporting effort—which meant they would pick as many fights as they could, as General Conway put it, in order to deflect pressure from the Army and to make the Iraqis think the Marines were the main effort. In effect, the Marines would defend the Army's flanks by rapidly defeating enemy forces in its zone. MEF's spearhead, Division, would have the city of Al Kut as its aiming point, while Task Force Tarawa would seize and hold objectives in the south, securing the division's rear from potential threats.[81] A quick look at the map reveals that Task Force Tarawa was to assume responsibility for at least one major city, Basrah, the surrounding oil fields, and thousands of square miles of territory, much of it inhabited—a breathtakingly ambitious mission that could succeed only if the optimistic assumptions about the nature of the opposition (or the lack thereof) were correct.

How Task Force Tarawa Got Its Name

General Conway did not like the colorless designation "Task Force South" for 2d MEB, and he asked Brig. Gen. Richard F. Natonski, its commander, to come up with something better. A Marine with a good sense of history, General Natonski wanted to think the matter through and began by asking the History and Museums Division for help in naming the task force. The chief of the division's reference section, Danny J. Crawford, reviewed the names of the task forces in Desert Storm—such as Grizzly, Papa Bear, and Ripper—and made a few suggestions for the new task force: Mameluke, from the name of the sword; Fortitude, one of the Corps' earliest mottoes; Chosin or Chosen Few, to commemorate the fiftieth anniversary of the Korean War (which had ended in 1953). Crawford added the incidental note that the Navy's code name for Iraq in World War II had been "Plughole," clearly a non-starter but an interesting bit of historical trivia. General Natonski agreed and said he would consider Crawford's other suggestions along with the idea that he pick the name of a mythical creature from the Arab world that his future opponents would recognize. In the end, Tarawa seemed to fit best. General Natonski happened to be looking at some artifacts from World War II in the Pacific, a reminder that Tarawa was a famous battle associated with 2d Marines and therefore a good name for a task force with that regiment as its infantry. When 2d MEB landed in Kuwait, it became known by that illustrious place name.*

*Interview with B. Gen. Richard F. Natonski, 26 March 2004 (MCHC, Washington, D.C.), Natonski-Crawford e-mail messages, 18 Dec. 2002 (Reference Section, MCHC, Washington, D.C.).

Exactly what the Marine Corps would do in Baghdad was once again unclear. Along with the elite forces that would most likely try to keep the coalition away from the capital, Baghdad had long been recognized as the enemy's center of gravity. MEF wanted to play a role in the fight for Baghdad and argued for a simple boundary—like the Tigris River—between Marine and Army units in the zone. By late summer 2002, the CFLCC commander, General Mikolashek, appeared ready to accept that approach. Then, in September his successor, General McKiernan, decided to change course and designated the V Corps staff as the lead on Baghdad. The Army was the main effort and it had the heavier force. It would fight in the city; the Marines would support the attack but remain outside the city limits. To be sure, there was always the possibility that this would change, both in General McKiernan's mind and in the minds of the Marine planners. To the general's way of thinking, the "base plan" was for V Corps to command the tactical fight for Baghdad. But "there was a branch plan that said, if . . . it makes sense . . . bring forces into Baghdad from both the . . . MEF . . . [and] . . . V Corps, . . . we ought to be sure that we can do that."[82] The bottom line was that both V Corps and the MEF continued to think about Baghdad and to try to come up with the right way to subdue and control the Iraqi capital.

The prospect of a joint British-American attack from the north lasted through most of December 2002, when it became increasingly clear that the Turks were not likely to allow the British to pass through their country. (It was only later that the Turks also refused to allow an American division to pass through Turkey.)[83] In January 2003 it was easy for CentCom and CFLCC to decide to redirect as many British forces as possible to Kuwait and to the MEF, which did what it could to encourage this development. The reinforcements came in the form of the 1 United Kingdom Division (Armoured), a composite made up of three more or less independent brigades, which began to flow into Kuwait in early 2003. MEF planners happily proceeded to include the British division in their plans, along with the 15th MEU(SOC), which was now officially slated to reinforce the British.[84]

With a full division at their disposal, the British could assume responsibility for Basrah and its surroundings. In the words of one staff officer, Lt. Col. Richard T. Johnson, USMCR, who worked on the plan at CFLCC, the Marines "hit the right numbers" (like a lucky gambler) when the British joined their team. Johnson's thinking—in retrospect—was that without the British, the Marines would have been hard pressed to control the powder keg that was Basrah and accomplish their other assigned missions.[85] Another planner, Lieutenant Colonel Smith, said the British were the MEF's "slingshot," propelling it much farther and faster than it could otherwise have gone.[86] With the British in the MEF, TF Tarawa's mission changed; its focus could shift westward, away from Basrah and the southern oil fields. But the type of mission remained similar: it was to secure crossing sites over the waterways in the south and to preserve combat power. General Natonski stated that he became aware of this change on approximately 17 January 2003.[87]

There were similarities—and dramatic differences—between the battle space assigned to the Marines and that assigned to the Army. Most of the Army's battle space was trackless desert, at least until it reached the cities of Najaf, Karbala, and Hillah, which lay southeast of Baghdad. Being heavily mechanized, the Army was, arguably, well suited for the desert. The Marine battle space, on the other hand, started off as desert but soon became a varied and complex mix of desert, scrub brush, agricultural land, rivers, and canals. It was defined—and largely contained—by the two great rivers, the Euphrates and the Tigris, and anchored in the south by Basrah, which lay on the Shatt al Arab waterway not far from the border with Iran, and in the north by Baghdad, some three hundred miles to the northwest. A small number of highways ran through the area, varying in quality from a good superhighway to two-lane local highways to dirt roads. Like the rivers, the highways mostly ran on a northwest to southeast axis. There was a prominent chokepoint at An Nasiriyah in the south of Iraq, some ninety miles west-northwest of Basrah, where three highways, one river, the Euphrates, and a canal came together. It was on the way for anyone going north or west from Kuwait or Basrah. The argument has been made that the Marine battle space was a good fit for the Marine Corps' capabilities—being closer to the ocean, calling for the ability to cross bodies of water, and encompassing cities that a Marine regiment, with its many infantrymen, could subdue more readily than an Army brigade, which had relatively few "dismounts."[88]

The MEF took CFLCC's "Cobra II" OPlan and used it to develop its own plan, which had four phases and came to include various branches and one sequel. Similar to contingencies that could become part of the plan, the branches included were early military collapse (a variant of "catastrophic success"), inundation (which could occur if Iraqi engineers intentionally flooded parts of the region between the Tigris and the Euphrates), and the seizure of the crossings over the Euphrates in and around An Nasiriyah. One sequel, a mission that the MEF could receive after completing the missions in the base plan, addressed the seizure of the oil fields in the north around Kirkuk. MEF did not view all of the branches and the sequel as equally likely—or any one of them as particularly likely—but wanted to err on the side of being prepared. Speaking about branch plans at his level, General McKiernan referred to "the old adage that you can have a great plan, but the plan could change at the line of departure for a variety of [reasons] . . . that we don't have a great deal of control over. . . . We ought to . . . have lots of options. . . . We can decide which one we are going to execute to obtain the initiative throughout the fight. . . . We need to go through the planning of different branches . . . so they don't become surprises to us." The general stressed that it was important for the various parts of the joint force to coordinate their branch plans in advance.[89]

The four phases of the plan ranged from reception, staging, onward movement, and integration, commonly abbreviated RSOI, a needlessly complicated acronym for Phase I, or "preparation," which was mostly about deploying the forces to theater and preparing them for combat, to "shaping the battle space" through preliminary attacks in order to degrade Iraqi command and control and seize key pieces of terrain. This was the phase when various special operations troops under CentCom's Joint Special Operations Command would engage the enemy, especially in the western and northern parts of Iraq, and there would be air attacks in the northern and southern no-fly zones, which had already done much to ensure air supremacy for the coalition. Then there was Phase III, which included the main air offensive and decisive ground maneuver. Finally there was Phase IV, postcombat operations, which encompassed security and stability operations.[90]

Phase III was the heart of the plan—there was amazing breadth and depth to the parts of the MEF plan dealing with this phase. Phase IV, in comparison, received very little attention.[91] There was very little guidance from higher headquarters on Phase IV, not even a basic policy decree. Some of the MEF planners found this troubling and got out ahead of their higher headquarters, making preliminary plans for Phase IV on their own. They realized that, like it or not, the Marine Corps would be involved in Phase IV operations, though hopefully for only a relatively brief period of time. This was, after all, the phase that had traditionally been left to the Army. But as General Conway put it later on, the Marine Corps had "always done windows" and would now do whatever the president, secretary of defense, or combatant commander directed.[92]

A maneuverist, especially if British, might argue that there was too much detail in Phase III of the MEF plan—that it was reminiscent of the bad old days when the Marine Corps prepared "to fight the plan" as opposed to the enemy. In this conflict, British plans tended to be very brief and to the point in comparison with American plans. One British planner, Lt. Col. Jim Hutton, Royal Marines, could not believe all of the time he spent at planning meetings with his American counterparts, especially the SEALs, who, he thought, tried to plan for every last possibility. It was, he said, "mind-numbing" and inhibited flexibility. He added the thought that the Royal Marines might appear slack by comparison, but they also felt they had more leeway to react to situations as they developed.[93] When asked about this topic, the typical MEF staff officer occupied the middle ground between the SEALs and the Royal Marines, believing that the plan itself was nothing but that planning was everything, because it forced the operators to prepare for a broad range of contingencies. As one of the lead planners, Col. George F. Milburn, the MEF's Future Operations officer, commented: "You have to replan continuously. I honestly believe [that] . . . as Americans we're going to do that anyway. We'll plan for the last day. Once we begin executing, we'll continue to plan. Our job is to make sure that we can take care of any contingency that comes up and give the CG . . . the game book of all the variations . . . to make things happen to win the campaign."[94]

There were various estimates as to the length of the war. While some of the early plans assumed a lengthy campaign, in the end the hope—and the expectation—was for a much shorter campaign. Two weeks if it goes well, two months if it doesn't—was what one of the Army generals told journalist Rick Atkinson.[95] In early March, General Conway commented that the three weeks predicted by the "talking heads"—the retired military officers who had been hired by the networks at home and were very free with their advice—was overly optimistic, because "Saddam has things he could do to slow us down."[96] After the war, General Conway's boss, General McKiernan, remembered that Phase III had been planned "as if there [would be] . . . determined fighting all along the way. . . . There were planning timelines that took it all the way [out to] 125 days."[97] One of McKiernan's planners, Major Huelfer, remembered that General Franks sometimes sang a jingle that went: "5–11–16–125," to do with timelines, 16 meaning the length of the air offensive in days and 125 referring to the days in the ground offensive.[98]

The uncertainty about timing matched the uncertainty about the enemy. CFLCC, and its major subordinate commands, seemed to be working off a set of assumptions that various agencies had developed for the contingency. General McKiernan explained those assumptions in an interview a few months later. The Iraqi forces were basically divided into three categories: the regular army, the Republican Guard, and the Special Republican Guard. The Iraqi navy and air force no longer posed a threat to anyone but themselves, but there were approximately twenty-one ground divisions of various kinds and strengths for an estimated total of some 330,000–430,000 men. The regular Iraqi army, which did not appear to be at a particularly high state of readiness, had up to six divisions in southern Iraq, including two that were relatively close to the border: the 51st Mechanized Division, in and around the city of Az Zubayr near Basrah, and the 11th Infantry Division, associated with the cities of An Nasiriyah and As Samawah on the border of the western desert. There were two other regular army divisions in the MEF area of operations that bore watching: the 10th Armored, in the vicinity of Al Amarah, and the 6th Armored, around Basrah.

General McKiernan surmised that Saddam Hussein probably intended his forces in the south to be no more than "a speed bump" for the coalition. They would not put up much of a fight, and the coalition's biggest problem would probably be what to do with all of the prisoners of war when they surrendered (as they had in droves in Desert Storm). However, he expected that there would be something like a cordon around Baghdad of four elite Republican Guard divisions at a much higher state of readiness to defend the regime's center of gravity. At least two of these divisions, the Baghdad and the Al Nida, were likely to stand between the MEF and Baghdad. If and when coalition forces approached the cordon, Saddam might attack them with weapons of mass destruction (WMD)— that is, chemical or biological agents—which virtually everyone in uniform in the area of operations expected to encounter at some time during a war with Iraq. Inside the protective cordon around Baghdad there was also a "missile engagement zone," which meant the Iraqis were thought to have good antiaircraft defenses ranging from missiles to antiaircraft artillery to handheld weapons.[99] The missile zone would be part of an urban Baghdad defense. The Special

Republican Guard, estimated at around fifteen thousand soldiers and more like a palace guard than an army unit, would be part of that defense. Finally, there were the various irregular formations of paramilitary thugs like the Saddam Fedayeen. They were mentioned in most prewar assessments of the opposition, but they were seldom highlighted. The bottom line is that whoever the enemy turned out to be, no one thought the Baghdad fight would be easy.[100]

Iraqi Weapons of Mass Destruction

After the various task forces and investigative committees concluded that Saddam Hussein did not have any weapons of mass destruction in 2003, it was easy to forget the dimensions of this threat in the minds of the men and women who were about to go into battle. It was a threat they prepared for and lived with, in many cases for months. Every Marine, soldier, and airman was inoculated for anthrax and smallpox before coming to theater. Once in Kuwait, he carried a set of protective overalls in his backpack everywhere he went—along with rubber boots, gloves, and gasmask—and was prepared to use his atropine injectors to save himself when the seemingly inevitable attack came and he was "slimed." When on high alert, the coalition forces wore the overalls over their uniforms in the desert heat and continued their mission. The best anyone could say about the heavy cloth protective gear was that it was not as hot as it seemed—and certainly not as hot as earlier generations of rubberized gear. Not only did the coalition expect to encounter WMD when its forces reached Al Kut on the way to Baghdad, but it also feared that Saddam could launch strikes against troop concentrations, headquarters elements, or airfields in Kuwait—targets that were lucrative, close, and, in some cases, well known to the Iraqis who, after all, had occupied many of the same bases in 1990.

CFLCC's assumptions were based in part on information collected by various sophisticated "national" means of collection. There was, for example, excellent overhead coverage—you could count the tanks in a tank park without any trouble. The Task Force Tarawa G-3, Col. Ronald J. Johnson, remembered he had voluminous order of battle information about the Iraqi army—in some cases, down to the cell phone numbers of the Iraqi commanders—a truly impressive collection of data. What was lacking was hard information, especially about intentions. No one seemed to *know* what the enemy was thinking. Who could and would fight? What was the relationship between the regular army and the Ba'ath Party or the various special military and paramilitary organizations that the party had created?[101] In another example from the fall of 2002, the 1st Marine Division was exploring these questions and came up short. General Mattis wanted to organize an understudy program whereby his officers studied enemy division and corps commanders in order to understand them. But, given the shortage of human intelligence, "it was very hard, even for these dedicated young officers who were doing everything they could to . . . get information, to determine what was the background, what was the military school, what was their combat record, what [was] their political record"—in short, to get a feel for their enemy based on the kind of information that military attaches traditionally collect.[102] As late as early March 2003, General Conway complained—in his diplomatic fashion—that there was "not as much intel coming in about Baghdad as we'd like" in order to plan that urban fight.[103]

Not much more was known about Saddam Hussein's plans. Even after the war it took months for the coalition to start to assemble a picture of his frame of mind, which appears to have lacked clarity and been unduly optimistic. He probably believed the coalition would begin by waging a long air war, which would enable him to buy time for a cease-fire brokered by his friends in Moscow and Paris. Coalition planners generally believed that Saddam placed his hopes in various kinds of delaying tactics, both political and military. But according to a thoughtful article in the *Washington Post* in November 2003, investigators had been unable to find evidence of a coherent strategy for a ground war—such as a plan to abandon Baghdad and fight a guerrilla war, or to use weapons of mass destruction when coalition forces penetrated too deeply into Iraq—despite interviews and interrogations of many former Iraqi officials and military leaders. A retired Iraqi general who had been a division commander, Abed Mutlaq Jubouri, probably summed up the situation accurately when he said that Saddam Hussein failed to prepare his defenses in any kind of rational, systematic way. "There was no unity of command. There were five different armies . . . no cooperation or coordination. As to the defense of Baghdad, there was no plan."[104]

Planners throughout the MEF also wanted more information to drive their planning for Phase IV. There seemed to be even less processed and readily available information about the nature of Iraqi society than about the Iraqi army—that is, information addressing the degree of popular support for the regime, or the challenges that the coalition would face in the wake of "catastrophic success," the shorthand for what was likely to happen if Saddam Hussein and his sons were overthrown by a sudden uprising. Another way to ask the question was, What will Iraq be like after a successful offensive by the coalition? What was the state of the infrastructure? How did the electricity work? How about the plumbing? What about the economy? Would the civil servants return to work and be able to do their jobs? All that existed in the way of answers to these questions were hazy assumptions that the coalition might face a humanitarian crisis—for which it did prepare, especially by stockpiling food—and that it would be able to rely, at least to a certain extent, on Iraqi civil servants to get things going again.[105]

3

Preparing the MEF for War

The Most Important Fight Is the First Fight

The MEF's major subordinate commands did not wait for a formal order to prepare for war with Iraq. General Conway, who commanded 1st Marine Division before taking command of the MEF, had exercised the division's capabilities for war with Iraq in the first half of 2002.[1] When he took command from General Conway in August 2002, General Mattis put the division on a virtual war footing. From the outset his guidance was "to physically and mentally focus on one task . . . the defeat of the Iraqi Army and the liberation of the Iraqi people."[2] A few hours after the change of command, he gathered his commanders together in a secure room at the MEF headquarters at Camp Pendleton and told them to enjoy the coming weekend because it would be their last weekend off for a long time. They could take the time to ask forgiveness from the Almighty for what they would do to the Iraqi army when the time came. In the meantime, he wanted them to train as if this week were the last week of peace.[3]

A general requirement for speed of execution and maneuver over distance governed individual and unit preparations. At many levels the division evaluated procedures, organization, and equipment with a view to being able to move and fight rapidly. For example, in September 2002 long-distance communications exercises took place, shifting control back and forth from the forward and the main command posts. Then the division structured its regimental combat teams to make them more robust and able to operate independently. The 5th Marines, for example, were reinforced with a battalion of tanks and a battalion of eight-wheeled light armored vehicles. Similarly, Mattis made sure there were enough tactical vehicles for everyone to ride to the fight and ordered modifications to enable the vehicles to carry extra fuel (by welding "gypsy racks" to them—an initiative that did not find favor with the traditionalists in the motor-transport chain of command).

This was not simply a matter of general conditioning and preparedness. The division soon went on to anticipate specific missions, assigning them to subordinate units and staging elaborate rehearsals. This was especially true for what would become known as the "Opening Gambit," the division's scheme of maneuver for the opening days of the war. Around the division, there were mockups of various objectives in Iraq. At one point the parking lot in front of the division command post was taken over by a vast model of southern Iraq for an astoundingly detailed set of exercises, with toys usually used to create a make-believe world:

> The CG decided [that] using . . . Lego blocks to represent every vehicle in the Division would be a fine way to visualize the . . . challenges . . . of moving massive numbers of vehicles down . . . the limited [number of] roads [in Iraq]. . . . Legos were available in a variety of sizes, and were color-coded. Specific colors and sizes would be assigned to a unit's vehicles, [and] then the blocks would be attached to the corresponding plates [!] [for] . . . each of the units of the Division. A scaled terrain model was built to replicate the major terrain features in southern Iraq. . . . Each battalion walked through its scheme of maneuver, moving [its] . . . Lego pieces in the proper sequence. . . . For each traffic jam of plastic blocks, the . . . audience was forced to ask itself, "Who owns the battlespace? Where exactly are the boundaries?" . . . These drills shaped the actions that would take place on the ground in Iraq. . . . For example, . . . the MAG-39 Operations Officer . . . [saw] that the AH-1 . . . [Cobras] were oriented to the east in support of RCT 7's attack on the 51st Mechanized Division . . . at dawn. . . . The pilots would be attacking into the morning sun. The . . . plan was changed accordingly.[4]

MEF addressed the issue of supplying Marines stretched from Kuwait to Baghdad. In Enduring Freedom, a relatively small force, Task Force 58, had operated successfully some four hundred miles from the beachhead. But now planners were talking about taking a MEF hundreds of miles into Iraq. By doctrine such a distance exceeded Marine Corps capabilities and spawned concerns that, logistically, the MEF was trying to go "a bridge too far." From the beginning, many senior officers, starting with the commandant of the Marine Corps himself, focused on logistics as one of the three potential show-stoppers in Iraq (the other two being weapons of mass destruction and urban combat).[5] Luckily for the Marine Corps, inventive and energetic logisticians were ready to take on the challenge.

The MEF's subject matter expert for logistics was the commanding general of the 1st Force Service Support Group, Brig. Gen. Edward G. Usher III. General Usher knew the doctrine: the FSSG typically entered a theater organized in stovepipes, that is, by function; there were Headquarters and Service, Maintenance, Supply, Engineer, Transportation Support, Medical, and Dental Battalions. Once overseas, FSSG tended to establish and maintain large stationary bases. If restructuring was necessary, it occurred in theater. Not flamboyant but thoroughly professional and forward thinking, General Usher decided he would task-organize to meet the challenge before leaving California, a process he started in the fall of 2001. The goal was to create combat service support (CSS) units that integrated the various functions—something like the combined arms approach applied to CSS to meet a variety of needs for the supported unit. For example, after Usher's reorganization there was CSS Group-11, which was to support 1st Marine Division through a CSS battalion in general support, and three CSS companies attached to the regimental combat teams in direct support. The battalion was expected to establish repair and replenishment points throughout the battlefield, while the companies followed in trace of the regiments, carrying one to two days' worth of Class I (food), Class III (fuel), and Class V (ammunition) supplies. Another command, CSS Battalion-22, was to support Task Force Tarawa, while CSS Group-13 supported the 3d Marine Air Wing and its innovative plans to push supplies deep into Iraq. Providing general support to the MEF was CSS Group-15, required to have four days of supply on hand, as well as a full complement of transportation, engineer, and military police assets.[6]

For this war there were to be additional innovations by way of putting medical support virtually on the front lines—the shock trauma platoons and the forward resuscitative surgical systems would win praise for saving lives—as well as thoroughgoing preparations to conduct assault bridging operations, which were expected to play an important role in the MEF area of operations. The ultimate goal of these preparations was better integration into the MEF scheme of maneuver—from the initial stages of the planning process through the execution of the plan—and to enable the MEF to push the envelope a good bit further than it had ever been pushed before.

If 1st FSSG operated at the retail level, its wholesaler was to be the Marine Logistics Command. Comprising over four thousand Marines, mostly from 2d FSSG, the MLC was under the command of Brig. Gen. Michael R. Lehnert and remained under the operational control not of MEF but of MarCent. It was intended to serve as a bridge between the 1st FSSG and the theater-wide Army support command, the 377th Theater Support Command. (The mission of the 377th was to support "Big Army" in a land war, as opposed to an expeditionary war, the Marine Corps' forte. But since the Marines were now preparing to fight a land war, they needed help from organizations like the 377th.) General Hailston remembered an initiative to establish an MLC in Korea in the 1990s, and General Usher commented that it was an organization that had grown out of the lessons learned from the Gulf War. That is, the Marine Corps needed something it did not normally have—an operational logistics capability, at the echelon above MEF. In his words, "the MLC basically [was] . . . our broker for overarching sustainment requirements for the theater."[7]

Apart from such general statements of intent and a study by the Center for Naval Analyses (the Navy's think tank), there was little guidance and virtually no doctrine for General Lehnert to follow in preparing to stand up his command. The general was left basically to follow his own instincts and to learn through trial and error. He was a good choice to run a start-up operation, having recently weathered the challenge of standing up the task force to establish and run the detention center at Guantanamo Bay for the Al Qaeda detainees from Afghanistan. He had done so with just the right mix of common sense, good people skills, initiative, and energy. Now, in the Kuwaiti desert, he would need the same skill set. The MLC might look to the 377th for certain categories of supplies or equipment that were not in the Marines' inventory, such as line haul (long distance trucking) and heavy equipment transporters (usually used to transport tanks to save wear and tear). But if the 377th did not have enough assets to support both the Army and the Marines, General Lehnert would have to find work-arounds to obtain what the Army could not provide—that is, in addition to maintaining wholesale stocks of Marine Corps supplies and ammunition.

Given the emphasis on speed and distance, it made sense for General Mattis to declare his intention to create the "most air-centric division in history" and to forge a close relationship with the 3d MAW under Maj. Gen. James F. Amos, a former fighter pilot with a good mix of command and staff time, including a tour as the head of the leadership section at the Basic School and combined/joint tours in Europe. Amos's personal style was, by Marine Corps standards, laid back; he was unusually approachable and looked for the commonsense solution as opposed to asserting his status or rank. That said, he was nothing if not results oriented.[8]

What General Mattis said was certainly true, but it was not just the division-wing relationship that mattered; what was forged in 2002 was a very effective division-wing-FSSG team in the best tradition of the MAGTF. The personalities of the leaders, technology, and doctrine came together to create an unusually powerful force. Precision weapons like the JDAMs, the joint direct attack munitions, and changes in the doctrine for close air support, which made it easier to run, even when no one could see the target, opened up a new range of options. The plan was for Marine air to take on its traditional missions—close air support, casualty evacuation, occasional resupply—but Generals Conway and Mattis also wanted it to be a maneuver element in its own right, to take on more "independent" missions for the MAGTF.[9]

This meant complicated discussions on what aircraft to bring to the fight and how best to use them. Through the process of global sourcing to augment its own resources, the wing put together an exceptionally robust team that would peak at 435 aircraft and some fifteen thousand Marines and sailors, making it the largest wing to deploy since Vietnam. The aircraft ranged from FA-18 Hornet and AV-8 Harrier fighter-bombers, to KC-130 Hercules tanker/transports, to the same workhorses that Marines on the ground have, quite literally, been looking up at since the Vietnam War: the UH-1 Huey and CH-46 Sea Knight helicopters. (It was amazing for some older Marines to remember that the CH-46 first came on line in 1964 and has carried three generations of Marines into battle since then.) Two other helicopters, the AH-1 Super Cobra, a remarkably versatile platform for close air support, and the CH-53 Sea Stallion, providing a heavy lift capability, rounded out the inventory.

Having more or less resolved the issue of who would control Marine air—CFACC or the MEF—in their favor, the MEF was largely free to use its air as it wished. The first priority was to gain and maintain air superiority, which would not take too much of the wing's time, given the state of the Iraqi air force and the drubbing that the Iraqi air defense system had taken in Operation Southern Watch, especially in the past few months. The next priority would be enemy command-and-control systems. At least initially, enemy artillery would rank almost as high as command and control on the list of priorities. This was in large part because everyone in the coalition was worried about Saddam's ability to deliver weapons of mass destruction. (Any other targets associated with WMD that presented themselves would also be a priority.)[10]

Many of these targets could be prosecuted as part of the "deep battle"—"deep" being more of a concept than a location, though many "deep" targets would be far from what would pass for front lines in Iraq. The wing would be charged with reducing threats to the MEF before they could close with the Marines, or vice versa. General Conway wanted the wing to be prepared to take on Iraqi divisions that were still many road miles away from Division's lead elements, and to reduce their effectiveness before they even started thinking about moving into battle. The Republican Guard divisions near Baghdad that were in the Marine AO were excellent candidates for everyone's list of deep targets. Closer in—but not necessarily that much closer in—General Mattis wanted the wing to defend his columns as they raced deep into Iraq, destroying enemy formations that could threaten the division's flanks and uncovering any other threats during the Marines' march up-country.

Since the battlefield would be fluid—without well-defined "friendly" and "enemy" lines—careful coordination would be necessary between the Marines in the air and on the ground. This called for some innovative thinking and organizing. The basic policy was to decentralize various functions and to keep them as close to the front as possible. This was true for "Direct Air Support Centers, Air Support Elements, imagery liaison cells from VMU squadrons [flying unmanned aerial vehicles for reconnaissance, which became very popular with ground commanders]," not to mention dedicated casualty evacuation and command-and-control aircraft.[11] Each regimental combat team would have its own dedicated aircraft and its own aviation support element (ASE). To enable this organization, the wing planned for a number of forward operating bases and especially forward arming and refueling points, the small mobile bases that would spring up alongside the advancing forces. In other words, for instance, if the commander wanted support from the wing, he would not have to work through some impersonal, centralized mechanism that would dispatch airframes from a base perhaps hundreds of miles away. Instead, he could call on the assets that were dedicated to him and that could be rearmed and resupplied locally.[12]

Typical of the intense preparations for air-ground cooperation was the rehearsal of concept (ROC) drill at the Wing Operations Center in Miramar, California, on 6 January 2003, with the MEF and Division commanders in attendance, along with all of the wing's group commanders. Intended, like the many other ROC drills in Operation Iraqi Freedom, to refine the plan and make sure that all of the commanders understood it in the same way, this particular evolution was the first of its kind for a Marine air wing, which gives you a sense of how much more integrated the wing, already a major constituent part of the MAGTF, would be in this fight.[13] The drill laid out the wing's plans for supporting both the MEF and the division; what was clear once again was the extent to which it would not only provide close air support to the ground combat element, but would also serve as a maneuver element in its own right as it attacked deep targets and moved its assets around the battlefield, both in the air and on the ground.

The "shared understanding" that emerged from the Marine Air Wing's (MAW) ROC drill was one more example of that phenomenon in late 2002 and early 2003. General Mattis used those same words when he described the synergy that developed among Marine commanders at various levels, especially but not exclusively among the general officers who worked so well together under General Conway, whose command style was to welcome newcomers to the fold.[14]

The commander of Task Force Tarawa, General Natonski, was happy to find General Conway ready to reach out to "the outsiders" from Camp Lejeune and make them "his own," narrowing the gap (which was as much perceived as real) between East Coast and West Coast Marines. "Shared understanding" continued to make it possible to work smoothly, both in the joint arena and within the MAGTF, to rely on mission orders and the commander's intent, and to operate with lean staffs and a "light" communications suite. The intended result was speed, the mantra that permeated MEF, Division, and Wing planning, even before General Franks ordered his commanders to execute Operation Plan 1003V with the memorable words, "Make it fast and make it final."[15]

As the drills, and the planning, proceeded, Marines flowed into the country in great numbers. Apart from the Corps-wide "stop loss/stop move" decree, which applied to individuals, one of the most significant events in January was the approval of the deployment orders that began the wholesale flow of MEF forces to Kuwait. According to the MEF's command chronology, the main deployment orders were 177A, issued on 2 January 2003, and 177B, issued on 14 January 2003. Together these two orders were ironically known as SOMODEP—"son of the mother of all deployment orders," the Army's deployment order being MODEP.[16] There has been considerable discussion of the use of deployment orders, with their ad hoc flavor, as opposed to the more traditional, and many would argue, orderly, sequenced TPFDD process.[17] The Pentagon decision to use deployment orders—apparently in search of strategic and political flexibility— did not meet with universal approval in the field. For one thing, it made planning that much more difficult, as each deployment, at least in theory, stood alone. Planners remember feeling that they needed to change the plan every time they generated a request for forces (or RFF, which would go to the Office of the Secretary of Defense for approval and, with luck, turn into a deployment order). But the basic problem was still about sequence, as when a frontline unit was separated from its enablers—that is, the units that supported it. A fair criticism from the Marine point of view was that the process could threaten the integrity of the MAGTF, which was less likely under the TPFDD process.[18] Finally, General McKiernan made what was perhaps the most telling criticism, from the warfighter's perspective, of the use of deployment orders. When asked about his reaction to this "just-in-time" approach to delivering forces and equipment to theater, he replied with the very sensible observation: "I don't want them just in time. I want them a little bit early."[19]

Once they received their orders, I MEF units traveled to theater by sea and by air. There were the two amphibious task forces, known as ATF East and ATF West, which set sail in January and carried some eleven thousand Marines and their equipment on thirteen ships to Kuwait. ATF East carried the 2d MEB command element, and the elements that would serve under the MEB in Kuwait and Iraq, and arrived on 15 February.[20] ATF West carried Regimental Combat Team 1 (or RCT 1, built around 1st Marines) and various aviation and CSS units, arriving in late February.[21]

The remaining units came over by air, using a mix of military and chartered civilian aircraft. Some Marines literally flew first class, but for the majority it was a long, uncomfortable trip under crowded conditions. The eleven ships of the Maritime Prepositioning Force (MPF) squadrons moved independently to Kuwait with equipment for the MAW and other MEF units. Working twenty-four hours a day, seven days a week, Marines and sailors unloaded the ships in record time.[22] In the end, MarCent moved some sixty thousand Marines and their equipment to Kuwait in less than sixty days, a staggering accomplishment. In December 2002 there had been only a handful of Marines in Kuwait, but by 1 March 2003, the MEF had about one-half of all the operating forces in the Marine Corps in country, facing north.[23]

Marine Order of Battle

By 0800 on 17 March 2003, the order of battle for the MEF, and the individual components strength and missions, were depicted in briefing charts at Mar-Cent.

I MEF Command Element: 4,638

1st Marine Division: 20,606: Secure the southern oil fields; conduct a passage of lines through Task Force Tarawa, and attack toward Baghdad.

3d Marine Air Wing: 14,381: Shape the MEF's battlespace; screen the ground combat element from attacks; support CFACC.

1st Force Service Support Group: 10,504: Provide direct combat service support to the MEF; interface with the Marine Logistics Command, a theater-level command OpCon to MarCent.

MEF Engineer Group: 3,121: Maintain roads and bridges along the I MEF lines of communication; this unit was a composite of U.S. Navy construction battalions and Marine engineers.

Task Force Tarawa (2d MEB): 5,091: Secure An Nasiriyah and crossings across the Euphrates River; secure lines of communication.

15th MEU: 1,739: Attach to 1 U.K. Armoured Division for Opening Gambit; attach to Task Force Tarawa.

1 U.K. Armoured Divisions: 21,045: Attack north from Kuwait; conduct relief in place in oil fields with 1st Mar Div; secure Basrah and vicinity.

I MEF Total: 81,125

Other Marine Forces in Theater

MarCent Command Element (Bahrain): 385
Marine Logistics Command (Kuwait): 4,525
CJTF/Consequence Management (Kuwait): 742
MARCENT Total: 87,184*

*This is the rendition of the MarCent Morning Report, 17 March 2003, captured by the field historian attached to MarCent, Lt. Col. Jeffery Acosta, and sent to the author by e-mail. The total does not show the Marines committed to CJTF Horn of Africa.

Upon arrival in Kuwait, Marines and equipment moved into camps in the desert between Kuwait City and the border with Iraq that varied from relatively comfortable to very austere. The MEF had established its headquarters at Camp Commando, a few miles from Kuwait City. It had originally been acquired to serve as a no-frills, low-maintenance expeditionary camp for Marine units passing through Kuwait on routine exercises.[24] In the fall of 2002, however, as the MEF and Division staffs trickled in, the camp had started its metamorphosis into a medium-sized military city. In February 2003 a member of the MEF staff, Maj. Grant A. Williams, USMCR, described Camp Commando in less than glowing terms:

The area we obtained was an isolated portion of a Kuwaiti commando training facility. Last year we contracted to start pouring concrete slabs, [for] rudimentary plumbing, drainage, and [to] stockpile building materials. . . . Commando Camp is [now] a fortress carved out of the sand. . . . The physical layout . . . is approximately 2 miles around the perimeter . . . surrounded by concertina wire and fences. On the inside of the perimeter is a seven-foot berm that encircles the camp. This is an anti-RPG [rocket-propelled grenade] . . . precaution that makes it difficult to get a direct shot into the camp. All the key points have guard towers with very focused young Marines manning them 24/7. In the center of the base is a seven-story tower the Kuwaitis use for repelling [sic]. . . . We have deployed a sniper team at the top of the tower. . . . With night vision goggles and infrared sights they can see and take out any bad Hadjis . . . a mile away day or night.[25]

Within the MEF compound, surrounded by the tents of various sizes, stood three windowless "Butler buildings" made of sheet metal that looked like small warehouses. These became the combat operations and information centers for MEF Rear when the war started. Set up inside the nearly featureless buildings were cafeteria-style tables where staff officers with laptop computers controlled the MEF. One of the few decorator touches was a poster of *The Scream* by the gloomy Norwegian artist Edvard Munch, contributed by the G-3, Col. Larry K. Brown, who liked calling his domain the "House of Angst."[26] There was also a mobile command post. Able to deploy to Iraq, MEF Main was to be built around a structure known as "the Bug" because of its strange shape and because it bristled with antennae and radar dishes. Major Grant explained:

> We recently procured some high-speed, low-drag command tents that are similar to your basic self-erecting camping tent . . . on steroids. We can put up an interconnected dome style tent that can shelter 100 fully functional terminals hooked up to satellite feeds within 4 hours. Large . . . projection screens can display real-time satellite imagery and video feeds from unmanned aircraft. Environmental systems keep the inside cool (relatively). . . . [These are] not for the people but for the computers. [This command center is intended for service] well behind the front lines but [able] . . . to move forward so that the general can remain close to his battlefield commanders.[27]

Apart from Commando, there was quite a range of living conditions for Marines in Kuwait. Less austere, but still far from luxurious, were the Kuwaiti air force bases at Al Jaber, to the south of Kuwait City, and Ali Al Salim, to the west of the capital, where, thanks in part to other tenants like the U.S. Air Force, there were some creature comforts like a good, air-conditioned mess hall and shower trailers. But even at a "developed" base like Al Jaber, virtually all Marines lived and worked under canvas. When you drove onto the base at Al Jaber, you passed under an archway where it was said Saddam Hussein's forces had hanged Kuwaiti air force officers when they took over the country in 1990, just to let everyone know who was now in charge—a potent reminder of why the coalition had returned in 2003.

Some Marines lived and worked at Camp Doha, a sprawling U.S. Army base between Commando and Kuwait City that looked like a prison in the desert, with its watchtowers and rings of security provided by U.S. contractors. (The guards were retired U.S. military personnel making good tax-exempt money.) Doha was home for the Marines who worked at C/JTF-Consequence Management (C/JTF-CM) and for the Marines on the CFLCC staff. CFLCC had an incredibly sophisticated command and information center—much more elaborate than the "Bug"—and some of the accommodations at Doha were among the best in theater. The camp even boasted some semiprivate air-conditioned trailers. But much of the accommodations were far more basic, like the warehouses where soldiers and Marines simply set up their cots in large, open bays in the withering heat.

Catching the Bug

The "Bug" was the brainchild of the MEF's intense chief of staff, Col. John C. Coleman. In the fall of 2002 he sold the concept to General Conway and then went to find the right tentmaker, whom he located in Virginia. Sitting on the floor of the tentmaker's shop, he had sketched his concept. A few days later the finished product appeared at MEF headquarters in California. The MEF took it to Kuwait, and tested it in the desert outside Camp Commando, passing command back and forth with MEF Rear. It offered the commander "an incredibly rich picture of the battlefield." Screens in the command center could display a mind-numbing array of data, from live CNN reports from the front lines, to customized maps, to satellite imagery. The software even allowed the commander to "test drive" potential routes through built-up areas. Colonel Coleman said that putting the "Bug" together was the easy part. The hard part was educating the staff, which he divided into the "Flintstones"—the Stone Age warriors—and the "Jetsons"—the space-age warriors. But Flintstones could grow into Jetsons only when they had the right equipment. The "Bug" replaced the old maps covered with clear acetate, overwritten with grease pencil, and updated with data from old-fashioned line-of-sight tactical nets. That is what many subordinate Marine units still had, where there were only a few technological marvels like the "Blue Force Tracker," a laptop computer screen with ground-satellite links showing the location of friendly units and even allowing their commanders to exchange a few words.*

*Interview with Col. John C. Coleman, 11 Dec. 2003 (MCHC, Washington, D.C.); David J. Lynch, "Marines' Mobile War Room Is Rich with Data," *USA Today*, 31 March 2003, p. A-6.

Apart from Commando, Doha, and the air bases, most of the camps in Kuwait were simply patches of desert where Marines pitched their tents and bulldozed sand to form a protective berm around the perimeter. General Mattis had said he wanted everyone in his division ready to live like an infantry lance corporal in the field, and, for the most part, circumstances obliged him. The division's Camp Matilda was in the middle of nowhere and comprised a number of large fifty-man tents, mostly rented from the Kuwaitis. They looked like the U. S. military's general-purpose tents but were much larger, designed for traditional Arab social gatherings in the desert. Now they were surrounded by oceans of equipment, mostly from the MPF ships—much of it still painted green or "Woodland" camouflage—and by two-man tents pitched here and there wherever there was a vacant bit of sand. No one knew for sure exactly how big these encampments were, but they weren't small. For example, the commander of RCT 7, Col.

Steven A. Hummer gauged the size of his regiment's encampment (within Camp Matilda) by the amount of time it took him to jog around it—thirty minutes.[28]

No matter which camp they called home, most Marines in Kuwait had to put up with frequent sandstorms that could blind a man as surely as a blizzard in the Dakotas, as well as temperatures that could sink to near freezing at night and soar to well over 100 degrees Fahrenheit during the day. Every Marine, soldier, and sailor in Kuwait knew he was within the "Scud fan"—that Saddam Hussein could fire missiles at the American forces that were concentrated in a small area. Many feared that Saddam would load the missiles with chemical weapons to "slime" his victims. (This was another bit of jargon peculiar to the Iraq War, often seen as a passive verb, as in "I know I am going to be slimed." There was not a lot of clarity about how this would happen, but one bit of scuttlebutt was that there could be an airburst that would shower contaminants on everyone within a grid square.) To guard against that possibility, U.S. Army Patriot antimissile missile batteries were on the ready throughout Kuwait. (Some Patriot batteries from the 108th Air Defense Artillery Brigade were under the MEF's tactical control and were slated to move with the Marines into Iraq. The Army was, by and large, generous with its attachments, sending some twenty-seven hundred soldiers to MEF with specialized talents that the MEF needed.) Most places also had crude bomb (or missile) shelters, which were often simply inverted U-shaped concrete culverts, about three feet high, that would have provided some protection from a blast but almost none from a chemical strike. Anyone doing the math could see there were not enough spaces in the shelters for everyone wearing a uniform in Kuwait.

If a chemical strike had occurred, each unit's organic decontamination teams would have sprung into action, helping to decontaminate people and things, which would have required a great deal of water and a lot of time. There was also an expectation that the Marines and some of the foreign experts in C/JTF-CM would pitch in. This was true even though the largely German and Czechoslovak international force was in Kuwait as part of Operation Enduring Freedom, not to participate in a war with Iraq but to "be prepared to" assist host nations in the event of a terrorist attack with chemical or biological agents. C/JTF-CM still answered to MEF, and its predominantly Marine command element, commanded in 2003 by Brig. Gen. Cornell A. Wilson, USMCR, routinely participated in CentCom planning conferences.[29]

After the Marines fell in on their gear, there was the process to test and calibrate equipment and to hone combat skills. MEF coordinated more planning and more drills, all of which were remarkable for their thoroughness. War games were carried out to explore the branches of the plan, the possible nightmares like "early military collapse" and intentional flooding. On 7 February, Division hosted a major ROC drill at its Camp Matilda for the MEF on a vast "model of the obstacle system of northern Kuwait, [and] the oil fields, the rivers, the ports, the roads [on the Iraqi side of the border]."[30] Framed on one side by four seven-ton trucks forming a kind of grandstand overlooking a piece of ground the size of a football field, the exercise went for three hours, with U.S. Marines, Royal Marines, and British soldiers, all in colored jerseys representing their units, literally walking through the moves that would occur during the first few days of the war. Major General Stalder, now deputy commander of the MEF, spoke about the utility of rehearsals and the need to form an image of the plan. This was already a familiar refrain—that Marines at all levels not only understand but also visualize the plan, "seeing" in their mind's eye the terrain, the enemy on that terrain, and their own actions in battle. As General Mattis had put it in a memorandum on 20 December 2002: "It is critical that each of us anticipate . . . what lies ahead and continue . . . to visualize (or image) our troops through the challenges . . . so well that they will move through [them] with a sense of déjà vu."[31] As he had done before, Mattis now warned against becoming wedded to the plan, reminding his listeners that once the MEF crossed the Tigris River, they would have many options for getting to East Baghdad and lots of room for individual initiative and action. (This was at a point when the plan for the Baghdad fight was still very much up in the air, although it was generally assumed by now that the Marines would approach Baghdad from the east, and, most likely, enter the city itself.[32]) Nevertheless, Mattis also made the point that the carefully choreographed plan would give his Marines confidence in the first days of the war, which would be the baptism of fire for many of them. He predicted that the MEF would have about thirty days more to prepare for war. The field historian who recorded the evolution noted that the mood was "very somber . . . no ooorahs, almost no laughter."[33]

Consequence Management

Morning formation at the C/JTF-Consequence Management at Camp Doha was an unusual sight—the largest body of troops was German. Seeing and hearing German spoken by men in uniform in the desert, anyone who had ever studied World War II couldn't help but think of another time, especially when next to the formation he could see the iron crosses painted on a tan background on the Germans' elaborate "Fox" vehicles. These vehicles, which looked like LAVs (light armored vehicles) to Marines, carried state-of-the-art technical gear to sample and sniff for NBC (nuclear, biological, chemical) agents. (The MEF had a few Fox vehicles of its own that would travel north when the time came.) What was very different this time was that standing in the formations next to the Germans were Czech and Slovak soldiers, many of them attractive women, with similar missions. The idea was that in the event of an attack, the Germans would "chase the plume"—following the fallout and figuring out what the agents were—while the Czechs and the Slovaks would concentrate on decontamination and on "turning victims into patients," meaning they would conduct triage and start medical treatment if there were mass casualties. Every so often, C/JTF-CM would conduct a field exercise. One such exercise occurred on 8 April 2003 in Tactical Assembly Area Fox, the home of the Marine Logistics Command in the gently rolling Kuwaiti desert, otherwise featureless but for a few tufts of grass. After drawing weapons and ammunition—a routine force protection measure even in Kuwait in April—the group set out from Camp Doha and bounced around in tactical vehicles for about sixty to ninety minutes, though the outskirts of Kuwait city, which looked like one big auto salvage yard (some of the material was "Iraqi surplus" left over from Desert Storm) and into the desert, from good highway to rough paved road, to gravel road, to desert track. Near the Marine Logistics Command's (MLC) headquarters, there was an exercise command post set up in a general-purpose tent without air conditioning. It was a wonder that the computers worked, since the temperature was in the low 100s (Fahrenheit) and rising. There had been a communications glitch, and the Germans had been held up at the gate to the MLC. Visibly annoyed, their commander took the astounding step of declaring that since the exercise was unrealistic, he was exercising his prerogative to cut short German participation and would return with his unit to Doha. The Czech contingent, however, turned to with redoubled enthusiasm and proceeded to practice decontaminating vehicles. The decon site looked like a car wash in the desert, except that the workers were working hard in completely sealed Soviet-style rubber suits in the staggering mid-afternoon heat. The Czech brigadier—who was cheerful, realistic, and easy to talk to—was in the thick of the action, an officer in his element.*

*Reynolds Journal, entry for 8 April 2003.

The next day, the MEF participated in CFLCC's four-day exercise "Lucky Warrior 03-2," intended to test command and control for the two-corps war plan that the CFLCC commander, General McKiernan, had called for after the last round of exercises in November and December. The exercise was labeled a "dress rehearsal" for war; the CFLCC OPlan had been published on 13 January, which meant MEF could finalize its plan, ultimately published on 10 February.[34]

Hard on the heels of Lucky Warrior came the CFLCC ROC drill around the only slightly smaller terrain model in one of the warehouses at Camp Doha on

14–15 February. It integrated the results of previous exercises and gave CFLCC components an opportunity to appreciate how their units would fit into the overall plan. Within the next month, there were at least two other major ROC drills, one at the division level on 27 February, and one at the MEF level on 10 March—not to mention similar evolutions at Task Force Tarawa—all serving to imprint the plan on the minds of the people who would execute it. At the 10 March evolution, General Conway made the point about the value of ROC drills in his terms, saying that the "most important fight is the first one"—the idea being that if the MEF could win the first battle, each succeeding battle would be that much easier.[35]

The ROC drill on 27 February was particularly memorable, a capstone event of sorts. Division engineers again prepared the ground with D-7 bulldozers, constructing on the desert floor a multitiered amphitheater, about one hundred meters in length, with an angled surface for better viewing from the cheap seats. The audience included Generals Conway, Amos, Natonski, and Usher, as well as Maj. Gen. Robin V. Brims, the British division commander. Once again, Marines and soldiers in colored jerseys on the "board" stepped through the actions that their units would take after crossing the line of departure. Division hosted the event, with the stated purpose of putting its intentions—and interactions with other units—on display. General Mattis repeated the by now familiar refrain: all of the "players" had to be able to visualize the "battlefield geometry" and the sequence of events in the first few days of the war, not unlike athletes who are trained to visualize what they are going to do on the playing field. He called it "anticipatory decision making," adding that he considered it "to be one of the most useful abilities of a field grade officer . . . [meaning the ability] to anticipate . . . both friendly requirements . . . and what the enemy's going to do."[36]

The commanders used the ROC drills, and other assemblies, to deliver a series of "go to war" speeches, speaking to their troops about the coming challenges in a more personal way—and continuing to erode the doubts among some that there would even be a war—not an unrealistic response to all of the clamor against the war throughout the world and the calls for a negotiated settlement of some sort.[37]

General Conway himself set out to visit as many units as possible and to deliver his message in person. On 1 March he went to nearby Camp Ryan to appear before Task Force Tarawa. Tarawa's headquarters group, and all of RCT 2, formed a box of companies in the desert. Armored vehicles formed one side of the box, and General Conway mounted the M-1 tank in the center of the side to give his talk, making his points over the high wind and dust.

The general had three main themes: why the MEF was there, what it was going to do, and the individual Marine in battle. The mission was to forestall future terrorist attacks like that of September 11. Either Saddam would disarm, or the coalition would go to war when President Bush gave the word. When and if that happened, the MEF would fight three battles: the deep fight, from the air, to reduce the enemy's combat effectiveness by up to 50 percent; the close fight on the ground; and the rear battle, that is, providing sustainment. The Marines had two things going for them: their reputation as the "meanest in the valley" had preceded them—it must have had an effect on their enemy—and, of course, their combined arms approach. Marines on the ground and in the air fought as one. At this point, on cue, there was a flyover by Cobra attack helicopters and jet fighters. When the noise of the flyover died down, General Conway reminded his Marines that they were not there to fight Iraq, but rather Saddam's regime, and they needed to distinguish between those who wanted to fight and those who did not. Finally, speaking to the individuals in front of him, Conway said that the next few days would govern how they saw themselves, and were seen, for the rest of their lives. Fear was a "natural battlefield phenomenon" that could sharpen perceptions and make Marines react more quickly. The Marines had better gear, weapons, and health care, but at the end of the day the battle was about people, and our people were better. He told the Marines to take care of one another, and themselves, and invoked a blessing before ending his talk.[38]

After addressing the formation at Tarawa, Conway gathered the officers of the task force together and dwelt on some of the same themes in more detail. One theme was the protests against the Iraq war—both at home and abroad—that looked like Vietnam-era antiwar protests on television. He suggested that Tarawa's leaders talk about the protests with their troops, making the points that this was not a war about oil and that his Marines would not be treated like Vietnam vets. They would be honored when they returned home. He expressed his belief that in the near future the president would issue an ultimatum and that when it expired the MEF would attack. The Marines needed to remain flexible; the plan was always changing, there was no guarantee that anyone would draw the same mission he had planned for. He said that while Tarawa's initial role was to be in support, that could change—the MEF might need to reorganize and "retask," say, to head to the oil fields north of Baghdad.

Conway stressed the standard rules of engagement (ROE), declaring that they were not as restrictive as they might have been. On the other hand, Marines had to be careful: the mission was to unseat a dictator, not necessarily to destroy his army, and certainly not to kill civilians. The four specific points he made with respect to ROE were:

(1) Commanders always have the right to self-defense.
(2) An enemy commander who purposefully places his forces near civilians has violated the law of land warfare.
(3) A commander is responsible for his actions based on the facts as they appear to him at the time, not as they will appear in retrospect. It boiled down to a matter of good judgment.

(4) Use "Wilhelm's Law" (named after retired Marine Gen. Charles E. Wilhelm, who had come to theater as a mentor in December to observe the MEF's preparations for war and offer his advice). If the enemy fires first, the Marine response should be proportional: use the smallest weapon first, then progress upward. If Marines initiate fires, they need to mitigate "collateral damage" (to individual civilians and civilian buildings).

Conway went on to express his concerns about fratricide; our weapons were more lethal than the enemy's, and Marines needed to be sure of their targets before they fired. No one wanted to live with the responsibility of having killed friendly troops. Next he returned to the subject of fear. He wanted Tarawa's officers to talk about it with their troops. It was a problem that each would solve in their own way—some thinking they were invincible, others, like Confederate General Stonewall Jackson, believing that all was in God's hands. That said, General Conway told his officers that their greatest fear should be that they let their fellow Marines down in some way—by choking or by being crazy-brave. He cited the example of a second lieutenant in Vietnam who wanted to go home with a Silver Star and was last seen charging the enemy with his .45 caliber pistol at high port. He did nothing for himself, his Marines, or his family.[39]

General Conway's speech varied slightly as he spoke both to other large formations of Marines and to smaller groups of officers, who were invited to ask questions. Generally, however, his remarks were brief, motivating, and practical. There were, for example, admonitions to leaders not to forget to sleep during battle, and there were moments of humor, as when he quipped that "when Abdul in the 51st Mechanized Division north of the border heard that he was taking on the 1st Marine Division followed by the 1st U.K. Division, he said, . . . '*Ana felaka beluchi*,' which is Arabic for 'Ain't that a bitch!'"[40]

On 14 March, Conway made his way over to the British encampment in the desert a few miles away for what he considered a most impressive welcome and what some British officers considered one of the most inspiring speeches they had ever heard.[41] To reach the formation of thousands of British troops of the 7 Armoured and 16 Air Assault Brigades he drove between two lines of Warrior armored personnel carriers, whose crews saluted him as he passed. Finally he reached the heart of the formation, dominated by two enormous cranes or mobile bridges that formed the letter "M"—ostensibly for "Marine"—where he was welcomed by pipers from the Black Watch. Then, using a loudspeaker that, the general was sure, could be heard in Iraq, the British sergeant major called the formation to attention and presented it to him.

Standing on top of a Challenger II tank decorated with a British Union Jack and the Stars and Stripes, Conway told the British that it was great to have them aboard. "Two hundred and fifty years ago the expression 'The British are coming' would scare [American] . . . children." But in Kuwait in December and January, that expression had been "a very positive thing." As he had in other speeches, he spoke about the reasons for war and about the strength of the Marine air-ground team. He said that one of four things would happen: Saddam could turn over his weapons of mass destruction; he could leave the country; "someone up there might kill him; [and] . . . if that doesn't happen, we are going to kill him." At the appropriate moment, Cobras and Hornets flew by—the Hornets blasting "into view in a split second" at two hundred feet before fanning out into the clear blue sky and disappearing from view. Speaking of the British troops' fighting prowess, Conway borrowed a quote attributed to George Orwell: "Our countrymen should rest well in their beds at night because rough men stand ready to visit violence on those who would do them harm."[42]

Subordinate Marine commanders echoed many of the same themes as they made the rounds and addressed their troops. Like General Conway, they spoke about honor and values in a way that was unfamiliar to many Cold War Marines. General Mattis had been preparing his troops for the inevitable for some time, most notably during the ROC drills in late February. On the twenty-seventh, he had spoken forcefully about "soldierly compassion and incredible violence."[43] One of the officers at the ROC drill, field historian Col. Reed R. Bonadonna, wrote he had heard that

> General Mattis was an inspiring and sometimes fiery speaker, and he did not disappoint. . . . He provided the words of inspiration to pass down to the troops. He said that the Brits and we were free people fighting for what we believe in. There are no war protests in Iraq . . . because Saddam would not allow them. He told us that, when we get home, we should shake the hand of a war protester and thank him for exercising the freedoms we had fought to protect, and then wink at the protester's girl. . . . [This] brought the house down, releasing the tension so many of us felt . . . Mattis . . . appealed . . . to our sense of justice and our sense of ourselves as men in the same breath. . . . He was like Patton, maybe better, because [he] . . . came across as natural, not performative.[44]

In a written message in March, General Mattis summarized the reasons for the war and declared that "together we will . . . close with those forces that choose to fight, and destroy them. . . . We will treat all others with decency, demonstrating chivalry and soldierly compassion." He warned his Marines to be ready for "chemical attack, treachery, and . . . other unethical tactics," exhorting them to keep their honor clean and to keep faith with their comrades on their left and right and with Marine air overhead. Finally, in an archaic turn of phrase, he charged them to "fight with a happy heart and strong spirit."[45] The general's intent was to evoke Sitting Bull and Crazy Horse on the Little Bighorn, not General Custer, who may have had a strong spirit but probably did not have a happy heart on the day he died. It was "the idea that . . . you sense that all is well in your world [as] . . . a Marine . . . you've got a good Marine on your left and [on] your right. . . . That sense of happiness [about] . . . who you're fighting alongside armors you . . . against the trauma of the battlefield."[46]

Like General Mattis, General Amos had been making the rounds of his squadrons. The gatherings on 4 March on the USS *Bataan,* now the "Harrier-carrier," were typical. He spoke first to the assembled Marines and sailors in the well deck and then met with the officers of the two embarked squadrons in the ready room. The general implied at each meeting that the war would start soon. He emphasized a number of themes: watching out for one another; the just cause of the coalition's impending actions, to be taken against Saddam Hussein, not the Iraqi people; the corollary need to limit collateral damage; and the belief that many Iraqi soldiers would surrender rather than fight.[47] Just before launching his forces against the enemy, General Amos wrote a more formal message to the wing, offering a "few thoughts" to his Marines about the honorable cause that they were embarking on and declaring that there was "a fear worse than death . . . that's the fear of letting down your fellow Marines." He predicted, "We will win this war and the respect of the Iraqi people . . . and we will do it honorably." He distributed the message to his air groups as an attachment to an e-mail, which he ended with "God Bless each of you . . . now let's go kick the shit out of them!"[48]

Perhaps the most eloquent "go to war" speech that anyone in the MEF delivered was that of Lt. Col. Tim Collins, commanding officer of the 1st Battalion, Royal Irish Regiment, delivered on 19 March. Known for his American-made gold Ray-Ban sunglasses, ever-present cigar, and kukri—the ferocious curved Nepalese blade he was entitled to carry for commanding the Gurkha company attached to his battalion—Collins was a flamboyant commander whose forebears had served with the regiment for generations.[49] Said to be a reflection of his upbringing and his professionalism—and not of a desire for publicity—his unusual eloquence was widely reported in the press and caught the attention of a number of prominent figures, including Prince Charles and President Bush:[50]

We go to liberate, not to conquer. We will not fly our flags in their country. . . . There are some who are alive at this moment who will not be alive shortly. Those who do not wish to go on that journey, we will not send. As for the others, I expect you to rock their world. Wipe them out if that is what they choose. But if you are ferocious in battle, remember to be magnanimous in victory. . . . If there are casualties of war then remember that, when they woke up and got dressed in the morning, they did not plan to die this day. Allow them dignity in death. The enemy should be in no doubt that we are his nemesis and that we are bringing about his rightful destruction. . . . You will be shunned unless your conduct is of the highest . . . We will bring shame on neither our uniform nor our nation.[51]

The speeches, along with the frequent air-raid—or, more precisely, missile-raid—drills, to prepare for a possible preemptive strike with weapons of mass destruction against the troop concentrations in Kuwait, all contributed to a sense that war was imminent. There was also a sense among some officers that the operation was a high-risk proposition on at least one other account, and that was the logistics challenge: Would the MEF be able to push supplies fast enough into the heart of Iraq to maintain the momentum of the attack?[52] But along with these concerns was a wish for the waiting to end and a determination to get on with the inevitable while the Marines were at their peak. If left too long in their desert camps, these young men and women might lose their edge. "Waiting [was]," the MEF historian wrote, "hard on morale . . . from [the] youngest to [the] most senior."[53]

4

The MEF's Opening Gambit

"Tally-Ho!"

The "Opening Gambit" that the MEF prepared so thoroughly in its drills and plans still had as its goal to seize the southern oil fields that were, very roughly, north of Kuwait and west of the city of Basrah, and usually known as the Rumaylah oil fields. For General McKiernan, seizing the oil fields was like a foreign branch to his base plan—separate from the core mission of driving to Baghdad, considered the enemy center of gravity.[1] It was the strategic imperative, imposed on CFLCC by CentCom rather late in the day, intended to keep Saddam Hussein from creating an environmental disaster by blowing oil wells as he had in Kuwait in 1991 and as he planned to do again in his own country when the coalition attacked. The way General Conway explained it, for CentCom the oil fields were as important as Baghdad, and money from oil was needed to rebuild the country.[2]

The final plan was for the division to seize the oil fields while the British, reinforced by 15th MEU(SOC) to make up for a British unit that could not make it to the fight, moved against the Al Faw peninsula and the port of Umm Qasr, which lay between Kuwait and Basrah. Once the Marines had secured Umm Qasr and the oil fields, the British Army would relieve them and become responsible for securing the southeastern part of Iraq. The 15th MEU would revert to Marine control, and the MEF would move to the west, on its way to the river crossings at An Nasiriyah before moving north.

So carefully choreographed, the plan for the first few days of war contrasted with the more general plans for the rest of the war. Even though the nature of MEF participation in the Baghdad fight was still up in the air, the Marine expectation, as of early March, was still that the MEF would pass through Al Kut to threaten Baghdad from the east. General Conway considered the danger of attack by weapons of mass destruction to be "highest" in and around Al Kut; it would be on the route to Baghdad but not too close to that city (the theory being that the enemy would hesitate to contaminate his own capital). That militated for getting the Marines as close to Baghdad as they could, as quickly as possible, whatever the final arrangements for the difficult fight inside the city turned out to be.[3] Nevertheless, General Mattis made it a matter of record that he was ready not only to cross the line of departure but to go on to the capital: "this division is prepared for rapid attack in the Iraq regime's center of gravity, Baghdad."[4]

On 17 March, President Bush gave Saddam Hussein and his sons forty-eight hours to leave Iraq. What followed was a confusing series of schedule changes for the MEF. Now on edge about sabotage in the oil fields, CFLCC sent a "be prepared to" tasker to MEF. This led MEF, in the early morning hours of 18 March, to issue Fragmentary Order (FragO) 046-03, which tasked its subordinate commands to be prepared, by 1800Z (or 1800 Greenwich Mean Time, a standard used to avoid confusion) on the same day, to seize the oil fields on four hours' notice. The next day, after seeing "feed" from a "Predator" unmanned aerial vehicle showing oil well fires that looked like sabotage, CFLCC contacted CentCom to request permission to launch the ground offensive early in order to limit the potential for further sabotage.[5]

The adrenaline was now flowing freely. Long lines of Marine vehicles now started to move to their dispersal areas and then to their intermediate attack positions near the border. The processions moved across the desert landscape on 18 and 19 March, while engineers finalized the complicated work of clearing lanes through the demilitarized zone on the border between Kuwait and Iraq. Though often called "the berm"—as in, "I'm going across the berm (into Iraq)"—it was actually much more than that. In most places there was at least one antitank ditch, a ten-foot berm, and an electric fence. With Kuwaiti assistance, coalition engineers had been working on the berm for quite some time to prepare lanes for the attack.[6] Ground crews and aircrews turned to at the large bases like Ali Al Saleem and Al Jaber, as they did at a few small expeditionary airfields like "Joe Foss" (which was little more than a rolled-sand landing strip for C-130s in the desert near the Iraqi border). General Amos reported that "strike aircraft . . . and assault support/attack aircraft . . . are loaded with ammunition, fueled, and ready. Casevac [casualty evacuation] aircraft are forward . . . with the maneuver elements. Quick-strike package is identified. Crews . . . [are] on 30 minutes alert . . . [for] counter-fire mission should Iraqi forces attack . . . prematurely. . . . Commanders are briefed, targets assigned. We are prepared to execute the quick start option or the base plan; 3d MAW is ready to roll."[7]

Before long MEF received another order from CFLCC establishing D-Day and H-Hour for 1800Z on 19 March, when the air war would start. Ground operations were to start two days later, on 21 March.[8] Now everyone knew that war was hours away. The word was passed that there was a high probability of Iraqi missile strikes during the night of 19–20 March. Many Marines had their gas masks and MOPP-suits staged for a quick run to a shelter from their sleeping mats, but nothing happened during the night.[9]

MEF's war started the next day, 20 March, with an unexpected bang. At approximately 0725Z, there was a sound like that of a low-flying jet, followed by an explosion that shook the ground, and then by a tall gray-brown plume of smoke, about two hundred meters north of the perimeter of Camp Commando. The very first effect was that it interrupted a staff meeting—General Conway and his principal staff members were in a briefing tent near the point of impact; they all dove under the tables.[10] Other members of the MEF staff wondered if the plume was poison gas, and if it was a terrorist attack—there had been no warning. Most reached for their protective gear, and NBC monitors swung into action. There was more than a little bit of confusion as Marines tried to figure out where to go and what to do. Many took shelter in the "Scud bunkers"—the inverted concrete culverts and sandbag concoctions—but the combat operations center continued to operate. As many Marines sat jammed in the bunkers, with gas masks on, the word was passed to go to MOPP IV—the highest NBC protective state. Four Cobras were scrambled to scout for possible enemy attackers on the ground. By 0825Z it was clear what had happened and the "all-clear" had been sounded, but there were many more missile-raid alerts throughout the day, announced by the siren/loudspeaker combination known as "the Giant Voice." By one count thirteen alerts had been sounded.[11]

By now CFLCC had received its answer from CentCom and was free to attack into southern Iraq to secure the oil fields. CFLCC passed the order to its subordinate commands to attack at 1800Z on 20 March, not on 21 March (as CFLCC had ordered earlier).[12] It was around this time that General Mattis called Col. Joseph F. Dunford, the commander of the lead element, and asked him how soon he could attack. Colonel Dunford asked for a few minutes to poll his staff, but soon came back with the answer: four hours. In fact, RCT 5 was ready to go in three hours, and that is what happened.[13]

At 1512Z MEF released the execute order, and on 20 March at 1742Z, which was 2042 local, RCT 5's tanks crossed the border into Iraq in the dark, about nine hours ahead of the last "regularly" scheduled time. Instead of an attack at dawn, the RCT was attacking at night—a much more complicated evolution, especially for a large, reinforced formation that was going into combat as a team for the first time. It was quite an achievement. When his troops crossed the border, General Mattis's official comment was "Tally-ho!"[14]

It was only later that the MEF learned that during the night of 19–20 March, the United States had begun the war by hitting select targets in Baghdad—an unplanned bomb and missile strike at Saddam Hussein and his entourage, who, according to U.S. intelligence, were spending the night in a bunker at a place called Dora Farms, a residential compound in south Baghdad. The report turned out to be false; a somewhat shaken Saddam Hussein soon appeared on Iraqi television vowing defiance. What was clear was that this was not an early start to the coalition's long-planned air war. The timing of the missile attack on Camp Commando on 20 March suggests that the attack—and those that followed—was in retaliation for the Dora Farms attack.

What Dora Farms and CFLCC's images of burning oil wells did was breathe new life into the old debate about the separation between G-Day and A-Day. The CFLCC request for permission to attack early amounted to a request to reverse the order of G-Day and A-Day. When CentCom granted CFLCC's request, it was official—rock and roll for G-Day, wait one for A-Day. That left the relationship between air strikes and ground attacks within the MEF's own sector. It is fair to ask whether there was to be any separation between them, and the answer was, not much at all, apparently for the same reasons. The Marines simply liked synchronicity, whether the context was the Iraqi theater as a whole or just the Marine battle space. As D-Day approached, the plan was for the MAW—along with Marine artillery—to strike some targets in zone hours before the infantry went over the top. A variant of the plan called for even greater simultaneity, with a "spike" of close air attacks during the first day of the ground war. In either case, the guiding principle was coordination between Wing and Division, and everyone knew that. As General Amos had written on 19 March, the "synchronization of major muscle movements is complete."[15]

On 19 March the MAW had started attacking Safwan Hill, the high ground on the border between Iraq and Kuwait, which was a great observation post for the Iraqis, and was flying over the 5th Marines when they crossed the border into Iraq late on 20 March. On that day, the first full day of war, the 3d MAW flew 259 missions—24 in support of CFACC, and 235 in support of I MEF, shifting its emphasis somewhat from generally "shaping" the battlefield to "preparing" specific objectives that Division was about to assault. The arrangement with CFACC was clearly working as the Marines intended. It is worth quoting the dry language of the wing's command chronology to get a sense of its activities on 20 and 21 March:

Maintained constant airborne CAS [close air support] coverage in support of RCT 5 . . .

   Maintained constant F/W [fixed wing] FAC(A) [Forward Air Controller (Airborne)] coverage for both RCT 5 and RCT 7, to enable interdiction of enemy counterattack or reinforcing elements.

Conducted F/W counter fire in support of RCT 7 . . .

Began . . . effort in earnest against Iraqi 2nd echelon forces, focusing on enemy indirect fire and SSM [missile] assets. . . . Shaping MEF battle space . . . Focus on MRL [multiple rocket launcher], artillery, and reinforcing armor in Al Amarah and Basrah areas . . .

Provided 8 F/W sorties to conduct CAS in support of UK forces engaged in Al Faw . . .

Pushed . . . units forward to commence establishment of FARPs [forward arming and refueling point] at Safwan and Jalibah.[16]

The last item does not look particularly dramatic on paper, but the words belie an impressive accomplishment. Ultimately, some four thousand ground personnel from the MAW crossed the berm and, according to plan, set up some fifteen small air bases and support points in Iraq. The concept was not new, but the scale was, as was the speed and flexibility of execution.[17] There were some dramatic, even heroic, moments for the support Marines who made it all happen. One of the most memorable interviews any field historian conducted during the war was that of Gy. Sgt. Melba L. Garza, the operations chief of Marine Wing Support Squadron 271. She recounted, in a deadpan voice, her memories of traveling north in one of the long convoys of support vehicles, which included a number of fuel tankers. These slow-moving convoys stretched literally for miles along the few highways through the desert. When the convoy was ambushed by Iraqis on the ground, there was not a great deal that any one individual, especially someone like an ops chief armed with a 9mm pistol, could do about it except hope that the accompanying Cobras would be able to deal with the enemy—that is, until the Cobras ran low on fuel and the support Marines decided to do some "hot" refueling on the spot so that the Cobras could stay in this particular fight until it was over. Refueling is normally done in a controlled environment, after the aircraft powers down. If time matters, it is all right to refuel "hot," while the blades are still turning. But there is no doctrine about refueling under fire. To say the least, this group of Marines redefined the term "hot."[18]

Within about eleven hours of crossing the line of departure, RCT 5 had seized most of its initial objectives. This was largely because the division was so well prepared and coordinated on many levels. A look at fire support coordination from an artilleryman's perspective suggests only some of the complexities:

During . . . the "Opening Gambit," the opportunity for fire support coordination to break down was at its greatest. Consider managing a fire support coordination line shift, a battlefield coordination line . . . shift, coordinated fire lines . . . shifting up to seven times, opening and closing multiple keypad variations of up to six different killboxes [the map grids used to coordinate fires], coordinating numerous no-fire areas . . . and managing a restricted target list of over 12,000 targets all within a matter of 12 hours. [At the same time there was coordination] . . . with a counterobservation post program of fire, breaching operations, three regimental combat teams attacking at separate times, . . . two counterbattery programs of fire, one counterarmor program of fire, attacking high-payoff targets of opportunity . . . a transfer of control between the division main . . . and division forward . . . and deteriorating weather conditions.[19]

On the same day, 21 March, the rest of the Marine division, as well as the British division, poured through the breaches in the border installations between Kuwait and Iraq on their way north, while the "official" air war, the "shock and awe" phase, finally began over Baghdad with the obliteration of a carefully chosen set of targets. The world watched on live television. This was certainly an impressive display of precision targeting and pyrotechnics that lit the night sky and offered one very fine photo opportunity for the news services. Some of the resulting photos of Baghdad in flames will be emblems of the war for years to come. But it did not spark an uprising, and the regime did not collapse.[20]

Back in the south, there was sporadic fighting, some of it sharp and deadly, which continued into 22 March when RCT 7 engaged isolated pockets of resistance in the Marine area of operations. One of the first Marines to be killed in Iraq died in one of these firefights. He was 2d Lt. Therrel S. Childers of 1st Battalion, 5th Marines, who was hit when Iraqi fighters in a civilian pickup truck attacked his unit in the oil fields. But by and large the Marines were pleasantly surprised by the relatively light resistance they encountered, which was much less than they had expected or feared. The local Iraqi command, the 51st Mechanized Division, had ceased to exist in any recognizable military form, and there were already hundreds of apparent deserters in civilian clothes fleeing to the west on 21 March. While some of the Iraqi wells near the border with Kuwait burned brightly after being sabotaged by their owners, there were also instances of Iraqi oil company employees waiting patiently for the coalition forces to arrive, after carefully following the instructions for preventing sabotage in the CFLCC leaflets that had rained down from the sky.[21] Overall, there was far less destruction to the oil infrastructure than many had feared. (That was the good news. The bad news was that the oil infrastructure had not been maintained for years and was in terrible shape.) By the end of the day, with most of the MEF's initial objectives having been seized, the division was getting ready to turn them over to the British. The official relief in place (RIP) occurred without incident on 22 and 23 March. When reporting the RIP, Division added the note that after receiving information about possible Iraqi infiltrators in American uniforms, the commanding general had "directed all Division Marines to remove their moustaches as part of the . . . effort to distinguish Iraqi infiltrators."[22]

With the British now protecting its right flank, the division could now turn west, moving in the same direction as Task Force Tarawa, which had rolled through the breach and crossed into Iraq on the early morning of 21 March and moved toward the town of Jalibah, paying special attention to Jalibah Air Base, where the MEF was soon to place its forward headquarters, and the key terrain at the small city of An Nasiriyah.

5

The Bridges of An Nasiriyah

"One hellacious of a fight"

The heart of An Nasiriyah is something like an island between two waterways—the Euphrates River on one side, running roughly northwest to southeast, and the Saddam Canal, which runs more or less parallel to the Euphrates on the other, eastern side of the city. An Nasiriyah controls the bridges over both river and canal that lead to Route 7, the main highway to the north through the center of southern Iraq. Route 1, a more westerly highway to Baghdad, passes within a few miles of An Nasiriyah but does not come within the city limits. Apart from the fact that if you approach from the desert, An Nasiriyah is like an oasis—with its palm trees and other greenery—the city has little to offer; pictures show an uninviting Third World "sprawl of slums and industrial compounds," with two- to three-story concrete buildings set on a grid of bad roads and alleyways, many strewn with garbage and raw sewage.[1] The city was all the more rundown because its largely Shia population was known to have opposed Saddam's rule, and he repaid the favor by neglecting even its most basic needs.

Task Force Tarawa's mission was to be the first Marine unit at An Nasiriyah and to secure the bridge over the Euphrates on Route 1, which lay a few kilometers west of the city. It had the follow-on mission to "be prepared to" secure the bridges over the Euphrates and the Saddam Canal on the eastern edge of the city, which the Marine division, especially RCT 1, would need to pass over on its way north on Route 7 toward Al Kut. (The plan was for RCT 1 to more or less keep pace with RCTs 5 and 7 as they moved up Route 1.) In a sense it was a straightforward mission, and it was one that had been assigned to Tarawa before it arrived in Kuwait. Tarawa officers, down to the company level, had performed map studies, war games, and rehearsals for An Nasiriyah.[2] That said, there was a difference between the East and West Coast Marines, who had been visualizing the first days of the war since the summer of 2002. By contrast, most Tarawa Marines did not begin to focus in on the mission until December 2002, and while the operational picture had come into progressively sharper focus as Ground Day approached, there were still a lot of unknowns about An Nasiriyah. One lingering question was just how "permissive" the city would be. The general assumption was that the Marines would receive a friendly welcome from the townspeople, and at worst some light resistance from Saddam loyalists. Certainly the Army, which would pass through part of the area before the Marines, would find out for sure.[3]

On 22 March the MEF announced that within the next twenty-four hours it wanted to secure the eastern crossing sites at An Nasiriyah and commence the forward passage of lines by 1st Marine Division through Task Force Tarawa.[4] On 23 March MEF reported that it had released its FragO 017-03 "that tasked TF Tarawa to conduct [an] RIP with 3ID at [the] Hwy 1 Euphrates River crossing and attack to seize [the] bridges east of An Nasiriyah iot [in order to] facilitate the unimpeded continuation of the attack by 1st Mar Div to the north and northwest."[5]

It was a mission fraught with potential complications. Tarawa's western boundary was with the Army, and the task force's first job was to relieve elements of the 3d Infantry Division that had passed through the area on their way to the western desert. Then, after seizing the bridges that passed through the city, Tarawa would have to coordinate the forward passage of lines with RCT 1. These missions are difficult enough in peacetime between units that have trained together, let alone units from two separate services, Army and Marines, and two separate chains of command, task force and division, which literally had trouble getting on the same frequency. There was a final complication: Marines, many of them new to combat, not to mention the demands of combat in a city, were beginning to get very tired. The burst of adrenaline that had carried them across the border and into combat could not keep all of the Marines on their feet forever, especially when everyone, from the MEF commander to the private on the firing line, had to work and fight in the hot, bulky NBC protective gear—usually with a flak vest as the outer layer—in the desert heat. The MEF was approaching a culminating point of sorts: the end of the first phase of the battle for Iraq.[6]

At An Nasiriyah, Task Force Tarawa was, briefly, the de facto main effort, and the burden of winning this particular fight fell on the shoulders of General Natonski. He has been described as a large man with a deliberate, confident bearing who was shaped by his experiences as a MEU commander and as a senior staff officer in the J-3 at CentCom as well as in Plans, Policies, and Operations at Headquarters Marine Corps. Senior members of Natonski's staff liked working for him and even called him a "model commanding general." An Nasiriyah was to be Tarawa's first major challenge. Both Natonski and many of his Marines knew it might be their only time at center stage. He was determined to get it right, even if that meant demanding sacrifices from his line commanders.

When they met late on 22 March, General Natonski and the commander of RCT 2, Col. Ronald L. Bailey, focused on the MEF order. Following up on the MEF FragO, General Natonski tasked Colonel Bailey, who commanded most of the ground troops in the task force, with seizing both the Route 1 and the Route 7 crossings on 23 March. This was a departure from the original plan to begin by seizing the Route 1 bridge to the west of the city, and then move on the "eastern," or "city" bridges "on order"—which meant there would be a delay between the two evolutions, a chance, however short, to fine-tune the planning for the next step. There was nothing new by way of intelligence about An Nasiriyah, but Colonel Bailey was warned to expect small arms fire. When he expressed some concerns—his troops needed rest and his mechanized assets were low on fuel—General Natonski told him it was important to press on, the Marines would have to run on adrenaline.[7]

Marines throughout the theater felt that the next day, 23 March, started bad and never got any better. Around daybreak, the Army's truck-borne 507th Maintenance Company lost its way and blundered into a bloody ambush in An Nasiriyah. One of the members of the 507th was PFC Jessica Lynch, who was wounded and captured by the Iraqis and after being rescued went on to become a celebrity of sorts. This helped set the stage for the events that followed, as did the relief in place to the west of the city between Tarawa, in particular "Charlie" Company, 2d LAR Battalion, and the 3d Infantry Division. This was accompanied by a boundary shift that put virtually all of An Nasiriyah in Marine battle space. The relief in place and the boundary shift were otherwise unremarkable, despite occasional allegations to the contrary.[8]

A few miles away, during the advance toward An Nasiriyah from the southeast, at about the same time as the 507th was ambushed, 1st Battalion, 2d Marines, with tanks and a combined antiarmor team in the lead, encountered small arms and mortar fire while still well outside the city. This was a portent of more to come. A short while later the Marines encountered a few survivors from the 507th, which fed the hope that there might be more survivors up ahead. This possibility put added pressure on the RCT.

Mid-morning on 23 March, General Natonski flew twice to the battlefield in his command Huey. When he looked down from the air, he did not see the RCT's troops where he wanted them to be. His impression was that the attack was not going quickly enough; what were they waiting for? He ordered the Huey to land at Colonel Bailey's forward command post, which was near a railroad bridge outside the city limits, so that he could urge him to move faster. On the first visit, the general spoke both with Capt. Troy K. King, USA, the commander of the 507th, who told him firsthand about the ambush, and with Lt. Col. Ricky L. Grabowski, the commander of the lead battalion, 1st Battalion, 2d Marines (1/2), in addition to Colonel Bailey himself.[9] General Natonski told Colonel Bailey and Lieutenant Colonel Grabowski that he could see nothing in their way, no enemy tanks or other mechanized assets, and that the MEF was relying on Tarawa to seize the bridges and hold them open. General Natonski believed that by moving fast, Tarawa would keep the enemy off balance and, ultimately, limit the number of friendly casualties. After talking to Colonel Bailey, General Natonski flew to the MEF command post at Jalibah, a few minutes' flying time from An Nasiriyah, and briefed General Conway on the situation. When he returned to Bailey's position an hour later, Natonski repeated his orders, which now contained the even more forceful pronouncement, seemingly from the MEF commander's mouth, that Bailey was holding up the MEF.[10]

Colonel Bailey did as he was told and made the general's intent his own, despite his personal reservations. This was, after all, a city that had not been thoroughly probed by reconnaissance in the recent past, perhaps because of the expectations that the natives would be friendly.[11] Similarly, there appears to have been no plan to conduct preparatory artillery or air attacks before the Marines entered the city limits, even though air and artillery support were on call and about to become very active participants in the battle. Cobras flew above the advancing Marines, and the artillerymen of 1st Battalion, 10th Marines were following in trace of RCT 2's lead elements, ready to emplace and process fire missions in very short order.[12]

After the first meeting ended and the three principals went their separate ways, Colonel Bailey had second thoughts and wanted to talk to Lieutenant Colonel Grabowski again. He wanted to be sure that Grabowski had not left with the wrong impression: Grabowski should proceed, but not at all costs. It was the kind of thought that passes through a commander's mind as he sends his troops off to battle, especially on the first day. Bailey was a conscientious officer with a reputation for taking care of his Marines. But Grabowski was already out of reach, moving into the attack, and it was too late to review the bidding.[13]

It was now sometime before noon; after the fight, Lieutenant Colonel Grabowski commented that it was difficult to remember exactly what happened when, given the intensity of the combat, which plays tricks on a person's sense of time. The sun was high, the day clear and hot. Two kilometers south of the Euphrates, the tanks detached to refuel, but the rest of Grabowski's battalion continued over the river and into the city. After the friendly tanks detached to refuel, Bravo Company encountered enemy tanks, which were engaged and destroyed by antiarmor Marines, including a "Javelin" team. Alpha Company secured the far end of the eastern bridge over the Euphrates. Then Bravo Company, with the battalion command group, crossed over the bridge and, looking for a route around downtown An Nasiriyah, drove onto apparently firm ground that turned out to be a kind of tarry quicksand. One Marine, Cpl. Jason J. Polanco, was looking at the two tanks in front of him that were running level with his own vehicle one second, and then, in the next, "just dropped in[to] the mud."[14] Bravo Company's plan to come up on the southeastern flank of the bridge over the Saddam Canal, and to support the assault on that bridge by fire, was on hold.

With Bravo Company stuck on its right to the east, Charlie Company forged ahead through four kilometers of cityscape that became known as "Ambush Alley," coming under "intense machine gun, small arms, and RPG fire" from a variety of combatants—a mix of regular soldiers and paramilitary fighters, almost all of whom wore civilian clothes. Sometime after noon, mindful of the pressure on the task force and the RCT, the Charlie Company commander, Capt. Daniel J. Wittnam, decided to keep moving ahead. He appears to have made this particular decision more or less on his own, although it was definitely consistent with his battalion commander's intent. Lieutenant Colonel Grabowski had effectively conveyed his determination to seize and hold the bridges. Not only was Wittnam's the first Marine company over the Saddam Canal, but it was now out ahead of the rest of the battalion, more exposed to the enemy than anyone else.[15]

Wittnam's company drove across the wide, flat modern bridge—it looked as much like a stretch of highway as a bridge—into what amounted to a kind of fire sack. The weapons platoon sergeant, Staff Sergeant Lonnie O. Parker, remembered the feeling: "We all came out of the door [of our amtrack], got . . . situational awareness of where we were, where the enemy was. They were located north of us, they were located to the west of us, they were located to the south of us, and they were located to the east of us."[16] The Marines found themselves on a roadway on the far side of the canal, surrounded by fields that were lower than the roadway, which made them good targets for the waiting Iraqi soldiers. They could see the enemy scurrying in and around their fighting positions and the plain concrete buildings that were all some distance away on the other side of the fields and the berms that helped to define the fields. Apparently emboldened by their success against the 507th, and now ready to fight the next wave of Americans, the Iraqis fired infantry weapons and, especially, mortars up to 120mm in caliber. (Task Force Tarawa later learned that the enemy's positions were primarily oriented to the north, in order to defend against an airborne attack that was never planned, let alone executed.) The enemy infantry showed no interest in closing with the Marines and getting within easy range of their small arms; they chose either to fire from their foxholes or to dart out from a courtyard or alleyway to fire off a few rounds. At least one Marine small unit leader had to keep his hard-chargers from rushing across the open fields at the enemy.[17] Instead, the Marines used their own weapons against the enemy and called in artillery— 1/10's guns soon fired to good effect. Sadly, the company's forward observer, 1st Lt. Frederick E. Pokorney Jr., was killed while calling for fire. But thanks in part to the enemy's poor marksmanship, and thanks in part to the Marines' good work, the company was soon making some headway against the enemy and consolidating its own position. Wittnam had seized an important objective, and he wanted to hold it until reinforced or relieved.

Then, a U.S. Air Force A-10 Warthog swooped by, circled, and lined up for a strafing run on the Marines as they watched in horror. Though a jet, the Warthog is designed to fly low for close air support missions and, with its depleted uranium rounds, was known as a good tank buster. It is usually a welcome sight on the battlefield and had already done good work on 23 March against other targets. But now it was bearing down on friendlies.

One Charlie Company Marine on the bridge, 1st Lt. Michael S. Seely, had been strafed by an A-10 before, in 1991, and he knew instantly what was happening:

> I didn't even have to look up, because I knew exactly what that sound was. . . . I ran up and found 2d Platoon scattered all around the area there, but I grabbed their [radioman and] said, "Put that damn thing on Battalion Tac now!" I got on Battalion Tac immediately and started calling, "Cease fire! Cease fire!" Timberwolf 6 [the battalion commander] came up, perfectly calm, and I started talking to him. He said, "What do you got?" I said, "We [are] having friendly air, [an] A-10 strafing our pos." I don't know the time that it took, but it was probably a couple minutes later . . . I don't know, 10, 15, whatever—the A-10 was still circling overhead.[18]

To make matters worse, the A-10 (apparently along with his wingman—the A-10 was flying in a two-plane section) made numerous deadly passes, while the Marines on the ground tried every way possible to end what arguably became the most notorious friendly fire incident of the war. By mid-afternoon each of the battalion's rifle companies was, in the understated words of the *Marine Corps Gazette* article about the fight, "decisively engaged in non-mutually supporting positions" throughout the city and only in sporadic touch with their battalion commander, whose tactical radio nets have been described as "clogged."[19] It was only later in the afternoon that the companies were able to support each other, which is what Wittnam had been waiting for, given his intent to hold the position until reinforcements could get to him. He estimated later that the wait was between two and a half and three hours.[20] He and his men had breathed an enormous collective sigh of relief when a pair of Marine tanks rumbled into their lines and suppressed the remaining Iraqi opposition once and for all. (There had been a couple of anxious moments when the Charlie Company Marines first heard tanks coming their way, and before they identified them as the friendly reinforcements they were hoping and waiting for.)[21] Exhausted, dirty, and bloody, they began to recover from the first day of heavy fighting for the MEF in Iraq, which cost the lives of eighteen Marines. With some pride and some sadness, Staff Sergeant Parker summed it all up when he said that it "wasn't supposed to be no really big conflict that day," but "we put up one hellacious of a fight. . . . It's really sad when it ends and you lose the majority of your people not from enemy fire but from friendly fire."[22]

Task Force Tarawa remained heavily engaged in An Nasiriyah for eight more days, working to clear the enemy from the route through the city. This included some bitter house-to-house fighting; defeating some one thousand enemy fighters massing for a counterattack; and on 1 April, support for the mission to rescue that most famous of survivors of the ambush of the 507th, Private First Class Lynch. The field historian attached to Task Force Tarawa, Colonel Bonadonna, commented that 3d Battalion, 2d Marines became "adept at collecting front-line intelligence and following up with what were termed 'House Calls' on the homes of officials of the regime," which, in turn, led to further contacts and a growing hold on An Nasiriyah.[23] Throughout this period there was good cooperation with Army Special Forces, whose detachments continued to operate alongside the task force and produced actionable intelligence, which often led to fire missions, air strikes, or raids like the Lynch rescue.[24] It is worth noting one such attack, early on, when Tarawa drove a band of fedayeen from a hospital that turned out to have a stockpile of "200 AK-47 . . . [rifles], 20,000 rounds of ammunition, 3000 chemsuits and masks, a tank[!], . . . 400 Iraqi uniforms, and four U.S. Army uniforms."[25] This was one of the first concrete indications to the coalition that Iraq was one vast ammunition dump-cum-armory, which would pose a disposal problem on an unimagined scale. Nevertheless, by early April, An Nasiriyah was taking its first tentative steps, under Tarawa, toward postcombat reconstruction—a few days ahead of the rest of Iraq.

Various controversies about 23 March were to continue for some time. There were questions, some of which made more sense than others, about such things as why the Marines did not bypass An Nasiriyah or in general do a better job of fighting in cities.[26] There were other questions about whether it was right for Task Force Tarawa to push into An Nasiriyah the way it did. Would it have made sense to wait for the tanks moving with 1st Battalion, 2d Marines to refuel before advancing into the city? Or to wait until the battlefield had been "shaped"—that is, why hadn't there been a more thorough reconnaissance before the Marines

The Other Ambush on 23 March

A few hours after Wittnam's Marines drove across the bridge over the canal into the enemy fire sack, another group of Marines had a similar experience in the desert north of the city. The story begins late on the afternoon of 23 March. One of Division's P-3 Orions, borrowed from the Navy, was flying high and slow above the battlefield to scout the route up Highway 1, while light armored reconnaissance (LAR) Marines did the same on the ground. Although one of the accompanying Cobra pilots who had been flying around the LARs thought he had seen some signs of enemy activity, the route seemed clear to Division. General Mattis decided he wanted the LARs to move even faster, and personally called one of his LAR commanders, Lt. Col. Herman S. Clardy III of 3d Battalion, code name "Wolf pack," to tell him to proceed up to the town of Hantush some distance up the road. Clardy told his commanders to pull off the road and gather around him for a five-minute briefing and a FragO. Minutes later the battalion went "screaming north" into the gathering dusk, well out ahead of any friendly formations and outside the artillery fan.

Capt. Charles J. Blume, Clardy's fire support coordinator, remembered in vivid terms what happened next:

> We definitely could feel [that] we were getting well out in front of the Division. We lost comms with the DASC-A [the airborne direct air support center] and it was starting to get dark. . . . We began to see abandoned weapons and equipment strewn along the highway. [We saw a] suspicious vehicle . . . to our front that [looked at] . . . us and sped away. . . . We could all feel the hair standing up on the backs of our necks. You could tell something was about to happen.

What did happen next, at 1607Z, was burned into the memory of one of the company commanders, Maj. Bruce Bell, USMCR:

> The fedayeen had actually laid out a decent "U"-shaped ambush spread over . . . 500 meters on both sides of the road. . . . They picked a tactically sound, defensively oriented bend in the highway . . . to exploit massed surprise . . . fires on the lead units of whoever fell into the trap. They also had assembled a column of approximately ten tanks, armored personnel carriers, and other various "technical" . . . vehicles [mostly pickup trucks with machine gun mounts] which they positioned on the eastern flank of the ambush position, hoping to use a north-south jeep trail . . . to move down and flank units caught in the kill zone on the highway.

When the enemy opened fire, at first it was only scattered tracers flying across the road, and then there was a torrent of fire all up and down the route of march. Some of the enemy appeared to be massing for an attack. The Marines fired back, but the enemy fire kept coming. The air officer tried to reach Clardy over the radio, but could not. Someone, either the air officer or the communications officer, called "slingshot," the heart-stopping code word for "I am being overrun." Division later reported that the call came over the Iridium cell phone, the official/unofficial alternate communications system in this war, and that "3d MAW immediately responded with 6 Harriers and 4 Cobras, followed shortly thereafter by a host of additional air assets." It was all over by 1741Z, the remnants of a battalion-sized Iraqi unit left smoking on the battlefield. The Marines, miraculously, emerged from the fight with only one WIA (wounded in action) and some battle scars on their vehicles, but were still able to continue moving up the road.*

*IMEF Sitrep 221800ZMar03 to 231759ZMar03 (Copy in Reynolds Working Papers, MCHC, Washington, D.C.); 1stMarDiv ComdC, Jan.–June 03 (MCHC, Washington, D.C.), section 2, chapter 5, pp. 5–8; Maj. Bruce Bell e-mails to author, 11 and 12 July 03 (Copies in Reynolds Working Papers, MCHC, Washington, D.C.).

entered the city, or why hadn't artillery and air struck Iraqi positions before the Marines reached them? Did Captain Wittnam's decision to advance Charlie Company by itself make sense? There are answers, some more compelling than others, to all of the questions about 23 March. General Natonski's pressure on RCT 2, and Captain Wittnam's decision to push on and then hold on, may have saved the day. One of the Iraqi commanders captured at An Nasiriyah commented that the fast tempo of the American advance had made it impossible for him to respond in time and that he had been "shocked" at the aggressiveness of Marine small unit leaders. "He said that his fighters were very confident initially . . . but became dispirited when the Marines kept coming at them."[27]

From the CFLCC and the MEF point of view, it would not have made sense to bypass An Nasiriyah. The layout of the roads and bridges around the city made it difficult to bypass. Not even assault bridging would have helped. When RCT 1's Col. Joseph D. Dowdy considered that option, he concluded it would add days to the journey north. Even if the bypass option had made sense, the Marines would still have had to find a way to deal with potential enemy threats to their lines of communication from within the city. Simply put, CFLCC forces needed to control all of the routes in and around An Nasiriyah and had had little choice but to go into the city. As General McKiernan put it: "Everybody had to go by An Nasiriyah, in either corps' sector, because that was the only place to cross the

Euphrates. . . . It was just the [nature of the] whole fight in the south. Our enemy concentrated out of urban areas."[28]

Perhaps the most bitter controversy about An Nasiriyah was in a class by itself: the controversy over the "friendly fire" by the A-10s, which led to a lengthy investigation and, in April 2004, to the release by Central Command of a nine-hundred-page report that concluded it was a Marine air officer who had cleared the A-10s to fire on any vehicles on the far side of the bridge over the canal. Located a few hundred yards away with Bravo Company, the officer apparently believed he was with the lead element of the battalion and therefore no Marines were in front of him. (Charlie Company did not have its own forward air controller.) The report essentially invited the Marine Corps to continue the investigation to determine whether any disciplinary action should be taken against that officer, which would perhaps prolong the controversy. One observer has argued that it is unfair to single out the air controller, since his actions followed, at least in part, from the actions of others in his chain of command, and since it appears that some of the battalion's communications nets failed at crucial points.[29]

The end result of the general confusion on 23 March and the attack by the A-10 was not only the painful casualty count but also a monumental traffic jam that lasted through 24 March and into 25 March.[30] The CentCom report stated that "eight of the deaths were verified as the result of enemy fire; of the remaining 10 Marines killed, investigators were unable to determine the cause of death as the Marines were also engaged in heavy fighting with the enemy at the time of the incident. Of the 17 wounded, only one was conclusively . . . hit by friendly fire."[31] Behind the Marines in the fight at the bridge and along "Ambush Alley" thirty kilometers of vehicles waited. In addition to Tarawa's vehicles, there were literally hundreds of vehicles belonging to RCT 1. It was still a particularly lucrative target for the Iraqis. But not unlike his counterpart in RCT 2, the commander of RCT 1, Colonel Dowdy, was reluctant to try to squeeze his regiment through Ambush Alley. And behind Colonel Dowdy a seemingly endless convoy of supply trucks was waiting to move north.[32]

This was the kind of evolution that attracted more attention than most subordinate commanders want in a decade. On 24 March there were a number of generals on site: Tarawa's General Natonski; the assistant 1st Marine Division commander, Brig. Gen. John F. Kelly, whom General Mattis tasked with roaming the battlefield to help him maintain situational awareness; and General Conway, the MEF commander. Even a retired general was nearby, Maj. Gen. Ray L. Smith, traveling with the division to gather material for a book, *The March Up*. (General Smith and his coauthor, Bing West, recorded many interesting vignettes for posterity, including the mood of a young infantryman on the line at An Nasiriyah who seemed to think that events had slowed because of the number of generals there. It is not clear whether the Marine knew that he was talking to a general.)

Being the kind of general who made it a point to see for himself how the fight was going, Conway traveled by helicopter to An Nasiriyah from Jalibah, where MEF Main was by now well established. On the way, he flew over what looked to him like a great deal of Marine combat power stretched out on the road, and he remembered thinking, with growing frustration, there should be no holding all of that power back. This made him all the more determined to deliver his message in no uncertain terms. After landing, Conway spent over an hour at Tarawa's command post. Then he and General Natonski drove forward in a "soft-skinned" HumVee, the vehicle that had replaced the jeep, through fires so intense that three Marines around them were injured. According to one account, the two generals talked matters over with Brigadier General Kelly and Colonel Dowdy while AK-47 rounds snapped overhead. General Natonski remembered later the topics discussed were whether the Marines could hold the bridges and whether 1st Marines could pass through Task Force Tarawa and over the bridges without delay. Throughout, Conway's basic message was simple: find a way to get things moving again.[33]

Word spread wide about the fighting in An Nasiriyah, along with reports and rumors of heavy U.S. casualties. Recordings of a disturbing Iraqi television broadcast mission showing the killed and captured soldiers made the rounds while corpsmen and doctors waited for the Marine wounded. There was a perception that U.S. forces had suffered a setback and that the war was not going according to plan, especially among the experts on television with their nonstop stream of commentary and free advice, usually from thousands of miles away. (They were not, almost needless to say, making themselves popular with commanders in Iraq and Kuwait.) Reflecting the views of many, the historian with Tarawa, Colonel Bonadonna, wrote on 23 March that "any hopes we may have had for an easy entry into An Nasiriyah, and any larger hopes for a campaign as a series of capitulations, have ended today." The war could be longer and harder than anyone had expected—or hoped.[34]

Underlying this new perception was the nature of the fight at An Nasiriyah, which General McKiernan characterized simply as "a damned tough urban fight."[35] It was that—and more. The general expectation had been that the Iraqi soldiers in the regular army divisions stationed in the south of the country would surrender in droves once the coalition crossed into Iraq, and that the population, at least in the south, where there was a Shia majority hostile to Saddam Hussein's Sunni ruling class, would welcome the coalition as liberators. But the number of prisoners had been measured in the hundreds, not the expected thousands. This did not mean that the Iraqi army was fighting hard. On the contrary, it seemed to be simply melting away. What was more surprising was that the irregular forces, especially the loosely organized Saddam Fedayeen—literally the "men of sacri-fice," soon to be renamed "regime death squads" by Pentagon edict—were will-ing to stand and fight. Typically in civilian clothes, they were hard to pick out from innocent civilians, whom they were often more than willing to use as human shields or to sacrifice in other ways. There were also numerous reports that they were willing to feign surrender and then open fire on anyone who advanced to take them prisoner.

Speaking about An Nasiriyah, General Conway said that the MEF was facing "hard little knots of fedayeen."[36] General McKiernan characterized the enemy as "a combination of several different sources, fedayeen, Special RG, some military, regular army that . . . took off their uniforms . . . but it was a pretty determined enemy."[37] General Mattis spoke for many when he declared that the fedayeen "lack any kind of courage. They literally hide behind women and children, hold-ing them in their houses as they fire . . . They really lack manhood. They're vio-lating every sense of decency. They're as worthless an example of men as we've ever fought."[38] General Amos was equally outraged, commenting later that An Nasiriyah was a turning point for him: "When the Saddam fedayeen came down and . . . were picking off our Marines, they became, in my mind, cannibals. And my whole perspective on how we were going to fight this war changed."[39]

It is difficult to escape the conclusion that An Nasiriyah was a turning point for many, if not most, Marines. Not only was it the first heavy dose of combat for the MEF, but many things did not go as planned or hoped. The enemy was dif-ferent than expected, more tenacious and committed, and he was having a certain degree of success. For him An Nasiriyah was a target-rich environment—a large number of Marines needed to pass through a relatively small area. For the Marines it came at a time when many were close to exhaustion, and the battle saw its share of misjudgments, mistakes, and bad luck. All things considered, it is not surprising that there was congestion and confusion, and that the pace slowed.

What is just as obvious is that no one in the MEF gave way under the pressure and that the Marines quickly recovered from the first day of battle in An Nasiriyah. It did not change the MEF's focus or slow operations for more than a day. On the contrary, there was a hardening of resolve among many Marines. For his part, General Conway did not lose his focus. He consistently pushed Division and Wing to move north in order to defeat the Republican Guard's Baghdad and Al Nida Divisions, which lay on the MEF's route to Baghdad, while General Natonski and Tarawa dealt with the fedayeen and other threats in the south.

Even though the firefights, sometimes heavy, continued in An Nasiriyah for a few days, RCT 1 had pushed through the eastern part of the city and started up Route 7 by the afternoon of 25 March. General Mattis's intent was for RCT 1 to move quickly to the north, in the direction of Al Kut, in order to fix the Baghdad

Division in place in the center of the country long enough for him to get the rest of the 1st Marine Division behind the enemy division, while blocking any Iraqi forces that might attack the Marines from the east. He did not want the Iraqi infantry to be able to fall back into Baghdad.[40]

Although the fighting in An Nasiriyah did not slow the division by much more than twelve hours, the weather did succeed where the enemy had failed. On the night of 24–25 March, the "mother of all sandstorms" moved into the theater, with high winds stirring up massive clouds of sand and slowing operations to a crawl. General Usher, the 1st FSSG commander, called it the worst sandstorm in twenty years.[41] In the words of the division's command chronology, "Marines choked on the dust and visibility was reduced to almost nothing. Soon, it was blowing so hard that it was difficult to breathe outside."[42] Most air was grounded, leaving fire support to artillery and mortars. But some pilots braved the weather anyway. On 25 March, Colonel Bonadonna watched "a breathtaking performance by two Hueys . . . trying to deliver ammo. They flew straight up the road at about the level of the telephone lines. Between the wind and the prop wash, visibility must have been less than zero. . . . The last I saw of them, they were flying [away] into the dust clouds."[43] Like the Huey pilots, Colonel Hummer of the 7th Marines was not ready to let the weather stop him or his regiment. He himself became a ground guide, personally leading his Marines north in the storm, with "connecting files" behind him, Marines walking between vehicles, literally holding on to the one in front and the one in back, guiding them slowly forward. But finally it was too much even for Colonel Hummer, and he stopped his Marines for the night, putting them in a defensive posture.[44] Hunkering down like this did not necessarily mean the Marines were safe. In one of the tragic, incomprehensible accidents that occur during wartime, the executive officer of 3d Battalion, 5th Marines, Maj. Kevin G. Nave, was killed by an earthmover while he was sleeping during the dust storm. A few miles to the southeast at Jalibah, the MEF was trying to operate out of the "Bug," its expensive custommade air-conditioned canvas command post. But on the twenty-fifth, the lights were flickering on and off and the canvas was flapping vigorously. MEF officers were worried that the Bug would literally blow away, and they took the precaution of passing control back to the rear at Camp Commando for a day.[45]

The sandstorm was followed by thunderstorms, which cleared the air somewhat but created mud, both on the ground and in the air. More than one Marine commented that when the thunderstorm hit, it seemed like it was raining mud; the rain hit the dust suspended in the air and drove it to the ground in wet, heavy drops. Many division Marines went to sleep in sand and woke up in mud on 26 March. For at least a day after the storm, there was a massive cloud of sand over Kuwait, which limited visibility, continued to keep many aircraft on the ground, and made it seem that the sun was shining through a dense, bright yellow filter.[46]

The *Washington Post* reported that now, in the wake of An Nasiriyah and the sandstorm, "some senior U.S. military officers" were convinced that the war would last for months and would require "considerably more combat power." The United States had kicked in the door, and the house had not collapsed; on the contrary, it seemed to be holding up fairly well in some ways.[47] General McKiernan was concerned not so much about the situation as about what his commanders might be thinking: "The going was a little tough. The fedayeen . . . and the urban defenses were something we were going to have to deal with. The weather was bad, and we had extended our supply lines." As a result, he felt the need to fly up to see the V Corps commander, Lt. Gen. William S. Wallace, to look him in the eye and to "know that we both saw the way ahead," which was Baghdad.[48]

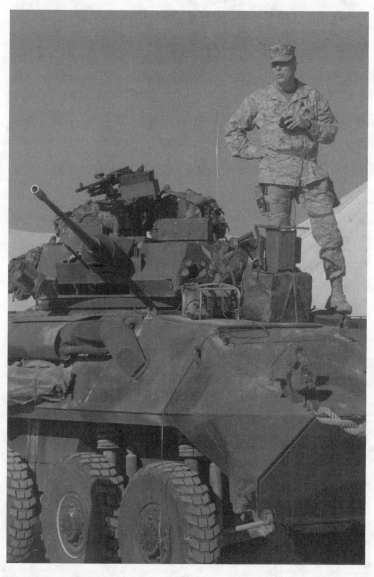

The MEF Commander, Lt. Gen. James T. Conway, set the tone for the combined Marine and British force in Operation Iraqi Freedom. In this photograph, he is addressing a British formation in Kuwait on 2 March 2003. *U.S. Marine Corps Photo*

I MEF welcomed the addition to its ranks of 1 UK (Armoured) Division, made up of a variety of long-serving—and highly professional—soldiers and Marines. *U.S. Navy Photo*

The commander of the British Division, Maj. Gen. Robin V. Brims, quickly established excellent relations with his American counterparts. He is shown here with Maj. Gen. James N. Mattis. *U.S. Marine Corps Photo*

Virtually all Marine units conducted elaborate Rehearsal of Concept (ROC) drills before crossing the line of departure. The layout for the 15th Marine Expeditionary Unit (Special Operations Qualified) at Camp Bullrush in Kuwait may have been smaller than most, but otherwise it was typical. *U.S. Marine Corps Photo*

There was a near-unanimous belief that Saddam Hussein would use chemical weapons on Coalition forces, whether they happened to be at fixed sites in Kuwait or on the road to Baghdad. Frequent alerts were taken seriously, as the expressions behind the masks suggest. *U.S. Marine Corps Photo*

Believing that Saddam was about to sabotage the southern oil fields, CFLCC wanted to accelerate the attack across the border. Early in the war, a Marine CH-46 flies over a burning oil well in the trackless desert that characterizes southern Iraq. *U.S. Marine Corps Photo*

After crossing the border into Iraq, British forces moved northeast across a bleak landscape marked by oil fires. *U.S. Marine Corps Photo*

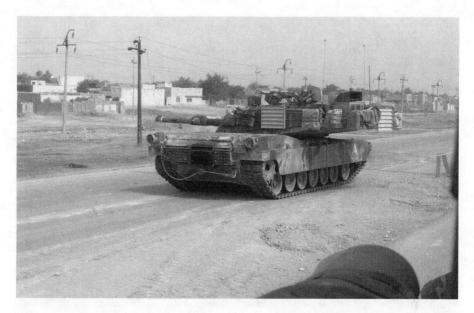

"Unprepossessing" would be a polite term for An Nasiriyah, the southern city where Marine and Iraqi forces fought for the better part of the day on 23 March. *U.S. Marine Corps Photo*

In the aftermath of the fighting and the friendly fire incident on 23 March at the bridge over the Saddam Canal in Nasiriyah, FSSG Marines went through the painstaking and heartbreaking process of recovering equipment and personal effects while a crowd of Iraqis stood silently by. *U.S. Marine Corps Photo*

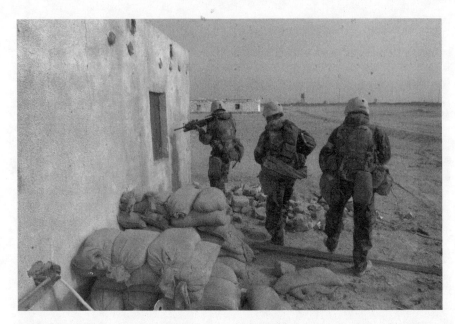

While the 1st Marine Division raced to the north, Task Force Tarawa took on the difficult work of clearing and securing towns and routes between the front lines and Kuwait. *U.S. Marine Corps Photo*

The Coalition did not fight many Iraqis in uniform. Here, on 30 March, a Marine from Echo Company, 2d Battalion, 1st Marines rounds up a motley crew of prisoners in southern Iraq. *U.S. Marine Corps Photo*

Commanders made good use of Marine artillery, which fired thousands of rounds in support of operations and, during the sandstorm of 24–25 March, helped to replace air as the supporting arm of first resort. The firing was largely computerized, especially when it came to counter-battery fire, and often occurred in a matter of seconds—a departure from previous wars. *U.S. Marine Corps Photo*

After An Nasiriyah, the Marines moved north as fast as they could, sometimes taking advantage of excellent highways, and sometimes confined to highways under construction or rundown secondary roads. *U.S. Marine Corps Photo*

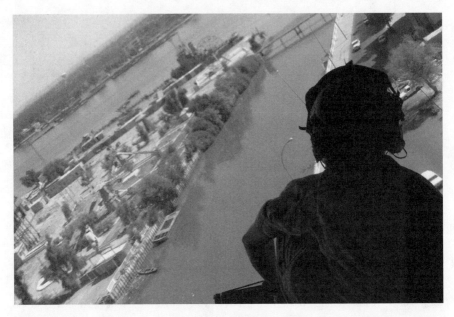

British forces found Basrah to be a sprawling, rundown port city. *U.S. Marine Corps Photo*

A war of movement needed fuel and ammunition, and there were seemingly endless convoys of fuel trucks running north from Kuwait virtually from the first day. *U.S. Marine Corps Photo*

The long convoys faced threats from irregular formations. 1st FSSG Marines provide security during a stop between Ad Diwaniyah and Babylon. *U.S. Marine Corps Photo*

General Usher of the 1st FSSG, shown here with his staff, was the principal architect of the adaptive support system that enabled the Marines to move quickly over long distances. *U.S. Marine Corps Photo*

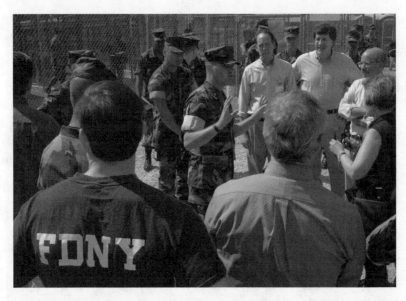

General Lehnert, center, of the Marine Logistics Command was General Usher's "wholesaler," receiving supplies in Kuwait and pushing them to the Front for distribution by the 1st FSSG. He came to theater after a successful tour as the commander of the joint task force charged with the custody of Al Qaeda detainees at Guantanamo Bay. *U.S. Navy Photo*

As MarCent commander, Lt. Gen. Earl Hailston was the senior Marine in theater. He spent much of his time creating the conditions for subordinate Marine commanders—especially Generals Usher and Lehnert—to succeed and, when circumstances allowed, interacting with young Marines. *U.S. Marine Corps Photo*

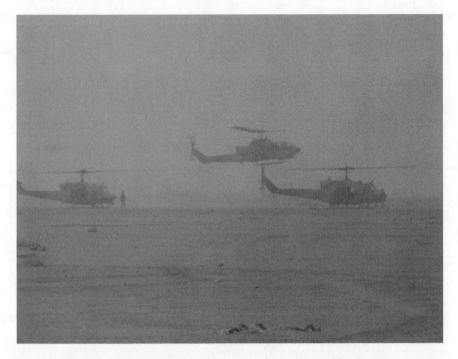

Marine aviation escorted Marines on the move whenever possible, but was sometimes grounded by bad conditions. *U.S. Marine Corps Photo*

The 3d Marine Air Wing established a string of Forward Arming and Refueling Points from Kuwait to Baghdad—and beyond—enabling Marine Air to be even more responsive to calls for support. *U.S. Marine Corps Photo*

Even the hardiest Marines began to tire after a few days of nonstop movement and combat. *U.S. Marine Corps Photo*

Marines sometimes went to considerable lengths to care for wounded Iraqis, both military and civilian. Marines of HMM 268 pick up a wounded EPW for an aerial medevac at a forward staging area on 8 April 2003. *U.S. Marine Corps Photo*

By early April, the Marines were facing the challenge of crossing the Diyala River in order to move on Baghdad. The FSSG's 8th Engineer Support Battalion provided assault bridging for the Division. *U.S. Marine Corps Photo*

Marines moved quickly through the outskirts of Baghdad and into the capital itself. *U.S. Marine Corps Photo*

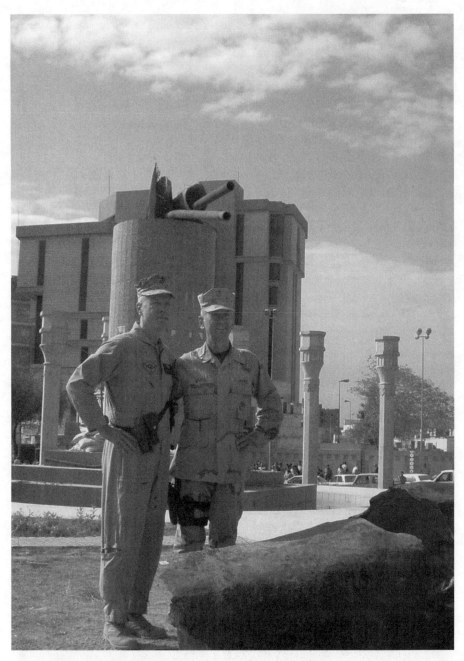

The commander of the 3d Marine Air Wing, Maj. Gen. James F. Amos, and Division's General Mattis—the "two talking Jims" who talked and planned virtually every day during the fighting—posed in Firdos Square in Baghdad on 18 April. Behind them is the pedestal that supported the statue of Saddam Hussein that Marines helped to pull down in the famous incident on 9 April which marked the regime's collapse. *U.S. Marine Corps Photo*

1st Battalion, 5th Marines fought two hard-pitched battles in Baghdad on 10 April. This photo appears to have been taken on the grounds of Al Azimiyah Palace. *U.S. Marine Corps Photo*

The Marines took pains not to leave any equipment on the battlefield. This photo shows an AAV guarding the recovery of a downed AH-1 helicopter near Hamid As Sayyis on Highway 6, southeast of Baghdad. *U.S. Marine Corps Photo*

The same could not be said of the Iraqi forces. Saddam had turned the country into one vast ammunition dump, probably to fuel guerrilla warfare against the invaders. Coalition forces saw rooms like this throughout the country. *U.S. Marine Corps Photo*

The country was also littered with other kinds of cast-off military equipment. At Diwaniyah in late April, a Marine used an Iraqi tank to proclaim his dedication to a loved one. *U.S. Marine Corps Photo*

There were portraits and statues of Saddam Hussein throughout the country. This one was at the entrance to the FSSG compound in Diwaniyah. *U.S. Marine Corps Photo*

During the war, then–Maj. Gen. Henry P. Osman led a small but important mission to the semiautonomous Kurdish region in the northeastern corner of Iraq. *U.S. Marine Corps Photo*

For most of the summer of 2003, MEF Headquarters was at the ancient city of Babylon, where Saddam Hussein had built a sumptuous palace for himself. *U.S. Marine Corps Photo*

During World War I, thousands of British soldiers fought and died in Iraq, and the British Army established a military cemetery at the site of their defeat at Al Kut. In this war, U.S. Marine engineers restored the cemetery and held a commemorative ceremony with their British comrades on 8 May 2003. *U.S. Marine Corps Photo*

Even though, by and large, Marines and Iraqis lived in relative harmony in the southern provinces of Iraq in the summer of 2003, there were occasional signs of unrest, like this angry demonstration on 9 June 2003 by Iraqi soldiers for back pay. Their claim was that the British had made such payments in their zone. *U.S. Marine Corps Photo*

The Marine Corps deployed a seasoned combat artist, SSgt. Michael D. Fay, to Iraq in late spring 2003. In this watercolor, he captured the essence of what many Marines were doing at the time: patrolling on foot and interacting with Iraqis on a personal level. *U.S. Marine Corps Combat Art Collection*

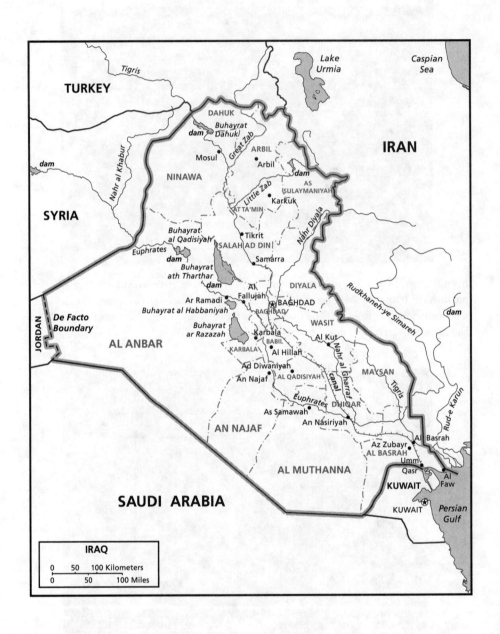

TURKEY

Tigris

Lake
Urmia

Caspian
Sea

dam

DAHUK

*Buhayrat
Dahuk*

dam

Nahr al Khabur

Great Zab

Mosul

ARBIL

Arbil

IRAN

SYRIA

NINAWA

Little Zab

AS
SULAYMANIYAH

dam

Karkuk

AT TA'MIN

*Buhayrat
al Qadisiyah*

Euphrates

dam

Tikrit

Nahr Diyala

SALAH AD DIN

*Buhayrat
ath Tharthar*

Samarra

dam

Al
Fallujah

DIYALA

BAGHDAD

JORDAN

*De Facto
Boundary*

Ar Ramadi
Buhayrat al Habbaniyah

BAGHDAD

Rudkhaneh-ye Simareh

dam

WASIT

*Buhayrat
ar Razazah*

Karbala

Al Kut

AL ANBAR

KARBALA

BABIL

Al Hillah

Nahr al Gharraf
canal

MAYSAN

Ad Diwaniyah

An Najaf

AL QADISIYAH

DHI QAR

Euphrates

Tigris

Rud-e Karun

AN NAJAF

As Samawah

An Nasiriyah

Az Zubayr
AL BASRAH

Al Basrah

AL MUTHANNA

Umm
Qasr

Al
Faw

SAUDI ARABIA

KUWAIT

KUWAIT

Persian
Gulf

IRAQ

0   50   100 Kilometers
0   50   100 Miles

military area

Saddam Canal

7

to
As Samawah

8

Euphrates

water
treatment
plant

hospital

thermal
power plant

H

water
treatment
plant

N

military
facility

H

hospital

railway
station

military
facility

military
training
area with
barracks

petroleum
refinery

military
storage area

Tallil
Airfield

to Al Basrah

AN NASIRIYAH

0   1   2   3
Kilometers

At Taji

At Taji
Airfield

N

BAGHDAD

0 1 2 3 4 5
Kilometers

Tigris

Abu Hanifa
Mosque

Saddam
City

Al-Azimiyah
Palace

Diyala R.

Muthenna
Airfield

Firdos
Square

Abu Ghurayb
Airfield

Qasr Tall
Airfield

Rasheed
Airfield

Baghdad
University

Saddam
International
Airport

Tigris

6

Toward the Enemy Center of Gravity

Ad Diwaniyah, Al Kut, and the Pause

Even before the storm had completely passed, Regimental Combat Teams 5 and 7 resumed their progress up Route 1, the northwest-southeast axis running to Baghdad, which was by turns a new four-lane superhighway and a roadbed under construction. On the way, they faced roadside ambushes by a variety of enemy formations that had prepared positions alongside the highway. An incident on 25 March that would ultimately mean a Navy Cross for 1st Lt. Brian R. Chontosh conveys a clear sense of the nature of the fighting. In the early morning hours of the day, Lieutenant Chontosh—an energetic, down-to-earth body-builder, who started his career in the Marine Corps on the enlisted side of the house and still shaved his head—was in the lead vehicle of his combined anti-armor team (CAAT) platoon, behind four M1A1 Abrams tanks as 3d Battalion, 5th Marines pushed north toward Ad Diwaniyah, a city some one hundred miles south of Baghdad that had been the home of a large Iraqi army garrison before the war. Suddenly the enemy, described as a mix of irregular and conventional forces, sprang an ambush from the berms on both sides of the highway. The enemy fire struck one of the CAAT vehicles, killing one Marine and wounding another. Lieutenant Chontosh wanted to move the platoon out of the kill zone, which was difficult because there were vehicles both in front of him and behind him. Noticing a break in the berm, he directed his driver to head through it and into a trench filled with enemy soldiers. Once in the trench, Lieutenant Chontosh jumped out, engaging the enemy with an M-16 rifle and then with a 9mm pistol until he ran out of ammunition. Then, in the words of the summary of action for his award:

> He . . . grabbed an enemy AK-47 [rifle] and continued to engage enemy soldiers as he continued the attack to clear the trench. . . . When the AK-47 was out of ammo he grabbed another and continued to engage [the] enemy both in and out of the trench under heavy enemy fire. A Marine following him found an enemy RPG [rocket-propelled grenade] and gave it to Lt. Chontosh who . . . used it to engage a group of enemy soldiers, eliminating the . . . threat. . . . His aggressive, violent action . . . undoubtedly saved the lives of many Marines along Highway 1 that day.[1]

Between 26 and 28 March, RCT 5 proceeded to crush fedayeen opposition in and around Ad Diwaniyah. Even before the fighting had ended in Ad Diwaniyah, one of RCT 5's battalions seized the airfield at Hantush after what has been described as "a fierce firefight." Hantush was some fifteen miles to the north of Ad Diwaniyah, located on Highway 27, an east-west axis that General Mattis intended to use in the coming days to approach Baghdad from the east. In the meantime, RCT 1 was fighting its way up Route 7 through towns and villages to the junction with Route 17, which was at roughly the same latitude as the city of Al Amarah, not far from the border with Iran, the home of the Iraqi 10th Armored Division, which was another potential threat, from the southeast, to Marines advancing on Baghdad.

The division was moving ahead despite the increasing distance from its base in Kuwait. General Mattis had been prepared to rely on organic supplies for a few days; he later said that the 1st Marines, when they crossed the river at An Nasiriyah, fully expected to cut their supply lines "and just break loose and head north," relying on emergency resupply by air when necessary (hence the interest in Hantush airfield) and not having to worry about protecting their supply lines back to the rear.[2] This was a reflection of General Mattis's "logistics lite" philosophy he had been inculcating in all of his troops for months, and of the benefits of General Usher's reorganization (the 1st FSSG having created a direct support structure for the division, especially the combat service support companies designed to move with the regiments). As stated in the division's command chronology, the reorganization "provided [for a] . . . shared situation awareness . . . [which enabled FSSG to] proactively calculate logistical needs and have them out the door before the customer even registered a request."[3] Although statistics are lacking, this approach most likely helped to reduce the demand for consumables and, perhaps as important, contributed to an expeditionary mentality that made his Marines believe they could go the extra mile without extra supplies.

On a larger scale, the Marine Corps supply system had generally kept up, even though it was stretched. As the deputy FSSG commander, Col. John L. Sweeney, commented on 24 March, "the plan is evolving" successfully; there had been "no operational pause due to logistics" because of "what those lance corporals are doing out there."[4] In the daily MEF situation report for the next day, General Conway reflected satisfaction with the FSSG's efforts to date, especially the hose reel system it had laid from Kuwait to Jalibah, a distance of some seventy miles, in order to deliver fuel. The FSSG Marines had accomplished this feat in less than half the projected time.[5]

There can be little doubt that it had been a challenge to get supplies from the beach to the forward bases of the FSSG, which quickly sprang up in Iraq behind the advancing Marines at places like Jalibah and Ad Diwaniyah. It turned out that the Army's 377th Theater Support Command had not been able to meet all the needs of both I MEF and V Corps as originally hoped; the 377th was a relatively late arrival in theater, its headquarters not "closing" until March 2003. Partly because of this and partly because of the challenges the operation would pose for any command planning to move men and equipment over such a long distance, logistics remained a concern for General McKiernan throughout the war, and there were some trade-offs. The main effort, V Corps, was typically supplied first, and the Marines were sometimes left to their own devices. Under Brigadier General Lehnert, the "wholesale" Marine Logistics Command (MLC) had done what it could to bridge the gap between the 377th and the "retail" FSSG and, in general, to meet the MEF's needs. After its arrival in country in December 2002, it had worked wonders in its nearly featureless stretch of Kuwaiti desert now known as Tactical Assembly Area Fox, turning it into a vast logistics base. The general and his Marines often had to improvise, which they learned to do well. For example, the MLC had to contract for three hundred tractor-trailers driven by third-country nationals, many of whom were to drive hundreds of miles into Iraq under dangerous conditions, and then find ways to motivate them to continue working under near-combat conditions. (One solution was to award "eagle, globe, and anchor" emblems to the more intrepid drivers.) As the Marines moved north, the MEF kept asking the MLC to keep pace, which it did by, in General Lehnert's words, "using every transportations means available including Marine Corps tactical trucks, Army line haul, contracted third country national . . . vehicles, C-130 . . . air delivery, and rotary-wing aircraft."[6] After the war, General Lehnert concluded that he didn't "know how much further we could have gone as the culminating point kept moving north. . . . We had every truck and every driver on the road to the limit of their ability. . . . We were always in a surge mode." There were some notable shortages, especially of spare parts (Class IX supplies), and there was no reserve.[7]

What the MLC delivered to the FSSG, the FSSG pushed forward to its front-line customers. General Usher said it was sometimes a matter of "brute force logistics." Despite all the FSSG's careful preparations, sometimes it came down to Marines muscling their way through a problem. When the system was stressed, the general added, "It wasn't pretty. It wasn't elegant. It was just sheer adrenaline."[8] This was especially true as the Marine division sprinted toward Baghdad:

> [Resupply] was accomplished by the integrated, rapid distribution of fuel, water, rations, and ammunition to the nearest SA [support area] or RRP [repair and replenishment point] to the fight, moved by [FSSG] assets . . . and in some cases [by] the MLC, at distances farther than anyone had imagined prior to the beginning of the war. At the height of the action, more than 250,000 gallons of fuel were moved on a daily basis from as far south as SA Coyote [in Kuwait] to as far north as SA Chesty at the An Numiniyah Airfield, stretching more than 300 miles over improved and unimproved highways [in the face of] . . . the unconventional threat along the . . . MSRs [main supply routes].[9]

The bottom line is that despite some serious challenges, the Marines of the FSSG and the MLC consistently managed to keep supply ahead of demand on the battlefield and thereby enabled operational success.

That helps to explain why, for many Marines, what happened next was as unexpected as many of the other challenges in this campaign: CFLCC ordered a halt in the march toward Baghdad. According to the MEF situation report for 27 March, MEF received a CFLCC order to halt the attack north and focus on securing its lines of communication. MEF in turn passed the order to Division. General Mattis "didn't want the pause. Nothing was holding us up." Moreover, he believed that his troops, especially 5th Marines in Hantush, were in an exposed position, and he did not want to leave them in what amounted to a holding pattern. As a result, he felt constrained to give "one of the toughest orders [he] . . . ever had to give to an assault battalion that had taken ground [and] lost men doing it": he told them to withdraw to a more defensible position, which they did despite the infantryman's "So, now what do they want us to do?" reaction to an order that didn't make sense to him.[10]

Underlying the order were CFLCC concerns about resupply, which had apparently percolated up from V Corps; during the sandstorm, some Army units had nearly exhausted their supplies. The obvious corollary was: now, with the fedayeen threat, who would protect the force's ever-longer supply lines, the long, dusty, slow-moving convoys from Kuwait to the front lines? There may be some validity to the argument that this thinking had its roots in the various prewar discussions about a lengthy "operational pause" between the opening phase of the

The Missile Attack on CFLCC

Marines and soldiers were increasingly becoming aware of the fact that this was a war without defined front lines and rear areas. Threats could come from any quarter, when least expected. But one week into the war, the rear areas, especially in Kuwait, seemed fairly safe, and the mood at Camp Doha was, if not exactly relaxed, at least moving into a smooth wartime routine. During the first few days of the war, everyone at Doha had worn their MOPP suits and carried their gas masks; now the soldiers and Marines had the suits and the gas masks with them but were not wearing them. CFLCC's Battle Update Assessment (BUA), which was "the" daily brief in the ultramodern command center, on 27 March was no exception. It was chaired by General McKiernan, dressed as usual in his freshly starched desert battle dress uniform. The staff was moving crisply through its agenda when the alarm came from one of the air defense liaison officers: "Lightning, lightning, lightning!" which meant that an Iraqi missile launch had been detected and that the target was Kuwait. Everyone in the large amphitheater paused to put on their gas masks, which would have offered some protection in case of a chemical or biological strike, but none against the effects of high explosives. With his gas mask in place, General McKiernan went back to work, speaking through its mouthpiece, his voice calm and only slightly garbled. A few seconds later there were two deep detonations nearby, and then a third and maybe a fourth detonation—the sounds of two outgoing Patriot missiles and of at least one Patriot striking the incoming missile. Bits of debris rained down on Doha as the Giant Voice—for once, late—sounded the alarm. In the BUA the gas masks stayed on for a few more minutes while experts tested for the effects of special weapons. Then it was back to business as usual, as if nothing had happened. But something *had* happened. The incident was captured on CNN (to be shown after the war in a documentary on CFLCC's "Warroom") and was analyzed and chewed over among the men and women at Doha for a few days. One German artillery officer, attached to C/JTF-CM, claimed to have learned from a good source that the Iraqi missiles fired at Kuwait had not been fired by a fire direction center; instead, the Iraqis were using a form of dead reckoning—calculating the distance and direction to a (well-known) target like Doha, and simply cranking in the right numbers. If so, they had done an excellent job. The computers at the Patriot missile battery showed that the trajectory of the missile, probably an "Ababil" missile, was such that it would have struck the command center itself or the building next door, which could have wiped out the CFLCC command group. That was not quite the end of it. In this war, neither CFLCC nor any other headquarters, especially in the rear, was a place where anyone showed much emotion of any kind. Maybe it was all the technology that made emotion seem out of place. Most soldiers and Marines were bone-tired, stretched close to their limits by impossibly long and stressful days. On the staffs, some never forgot that what they did, or did not do, could mean life or death for someone a few hundred miles away and pushed themselves even harder. But few ever seemed particularly happy or sad, except for the time when a few days later, during another BUA, the officers in the command center offered the Patriot missileers a spontaneous round of applause.*

*Interview with Maj. Gen. Robert R. Blackman, 31 May 2003 (MCHC, Washington, D.C.); Reynolds Journal, entries for 27 March and 8 April; CNN, "The Warroom" (Published as CNN DVD or Video: Atlanta, 2003); Maj. Robert K. Casey interview, 27 April 03 (MCHC, Washington, D.C.); Fontenot, et al., *On Point*, p. 98; Franks, *American Soldier*, pp. 506–7.

war and the fight for Baghdad in order to build up supplies and reinforcements. After the war, some Marine operators talked about a link between the prewar discussions and the wartime pause.[11] While MEF consistently opposed a lengthy operational pause and Division opposed any kind of a pause, General Conway opted for the middle ground: a brief pause for the MEF to catch its breath, not to mention staying in synch with the Army corps on his flank, which was, after all, still the main effort. On 25 March, for example, he had discussed the situation with his staff, saying that the enemy attacks "will effect . . . our CSS convoys. These huge long supply lines are a problem. . . . Rear area security continues to increase in importance. . . . You might need to look at pulling combat power in order to secure the key areas."[12]

One of the threshold issues was just how long the pause would last, and what effect it would have on "the plan." On 28 March, General McKiernan flew from his headquarters in Kuwait to Jalibah, because he wanted to meet face to face with his two corps commanders, Generals Conway and Wallace, to discuss the situation and its implications for the upcoming attack on Baghdad, the next phase of the war. For General McKiernan, two enemy centers of gravity were now Baghdad and the Iraqi paramilitary forces, which could impede further progress to the north.

Accounts of the conference vary somewhat, but there is general agreement that both commanders talked about the threats they wanted to address before moving closer to Baghdad.[13] Wallace said he needed time to position his corps. Conway mentioned what sounded like tasks he wanted to accomplish before the attack on Baghdad: the MEF was committed to "a systematic reduction of the bad guys in An Nasiriyah," a reference to the ongoing fight for that city to secure the MEF's rear; the British division needed to execute some "pinpoint armor strikes"—that is, raids—into Basrah. Referring to RCT 1, he commented that "Joe Dowdy was in a 270-degree fight" on Highway 7 as his command made its way north through the heart of the country, occasionally encountering stiff resistance. General Conway later remembered making the case for a pause of approximately three days.

The upshot of the conference was a relatively open-ended decision by McKiernan for both MEF and Corps to "take time to clean up . . . before we commit . . . to the Baghdad fight, because once we commit to the Baghdad fight, we can't stop."[14] There would be a pause, a chance for securing the rear areas and for supplies to catch up, which, if all went well, would be relatively short, no more than "several days." It would not be a lengthy operational pause to wait for heavy reinforcements, and it would not keep CFLCC from the main event. When he spoke to his staff later on the same day, General Conway downplayed the pause and stressed that the focus remained on Baghdad.[15]

As the "operational pause" began, the MEF shifted its focus somewhat, attacking pockets of resistance in its area of operations while keeping its eye on the ultimate goal. FragO 040-03 outlined the missions of defeating "paramilitary forces in zone [in order to] protect MEF lines of communication and set conditions for continued attacks north to defeat the Baghdad and Al Nida [Republican Guard] Divisions."[16] General Conway and his staff seem to have made it a point even to avoid the word "pause"; they preferred to talk about "throwing elbows" in a different direction. When on Saturday, 29 March, the general quipped, "Enjoy your Saturday night, kick back and relax, and we'll tell you when the war starts back up again," he did not intend for anyone to take him seriously.[17] Nor did he want anyone to think the MEF had shifted to conducting counter-guerrilla operations. In his view, the MEF was simply "recocking" for the next phase—attacking pockets of enemy resistance, shoring up logistics bases, building air bases, giving the MAW time to conduct the "shaping" operations that had not been possible earlier. As General Conway was to remark on 30 May, "while we were stationary [on the ground], we were in fact attacking with our air," putting out 300 to 320 sorties per day on the enemy.[18] The Baghdad Division, arrayed around Al Kut, received constant pressure from the MAW, as did the 10th Armored Division to the south in the vicinity of Al Amarah. Both were ultimately degraded virtually to the point of ineffectiveness by the air attacks.

Division did not hide its impatience to move on toward Baghdad. Again and again, in its formal and informal communications, it spread the message that it was "anxious to resume the attack . . . [because] the best way to secure our locs [lines of communication] is to rapidly move north to collapse the regime."[19] General Mattis himself penned the comment on 29 March that he was "convinced that the enemy situation is such that we could cross the Tigris and destroy the Baghdad Division without interference from the 10th Armored Division within the next 72 hours."[20] General Conway was only slightly less forward-leaning, reporting on 30 March that "the conditions for attacking north are rapidly being set and should be in place within 2–3 days." It was his view that the MEF had nearly all the supplies it needed to move forward, and he was hearing that after the continuous air attacks, the enemy simply was not there in large numbers.[21]

The Battle of the Icons

The MAW's "kinetic" and "non-kinetic" effects—shorthand for bombs and leaflets—on the Iraqi 10th Armored Division were so powerful that it was soon little more than an icon on U.S. computer screens. MEF had monitored the situation and was satisfied that the 10th was no longer a threat, but the icons worried higher headquarters, perhaps even someone at the Pentagon, and the order eventually came down from CFLCC for the MEF to "neutralize" that division. And so, in early April MEF directed General Natonski to either capture or destroy its remnants. Tarawa put together a smaller task force from 1st Battalion, 2nd Marines and the 24th MEU(SOC), which advanced some three hundred kilometers across Iraq in short order—no small feat in itself—and, though prepared for heavy fighting, found nothing but cheering crowds when they drove into the flat, dusty town of Al Amarah on the Tigris.*

*Acosta Journal, entry for 20 May 03; 2d MEB ComdC, Jan.–June 03 (MCHC, Washington, D.C.); Michael Wilson, "Two Marine Battalions Turn to Confront the Remnants of a Lurking Iraqi Division," *New York Times*, 8 April 03, p. B-8. Tarawa's attack spanned 8–10 April.

On 30 March, General Mattis flew to Jalibah to meet with General Conway and outline his plan for getting things moving again. General Mattis found that he was preaching to the choir, the MEF planners being just as eager as he was. General Conway agreed that the security situation would allow the division to proceed with its plan for a limited objective attack across the Tigris to isolate Al Kut, which in turn would open up a number of further options for both Division and MEF. This was true even though MEF believed that Saddam would order an attack by weapons of mass destruction once the Marines reached Al Kut. "CW [chemical warfare] attack likely when attacks on Baghdad resume" were the words of the MEF situation report for 28 March. "Trigger depends on U.S. success against . . . forces [in the vicinity of] Al Kut."[22]

The MEF's plans weren't just about Division. Tarawa's status was especially important, since once An Nasiriyah was secure, the task force was to "expand its battlespace to the north" along Routes 1 and 7 to guard the division's rear as it moved farther north. Between 1 and 6 April, Tarawa focused RCT 2 on this task

while continuing its increasingly successful "three block war" in An Nasiriyah—
that is, the mix of combat patrols and civil affairs work that was required after the
major battles had been fought. Tarawa having been augmented by 15th
MEU(SOC) and 2d Battalion, 25th Marines, which assumed joint responsibility
for An Nasiriyah, freeing RCT 2 was free to operate to the north.[23]

During the preparations for the final phase of the war, the division and the
wing continued to place a premium on face-to-face meetings. The meeting
between Generals Amos and Mattis on 31 March is representative. On that
morning, General Amos, the former fighter pilot, flew himself and a few members of his staff in a CH-46E Sea Knight helicopter from Kuwait to the division's
forward command post alongside Highway 1, a few miles south of Ad Diwaniyah
in the center of southern Iraq. Even though the visibility was still poor—and the
desert below largely featureless for long stretches—the general flew at about one
hundred feet on account of the surface-to-air missile threat. It was an exhausting
six-hour round trip.

General Mattis met the helicopter when it landed and walked his guests to the
command post, which was little more than a few tents and camouflage netting.
He began by praising the wing for its support, especially for flying unmanned
aerial reconnaissance vehicles for the division. (This was like having a small television camera in the sky to scout the terrain just ahead, which, together with the
high-flying Navy P-3 Orions that General Mattis had arranged for, delivered an
excellent picture of the battlefield.) The generals then discussed the upcoming
offensive, with General Mattis describing his plan and asking for more support
from the wing. Two issues stood out: one was bridging the canals and rivers that
stood between the division and Baghdad; the other was resupply. Since the
FSSG's convoys had to drive literally hundreds of miles to reach the front, the
obvious alternative was for the wing to airlift supplies when shortages loomed.

After two hours of talks, General Amos and his staff flew up to Hantush to
personally evaluate the suitability of a field-expedient "highway airstrip" for
Marine cargo planes. General Mattis, who was immensely grateful for the wing's
support and his good relationship with General Amos, quipped later that General
Amos showed "more bravery than good judgment" when he flew himself on to
Hantush. They "approached by circling over a large date palm grove [which later
turned out to have contained enemy fighters] . . . and landed on the superhighway which was lined with [the] vehicles of the 5th Marines," who had moved
back into the area a few hours earlier. Amos found the eight-thousand-foot run-
way suitable for his pilots even though it was little more than a four-lane highway
from which the Marines had recently removed the centerline traffic dividers.[24]
That night, flights of heavily loaded KC-130s Hercules aircraft landed at Hantush using night-vision goggles. (The division later described Hantush as a "criti-

cal logistics hub" for the final push north.) Finally, before returning to his head-quarters in Kuwait, General Amos stopped briefly at I MEF's forward command post in Jalibah to touch base with General Conway.[25]

Writing about the meeting, one of the officers in General Amos's party, retired field historian Col. Charles J. Quilter II, USMCR, observed how much things had changed since Desert Storm, especially in terms of communications between the actuals: "There was the twice daily . . . video teleconference. They also talked on the phone a lot. That really struck me. Compared to Desert Storm . . . they talked far more than their predecessors [in that conflict]. . . . [They] often talked late . . . [into the night] about . . . the latest developments and what kind of air support the Division would need the next day. . . . They were called the 'Talking Jims' by their staffs."[26]

The MEF resumed the offensive to the north on 1 April. With RCT 7 follow-ing in trace, RCT 5 advanced northeast along Route 27, seizing a bridge over the Saddam Canal, a continuation of the north-south waterway the Marines had encountered near An Nasiriyah. The next day, RCT 5 seized two crossings over the Tigris, putting it astride a major route that ran between Baghdad and the city of Al Kut, where the British had suffered a disastrous defeat against the Turks in 1916 during World War I. This enabled Division to complete the destruction, in the vicinity of Al Kut, of the Baghdad Division, which RCT 1 had fixed in place by advancing from the south, thereby putting it at the mercy of RCT 7 advanc-ing from the northwest. The division history records 3 April as the day RCT 7 destroyed the enemy division's two western brigades.[27]

General Mattis made a point of keeping his troops from actually going into the city of Al Kut; he did not want to become bogged down in urban combat, and he did not want to assume the responsibility for governing the city, which he could incur under the Law of War if he entered the city limits. When he was con-tent that the enemy was surrounded, largely combat ineffective and unlikely to attack, he left Al Kut to its own devices, posting a recon battalion outside the town to make sure the Iraqi commander did not "get brave."[28] Division was now free to turn its attention to Baghdad.

It was in the wake of this attack that General Mattis, in a move that attracted considerable attention and stirred some controversy, relieved Colonel Dowdy as the commanding officer of 1st Marines and replaced him with his G-3, Col. John A. Toolan. Colonel Dowdy, a well-respected Marine who placed a premium on the well-being of his Marines, apparently fell victim to the general's overriding quest for speed. The division spokesman said, simply, "It was a decision based on operating tempo." On 4 April, in a tent at the division's command post, there was a difficult meeting between General Mattis and his assistant division com-mander, Brigadier General Kelly, on the one hand, and Colonel Dowdy on the other. Dowdy stood on the record of his Marines, who had been fighting their way up-country and getting the job done, perhaps not as quickly as Mattis and Kelly wanted. According to Dowdy's account of the meeting, Mattis told the colonel he was being relieved and asked him to empty his sidearm and turn over his ammunition, which Dowdy said would not be necessary. Before long, Dowdy was on a helicopter to Kuwait. A considerate man not given to undermining his brother officers, Colonel Toolan had not known what was coming but obeyed the order to replace Dowdy. When he arrived at the regiment, he let it be known that he would carry on where his predecessor had left off, that the regiment was bigger than any one man. Colonel Dowdy could not have agreed more, posting a message on an Internet Web site saying he remained loyal to the division and its leaders. He spent the rest of the war serving as an aerial observer in one of the P-3s flying over the battlefield.[29]

7

Baghdad

Going Down Fast, Going Down Final

The mantra had always been: Baghdad is the enemy's center of gravity; the purpose of the campaign is to remove the regime, the means to that end is capturing Baghdad. It was where Saddam's power resided, both symbolically and otherwise. CentCom and its subordinates were consistent in their assumption that Saddam had to defend the capital. While he had stationed relatively weak regular army divisions in the south, Saddam had kept his best forces around Baghdad—the Republican Guard and the Special Republican Guard. The thinking was still that the Iraqis would set up concentric rings of defense around Baghdad. CFLCC maps showed a ring around Baghdad and an area labeled the "Red Zone." The deeper the U.S. forces penetrated into the Red Zone, which took in Al Kut in the east and Karbala in the west, the tougher the fight would become. Supported by fanatic militiamen, retreating Iraqi forces would make their last stand in and around the capital. There might even be scenes like that portrayed in the movie *Blackhawk Down,* about U.S. soldiers mired in a fight in 1993 in downtown Mogadishu, where U.S. technology was hard put to overcome paramilitary fighters in a warren of alleyways and ruined buildings. It was the kind of place where helicopters became vulnerable to rocket-propelled grenades fired by young men and little boys, and elite troops lost their way and their lives. The vivid images from that movie, based on the gripping and carefully researched book by journalist Mark Bowden, were familiar to virtually every American soldier and Marine in the Iraq War. Those images were the stuff of nightmares for planners and commanders. Last, but certainly not least, the Red Zone was where Saddam Hussein was most likely to order the use of weapons of mass destruc-

tion—especially if the fight went badly for him and he had little or nothing left
to lose by way of international support. He would, presumably, prefer to stop
the coalition with WMD outside his capital. But with Saddam Hussein, who
could be sure what the plan was?

Since Baghdad was the one city that CFLCC could not bypass, the question,
as early as the summer of 2002, was how best to attack it and turn the nightmares, if not into pleasant dreams, at least into tolerable slices of reality. V Corps
and CFLCC planners, including Colonel Benson, the G-5 who had solid relations with the MEF planners, took the approach described as "systems-based
planning," which had grown out of the work of some very good military theorists
at the Army's School of Advanced Military Studies, the Marine Corps University,
and the Warfighting Laboratory at MCCDC in Quantico. Soon these theorists
engaged MEF planners, who made a contribution of their own, and learned an
approach that the MEF could adapt to fit its plans. The idea was to think of a city
as a system or, better yet, as a system of systems. On the one hand were the systems used by the regime to control the city, the other kind of "power points,"
such as the police and the military or the government-run media, not to mention
symbols of power, such as palaces. On the other hand were the systems that made
the city run—water, electricity, and transportation. There was of course some
overlap between the two categories. An airport, for example, could fit into two or
three categories. By analyzing a city, planners could map the relationships
between systems and identify the "key nodes." These could be attacked with
precision-guided weapons from the air or with raids on the ground. Then there
would be no need for costly house-to-house, block-to-block fighting, let alone
the wholesale destruction of the infrastructure, which the coalition wanted to
preserve for the postwar phase.[1]

To turn theory into practice, conferences and seminars on urban warfare were
held in late 2002, like the ones at CFLCC in Kuwait in December.[2] The Army,
and CFLCC, came to favor a concept of operations with two basic steps. The first
was encircling and isolating Baghdad. This would prevent reinforcements from
entering the city and keep prominent members of the regime, especially Saddam
Hussein and his sons, from escaping. The second step was to establish bases outside the city limits and then conduct "in and out" armored raids to attrite the
enemy. Supported by attack helicopters, with fixed wing support on station
nearby, the raiders would identify points of resistance, hit them "hard and
quick," then get out. Another option was simply to advance along a particular
axis and destroy whatever opposition presented itself. In December 2002 General
McKiernan summed up the plan as one to "isolate Baghdad, establish an outer
cordon which controls movement in and out of the city, and then a series of forward operating bases . . . to . . . attack . . . specific targets in the city [and return

to base,] . . . or [to] seize and secure specific targets." The process, which could be lengthy, would continue until the enemy was too weak to oppose an occupation.[3]

The CFLCC plan made sense for a force made up of mechanized infantry; the 3d Infantry Division, for example, had many tactical vehicles at its disposal, but surprisingly few—1,200 to 1,600—"dismounts," that is, infantrymen who were trained to fight on foot. Baghdad was an open city in the sense of having broad boulevards leading in and out of town that were not too bad for armor. This made for an exception to the Army's doctrinal reluctance to use heavy armor in urban areas. V Corps had tried the concept on a limited scale in the city of Najaf on the way to Baghdad, and the results were not inconsistent with the British example in Basrah. From their base at the airport outside the city, the U.K. division was staging carefully planned raids against specific targets. Intelligence collection on the streets of Basrah drove some of the targeting, a modus operandi that the British had learned the hard way in Northern Ireland over the preceding thirty years. Compared to the Americans, the British tended to use less armor and more infantry, and to drop off snipers and spotters when the main body withdrew. By early April they appeared to be enjoying a modicum of success.[4] Their success was contrasted with perceptions of Marine problems in An Nasiriyah. The comparison was not apt, as the goals of the two operations were different. The Marines needed to go into An Nasiriyah to get to the other side of the river in a hurry, while the British goal was to secure Basrah when the time was right. But at least for some, the perception was there. Planners at various Army, Marine, and joint headquarters were aware of what was happening in Basrah, and while it is impossible to pinpoint an instance when anyone copied a particular British tactic, the British approach seemed to confirm some of what the planners had been saying about urban tactics.[5]

The 1st Marine Division concept was different both from the CFLCC/Army concept and from the British concept—not surprisingly, since it was a more traditional infantry division, with some six thousand riflemen. As early as 1999, the Corps' Warfighting Laboratory had used Division forces to run the "Urban Warrior Advanced Warfighting Experiment," exploring some of the problems Marines would face in cities in the twenty-first century. In California, in December 2002, Division had conducted its own seminars and training on urban warfare, spending three days talking about how it would fight in Baghdad. Among the attendees were representatives of the Warfighting Lab, Marine Aviation Weapons and Tactics Squadron (the legendary MAWTS—the Marine equivalent of the Navy's "Top Gun" School), the MEF, and the wing. The seminar was followed by an "Urban Combined Arms Exercise" (UCAX) at the abandoned air base at Victorville. The UCAX ran two battalions through the kinds of challenges they might face in Baghdad, including "militias competing for power on the streets, the breakdown of civilian authority, unruly crowds at food distribution centers, car bombs, and snipers hiding in crowds."[6] The upshot was that Division did not like the idea of seizing objectives, giving them up, and then having to seize them again later. "Withdrawals from portions of the city after seizing raid objectives would embolden the enemy and lessen the 'dominating effect' the Division wanted to portray to the enemy and to the international media." Moreover, "identifying important targets by raiding and then abandoning them would give the Iraqi fighters the opportunity to reoccupy, mine, booby trap, or preplan fires."[7] In a postwar interview, General Mattis said, "We were not eager to set up . . . bases around the . . . city and raid into it and back out at any point."[8]

The division staff followed its commander's thinking about raids. First Mattis directed his G-2 to prepare a list of target packages—worthy objectives in the eastern half of the city, which ranged from military installations to media centers to government offices—that could be raided or seized and held. The list kept on growing. As the list grew, it seemed to make less and less sense to think of the operation in terms of "in-and-out" raids. Why seize one site, then give it up only to return the next day to seize a nearby site? Ultimately, the division began to consider breaking the city into zones and assigning them to the maneuver regiments, and even to its artillery regiment, 11th Marines.[9]

What the division or MEF thought about how to run the urban fight did not matter as much as what two other commands thought about the city. After all, CFLCC had long-since "assigned" Baghdad to the Army's V Corps to avoid the problems that came with having two corps-level commands responsible for the same objective.[10] In late 2002 it seemed that V Corps would be able to split the city between the 3d and 4th Mechanized Infantry Divisions while the Marines helped to maintain the cordon around it. But then after the Turks refused to allow the 4th Division to pass through their country into Iraq, CFLCC had considered using Marine units in place of that division. One proposal was to put one or more RCTs under V Corps' tactical control. (A version of this proposal surfaced in a CFLCC draft of the order for Baghdad as late as 25 March.) This did not sit well with MEF planners, who argued that a Marine regiment did not have the kind of robust communications suite needed to communicate with a corps-level headquarters, and that, besides, the best way to employ Marines was as a MAGTF. Even without a boundary shift—that is, even if Baghdad proper were the province of the Army, and the Marines stayed outside the city limits— an intact MAGTF could support V Corps more effectively, especially if given some latitude to control its own operations. "How to fight the MAGTF" was one lesson that seemed to be on the curriculum every semester.[11]

CFLCC gave fair consideration to MEF's arguments but did not come to a final decision about Baghdad before G-Day. General McKiernan had approved a branch plan to bring forces into Baghdad from both the MEF and V Corps if it made sense to do so.[12] Earlier, he had said, "If there is a decision . . . about introducing I MEF forces into Baghdad . . . I will establish the boundary . . . [which] would logically be . . . the Tigris." The assumption was clearly that MEF would come from the East and V Corps from the West.[13] In the words of the MEF planners: even after "the battle [for Iraq] began, the issue continued to evolve, and, as the coalition neared Baghdad, the decision was made to [ap]portion the city along the Tigris River," assigning the eastern half of the city to the Marines.[14]

It appears that General McKiernan made that decision in early April when the "Baghdad fight" was finally taking shape, and he was ready to predict that the regime was "going doing fast, going down final." By 3 April his staff had issued CFLCC FragO 124, which delineated the boundary between MEF and Corps. This would, McKiernan emphasized, be a "coordinated two-direction attack with I MEF attacking to seize [an intermediate objective] . . . and then beginning to work into Baghdad from the southeast."[15]

Was it a last-minute decision, one that had to be made earlier than expected? The watchword for the campaign had always been *speed*. Few had thought that CFLCC troops would be on the outskirts of Baghdad in early April. Even a forward-leaning officer like General Amos thought it would take some fifty-five days just to get to Baghdad.[16] Did the quick tempo outstrip prewar plans or, more precisely, the planning process? Perhaps, but only to a small extent. This was an issue that General McKiernan had been thinking about for months. He had a base plan, one with branches, designed to allow him the flexibility to change circumstances that no one could predict in advance. In that sense, everything was going according to plan.

While 1st Marine Division had been reducing the Baghdad Division near Al Kut, the Army's 3d Infantry Division, with the 101st Airborne Division in trace, had continued its march up through the western desert, reducing resistance in and around the cities of Najaf, Karbala, and As Samawah. The relationship between these two divisions was not unlike the relationship between 1stMarDiv and Task Force Tarawa, with the heavier force in the lead and the lighter force securing the lines of communication. By 3 April, the 3d was on the outskirts of Baghdad, ready to move on Saddam International Airport, soon to be renamed Baghdad International Airport, or BIAP, as it came to be known to most American military personnel. (General McKiernan himself viewed BIAP as one of the enemy system's key nodes, both as a symbol and as a useful piece of real estate; he placed considerable emphasis on seizing it and planting his own flag on it.) On the same day, the Marine division was once again on the march toward Baghdad, from the southeast. Along the way, the 5th Marines fought one of the fiercest engagements of the war on Route 6 near the town of Al Aziziyah.

The enemy was a mix of Republican Guard troops, Saddam Fedayeen, and foreign "volunteer" fighters from Syria, Egypt, and other Arab countries. During the day, the division lost an M1A1 Abrams tank to a mobility kill and three more to bad luck—transmission problems and mud—making it one of the worst days of the war for Marine armor. Nevertheless, there was no stopping the advancing Marines, or the tank recovery teams, for that matter, which overcame significant obstacles to get the tanks off the battlefield and back to friendly lines.[17]

By 5 April the 3d ID was ready to launch the first of its "Thunder Runs" from the west—its version of the "in-and-out" raids into Baghdad. There was some hard fighting on the way in and out of town. As usual the losses were disproportionate. The Army lost one M1A1 Abrams, but the Iraqi losses were far greater. At the same time, other units from the 3d Division moved west and north to isolate Baghdad.

One of the most amazing things about the "Thunder Runs" is that they—and subsequent forays into Baghdad—were filmed by television crews and broadcast, in real time or near real time, almost as if they were sporting events. But not everyone could watch. The frontline commanders at, roughly speaking, the regimental level and below did not have much information about what was going on in the "outside" world—the world outside their regiment, perhaps their division; there was a "digital divide" between them and their seniors in the rear, where the amount of information available was simply staggering. The more senior headquarters had a staff with a mind-numbing array of computers, televisions, telephones, and the like. The CFLCC command center at Camp Doha, Kuwait, looked something like mission control in Houston, an amphitheater with enormous screens at the front of the room and rows of desks with computer terminals and telephones. MEF Main was in the "Bug," the somewhat less comprehensive but still very well-connected portable command post. Television sets tuned to news channels were ubiquitous at the higher headquarters—in offices, mess halls, gymnasiums, and berthing spaces. It was almost literally impossible to get away from TV images of the war on the Cable News Network or on the Fox News Channel, whose reporters were popular both with military audiences and with the troops themselves.[18]

On this, the "high" side of the digital divide, there was, arguably, too much information available. It was difficult to know which data stream to enter, how to extract what was relevant, and how to combine streams. Assessment played an important role in managing data. At MEF, the Future Operations section was charged with assessing progress toward goals and laying out upcoming decision points. In the vernacular, the calculus was: here's where we are, here's where we are trying to go, and here's where we will have to make a decision about the route we need to take in order to get there.[19] At CFLCC General McKiernan and his chief of staff, General Blackman, had organized the staff by function rather than by traditional Napoleonic section, and created the effects board in order to think of the battle in terms of the effects they wanted to create, rather than the objectives they wanted to seize. Then they instituted the "Battle Update Assessment" (BUA) in place of the "Battle Update Brief" (BUB). On most days during the fight, either the commanding general or one of his principal staff officers chaired this virtual staff meeting, which was an attempt to manage the data flow and distill it into a useful form. Run by the CFLCC staff, it was conducted by secure video teleconference and included as participants senior officers (usually flag rank) from all of the major subordinate commands. Eschewing the awkward-sounding acronym "BUB," General McKiernan had opted for the more euphonious "BUA" because he wanted to make the point that the meeting was not about information as much as assessment. He described the BUA as an attempt to lay the foundation for "decision superiority." It was to enable the commanders to make decisions in the course of their duties after the BUA. He wanted to hear how the major subordinate commands assessed their current and future situations—on the operational level of war, thinking ahead at least ninety-six hours.[20]

Both General McKiernan and General Blackman thought the BUA often fell far short of the mark. Some briefers simply recited staggering laundry lists of events as opposed to concise, conceptual summaries of how they saw the battle, and were cut short by McKiernan or Blackman, once with "No, no, no, no—just tell me what I need to know." The various service cultures were on display during the BUA, with Army commands tending to report in great detail, while the Marines reported more concisely though not necessarily more conceptually, and the British Army seemed to want to report as little as possible. As time went on, the presentations became longer, less conceptual, and more factual, perhaps because of the press of battle. Usually run at 1000 or 1100 local every morning, the BUA could occupy a large chunk of a staff officer's or even a commander's day, since it generated its own set of pre-meetings and post-meetings, and there were complicated slides to prepare on PowerPoint. Some commanders decided to delegate the BUA function to others and seldom appeared on the CFLCC screen.

One thing that distracted staff officers and commanders from assessment was the factual reporting they believed they had to focus on, in part on account of pressure from higher headquarters. Many military reporting procedures hadn't changed much since World War II or Vietnam—the battalion reporting to the regiment to the division, and so forth, a system that worked well enough when the front was relatively static but did not work well when there were multiple, simultaneous lines of operation. It was difficult for units on the move to communicate, especially in built-up areas, because they were busy with other tasks and because the technology often let them down. The MEF Current Operations officer, Col. Dennis Judge, commented that he always knew where his forces were—no thanks to combat reporting, which, he said, "just wasn't there." Instead he was able to rely on automated systems like the Blue Force Tracker (BFT), which didn't require anyone to stop what he or she was doing during combat operations to write and send a report. The BFT included a transponder that transmitted its location and received the location of all other transponders on the same system, displaying them on a small screen. Since it was not line-of-sight but relied on satellites, it had clear advantages over some "legacy" systems to identify friend and foe.[21]

There were others whose job was to report in real time and who had the technology to do so without having to work through a military chain of command: the embedded journalists, whose work appeared on the ever-present TV screens. The media had been "embedded" (this war's jargon for "assigned") down to the battalion level for the duration of hostilities and had the ability to report directly to their home offices, which in turn were able to rebroadcast their stories in very short order.[22] What often happened was that higher headquarters would pick up a breaking story on the media and then go back down the chain of command to get the official reporting about it, which would painstakingly work its way back up the chain and seemed often to be wrong, at least initially. Some staff officers concluded either that "first reports are always wrong" or that they needed to browbeat their subordinates into doing a better job of reporting. But the problem persisted throughout the campaign. As one CFLCC staff officer quipped, "If you want information bad, you will get bad information."

In early April, as events unfolded around Baghdad at dizzying speed, every commander desperately wanted up-to-the minute information, however he could get it—whether from the television newsmen, with their amazingly vivid and reasonably accurate reporting (on TV you could literally hear and see the tanks fire their main guns at Iraqis along the main streets of Baghdad), from the battle update assessments (BUA), or even from the official spot reports and sitreps, which were less timely and far less vivid but, when they trickled in after the battle, a little more accurate.

In the absence of other guidance, the Marines operated in accordance with the next senior commander's intent, which remained simple and consistent: encircle the capital and conduct raids. The MEF staff officers reported that their plans were to "continue to establish the eastern outer cordon of Baghdad . . . and bpt [be prepared to] support further CFLCC missions iso [in support of] regime removal."[23] Since there was little by way of amplifying instructions, they had the leeway to exploit opportunities as they saw them. During a conversation on 6 April, Colonel Hummer of 7th Marines commented that CFLCC had not issued orders telling the field *how* to conduct raids, and he planned to do it his own way.[24]

On that day, the Army was still planning in-and-out raids. On 7 April, the day of the second "Thunder Run," the 3d Infantry Division reported that it controlled a zone from BIAP to one of Saddam's palaces, with armor at all the main intersections in between, but planned to pull back to BIAP. Soon the plan changed; the troopers believed they could hold their ground in downtown Baghdad. This was fine with General McKiernan, who endorsed the idea when General Wallace told him about the situation. General McKiernan made it plain that it was the corps commander's call; this was a tactical decision, best left to the commander who was in contact with the enemy.[25]

While the Army was raiding into Baghdad, the Marines were working to cross the last major obstacle on their way to Baghdad. That was the Diyala River, located east of the city and flowing roughly north to southeast into the Tigris. It had been briefed as a minor obstacle with numerous fording sites.[26] But this was definitely not the case for the Marines, who found it a challenge just to get close enough to the river to take a look at it. Even with engineering support, crossing did not look easy; the problem was that the riverbanks were either steep, muddy, or both, and the local roads were bad. On the afternoon of 6 April, Division reported with some frustration that it had completed a reconnaissance of some sixty kilometers of the Diyala and had "found no viable crossing."[27] It had also encountered stiff resistance in some places.

On 7 April the frustration continued, preventing forward movements, which may have been a blessing in disguise. General Mattis's comments for that day—and the next—in the daily MEF sitrep reflected his concern that the logistical situation was "tenuous" and that his command could be nearing a "logistical culminating point," fairly grim words for a very "can-do" commander. He concluded that he was determined to continue "all previous measures to lighten the logistical burden in hopes of building up substantial stocks . . . for future operations," which included conserving artillery ammunition.[28] On 8 April he wrote that the division had only one "day of supply" of food and that it was so low on artillery ammunition it had decided to rely more heavily on the MAW than on artillery for counter-battery and preparatory fires.[29] But on 8 April he was able to report that his regiments were all across the Diyala. They had crossed using a variety of means—from seizing bridges, to building bridges, to swimming vehicles across. At two locations, the FSSG's 8th Engineer Support Battalion played a critical role, putting in assault bridging while under fire—something the Marine Corps had not done for decades. At one RCT 1 crossing site, Iraqi resistance had ebbed as the amphibious tractors entered the water. One of the Iraqi prisoners of war explained why: "When we saw the tanks floating across the river, we knew we could not win against the Americans."[30]

After crossing the Diyala, 7th Marines had gone on to conduct a raid on the Rashid military complex on the outskirts of Baghdad, the ideal intermediate objective, not quite in the city but a good platform for attacks into it when the time was right. At the same time, 5th Marines was attacking first to the north and then to the west to extend the cordon around the city.[31]

By now, most units in the division had shed their MOPP suits—the protective overalls in the "Woodland" green pattern that contrasted with the desert camouflage uniforms and constricted movement—not to mention how hot they could make the Marine or sailor inside. The general assumption had been that Saddam would use chemical or biological agents outside but not within the Baghdad city limits. The MEF had been on tenterhooks, waiting for the seemingly inevitable report and enduring the almost eerie absence of bad news. But it never came, and the word was passed that since the Marines were now at the city limits, commanders could make the call on the right protective posture. For most Marines, shedding the unwanted second skin was an incredibly liberating and energizing experience— energy that General Mattis wanted them to use on the enemy in Baghdad.[32]

For their part, the MAW and the FSSG had continued to do incredible work, pushing supplies to the front, especially through the airhead at Qalat Sikar, which was south of Al Kut, and getting ready to set up shop at another airfield, Salman Pak, on the outskirts of Baghdad. The Marines soon had the food and ammunition they needed, and the cordon around the city was nearly complete— CFLCC's precondition for the next phase. In the words of the command chronology, "By establishing a cordon, the Division had closed the door for the enemy's escape, and opened the door to operations inside the city."[33] Now all they needed was permission to proceed beyond their limit of advance.

By 1800Z on 8 April, MEF was planning to conduct "armed reconnaissance in force into Baghdad" on the next day, and Division reported that it was contemplating specific "offensive operations within Baghdad iot [in order to] complete the removal of the Regime." This was quite a change from the day before, when the focus had been on crossing the Diyala.[34] Finally, early on 9 April, the division received the go-ahead from General Conway to attack its targets.[35] A few hours later, the field historian at MEF, Maj. Theodore R. McKeldin III, USMCR, noted that MEF had been "cleared hot" by CFLCC for the eastern part of the city.[36] By the time McKeldin penned this note late in the morning, the RCTs had started to move toward the objectives that the division staff had so carefully selected. As one of the embedded reporters, Peter Baker of the *Washington Post,* wrote, they were executing the plan for the day, which "was to keep chipping away at . . . Saddam Hussein's power structure. The Marines would stab into Baghdad and seize a paramilitary base, a secret police headquarters and a presidential palace."[37]

No one was entirely sure what the day would bring. At the morning staff meeting, General Conway commented to his staff that he thought there would be a "big fight" for Saddam's palaces.[38] Division had concluded that the threat from conventional forces had been "nearly eliminated," that there would be little by way of centrally controlled, organized resistance. But there were reports of irregular formations.[39] The regiments were ready to fight if they had to. Soon many of the reports from the front showed quite a different picture. CNN was with 1st Battalion, 7th Marines as it went into the city, and Fox News was with 3d LAR Battalion to the northeast. Instead of fighters, both battalions encountered crowds of jubilant Iraqis who welcomed their liberation. One of the LAR company commanders, Capt. Brian B. Smalley, said later that it was "like driving through Paris in 1944."[40]

In his trailer at MEF headquarters, now at An Numiniyah, General Conway watched the dramatic television footage, some of it showing the poor Shia neighborhood known as Saddam City (and later as Sadr City), which the Marines had originally bypassed. The images impressed him so much that he decided to approve Division's request, which had apparently percolated up from the regiments, simply to advance in zone until they encountered opposition. But his optimism was guarded: "Our intent was to constrict the city using various key objectives as lily pads to reduce the regime on the east side. What we're seeing on TV is happening in some Shia neighborhoods. We can't make the mistake to say that's happening all over Baghdad. We still have a military imperative to conduct operations to reduce . . . regime-related facilities."[41]

The MEF commander discussed the issue with his Army counterparts at a midday video teleconference, and ultimately there was broad agreement on "a plan for a decisive assault on the city" by the Marines and the Army.[42] This was the end of the various plans for a methodical advance to seize particular objectives, let alone the plan for in-and-out raids. The division finally had a free hand in Baghdad.[43]

The result was that RCT 7 happily assaulted through its assigned area of operations, moving from the southeast to the northwest on the north bank of the Tigris. The list of sites they secured on that day was impressive: the Ministry of Intelligence; the Ministry of Oil; Uday Hussein's offices, which were already burning when the Marines arrived; the Iraqi air force headquarters, which had been destroyed; and the Fedayeen headquarters, which was listed as "rubbled." At the end of the day, the division's plans were just as ambitious as its accomplishments: "to have made [the Marine] presence known in all of [our] city zones by morning tomorrow [and] over the next few days . . . allowing the local populace . . . to return to some sense of normal life."[44]

Among the sites in the 7th Marines area of operations was Firdos Square in downtown Baghdad. It was dominated by a six-meter-high statue of Saddam Hussein with his right arm raised in a heroic gesture. The 3d Battalion, 4th

Marines rolled into the square late in the day on 9 April. A crowd quickly gathered. Given the proximity of the local haven for journalists, the Palestine Hotel, there seemed to be as many foreign reporters as Iraqi citizens in the crowd. An Army psychological operations team attached to the Marines arrived and announced over a loudspeaker in Arabic that the Marines had decided the statue should come down. Millions around the world were able to watch the events in real time on CNN and other television networks. A Marine named Cpl. Edward Chin, of Bravo Company, 1st Tank Battalion, climbed onto a kind of derrick that extended from his M-88 tank retriever. He reached up and placed an American flag over Saddam's face. Some of the Iraqis said, *No, we want an Iraqi flag,* and, within one or two minutes, Chin took the flag down and replaced it with an Iraqi flag. Next a stout rope was fitted around the statue, and then to a cable on the tank retriever. When the tank retriever pulled, the statue came down, slowly, as the metal bent and Saddam slipped off the pedestal. The crowd rushed forward, swarming over the fallen statue. One group of Iraqis dragged its head to an unknown but no doubt unpleasant fate.[45]

There are a few arresting images in every war, and the toppling of the Saddam statue was one of them for the Iraq War. It was not exactly what the high command wanted. Generals Franks and McKiernan, each at his own headquarters, had been watching the scene unfold on television, and when the American flag went over Saddam's face, Franks picked up the telephone to call McKiernan, who did not need to be told why his boss was calling. Even before General Franks could say anything, General McKeirnan said, "We're already on it."[46] As commanders from General Franks to General Mattis had told their troops over and over again, this was not a war of American conquest, but of Iraqi liberation. The flag that mattered was not the American flag, it was the Iraqi flag, flown by itself, in sites no longer dominated by statues and murals of Saddam Hussein. Nevertheless, the Saddam statue's fall marked a turning point; the end of Phase III seemed to be in sight, even though there would still be some hard fighting.

While the statue had been coming down, Marines a few blocks away had been exchanging fire with Iraqi loyalists, and the next day, 10 April, was little better. On the contrary, 1st Battalion, 5th Marines spent the better part of the day securing two objectives, Saddam's Azimiyah Palace (one of many throughout the capital and the country) and Imam Abu Hanifah Mosque. First they had to drive through a hail of rocket-propelled grenades and "a torrent of heavy machine gun and small arms fire," and then, perhaps the ultimate nightmare, they got lost and had to make a U-turn while under fire. (If you think it's bad enough to drive in an unfamiliar city in the Middle East, imagine what it is like to do so with people shooting at you.) The Marines were encountering more foreign "jihadis"— Islamic fundamentalist paramilitary fighters. The mosque was a target because it had been the location of what someone called an "Elvis sighting"—Saddam Hussein was said to have entered the mosque—and the Marines were told to secure the perimeter to keep anyone from entering or leaving. The report turned out to be false, but the jihadis still fought with determination. By the end of the day, RCT 5 reported it had lost one Marine killed in action, and forty-two wounded in action, along with two tank mobility kills—another unusually bad day for tanks in this war. The commander of RCT 5, Colonel Dunford, remembered 10 April as both the worst and the best day of the war. It seemed like the worst day while his regiment was heavily engaged in downtown Baghdad. His fear was that there would be many more days of heavy fighting. But it turned into the best day when his 1st Battalion reported that the situation was well in hand and that after the fight it was encountering crowds of cheering people, some eight or nine deep, shouting in broken English, "Good, good, Mister!"[47]

The fighting tapered off rapidly—the regime's "last stand" in Baghdad turned out to be so short that it was anticlimactic. There was no sign of Saddam. Some thought (erroneously, as it turned out) he could be lying under the rubble of a restaurant in the Mansour district that had been struck by smart bombs on 8 April. His government had simply evaporated. The civil servants, including "Baghdad Bob," the infamous spokesman who kept predicting on television that coalition forces were on the brink of annihilation, had simply stopped coming to work. Very soon looters took over the city. If the focus on 9 and 10 April had been on crowds who were literally applauding the collapse of the Saddam regime, it quickly shifted to those who were taking advantage of the situation. The TV news broadcast one scene after another of Iraqis, young and old, carrying away anything that was not bolted down—from government offices, from official residences, from army bases, even from schools and hospitals. Particularly upsetting for some westerners was the looting of the antiquities museum, a repository of ancient and irreplaceable treasures.

The extent of the looting, and what to do about it, certainly seemed to catch the coalition by surprise. The basic outlines of OPlan 1003V did not extend far beyond the goals of securing the oil fields, removing the regime, and finding weapons of mass destruction; there had been a great deal of detailed planning, and rehearsals, for Phase III, but the postcombat Phase IV had, by comparison, been virtually neglected. If Phase III had been the favorite son, Phase IV was the redheaded stepchild—and now he was acting out.[48] When asked about the looting, American officials were low-key. On 9 April, Secretary of Defense Rumsfeld downplayed the problem, as did Generals Conway and Mattis and other senior coalition commanders. They implied that the Iraqi people had earned the right to profit at the expense of their dictatorial government, and that there was, in any case, only so much the U.S. forces could do, given their limited numbers. General Conway said, "Does it bother me . . . that I see people taking an office chair or the guts of a refrigerator or an air conditioner? Not really, . . . at least [not] at this point. . . . It's got to be the pent-up frustration they've experienced for the better part of their lives."⁴⁹ General Mattis offered the uncharacteristically mild observation that the coalition was "in that kind of never-never land right now . . . we're not in full control [yet], so you're in that transition period."⁵⁰

Phase IV in Baghdad

Lt. Col. Christopher C. Conlin, commanding officer of 1st Battalion, 7th Marines, wrote a vivid account of the quick and dramatic shift from Phase III to Phase IV on the streets of Baghdad:

> Within minutes of our seizure of the capital, one of my lieutenants was presented with the rapidly expiring body of an Iraqi who had been pried from a vehicle accident seconds before. He was not a war casualty, but a simple victim of a "routine" incident. The fact that the locals brought him to us as he was in his final death spasms was their unequivocal realization that the normal procedure, going to the hospital or calling the police, was gone. This episode was duplicated throughout our zone with geometrically increasing frequency. Frantic locals ran up to tell us phones were out, doctors reported hospitals being looted, and that the water was off. They were desperate to know where they should dump the trash, could they use cell phones, or was it OK to drive to their father's house in Mosul? They approached us to arrest a strange man with a gun lurking in their neighborhood. We were approached by alleged sheiks who demanded to [see] "his Excellency the General" about their tribe's loyalty to Mr. Bush. . . . On and on the requests came. All being diligently received and somehow answered by our young squad leaders and platoon leaders. We too were in transition. Having overwhelmed organized resistance, we were hot on the trail of Saddam's . . . Fedayeen. . . . Our aggressive small unit leaders were able to hit them in their homes and offices in ever quickening succession. We created hunter-killer teams on the fly, sending our very talented Humint Exploitation Teams, . . . PsyOps and Civil Affairs . . . Teams down to the platoon level . . . Companies worked huge urban sectors usually rotating platoons to achieve a 24/7 battle rhythm. The effect was dramatic. . . . Within a week of liberation, the markets were open again, . . . many were going back to work, there was a new police force reorganizing, neighborhoods were organizing. . . . Lessons Learned: . . . Press flesh, kiss the babies, and kill the enemy.*

*Col. Christopher C. Conlin, "What do you do for an encore?" *Marine Corps Gazette*, Sept. 2004, pp. 74–80.

By the next day, the coalition forces were shifting their approach and trying to address the problem as best they could with the limited resources at their disposal. Early on the morning of 10 April, a pedestrian suicide bomber blew himself up and injured five men from 5th Marines. The incident caught General Conway's attention. He called it "a sobering reminder . . . that much work remains to be done." The MEF "must . . . quickly transition to Phase IV Stage B civil-military/humanitarian assistance operations to stabilize the situation and demonstrate our resolve to . . . the newly liberated . . . people" of Iraq. The theme at the MEF's morning staff meeting was that the Marines needed to switch from a combat role to a stabilizing role. For that reason, Marines were ordered to take steps to control the looting, which included the protection of International Red Cross facilities by 7th Marines.[51] On the same day, 7th Marines took the initiative to establish a civil-military operations center (CMOC) in the centrally located Palestine Hotel. The other regiments followed suit in short order, reaching out to local leaders and generally establishing useful contacts in the interests of restoring some semblance of order and basic municipal services. The division's artillery regiment, 11th Marines, played its part. Realizing he was unlikely to need much more artillery support, General Mattis took the unusual step of turning the Division CMOC over to 11th Marines and assigning the artillerymen their own sector of Baghdad along with the infantry regiments.[52] Late in the day, he was feeling upbeat about the situation: "The city in our zone is . . . [almost] entirely in USMC hands. While it will remain a dangerous place for days to come, the local populace is wholly supportive of our efforts and active patrolling will impose our will. . . . We will calm the situation and . . . build on the goodwill we have experienced to date."[53]

That Baghdad was still a dangerous place was an understatement. The Marines faced a number of daunting tasks from turning the lights back on to explosive ordnance disposal. One problem was, in the words of the division's command chronology, it seemed that "virtually every block" in Baghdad had its own weapons cache. Some of these caches were enormous, "containing every conceivable type of weapon and ammunition, to include tanks, mortars, artillery pieces, and even . . . surface-to-surface rockets."[54] On the march up to Baghdad, Army and Marine units had, like Task Force Tarawa in An Nasiriyah, found weapons caches throughout the country—often in schools, hospitals, and mosques—to say nothing of the enormous ammunition supply points that covered acres and acres of ground. In the convoluted logic of the Saddam regime, it was only fitting that the capital itself be lavishly supplied and ready for a drawn-out fight. Although Iraqi intentions remained unclear, the discoveries suggested that the regime had been getting ready to back up its threat that the coalition would face a people in arms, or some kind of guerrilla war, if it invaded Iraq.[55]

Well to the south of Baghdad, Task Force Tarawa had already been conducting Phase IV operations over a vast stretch of country with its approximately thirteen thousand Marines and sailors. When it had expanded its battle space to the north, it had become responsible for providing security along the major supply routes, Routes 1 and 7, which meant it had to occupy or neutralize threats in the area. This was in addition to remaining responsible for An Nasiriyah, where Tarawa Marines continued to make notable strides in eliminating enemy resistance and establishing city government. The city of Ad Diwaniyah astride Route 1 posed a typical challenge, which the Marines met in ways that were becoming typical. In early April, various kinds of enemy formations continued to pose a threat to convoys passing through. While cordoning off the city, Tarawa made good use of its Operational Detachment–Alpha (ODA), a U.S. Army Special Forces unit that cultivated the population and gathered actionable intelligence. This in turn led to attacks on specific targets with precision munitions. Similarly, in the nearby city of Al Hamsha, information gathered by Special Forces led to a strike against the Ba'ath Party that caused the death of the local Ba'athist leader and was followed by a successful revolt by the local citizenry.

In much the same way, Tarawa prosecuted attacks against enemy forces in several other cities along Route 7, the other major supply route. These cities were Al Hayy, Qalat Sikar, and Ash Shatrah. Another city that more or less liberated itself was Al Amarah, where elements of the task force had gone to eliminate the 10th Armored Division from 8 to 12 April in the "Battle of the Icons." In mid-April, after the British expanded their zone to the north and took charge in Amarah, Tarawa shifted its focus to the cities of An Numiniyah and Al Kut. The task force placed a battalion of infantry in An Numiniyah, where MEF main had set up an interim command post, and set up its own headquarters on the airfield at Al Kut in hardened aircraft shelters that were mercifully cool, a brief respite from the heat but not from the high tempo of operations.[56]

8

No Smell of Saltwater

North to Tikrit, South to Ad Diwaniyah

The MEF's focus had always been on Baghdad. The events of 9 and 10 April signaled the end of the combat operation that most Marines had expected to conduct. Those with longer memories remembered that before the war began, CFLCC had gamed a scenario for securing the oil fields around the city of Kirkuk from the south, instead of the north or the east, and that the MEF had written a branch plan for Kirkuk.

Some 150 miles north of Baghdad, Kirkuk was the oil capital of the north. The surrounding oil fields were comparable in significance to the southern oil fields and represented an objective far too important to ignore. There had been various plans for the Army to secure the area, especially by introducing the 4th Infantry Division through Turkey. But if that proved impossible, other CFLCC troops might have to advance from the south. After the war, General Conway remembered being asked by CFLCC if the Marines could take on the mission if necessary, and he answered that it could be done—if necessary. The MEF was not looking for yet another mission at the end of its supply tether but would take it on if tasked. As General Conway commented to a journalist on 9 April when asked about ordering the MEF to advance to the north: "That would be tough for us. We are a long way from our sea base. As Marines, [if] we don't smell saltwater . . . that makes us a little uneasy. That said, our logisticians, . . . augmented by our [air] wing, have done a magnificent job. . . . To take [it] . . . another couple [of] hundred miles would be extremely difficult. It's difficult right now—that would be extremely difficult. But it might be something that we have to ask our people to do."[1] A few days later, during a staff meeting, Conway made the sensible comment: "We're not putting our hand in the air for that . . . [we] have enough [to do] already."[2]

CFLCC's prewar questions meant it was not a complete surprise when the issue came up again and occupied General Conway and his staff on 10 April. MEF issued a verbal order to Division to "be prepared to" proceed to Kirkuk, and to FSSG and Wing to be prepared to support the attack. The guidance was to focus on the objective and to avoid being sidetracked by enemy formations along the way.[3]

Division had already been thinking about the north. Amazingly, it had recently gone on record as being "prepared to continue the attack to Kirkuk . . . and secure the . . . oilfield." This was on 8 April, the day when it was worried about running out of ammunition while it was finishing the struggle to get across the Diyala River, just before what would be, for many of its Marines, the fight of a lifetime in Baghdad.[4] Even though Division had apparently long had a contingency plan on the shelf for an attack to the north, this was just about as far forward as anyone could—or did—lean in his foxhole during Operation Iraqi Freedom.[5]

Division then announced that it could "collapse" its cordon around Baghdad and form a task force, to be known as "Tripoli" (after another Marine march across desert sands, that of Lt. Presley O'Bannon to Tripoli, Libya, in 1805), to conduct the operation. The assistant division commander, Brig. Gen. Kelly, would command, using the nucleus of the division's forward command post.[6]

Preparations intensified on 11 April. MEF issued a formal warning order for the continuation of the attack to Kirkuk. Division decided on the composition of the force. It would be the division's three light armored reconnaissance (LAR) battalions—1st, 2d, and 3d; 5th Battalion, 11th Marines; and Golf Company G of infantry from 2d Battalion, 23d Marines. This would amount to the equivalent of a reinforced LAR regiment. Logistics would roll with the task force, which would have a dedicated combat service support element; but some resupply would have to come from the wing, which pitched in with plans to establish forward arming and refueling points (FARPs) as the task force moved north and secured suitable pieces of terrain. Cargo helicopters and KC-130 Hercules cargo haulers, the workhorse of choice for many missions in Iraq, would deliver supplies to the FARPs. (By this point in the campaign most acknowledged that the Marine KC-130s—many of them piloted by Reservists—were ideal for the distances and the loads in Iraq; General Amos was to call them "the queen of the prom" in a postwar interview.[7]) For its part, the division staff went so far as to analyze the makeup of the oil fields, build objective folders, and recommend schemes of maneuver to General Kelly.

The MEF plan for Kirkuk was overtaken by events that had been set in motion before 10 April. Kurdish forces, advised by U.S. Army Special Forces teams, seized the oil fields. As of 1800Z on 10 April, CFACC stopped bombing the city of Kirkuk, because organized enemy resistance was crumbling. On 11 April the city was in Kurdish hands. By late afternoon on the same day, CFLCC changed the MEF's target to Tikrit, Saddam Hussein's hometown, which was only about one hundred miles north of Baghdad. General Conway commented to his staff by way of explanation that the Marines "were the best force available now to do this."[8]

Tikrit was assessed by various G-2 and C-2 elements as a logical place for the regime to make a last stand; the division framed the operation as an attack to deny the enemy safe haven and to prevent the escape of high-value targets. The enemy forces that the division expected to encounter were one or two brigades of the Special Republican Guard and a few hundred paramilitary fighters. The general assumption was that the paramilitaries would fight but that the uniformed soldiers would not.

The change may have been frustrating to some MEF and Division planners, but overall it was a positive development, since it was relatively easy to substitute Tikrit for Kirkuk, and Tikrit was closer to Baghdad; the supply tether would not have to stretch as far. In General Mattis's words, "The Division is stretched, but not to the breaking point, with stabilization ops in Baghdad [and] TF Tripoli focused on Tikrit. . . . We are green on logistics, but will require a new . . . estimate of supportability if ordered to the Kirkuk or Mosul area."[9]

What General Conway called "the final attack" officially began on the afternoon of 12 April—at 1255Z, to be precise—and proceeded rapidly up-country. It was, in a sense, a quintessential OIF operation. It was short-fused and had a commander who stressed the need for speed. He task-organized in a matter of hours, making good use of two weapons systems that also seemed to have been made for a place like Iraq: the eight-wheeled light armored vehicles and the Cobra gunships. "It was," the command chronology recalled, "comforting [to have] the Cobra escort. They were masters at rooting around the enemy's potential hiding spots and building our situational awareness around every corner. . . . We [had] gained a deep respect for the Cobra pilots during the war."[10] The wing's airborne forward air controller (FAC[A]) complemented the work of the Cobras and kept in touch with a section of Harriers that were dedicated to the task force. When this piece of division-wing coordination was reported to MEF, the word was that if anyone opened fire on the Marines, he would not live to regret it.[11]

After leaving its assembly area, Task Force Tripoli passed first through friendly territory, with Iraqis lining the roads to wave and shouting greetings like "Good, good!" In Samarra, a city between Baghdad and Tikrit, there was a happy event when the 3d LAR Battalion found and freed seven American prisoners of war on

13 April. Then, closer to Tikrit, the locals became less friendly and in some cases downright hostile. There were even more murals, portraits, and statues of Saddam here than in other parts of the country—where they were certainly plentiful enough—but, the Marines noticed, only a few had been defaced. Both on 13 and 14 April there was "minimal contact" with enemy formations—occasional firefights, some of them intense—on the way to the objective.

The Other Prisoner-of-War Rescue Operation

Some of the most high-profile stories of the war were about POWs, especially the rescue of Army PFC Jessica Lynch, who had been captured early in the fighting around An Nasiriyah and later became something of a media figure in the United States. On the night of 1–2 April, Task Force Tarawa had facilitated the rescue. But the rescue at Samarra was as memorable, if not as celebrated. It was a victory for the Marine traits of getting out to meet the locals and taking calculated risks. On 13 April, HUMINT Exploitation Team (HET) 3, led by 1st Lt. Nathan M. Boaz, entered the city to meet with tribal elders. While the team was in the city, an Iraqi policeman approached with information about U.S. POWs. To pinpoint the location without compromising the source, the HET's chief, Staff Sgt. Randy Meyer, gave the policeman a GPS receiver and told him how to use it to record the location of the POWs, which the policeman did. Even though he was under pressure to continue on to Tikrit, 3d LAR Battalion commander Lt. Col. Herman S. Clardy III decided on his own that the information was reliable enough to act on, and that trying to rescue the POWs was worth the time. LAR scouts and HET members proceeded to storm the house pinpointed by the informer and, without firing a shot, freed the seven grateful soldiers—two pilots and five members of Jessica Lynch's unit, who had also been captured in An Nasiriyah on 22 March. One of the pilots later described the rescue on television in vivid terms, cheerfully recounting that he had never before been so glad to see a group of men who looked like hollow-eyed killers coming to get him. The news of their release was immediately briefed throughout the theater, and the POWs were whisked to the rear.*

*In addition to the division command chronology, see Lt. Col. Herman S. Clardy III e-mail to author, 28 April 04 (Copy in Reynolds Working Papers, MCHC, Washington, D.C.).

"Minimal contact" is the kind of phrase that senior commands put in situation reports. To the Marine on the ground who is risking his life during one of the few firefights of the day, it certainly does not seem "minimal," and the division's command chronology contains vivid descriptions of fights with fedayeen in and around Tikrit. Even by the Iraqi standard—which seemed to call for every school and mosque to be filled with munitions—there was a great deal of military hardware in the area. The Marines of 1st LAR Battalion, for example, passed through a "large area [south of Tikrit] . . . with multiple revetments that contained enemy vehicles" and then called in air strikes on the vehicles before proceeding on to a crossroads where they took a number of RPG rounds, one of which struck the tailpipe of a light armored vehicle. The Marines returned fire, destroying two trucks and killing five of the enemy. Once inside the city, the Marines found massive amounts of ordnance, including a compound with thirty warehouses of weapons and a cache at a hospital containing literally thousands of AK-47 rifles. The division concluded that "the amount of ordnance . . . is overwhelming and will require months of dedicated lift to remove it all"—a telling reflection of the Pentagon's troop-to-task calculus.[12]

By 15 April fighting had tapered off, and Tripoli found itself the de facto source of power in Tikrit. The question was how to use that power to address the bewildering array of problems that the city faced. The existing power structure—the tribal sheikhs—approached the task force, outlined the situation as they saw it, and wanted to establish a leadership council. General Kelly was reluctant to deal with the sheikhs, who were hardly a democratic body and had done business with Saddam Hussein. In the end, he decided that the sheikhs represented as good an interim local government as any and met with them on 15 April to lay out his view of the situation. He repeated a number of basic themes: the Marines would take responsibility for the security of the area; the locals would help the Marines hunt down any remaining foreign fighters or Saddam loyalists; and, finally, the sheikhs would bear much of the responsibility for restoring power, water, food, and medical services. All of this was easier said than done; the 15 April meeting was simply the beginning of a process that entailed numerous meetings between the sheikhs on the one hand and General Kelly on the other, as men conditioned by long-simmering feuds and unaccustomed to democracy took their first tentative steps away from a dictatorship that had dominated their lives for thirty years. A by-product of the good relations between General Kelly and the sheikhs was their assistance in the peaceful "liberation" of the city of Bayji about twenty-five miles north of Tikrit.

Meanwhile, out on the streets of Tikrit, the Marines dealt with such challenges as a panicky crowd of citizens who wanted to cross over a bridge that had been weakened during the war; a group of vigilantes who established their own checkpoints outside the city, apparently to harass people they didn't like; and marauding Kurds, the ethnic minority who had suffered at the hands of Saddam's regime and were not inclined to treat the citizens of Tikrit gently. The Marines' aggressive patrolling—typically by dismounted infantry without flak vests and in soft covers—along with their commonsense solutions to problems, restored more than a small semblance of order to the city within a few days.

Between 19 and 21 April, Task Force Tripoli conducted a relief in place with the Army's 4th Infantry Division and prepared to rejoin the main body of 1st Mar Div. The 4th ID had spent the war en route first to Turkey, where it had been unable to land, and then to Iraq through Kuwait. Although major combat operations had ended, this division characterized its move north to the zone it would occupy as an "attack," which led to some unfortunate incidents. On 19 April the Marine division complained about U.S. Army Apache helicopters entering Marine battle space "without permission or clearance to engage"—and then firing at abandoned enemy armor located between the 2d and 3d LAR battalions. The 4th ID also seemed intent on treating the Tikritis as hostile, which distressed the Marines, who had gone to some lengths to establish good relations with the locals. General Mattis himself noticed that like the 3d ID, the 4th ID had a lot of armored vehicles and only a limited number of dismounts and went on record with a prediction that "the lack of Army dismounts is creating a void in personal contact and public perception. . . . Our forces need to project confidence in the security environment we have created. That is best exemplified in light, mobile forces in contact with the local citizenry sans helmets and flak jackets and without armored vehicles. If we cannot engender friendship and confidence in the local security environment, we cannot set the conditions for good order integral to a return to civil control."[13]

General Mattis's comment applied not only to Tikrit but also to Baghdad. While Task Force Tripoli was securing Tikrit and preparing for a relief in place with 4th ID, three regiments of the division had been consolidating their gains in Baghdad and getting ready to turn their zones over to 3d ID in accordance with the plan for the occupation of Iraq. The civil-military operations center— the CMOC—run by the artillerymen of the 11th Marines, continued to find stopgap solutions for the many problems they faced; with remarkably little assistance or guidance from anyone, it had established cells for police, fire, electricity, water, and medical care, and the instant experts worked their issues as best they could. The CMOC appointed an interim police chief and opened an Iraqi police academy. It facilitated and coordinated the work of nongovernmental organizations like CARE, the Red Cross, the Red Crescent, and the World Food Program. Meanwhile, out on the streets, the RCTs maintained checkpoints to control movement in their sectors (which they moved often to frustrate any attempts to target them). The division took some additional steps—such as delivering public safety messages—in the hope of controlling the rampant looting and widespread crime that had broken out when the regime collapsed and left a power vacuum in Baghdad. Since this was something no one had really planned for except in the most general terms, there had been an ad hoc quality about the guidance from CFLCC and MEF about looting and crime that seemed to boil down to "stop it if you can" and left it up to the units in contact to come up with workable solutions.[14]

Even though there was only so much the Marines could do in the few days between the collapse of the regime and their scheduled departure from Baghdad, there were signs of progress. One Marine, Maj. Jason L. Morris, of 3d Battalion, 5th Marines, observed that the eastern half of Baghdad seemed to him to have returned to something like normalcy within ten days of the fall of the Saddam statue on Firdos Square. Morris attributed this to the division's approach, which he characterized as relatively low impact. Even in the days immediately after 9 April, Marines allowed the local citizens to go about their business so long as they did not interfere with Marine business. There was certainly an active Marine presence in the streets, especially by dismounted infantrymen, but he did not think they gave the city the feel of being under martial law. He supported General Mattis's argument that infantrymen are better suited for patrolling a city than armored vehicles.[15]

As impressive as its beginnings were, no one will ever know how effective the division's occupation of Baghdad would have been in the long run. By 15 April, if not before, the division staff had begun to prepare for a turnover to the 3d ID, with the assistance of the Army's 358th Civil Affairs Command's Deliberate Assessment Team. Detailed staff work and command interaction followed at various levels, more or less spontaneously—"without written orders, instructions, or doctrine of any kind," to quote the division's command chronology.[16] The actual relief in place in Baghdad occurred between 18 and 20 April, another eventful day. While elements of the division moved south to Ad Diwaniyah, where it relieved the Army's 82nd Airborne Division and established a new headquarters, MEF convened a combined Phase IV and R3 (retrograde/reconstitution/regeneration) conference at its dusty field headquarters in An Numaniyah.

Phase III, the war from the line of departure in Kuwait to the enemy center of gravity in Baghdad, had gone by in the blink of an eye, a remarkable performance by any standard. But there had been a cost. For the MEF the casualties were on the order of seventy-five killed in action and three hundred wounded in action. Even if statistics did not lessen the heartbreak of loss for each man who died, the numbers were far smaller than had been feared, which was something to be thankful for.[17] The MEF honored its dead and wounded and prepared for the next phase of the operation.

9

The Other War in the North

Marines in Kurdistan and Mosul

Task Force Tripoli was not the only Marine command that operated north of Baghdad, which included great stretches of territory that fell under Joint Special Operations Task Force-North (JSOTF-N), commanded by Col. Charles T. Cleveland, USA. Cleveland, who had apparently been in Iraqi Kurdistan for months, reported not to CFLCC but to Coalition Forces Special Operations Command, another CentCom dependency. Using various kinds of paramilitary forces, he ran the war in the northeast corner of Iraq, responsible for its defense from the Iraqi army and for preparations to secure the cities of Mosul and Kirkuk and their surroundings. He had, in a sense, taken on the mission that had been assigned to the 4th Infantry Division: to put pressure on Baghdad from the north, or at least to manage the situation in the north in order to prevent any surprises that might undermine the offensive in the south. To do this he had at his disposal a Special Forces (SF) Group, made up of three SF battalions, and Kurdish formations as well as coalition air power in general support. There was an Air Force contingent with some air and ground assets complementing the SF, and Colonel Cleveland could also request sorties from CFACC. As for the Kurdish fighters, there were some seventy thousand of them, grouped into two militias identified with the two main Kurdish political parties, the Patriotic Union of Kurdistan (PUK) and the Kurdish Democratic Party (KDP), which were now cooperating against the common enemy but had in the past turned on each other, exhibiting some of the less attractive aspects of a warlike culture. The SF had been working with these fighters for at least a few months.[1] There was another group working in the north that did not come under Cleveland but cooperated

with his command. It was the handful of Marines known as the Military Coordination and Liaison Command (MCLC), led by Maj. Gen. Henry P. Osman, the
commanding general of II Marine Expeditionary Force (II MEF) from Camp
Lejeune, North Carolina, another one of the low-key but very effective generals
who left their mark on Operation Iraqi Freedom.

The MCLC had a complicated history. In the fall of 2002, General Osman
had watched General Natonski and 2d MEB's preparations to join I MEF in
Kuwait for the attack from the south. This was neither unexpected nor a particular hardship to II MEF; since the end of the Cold War, and the shift in focus
away from the North Atlantic, II MEF had served largely as a force provider for
other theaters. The 2d MEB was by design a detachable module of II MEF. General Natonski himself was the deputy MEF commander, as well as the commander of 2d MEB. Similarly, many of his officers were dual-hatted, with both
MEF and MEB functions. The deployment of the MEB meant the MEF staff
had only a small residual capability, but it was still a capability that could be put
to good use in the CentCom theater. General Osman believed that II MEF could
field a small joint task force and told Headquarters Marine Corps as much.[2]
What happened next was a dialogue between II MEF and HQMC over the
potential uses of II MEF's staff, animated at least in part by the commandant of
the Marine Corps' continuing interest in northern Iraq, especially the northeast
corner of the country with its large Kurdish minority.

In 1991, in the wake of Operation Desert Storm there had been a humanitarian crisis in northern Iraq following Saddam Hussein's brutal suppression of a
Kurdish revolt. After a delay, President George H. W. Bush had directed the
Commander in Chief, European Command (EuCom) to conduct an operation
to provide humanitarian assistance to the tens of thousands of Kurds who, in the
aftermath of the revolt, had become refugees in their own homeland. The result
had been Operation Provide Comfort, a multinational effort that had lasted for
about four months and created the basis for de facto Kurdish autonomy for the
next decade. Iraqi troops stayed out of Kurdish territory, part of the northern no-
fly zone enforced by Operation Northern Watch. That said, in 2002 there were
up to twelve Iraqi divisions north of Baghdad, at various stages of readiness,
grouped in I Corps and V Corps. A number of them were assessed as capable of
advancing into Kurdistan. Both the Iraqis and the Kurds actively manned and
patrolled the "Green Line" that divided their spheres of control.[3]

The commandant of the Marine Corps, Gen. James L. Jones Jr., had been the
24th MEU(SOC) commander during Provide Comfort, and he had not forgotten the experience. Now, in late 2002, as he prepared to step down as commandant and take up the responsibilities of Supreme Allied Commander, Europe
(SACEur), he wanted to do what he could to support CentCom in the coming

war against Iraq. One of his agenda items was to explore the need for another such mission with Marine participation.[4] Would the CFLCC attack from the south lead to another humanitarian crisis in the north? If so, it would involve Turkey, a NATO ally. Southern Turkey was the obvious location to stage the mission. This was therefore a matter that SacEur, like his predecessor thirteen years earlier, needed to consider. (The border between Iraq and Turkey was also the border between CentCom and EuCom; anything that happened in northern Iraq would affect both commands.) General Osman and the II MEF staff were natural candidates for a military-political mission to the region, and after he had more or less volunteered his services, Osman discussed the contingency with General Jones in November and December 2002. He also met twice with General Zinni, another veteran of Operation Provide Comfort, who, while at Central Command, had spent much of his time traveling around the region practicing military-political diplomacy.[5] By late January 2003, after 2d MEB had left Camp Lejeune, General Osman was in touch with the senior Marine in U.S. European Command, Marine Forces Europe (MarForEur) commander Lt. Gen. Martin R. Berndt, about standing up a joint task force to coordinate Phase IV— that is, postcombat—operations in northern Iraq. To consider, first, how to staff the JTF and, second, how it should operate, II MEF had created an operational planning team.[6]

On 17 February 2003 General Osman and a few of his principal staff officers flew to the EuCom headquarters at Stuttgart, Germany, to discuss the potential operation with military planners at MarForEur (which is part of EuCom). Next they visited Ankara, Turkey, for meetings with subject matter experts at the American embassy and the Turkish General Staff. To put it mildly, the Turks were able to contain their enthusiasm for a mission to help the Kurds, especially one operating out of southern Turkey, and did not offer much by way of help or encouragement. Since they wanted to keep their own Kurdish minority in check, the last thing the Turks wanted was for the Iraqi Kurds to assert themselves. The Turks and the Kurds had a long tradition of enmity, and the United States had to strike a delicate balance between using the Kurds against the Iraqis and not upsetting Turkish sensibilities. (This was one of the reasons why the United States could not use the Kurdish militias as proxies in the quite the same way it had used Afghan militias in late 2001 and early 2002.) Throughout the operation, as General Osman and his officers encountered strong, even visceral, anti-Kurdish sentiments among the Turkish officers they met, they made it part of their mission to do what they could to keep such sentiments in check. It did not help that General Osman had a typically Turkish surname but was not of Turkish descent, leading his Turkish contacts first to imagine that they were speaking to a compatriot, and then to disappointment when they were disabused of that notion.

General Osman's small group went on to Camp Doha, Kuwait, to meet with General McKiernan and his staff, whom they found to be, understandably, pre-occupied with other matters and not able to devote much attention to northern Iraq. The group's last stop was CentCom headquarters at Doha, Qattar, where there were more discouraging meetings. A down-to-earth son of Georgia who called it like he saw it, Col. Robert L. Hayes III, the MEF G-3, remembered thinking that no one really seemed to want the mission to happen. He himself was beginning to question its utility, especially since his mission analysis showed that the conditions that had called forth Operation Provide Comfort in 1991 simply did not exist in 2003. There did not appear to be an impending humanitarian crisis; on the contrary, this time the Kurds appeared to be well prepared for any such eventuality. The joke among members of the staff was that this task force without a mission should be known as "JTF JDK"—for "just don't know." Someone even went to the length of ordering coffee cups with an official-looking "JTF JDK" logo.

Virtually at the last minute, during a meeting with Gen. John P. Abizaid, USA, the deputy commander of CentCom forward and another veteran of Operation Provide Comfort, the mission was saved. General Abizaid analyzed the current situation from another angle and came to the conclusion that the presence of the right American flag officer would definitely be value added. That officer's mission would be to preserve the status quo during combat operations—in effect, to help secure the northern flank—and not just to prepare for humanitarian assistance after the war. He would work to keep the Kurds (and the other minorities) in check, which in turn would keep the Turks from intervening "to protect their equities"—a distinct possibility if the Kurds seized Kirkuk, the medium-sized city that was the key to the northern oil fields, and/or Mosul, its larger neighbor to the north, with a population of more than 1.5 million that many senior Ba'athists called home. Even without the Turkish factor, there were so many different groups with ancient conflicts against one another that the region was a powder keg. The Turkish threat to intervene if the Kurds "got out of hand" was the match that could have set it aflame. With this vision, General Abizaid played the leading role in converting the EuCom initiative into a CentCom mission and became the mission manager to whom Osman reported, on an almost daily basis. General Abizaid told General Osman that the best place for the MCLC was in northern Iraq, not southern Turkey.[7]

Even though Kurdish Iraq was more or less autonomous and enjoyed the protection of its own forces, this was technically enemy territory. Getting ready to operate in Saddam's backyard during the war made matters more interesting and called for a lot of creative preparations. Leaving roughly thirty members of his staff in Stuttgart, General Osman decided to enter Iraq with only a handful of

Marines—a total of six. Through a portable communications suite, they would "reach back" for support to Stuttgart from members of the II MEF staff who had deployed to EuCom, and rely largely on the Kurds and Special Forces for situational awareness, security, and other forms of support. They acquired a mix of civilian sports utility vehicles and one pickup truck, a Ford F-350, through a mix of open purchase and barter with the U.S. Air Force. They planned to travel in uniform, with a mix of light weapons. Just about everyone had more than one job on this tiny staff. Col. Keith A. Lawless, for example, was not only the G-2 (his normal job) but also the political adviser and a bodyguard armed with an M-4 assault rifle. Colonel Lawless's colorful ops chief, Master Gy. Sgt. Richard C. McPherson, doubled as an interpreter/translator in addition to his normal duties and his additional duties as driver and bodyguard. Born in Jamaica to Scots-Lebanese parents, "Top" McPherson had served a number of tours in the Middle East and was an accomplished Arabist.[8]

Just getting the approvals to travel through Turkey, and then to cross the Turkish border into Iraq, was no simple matter—requiring at one point the personal intervention of General Jones, the SACEur, with the Turkish high command. Finally, on 23 March the small task force made it out of Turkey and found itself very much alone on the Iraqi side of the deserted border crossing, until two heavily armed U.S. Army Special Forces noncommissioned officers appeared, seemingly out of nowhere, to serve as escorts and advisers. They made no secret of their initial lack of enthusiasm for the newcomers who were taking them away from their primary duties of training the Kurds and helping them to kill Iraqis. But, like others in JSOTF-N, they soon discovered that General Osman's group was low-maintenance and that its work could complement that of the Special Forces.[9]

Within two hours of crossing the border, Osman's work started in earnest. At a town called Dahok near the Green Line, he stopped to meet Gen. Babekir al-Zibari, the senior KDP military leader in the region, whom General Osman came to appreciate as "a great warrior and a great . . . patriot."[10] Babekir's troops, and those of other Kurdish organizations, were known generically as the "Peshmerga"—literally, "those who face death." The average Peshmerga fighter looked like a cross between a mountain man and a Bedouin horseman, but there was little doubt about his motivation or his fighting ability. Peshmerga groups ranged from loosely organized militia to semiprofessional paramilitaries, with about 45,000 loyal to the KDP and some 20,000 answering to the PUK.

Over the course of a meeting that lasted many hours and included an elaborate lunch, General Babekir talked about his appreciation for what the United States was doing in the region—and especially for the work of the Special Forces, with whom he had a strong ongoing relationship. He said he was eager to do more,

which was his way of saying he wanted to cross the Green Line and fight the
Iraqis. In what was to become a familiar refrain, General Osman counseled
patience, explaining the instability that Kurdish action could unleash, given
Turkish sensibilities. General Babekir took this on board and asked if General
Osman could do anything about the Iraqi artillery on the other side of the Green
Line that could range Dahok. Osman made no specific promises but said he
would see what he could do. By chance, a few hours later a heavy coalition air
raid was made on the Iraqi lines, and General Osman's penny stock with the
Kurds increased in value a hundredfold. The result was, in the words of the mission's communications officer, Lt. Col. James E. Bacchus, USMCR, "efferves-
cence" among the Kurds, who felt the Americans had abandoned them in the
past. Perhaps this time it would be different.[11]

General Osman and his party went on to the town of Salaheddin, where they
stayed in a guesthouse belonging to the KDP, the somewhat more westernized,
and larger of the two Kurdish political parties. The next day, 24 March, General
Osman held a press conference—there being a large contingent of media in
Salaheddin—during which he explained the Military Coordination and Liaison
Command's (MCLC) mission in general terms, outlining such functions as "the
deconfliction of military activities," synchronizing humanitarian assistance, and
"the maintenance of stability."[12] Reports of the conference described the MCLC
as a "special military command to protect northern Iraq and satisfy Turkish
security concerns along the Turkey-Iraq border," and especially to "dissuade
Turkey from sending troops to northern Iraq."[13] The presence of a two-star general had clearly caught the attention of the players on the field and demonstrated
that the United States wanted to make sure the game was played by its rules. It
also contributed to the "information operations" against the Iraqis, who had to
be asking themselves what a senior American officer was doing in Kurdistan—
was he paving the way for a larger force? General Osman did nothing to dis-
courage this speculation, especially when he reached out to the Iraqi generals on
the Green Line, passing a very direct written message from General Franks:
"Decide now. I, General Franks, will help you destroy Saddam's regime, or I
will destroy you."[14]

The next few days saw a round of seemingly endless meetings with a bewildering array of local groups, from the routine, such as coordination with JSTOF-N,
to the conventional, such as meetings with the KDP and the PUK, to the exotic,
such as the Iraqi Turkomen Front, representing the Turkish minority in the
region, and the Supreme Council of Iraqi Revolutionaries, an anti-Saddam group
supported by Iran. Most of the time General Osman drove long distances to meet
the local politicians and functionaries, choosing to meet them on their own turf
rather than summoning them to his headquarters; he did not want to seem like

an imperial envoy. This entailed some risk of attack on the road from Iraqi oper-
atives (who were said to have targeted the general for assassination) and considerable risk to gall bladders and stomach linings. Although sometimes accompanied
by a small Kurdish security detail, along with one or two U.S. Special Forces soldiers, force protection for the small group was mostly a matter of not making its
destination known until the last minute and then traveling at breakneck speed on
bad roads. (In the end, the general told his drivers to slow down; he said he would
rather die from a sucking chest wound than from the seemingly inevitable car
crash.) Once they arrived at a home or office, there were elaborate rituals of cour-
tesy to follow, which typically meant drinking a lot of tea and eating large quantities of unusual food. Some of the food was easily identifiable, like roast lamb
and rice, two local staples. But there were also unusual foods, like one that a
member of the mission could only describe in his notes as a "strange veggie." This
routine, and General Osman's personal style, which was characterized by
patience, politeness, and persistence, enabled him to build relationships with virtually all of these groups. Although Osman did not supplant Colonel Cleveland,
he became something like the senior adviser to call in order to discuss a plan, or
the honest broker who could keep the peace between warring factions.

The value of these relationships emerged as the Iraqi regime collapsed at the
end of the first week in April, and the Iraqi soldiers in the north either surrendered or simply changed into civilian clothes and went home, like thousands of
their comrades throughout the country. One result of the collapse was a power
vacuum in Kirkuk and Mosul that some Kurds wanted to fill. There had been
substantial Kurdish minorities in both of these Iraqi cities, and many Kurds had
lost property when Saddam Hussein had "Arabized" the region. Understandably,
the Kurds wanted to protect and assert their interests in both cities, while the
Turks wanted to make sure the Kurds did not turn them into centers of Kurdish
power. Apart from its interest in removing vestiges of the former regime, especially in the "loyalist" city of Mosul, and stabilizing the region, the United States
was as dedicated to protecting the oil fields around Kirkuk as it was to protecting
the southern oil fields around Basrah. With its blue-collar outlook, Kirkuk
reminded General Osman of a frontier oil town, while Mosul seemed to be more
developed and sophisticated, even attractive in parts.

The Kurds became increasingly anxious as rioting and looting spread through
Mosul, where there were few coalition troops in evidence. In Kirkuk, the KDP
and its Peshmerga took the initiative to fill the vacuum. Its leader, Jalal Talibani,
literally moved into city hall. His PUK rival, Massoud Barzani, immediately
complained to General Osman that Talibani had broken the rules and expanded
his sphere of influence at Barzani's expense. Barzani claimed to be losing ground
because he had listened to General Osman's pleas for restraint. Osman's response

was to drive to Kirkuk on 12 April—through a kind of no-man's land—and find Talibani, whose reaction on seeing the general was to try to embrace him in order to celebrate the day the Kurds had returned to Kirkuk. Within seconds Talibani saw that the general did not share his mood. The two stepped into the former mayor's office, where General Osman told Talibani in no uncertain terms why he and his forces had to leave Kirkuk. If they stayed, the result could be Turkish intervention, and a war within a war. This was no idle threat; there were Turkish liaison officers and a few Turkish Special Forces soldiers on the ground pursuing their own, crosscutting interests. Talibani, who spoke good English and wore western-style clothes, reluctantly came around to the general's point of view and agreed to withdraw himself and his troops from Kirkuk. Even General Osman's staff was impressed with this result, remarking, "Gee, Sir, you threw Talibani out of town."[15]

The townspeople of Kirkuk had seemed to be favorably disposed to the coalition and eager to return to a peacetime routine. At first they had not known what to make of the unusual group of Marines driving into town in black SUVs. But when they had realized they were looking at Americans, they had started to applaud. Mosul, by contrast, felt hostile—not unlike Tikrit. The locals appeared glum, and there were Iraqi flags flying everywhere, even from mosques. It did not help that Peshmerga elements were active in the city, which inflamed tensions between Iraqis and Kurds. While the city was quieter on 13 April than it had been the day before, General Osman agreed with the JSOTF officers that pockets of unrest were still apparent and that the United States needed to increase its military footprint as quickly as possible.[16]

As if on cue, 26th MEU(SOC) appeared over the horizon. It was the only readily available, uncommitted force in the area and was still in the Mediterranean, under the cognizance of 6th Fleet, which meant it was ultimately under the command of General Jones. It had been natural for him, a Marine with an interest in northern Iraq, to discuss and plan its employment with CentCom. General Jones had always been a keen proponent of putting a MAGTF into northern Iraq, and a MEU fit the bill.[17] Commanded by Col. Andrew P. Frick, the 26th was another MEU that had had an incredible existence, so different from most peacetime Marine Expeditionary Units (MEU) that simply went from one landing exercise to another until their time was up. The 26th MEU had flown from expeditionary shipping into Afghanistan the year before in what was viewed at the time as validation of the Marine doctrine and was now about to launch a new long-distance operation over semihostile territory.[18]

Part of the MEU soon flew by KC-130 Hercules aircraft from Naval Air Station, Souda Bay, on the island of Crete, to northern Iraq, a distance of some 975 nautical miles, while its air combat element, HMM-264, self-deployed from the

USS *Iwo Jima* in the Eastern Mediterranean to fly nearly 500 nautical miles into Iraq, possibly a new record. (The MEU's historian, Capt. Arnaldo L. Colon, noted that the "HMM-264 self deployment into Iraq was the farthest a MEU[SOC] ACE had ever flown. Prior to that flight, HMM-365 had flown the farthest with 380 nautical miles into Afghanistan in support of Operation Enduring Freedom."[19]) The route flown on 12 and 13 April skirted the Turkish/Syrian border and led to a U.S.–run expeditionary airfield at Irbil, in northern Iraq, where the MEU came under the tactical control of JSOTF-N. Although they welcomed the arrival of the MEU, General Osman and the MCLC had no command relationship with the MEU.[20]

The MEU had been briefed for a mission to establish security checkpoints to prevent "high-value targets"—mostly senior Ba'athists—from trying to escape to Syria. One officer, 1st Lt. Sunny-James M. Risler, later recalled he had not known what to expect on arrival in Iraq; he was under the impression that he and his men needed to be ready to fight their way off the aircraft. But once they landed in Irbil, the Marines found that JSOTF-N had the situation very well in hand; not only was the airfield secure, but there was a base camp complete with a good chow hall![21]

The only problem was that they were not going to stay long in Irbil. Soon after landing, Colonel Cleveland asked the Marines if they could take on a new mission: provide a stabilizing presence in Mosul. Both the battalion commander at the airhead, Lt. Col. David K. Hough, and Colonel Frick were ready to adapt and respond, which pleased Colonel Cleveland, who is said to have been frustrated at times by other services' lack of responsiveness. So, within a short period of time, the leading elements of 1st Battalion, 8th Marines went on to Mosul without even having had a chance to find a good map of the place, let alone to plan. Over the next few days, the MEU flowed the rest of its assets to Mosul and established a presence around the local airport.

On the morning of 15 April the MEU was involved in an incident that could have occurred almost anywhere in Iraq during this period. Tasked to conduct security operations for a regional coordination center in downtown Mosul, Bravo Company drove to the governate building—the former Ba'ath Party headquarters—along with civil affairs and Special Forces personnel. An angry crowd near the building became progressively angrier after a loudspeaker mounted on an ambulance began to broadcast a message in Arabic and a supposed "peacemaker" spoke to the crowd. (It turned out that the crowd was angry because they believed that certain Iraqis who had benefited from Saddam's rule were to remain in power under the American occupation. Since none of the Americans at the governate that day spoke Arabic, they did not know what the problem was until much later.) Some members of the crowd tried to punch at the Marines and to spit on them. Others tried to get close and, in the words of Sgt. Bryan L. Gilstrap, reach "into their pockets."[22]

The tension was palpable for the Marines, who were still getting adjusted to being in Iraq, to say nothing of a mission that was neither full-blown combat nor peacekeeping. True to their training, Marines checked the compound, manned the perimeter, and, according to Captain Colon, reacted to the first rounds that were fired at them by firing over the heads of the crowd. Sergeant Gilstrap, who was the scout-sniper team leader, remembered seeing an Iraqi raise an AK-47 rifle to a firing position, which made him a legitimate target under the rules of engagement. Gilstrap fired at, and hit, his target. This was followed by an intense firefight as the Marines and the crowd fired at each other. Sergeant Gilstrap said it was like the scene in the movie *Rules of Engagement* that showed Marines defending a U.S. embassy in the Middle East against a mix of demonstrators and shooters (the movie also raised questions about how much force the defenders were authorized, or entitled, to use). At some point a number of armed men tried to breach the perimeter and were killed or wounded by the Marines. According to the command chronology, the "crowd dispersed only after fixed wing aircraft, coordinated through JSOTF-N, made low-flying passes over the area." There were no Marine casualties.[23]

Lieutenant Colonel Hough, the battalion commander, decided to keep his Marines at the site overnight, and the company spent the night improving its positions. The next day, the hostile sniping started back up. The Marines used a CH-46E helicopter as a countersniper platform—with some success. But later in the day, Iraqi fighters began preparing to fire rocket-propelled grenades and crew-served weapons against the Marines from urban high ground. After consulting with his Special Forces counterpart, Colonel Frick decided to withdraw Bravo Company. Given the force ratios and the general hostility in Mosul, it made sense to leave the exposed position at the governate building. After dark, Alpha Company and Special Forces soldiers ran a convoy of trucks into the site to return Bravo Company to friendly lines. Although the evolution occurred without further incident, officers in the MEU S-3 commented that they would have felt more comfortable running light armored vehicles or amphibious assault vehicles, which they had not brought with them into Iraq, into the heart of town.[24]

For the remainder of its time in Mosul, which lasted until it was relieved by the 101st Airborne Division in late April, the MEU conducted a variety of security missions in and around the city—none quite so dramatic as the first, but still important and useful. The MEU also put its aviation assets to use for the mutual benefit of the Marines and the Special Forces. This was especially true of the Marine KC-130 at the MEU's disposal, which again proved their flexibility and their worth. On 23 April elements of the 101st began relieving the Marines at the airfield, and the MEU began the process of disengaging and redeploying. By 2 May its redeployment to Souda Bay was complete. Colonel Frick's view, in retrospect, was that the MEU (like the MCLC) had successfully bought time for the coalition—a stopgap force that had helped to make up for the general shortage of troops to take on occupation duties.[25]

As the 101st took over from the JSOTF, the MCLC contributed its insights on the situation. General Osman spent a good part of 22 April with the incoming commander, Maj. Gen. David H. Petraeus, explaining his work and passing on his views on recent developments in northern Iraq. In particular, Osman described Mosul as "different than any other city in Iraq" with its "feeling of having been defeated vs. liberated." He believed a strong U.S. presence was needed to enable key leadership to "feel comfortable enough to come forward." He concluded that as soon as the new leadership was able to establish itself, "we will want to remove the U.S. presence quickly."[26] General Osman conducted similar briefs with, among others, the commander of the 4th Infantry Division, Maj. Gen. Raymond Odierno, and representatives of ORHA, the Office for Reconstruction and Humanitarian Assistance. Some members of General Osman's staff thought ORHA was better prepared for a reprise of Operation Provide Comfort than for the situation that northern Iraq actually faced. (Since its chief, retired Maj. Gen. Jay Garner, was yet another veteran of that operation, this was understandable.) Once he had conducted out-briefs with all of these officers, General Osman determined his mission was at an end and had arrangements made for his group to fly home.

What was the significance of General Osman's mission? What did the MCLC contribute with some measure of success to a situation that was already being handled by the Special Forces? Arguably, the presence of a general officer freed the Special Forces from having to focus so heavily on day-to-day political relationships, thereby enabling them to focus more on the military side of things. At the same time, the MCLC accomplished its own mission. General Osman did not win a war. The MCLC did not receive or return fire (though it came close on some days). But it did help to prevent a small war within a war, and it did contribute to the success of Operation Iraqi Freedom as surely as if it had maneuvered a MAGTF over northern Iraq.[27]

10

A Marriage of Convenience

Cooperation between the MEF and the British Division

Like the war in the north, the war in southeast Iraq had some of the character of a private war. It was conducted by some sixteen thousand colorful fighters who had been fighting small wars for centuries, did things their own way, got along famously with Marines—and even spoke English.

The habitual relationships were there. British and American forces had been cooperating in the Persian Gulf since Desert Shield/Desert Storm. Their air forces jointly enforced the no-fly zones. After September 2001 there had been British liaison officers at CentCom and joint operations in Afghanistan. Some senior American and British decision makers already knew one another, which made planning that much easier, and there were a number of established joint procedures. The shared knowledge of the area, and of each other's procedures and personalities, made it easier for the British to succeed even though it was very late in the day when they started appearing in Kuwait in significant numbers to join I MEF.

Some of the unknowns about British participation were resolved only during the combat phase. The threshold issue was whether the British would fight alongside the Americans at all. Although the British prime minister, Tony Blair, proved to be a staunch ally before, during, and after the war, he faced a good deal of political opposition to his Iraq policy at home. This introduced an element of doubt, almost up to the last minute before D-Day, as to whether the British government would be able to order its troops into battle.

Even assuming that London would give the word to fight, there were still other significant unknowns. One was where the bulk of the British forces would attack from. Until December 2002 there were the plans to introduce most of the British from the north, that is, from Turkey, alongside the U.S. Army's 4th Infantry Division. According to testimony given to the British House of Commons: "In the very early planning, the Americans had decided to attack only from the south. . . . Militarily it made more sense to . . . attack on two axes, because there was going to be congestion. That was suggested to the Americans, who seized it with both hands, and that is why there was thought . . . of putting an axis through Turkey."[1] The truth is a little more nuanced. General McKiernan, for one, commented in December 2002 that he had "always wanted a supporting attack out of the north that makes Saddam Hussein . . . look in two directions at large conventional forces."[2]

If a British division had attacked from the north, the British contribution to I MEF would probably have been nothing more than the one Royal Marine unit earmarked for an amphibious operation against the peninsula in the southeastern corner of Iraq.[3] Always considered a piece of key terrain, Al Faw was an obvious choice for an amphibious assault of some sort. It faced Kuwait across a bay, making it a perfect launching pad for short-range missiles against Kuwait City or coalition forces packed into the desert camps north of the Kuwaiti capital. It also straddled two important waterways, the channel to Iraq's only deepwater port, Umm Qasr, and the Shatt al Arab, which ran between the Persian Gulf and the "capital" of southern Iraq, Basrah.

By late December 2002, in the face of continued Turkish intransigence, the British had begun to explore "the southern option."[4] That was the month when there were preliminary talks between General Conway and the senior British Army liaison officer at CFLCC, Brig. Gen. Albert E. Whitley, which helped to lay the groundwork for British cooperation with the MEF. Around the same time, British military officers were attending various CentCom conferences and exercises like Internal Look, but they were there only as observers, not as participants.[5]

By early January 2003, MEF and British planners were working hard to make up for lost time. Switching from the northern to the southern option meant the British would have to change their force mix. Instead of a predominantly armor/mech package, suitable for traveling and fighting over long distances, it now made sense to put together a lighter package, especially since there might be more fighting in the built-up areas of Umm Qasr and Basrah. So the British division, whose formal title was 1 (United Kingdom) Armoured Division, evolved into a hybrid of forces, the more or less independent units from various commands and regions being roughly comparable to U.S. Marine regimental combat teams: 16 Air Assault Brigade, 3 Commando Brigade, and 7 Armoured Brigade (the only one that was an organic part of the division). The Commando Brigade was the parent unit of the battalion-sized Royal Marine commando that had been aimed at Al Faw; it was now reinforced by another Royal Marine commando, but since it was still short of its full complement, the resulting gap was ultimately filled by the 15th MEU(SOC).

The headquarters elements arrived in theater first, and, aware that CentCom was planning to be ready to fight sometime in March, did a remarkable job of orchestrating the surge of forces into Kuwait, running them through the CFLCC reception/staging/integration process and establishing not only internal but also external command and control mechanisms. The man who made this happen was Major General Brims, the division's commanding general, who was tall, thin, articulate, approachable, and full of energy. A career officer who had been commissioned into the Light Infantry and subsequently served in Germany, Northern Ireland, and the Balkans, he was the kind of soldier Americans did not meet every day. There was a trace of old-school eccentricity in his official biography, which described him as "single, a cricket fanatic, Newcastle United supporter, and outdoor enthusiast whose specialty area is bonfires."[6] It was a trait that made him all the more attractive to Marines, whose values sometimes seem to be from another era. In this he was not unlike General Mattis, with whom he was to forge a good working relationship.[7]

Quick to visualize the desired outcome, General Brims put his stamp on the division, issuing his "GOC [General Officer Commanding] Directive 1" on 3 February 2003:

> We are TACOM CG 1 MEF [*sic*]. We create tactical effects to enable decisive delivery of his plans. We are integrating with HQ 1 MEF and its subordinate formations. Whilst we have been planning within 1 MEF for barely a month, much of 1 MEF has been planning, even conducting scenario related training, for many months. . . . We have identified 5 critical elements of 1 (UK) Armd Div's AO upon which we need to have an effect:
>
> a. Iraq's Armed Forces
> b. Irregular forces working against the Coalition
> c. Oilfield infrastructure
> d. UMM QASR
> e. BASRAH . . .
>
> We must also establish all our personal and electronic connectivities and processes with HQ 1 MEF. Our force is designed to be supported by 1 MEF deep assets. We must establish the techniques for delivering this in a timely, effective, and safe manner . . .

We are manoeuvrists. We must grasp opportunities to deliver our missions with minimum kinetic force. Iraq must still exist after the conflict as a
sovereign state, stable and able to defend itself. . . . We shall probably be the
first Coalition forces to implement Phase IV. We can set the pace.[8]

Despite their late arrival, the British received a warm welcome from MEF. To
review the bidding: the MEF could now assign some of its missions to the British
and would not be stretched as thinly as it would otherwise have been. It could
even ratchet the tempo of operations up still higher. With respect to the "Opening Gambit," the MEF decided not to change the carefully rehearsed plans to
seize the oil fields in the first few days of the war. The planners considered the late
date, and the extensive rehearsals that 1stMarDiv had already conducted, and
decided it made more sense to leave well enough alone. The Marine division
would still seize the objectives, but the British units, following close behind,
would take over the security mission soon after the initial assault. Similarly, 15th
MEU, operating under British control, would seize Umm Qasr but then turn the
city over to the British and revert to USMC control.[9]

The MEF was so pleased with the presence, and the potential, of the British
that by early March it had decided to expand its area of operations by a further
250 kilometers to the north. According to the British division's war diary, written
in somewhat archaic English, "it was envisaged that after the execution of the initial Base Plan, which sees the Division seizing the Al Faw peninsula, subsequent
operations would involve a push north by a brigade to the vicinity of Al Kut and
Al Amarah. This would be conducted in parallel with 1 MARDIV and TF
Tarawa to secure and screen the Eastern Flank. The origins of this increased role
apparently came from a mutually registered desire at all levels to maximize the
full potential of the Division's combat power."[10]

General Conway remembered later that one of the deciding factors in the distribution, and timing, of tasks was the amount of equipment available to the
British as G-Day approached. Quite simply, the U.S. Marines had more at their
disposal, while the British would not be fully equipped until after the war had
begun.[11] It was, as the British parliamentary report was to conclude after the
war, a "close run thing."[12]

By D-Day the division itself was combat ready—that is, ready for what in
American terms was a running start—even though some of its units were not
ready. It could carry out the missions that were to occur on the first days of the
war, and would have to continue to prepare for the missions that were to occur
after the initial battles. General Brims explained: "Sometimes you have to be positive . . . you are dealt a hand of cards . . . you would like to have 52 cards in the
deck. . . . But, in this case, we had actually declared readiness with 46 cards."[13]

His subordinate, Brig. Graham J. Binns, the commander of 7 Armoured Brigade, was not quite so sanguine, saying he "felt that we were carrying a lot of risk. The mood was one that we were not ready, . . . that the soldiers . . . were not properly equipped."[14] But throughout the process there was a great deal of creativity and adaptation that made the British ready to cross into Iraq on 20 March.

The synergy that developed between the British division and the MEF between January and March 2003 certainly eased the joint preparations for combat. Over the years, the U.S. Marines had nourished a relationship with the Royal Marines, while the British Army had tended to forge its relations with other armies on the continent, and the Royal Air Force had cooperated with the U.S. Air Force in the Persian Gulf—all good preparation for fighting as part of a coalition. It was something new for U.S. Marines and the British Army to work closely together, but it did not take either side long to discover the common ground. The two forces had similar cultures: traditionally oriented to "small wars," independent operations, and mission orders. The leaders' personalities meshed—not only between those of the same rank, as in the good relationship between Generals Mattis and Brims, but also between superior and subordinate. General Conway's command style sat very well with General Brims, who said that throughout his association with the MEF, he consistently felt empowered and never constrained.[15]

The process was strengthened by the exchange of liaison officers who actively interpreted their charters. The head of the U.S. liaison team to the British headquarters was Col. Thomas C. Latsko, USMCR, who embedded most of his Marines in the division's G-3, where they became active participants in planning and operations. The Marines found that the British division was far more map-centric than any American command. Battle updates took place around the "bird table"—a large table covered with maps and overlays for what looked to American eyes like World War II briefings. No one used PowerPoint software. The demeanor of the British officers around the table seemed informal, even casual; for example, there was little apparent consciousness of rank, and first names were used freely. But there could be little doubt about their professionalism. Units—and individuals—typically reported only what the next higher echelon needed to know. Briefers were held to time limits. Most British officers had a strong ability to visualize the situation, enter into creative (and occasionally pointed) debate about possible courses of action, and issue clear mission orders, which were far less detailed than American operations orders but, like most coalition orders in this war, focused first on the desired effect, as opposed to simply directing a particular action.[16] Marines working with subordinate British commands said that they found British briefs to be straightforward, person to person, and not cluttered with detail—overall, a "nice change of pace."[17]

Colonel Latsko and his executive officer, Lt. Col. Edward J. Quinonez, USMCR, made it their business to bring the British command-and-control system closer to the American and, holding school at the British command center, introduced their new comrades in arms to various computerized American systems. By the end of the fighting in Iraq, the two systems were literally operating side by side, and British and American staff officers could work both at the same time to mutual benefit—although the gap between them, at least in terms of hardware, remained significant and was the subject of a British lessons-learned article.[18] One significant technological issue was SIPRnet connectivity. This secret Internet channel was arguably the primary means of communication for U.S. forces in this war. Without access to SIPR, the British often felt at a loss—and liaison officers had to develop some awkward work-arounds.[19]

Alongside Colonel Latsko's officers in the G-3 was a U.S. Marine air support element (ASE), which was able to provide the rapid response and coordination of close air support that is the function of the Marine Direct Air Support Control Center. The ASE operated mostly out of the British combat operations and information center—built around the "bird table"—but also sent its Marines down to the two British brigades that wanted their services. There they joined forces with Reserve Marines from the 1st and 3d Air-Naval Gunfire Liaison Companies (ANGLICOs), small numbers of whom had been deployed to the British division and immediately integrated into its training cycle. Recognizing their usefulness in joint and combined operations, General Jones had wisely brought the ANGLICOs back on line during his tenure as commandant. This was proof of concept.[20] The 7 Armoured Brigade had made a point of getting its ANGLICO Marines to participate in training on British simulators in Germany, where they also made a point of exploring local drinking establishments together. As British officer Lt. Col. Nicholas D. Ashmore commented, if shedding blood is the best way to build comradeship, drinking together is the second best.[21] The officers of 7 Armoured viewed Marine air as the great "get out of jail" card, but thought that ANGLICO alone would be enough and passed up an opportunity to have its own ASE, a decision it came to regret once its sister brigades discovered what a useful and flexible tool Marine air control was.[22]

For the British the war began in much the same way as it had for MEF headquarters. On 20 March one of the incoming Iraqi theater ballistic missiles flew directly over the division headquarters, certainly capturing the attention of the staff. With British understatement—and humor—General Brims commented at the evening update brief that the "Iraqis were showing that they too had a vote" in how the war would run.[23] By the afternoon of 21 March, 3 Commando Brigade, the Royal Marine formation, had successfully deployed into the Al Faw peninsula, despite "blackened skies from burning oil infrastructure" and a deadly crash of a USMC helicopter carrying Royal Marines.[24]

In the meantime, 15th MEU(SOC) took the port of Umm Qasr, encountering some stiff resistance, particularly from Saddam Fedayeen, but not enough to
prevent it from making "excellent progress."[25] The next day, 3 Commando
Brigade reported Umm Qasr "clear though 15 MEU continued to have sporadic
contacts," while 7 Armoured Brigade and 16 Air Assault Brigade each carried out
a relief in place with the 7th and 5th RCTs, respectively, in the Rumaylah oil
fields. There was some friction: a blue-on-blue (friendly fire) incident with no
casualties between 15th MEU and 7 Armoured Brigade on 21 March, and some
confusion "due to the large volume of coalition traffic" when the British division
relieved the American division in the oil fields—not surprising considering the
volume of friendly forces passing through the area.[26] But overall, the first days of
the war went very well, and the British were pleased with the situation.

The 15th MEU(SOC), which was to chop back to U.S. control on 25 March
after being relieved in Umm Qasr on 24 March, had meshed almost seamlessly
with the British brigade. The MEU commander, Col. Thomas D. Waldhauser,
found it to be a great experience "by design and by default." He commented that
even though the MEU's ground combat element had more organic combat
power, there was a lot of congruence in the way both sides were organized. The
Royal Marines were true to their doctrine, giving the U.S. Marines mission
orders and then giving them the leeway to execute those orders, which were four-
fold: to annihilate the enemy who fought; to accommodate the enemy who capit-
ulated; not to destroy the infrastructure of the city; and not to get bogged down
within city limits. Given the opportunity to make a contribution under unusual
circumstances—this was not your normal cruise—the Marines of the MEU
(which, Waldhauser noted, had never carried out an exercise but only real-world
operations) accomplished the mission with gusto.[27]

Overall, the British were on plan and the Iraqis were not; in particular, the
British had been able to seize petroleum and shipping infrastructure before the
Iraqis could do much harm to it. While it would prove impossible to get the oil
flowing again quickly, it was soon possible to get ocean-going ships into Umm
Qasr, especially to unload large quantities of supplies for the expected humanitarian crisis. *Sir Galahad*, the first ship with a humanitarian load, began to unload
on 28 March. Considering the overall situation, the Ministry of Defence postwar
study concluded that

> Four days into the campaign the Iraqi 51st Division had been removed
> from its defence of the oilfields. 3 Commando Brigade held critical oil
> instructure at Al Faw and the port of Umm Qasr. 16 Air Assault Brigade
> held the vital oilfield at Rumaylah and threatened Iraq's 6th Armoured
> Division to the north of Basrah to such an extent that it could not interfere

with coalition operations. 7 Armoured Brigade held the bridges over the Shatt-al-Basrah waterway to the west of Basrah [a canal that ran from Basrah to Umm Qasr to the sea, paralleling the much larger Shatt-al-Arab to the east]. . . . This was the most crucial ground to hold in order to achieve the overall plan of protecting the right flank of the US advance to isolate Baghdad.[28]

Like their American allies to the west, the British were finding that the regular Iraqi army was not as much of a threat as had been feared but that there might be more of an irregular threat than had been predicted. On the evening of 23 March, General Brims spoke with 7 Armoured Brigade about "the changing nature of our understanding of the conflict. . . . There was not to be a solely conventional battle, rather resistance especially focused on urban areas, and troops either bypassed or deliberately inserted behind the forward line of our own troops."[29]

The issue confronting the British was what to do next. Ultimately they would have to occupy Basrah, Iraq's second city—that was not up for discussion. As General Brims commented, "to remove a regime you cannot leave [it] . . . in control of an urban area."[30] So it became a matter of timing and method. As for timing, CFLCC did not want the British to get ahead of the rest of the force; General McKiernan had directed them not to occupy Basrah proper until he gave the word. He told General Brims that he wanted the fight for Basrah to wait until the coalition had isolated Baghdad, because he did not want to risk a dramatic urban fight in the south that could drive Iraqis into the arms of the regime and make the overall mission that much more difficult.[31] General Conway's guidance was similar but keyed to the MEF's scheme of maneuver; he directed Brims simply to make sure that whatever he chose to do in Basrah, he should remember the paramount goal of protecting the MEF's flank.[32]

What Generals McKiernan and Conway wanted was the reverse of what the Ba'athist strongman in Basrah wanted. He was Saddam Hussein's cousin, Ali Hassan Al-Majid, commonly known as "Chemical Ali" for his murderous suppression of the Kurds in 1988 with chemical weapons. He had been equally brutal in his dealings with the Shia in the south in the 1990s after the Gulf War, and was one of the prime movers in the draining of the swampland north of Basrah, the ancestral home of the "marsh Arabs" and their distinctive culture, in order to eliminate it as a haven for potential or actual rebels. The result was an ecological and economic disaster. Since Basrah's approximately 1.25 million citizens were predominantly Shia, he was feared far more than respected. At the beginning of the war, he presided over a mix of unreliable regular army units and more reliable but not particularly skilled irregulars like the Saddam Fedayeen. To the extent that he had a strategy, it appears to have been one of trying to draw the British into a drawn-out fight within the city limits of Basrah, with the attendant collateral damage to cultural and religious sites, and of course civilian casualties—the kind of thing that hurts the coalition when it appears on the front page of an Arab daily, not to mention the *Washington Post* or *Le Monde*. British intelligence reports suggested just how basic the Iraqi plan for Basrah was: "Whenever the British intercepted enemy communications, Saddam's henchmen were merely urging loyalists to fight, fight, fight—without specifying how."[33]

This was exactly what the British were determined not to do, whatever the timing of the attack. British officers commented repeatedly that they were always determined to avoid the kind of bitter, costly, house-to-house, street-to-street fighting that had recently occurred in Chechnya, where the Russian army had become bogged down in its fight with Chechen rebels, or on the Eastern Front in World War II. "We were determined," Brims commented after the war, "not to have any sort of Grozny or Stalingrad scenes."[34]

Over the period between 25 March and 6 April, through a process of thinking and experimentation—almost like a Warfighting Lab evolution—the British came up with the alternative approach that fit the situation. The preliminary "lab experiment" took place in the much smaller city of Az Zubayr, population about one hundred thousand, to the southwest of Basrah in 7 Armoured Brigade's zone of action. The soldiers of 7 Armoured—who wore the "Desert Rats" patch their grandfathers had worn at the battle of El Alamein in 1942—found themselves taking heavy machine gun and rocket fire from irregulars every time they came near the city. The 7 Armoured had the combat power to enter and reduce the city, but exercised restraint, starting out small—with a raid into the city by 1 Black Watch battalion on 25 March. On 26 March, 7 Armoured proceeded to isolate the city, which was not the same as besieging it but rather a matter of controlling ingress and egress or, just as important, demonstrating its ability to do so.[35]

General Brims tells the Basrah story in a very English way—as if he and his subordinate, Brigadier Binns, had "casually" solved the problem in the same way a Londoner might "casually" solve the wickedly convoluted *Times of London* crossword puzzle, when in fact it was their lifelong devotion to the art of war that was manifesting itself:

> I talked to the Brigade Commander . . . about four or five days into the thing . . . and he said, "I'm going to work out how we're going to take Az Zubayr," and I said, "Good, I'll go away and consider Basrah." And he said, "I've got the most powerful armoured brigade the British Army's ever put in the field, and I'll back-brief you on my bit, of Az Zubayr, tomorrow morning." I arranged to see him first thing . . . and he asked me to come aside of him for

a short time, and he said to me, "I've worked out, we can't go into Az Zubayr . . . because that's what the regime want; we'll inflict undue casualties, we'll take undue casualties, we will hurt the civilians . . . that's what he's after. We've got to do it in a more cunning way." I said to him, "Well, that's funny, because I've worked out precisely the same thing for Basrah."[36]

On 26 March, General Brims convened a commanders' conference at Brigadier Binns's headquarters, where they discussed the issue among themselves. Brims took the opportunity to announce the decision to make Basrah a divisional responsibility rather than delegating it to one of the brigades, as British commanders were more likely to do. The U.K. division would hope to foment popular unrest by conducting "deep operations" through the destruction of key targets while at the same time providing an opportunity for the people to receive humanitarian aid.[37]

What came next, in both Az Zubayr and Basrah, was a series of carefully orchestrated events, aimed as much at the enemy's mind as at his body. One of the prerequisites was the collection of the kind of citizen-by-citizen, neighborhood-by-neighborhood intelligence that can seem more like police work than part of a military operation. This may have been something that the British government had been pursuing for years in southern Iraq. It was also a skill that the British Army had learned in Northern Ireland and the Balkans. By working with recruited agents, some of whom were reporting by cell phone, and by simply networking, the British were able to create a detailed picture of the life of the city, from the bottom up.[38] Next came a round of carefully calculated raids, sometimes synchronized with raids by JDAMs or other precision munitions, which could lead to sniping or to "lodgements," something like the establishment of patrol bases that ranged in size up to the battalion level. For example, a British unit might stage a nighttime raid and then, when withdrawing, leave a sniper team behind to observe the neighborhood for a few days, or to snipe at Ba'ath and fedayeen leaders.[39] At the same time, information operations worked on the minds of the citizenry—by means of leaflets, broadcasts, or even targeted mobile telephone calls by General Brims himself. Then there might be a carefully planned air or artillery raid against a pinpoint target, whose effects the division could observe on the live feed from the "Phoenix," the British unmanned aerial vehicle. "The way we did it," General Brims reported to the House of Commons, "was to build up an intelligence picture, focused raids, ground raids, air raids, mind raids . . . [the people] wanted to be freed but they could not do it themselves, they needed our support, and therefore actually we had them helping us, and they were feeding us . . . accurate intelligence, worthy targets . . . and we were able to conduct these raids, and they had a very significant effect."[40]

General Brims made it clear he wanted some operations to occur simultaneously even though the focus of main effort would shift. Initially it would be on
7 Armoured Brigade and Az Zubayr. After Az Zubayr was determined to have
fallen on 4 April—there was of course no formal surrender ceremony—the
lighter 3 Commando Brigade took over in Az Zubayr and 7 Armoured moved on
to augment the effort against Basrah, which remained a division-level operation.
Resistance was becoming progressively lighter, while the population seemed to
become more welcoming of the British.[41] As time went on and the British
became more successful, they received more information from the citizens of Basrah. On 5 April they received a tip about the whereabouts of Chemical Ali, and
the coalition launched a JDAM, or smart bomb, attack on the building where he
was believed to be hiding. Although unsuccessful, it was believed to have been
successful at the time and, at the least, a potent demonstration of coalition power
for all on the Iraqi side to see.[42]

By now the U.S. Army and the Marines were launching probes into Baghdad,
and there was little chance that anything that happened in Basrah could disrupt
operations in the north. The most recent raids having been deemed "very successful," General Brims ordered his division to execute "Operation Sinbad," the
final push against Basrah, which was to come from a number of directions. It met
with "a minimum of resistance from individuals with small arms" who were
apparently either Ba'athist Party members or fedayeen.[43] One objective after
another—the sewage plant, the party headquarters, the governor's palace—fell
without heavy fighting, something of which Brims was justifiably proud. Each
success created the next opportunity, which Brims exploited; he commented later
that his intent was to seek the right opportunity to execute each phase of the plan.
By twilight on 6 April, most of Basrah was in coalition hands, if not secure.[44]

Murray and Scales recount a story about the next day that speaks volumes
about the British Army's work in Iraq. On 7 April the division committed
paratroopers to the "old town" quarter of Basrah to finish off any lingering
resistance. But the paratroopers found there was little for them to do and began
to withdraw: "As the paras withdraw, Shia crowds began throwing rocks at
British tanks and armored personnel carriers. One of the battle group commanders immediately sensed what was happening. He ordered his . . . crews, as
well as the infantry, to get out of their vehicles, take off their helmets, stow
most of their weapons, and walk out into the agitated crowd. Immediately the
rock throwing ended and members of the crowd again smiled and clapped
hands for the British troops."[45]

This remarkable story, which begins by reflecting Shia fears of abandonment
by the coalition, conveys something of the British sense for how to handle the
transition to Phase IV, postcombat operations. With his experience in Northern

Ireland and the Balkans, the average British soldier may be one of the world's foremost experts on the three-block war. He could fight a conventional battle, defend himself against a guerrilla or paramilitary threat, and conduct humanitarian operations. He excelled at most of these tasks in southeastern Iraq. As early as 1 April, in Az Zubayr, British soldiers started to shed their helmets and patrol in berets. In Az Zubayr, Basrah, and, later, in Maysan province to the north, the same kind of bottom-up intelligence gathering that served the British well in combat was very useful in the transition period. Nevertheless, there was only so much this small force could do among a population of millions.

Like their American counterparts, the British did not have a definitive plan for Phase IV other than to be ready to handle a humanitarian crisis (which did not develop anywhere in Iraq), and to hand off to the Organization for Reconstruction and Humanitarian Assistance (which had focused much of its planning toward the same end). The British government as a whole and the British military in particular were in step with the rest of the coalition in assuming that "post conflict . . . there might be humanitarian or environmental disasters of various sorts, refugee flows, shortage of food . . . and those kinds of issues. . . . ORHA was really designed, as far as we [British] could see, to prepare mainly for humanitarian issues."[46] Another similarity was their response to the looting that occurred in their zone. Like the Americans, the British expected there would be some residual Iraqi police or army structure with which they could cooperate, and they had considered the possibility that there might be some looting, but they were taken aback by its scope and breadth.[47]

As in most other areas in Iraq, once the fighting stopped, virtually all levels of Iraqi government in and around Basrah simply ceased to exist. The looters stepped into the resulting power vacuum and went to work with a vengeance: in southeast Iraq, "they ransacked schools, hospitals and took away things . . . beds, chairs, and so on, or they just wrecked things."[48] The House of Commons Defence Committee judged that "the impact of this looting on the task of post-conflict reconstruction has been enormous," in terms of testing the goodwill of the people, making it difficult for them to return to work or school, get health care, or even accomplish the mundane tasks that local government performs for its citizens.[49] They were not prepared to cope with it; even if they had had the will to do so, they clearly lacked the numbers and, except in a few dramatic cases, did not intervene. (The MEF situation report for 7 April contained the laconic comment about Basrah: "looting ongoing, looters are only engaged if looting arms depots."[50]) The committee concluded that the scale and shape of the force provided were best suited to achieving the coalition's desired effects in the combat phase, but not to carrying those effects through into the postconflict phase.[51]

In the spring of 2003, the situation in southeast Iraq did not seem as bad as the House of Commons and others would later say it had been. The forces on the ground were generally upbeat and believed they were making good progress. Examples from the division commander's diary include, on 9 April, the observation that "the mood in the city is still jubilant and . . . the buses continue to run"; on 12 April the report that 16 Air Assault Brigade was able to proceed north to Al Amarah in Maysan province for the relief in place with Task Force Tarawa without incident; on 13 April the fact that "joint patrolling with the local police force commenced . . . in Basrah"; and the conclusion on 21 April that "the local population are becoming increasingly committed to policing themselves and preserving their own resources." Shortly thereafter, on 22 April the United Nations declared the British zone permissive, a few days before President Bush made his declaration that major combat operations had ended. For the British this was the end of the combat phase; parts of the division, to include General Brims, made preparations to rotate home, with a sense of having accomplished their mission.

One of this British general's last official acts before leaving Iraq was to host a farewell reception for I MEF commanders and staff at his headquarters in Basrah International Airport on 10 May to celebrate not just success on the battlefield but also the bond between the MEF and his division. Feelings that went beyond the usual routine expressions of official goodwill were on display. Senior Marines took the trouble to fly in from other parts of Iraq on KC-130s and went into the reception area in the airport's VIP quarters, which were opulent beyond belief or good taste, with gilded trimmings, high ceilings, marble floors, and thick carpets (but no working plumbing). Apart from the ultramodern Marine pattern desert digital utility uniforms, and the unusual British desert camouflage uniforms, it could have been a scene from the movie *Patton,* as white-coated stewards served gin and tonics to tired but happy officers who felt they had something to celebrate. The division band, very British and old school, beat retreat as the sun went down as if trying to close a chapter in history.

11

Postlude to Combat

Marines in the Occupation of Iraq in 2003

Occupation was not a mission that General Conway relished. He wanted his MEF to fight the war and then to "recock," to get ready for the next war. This was the pattern that came naturally to him and to many other Marines; the idea was to assault the beaches, seize the objective, and then move on to prepare for the next assault, leaving the occupation duties to others. When he discussed the issue with a journalist before the war, General Conway enumerated some of the issues that an occupier would face in Iraq—including some no-win choices, such as whether to intervene when Iraqis turned on one another after Saddam's fall—and concluded, "If I had a vote, I'd say let's get [the MEF] out of here." But he was quick to add that the Marines would probably have no choice but to involve themselves in the postwar occupation of Iraq in some form.[1]

There followed the decision for the MEF's G-3 Future Ops and G-5 Plans officers to think about Phase IV and to draft an operation plan, even before the shooting war started. One of their starting points was liaison with CFLCC planners and their counterparts at 1(U.K.) Armoured Division. By design or default, CentCom had left much of the responsibility for Phase IV planning to CFLCC, a dramatic change from its approach to Phases I–III. MEF turned to the British because they had some recent experience, as well as a useful staff study on the restoration of law and order after combat. (The State Department's comprehensive "Future of Iraq" study, which laid out many of the challenges the United States would face in Phase IV, was considered taboo for military planners, because it was not compatible with Pentagon policy-makers' vision of postwar Iraq.) CFLCC also had a loosely defined relationship with a group known as

Combined Joint Task Force IV (C/JTF-IV)—so poorly funded that its members had had to attend trade shows to obtain office supplies—and with what was, in effect, C/JTF-IV's successor organization, the Organization for Reconstruction and Humanitarian Assistance. Both organizations were more or less TaCon to General McKiernan, but it was no secret that ORHA's chief, retired Lt. Gen. Jay M. Garner, had direct lines of his own to the Pentagon.[2]

CFLCC came to assign nine governates (roughly equivalent to provinces) in southern Iraq to the MEF, covering a territory three times the size of Virginia with a population of nine to ten million people, and eventually issued a formal plan known as "Eclipse II" to guide its subordinates in Phase IV. ("Eclipse I" had been the plan for the occupation of Germany after World War II.) CFLCC focused on security and emergency repairs to the infrastructure. The assumption was that parts of the Iraqi government would still be in working order when the shooting stopped, able to maintain the infrastructure, and that ORHA would be able to step in to take on many tasks, especially those dealing with humanitarian assistance. As General McKiernan's special assistant, Terry Moran, commented, CFLCC planned to "leverage the Iraqi Army and . . . the [Iraqi] bureaucracy."[3] The Pentagon's original assumption was that even ORHA would not have to conduct operations for more than a few months in Iraq, and that after a relatively brief occupation, the coalition could turn the country over to an Iraqi government.

Within the framework of Eclipse II, MEF had a considerable amount of leeway, and its planners developed their own approach to the matter. First they did an "intelligence preparation of the battlefield" (IPB), looking at the tribes in the various regions, their infrastructure, and the various threats Marines were likely to face. They came up with two assumptions: that the first six to twelve weeks would be critical—this was when precedents would be set—and that it was important not to try to do too much. The Marines had to keep from involving themselves too deeply in local affairs and to let the Iraqis solve as many of their own problems as they could. One of the G-3 Future Operations officers, Lt. Col. Brian K. McCrary, remembered the many and varied unknowns that he and his counterparts discussed: how to vet and pay local police; how to provide routine municipal services (power and water); how to find, secure, and exploit suspected WMD sites; how to secure the many weapons caches from looting; how to secure and "process" mass grave sites of victims of the regime; even how to run prisons.[4] This list did not include searching for Saddam Hussein and his sons, along with other prominent members of the regime; such high-priority tasks were taken for granted.

The interim result of the planners' work was a scheme for dividing the various responsibilities among the Marine division, Task Force Tarawa, and the British division (which declared it did not need much U.S. assistance with Phase IV).

During a briefing to General Conway in early March, the planners provided him with options for "transitioning the force" and "enabling" the subordinate commands, especially by way of groups that would be known as "governate support teams"—small teams of experts that could deploy to a locality. As Lieutenant Colonel Smith of the G-5 remembered thinking, it was a good beginning; the MEF had defined the problem. But, he felt, the planners had only been able to point in the general direction of a solution but not to lay one out in detail.[5]

MEF announced on 15 April that it would soon take up its postwar stance in southern Iraq. The announcement contained the Marines' trademark tinge of remorse about even having to conduct Phase IV operations. Lieutenant Colonel Smith, who doubled as the MEF spokesman, explained to the press: "It's a tremendous responsibility and it's very complex. We focus the majority of our efforts on war-fighting. That's what we do. And so post-hostilities introduces a whole new spectrum of challenges. . . . We see that [fighting remnants of the *fedayeen*] . . . as the number one threat. . . . We're going to aggressively hunt these guys down and . . . destroy them."[6]

The next day, General Franks convened a meeting of his senior commanders at Saddam Hussein's Abu Ghraib Palace in Baghdad—"an extravagant amalgam of marble, tile, gold fittings and massive chandeliers, all surrounded by an azure moat"—to seal the coalition's victory over the dictator and to ratify the plans for securing the country.[7] MEF apparently held its commander's conference on Phase IV on the same day, and Division followed suit shortly thereafter.[8]

With input from the Army's 358th Civil Affairs Brigade, which remained a welcome adjunct to MEF during the occupation phase, MEF published its order for Phase IV four days later. The planners' assumptions, and the MEF's preference for keeping the occupation short and looking to the future after leaving Iraq, are clear from the text:

> On order, I MEF transitions to security/stability operations: establishes military authority, defeats remaining Iraqi combatants, maintains Iraqi territorial integrity, secures WMD in sectors, and supports humanitarian assistance [and] the restoration of Iraqi civilian administration/infrastructure IOT [in order to] . . . enable a rapid transition to follow-on coalition forces. . . .
>
> A guiding constant, to "enable," will be the basis for all that we do. We must enable IOs/NGOs [international organizations/nongovernmental organizations] and follow-on coalition partners to support the Iraqi people. . . . We must enable the Iraqi people to support and govern themselves. . . . Our overarching focus will be establishment of a secure environment as we disarm remaining Iraqi forces, . . . [re-create] local police forces . . . and develop . . . [a small new] Iraqi military. . . .

We must clearly communicate to the Iraqi people the temporary nature of our mission and our desire to quickly transition to Iraqi self-determination. . . . While accomplishing . . . Phase IV, I MEF must also look "deep" toward the requirement of reconstitution, regeneration and redeployment [of the force].[9]

There had been a blurred transition to Phase IV. Task Force Tarawa and the British and American divisions were conducting Phase IV operations before the MEF published its order—in Nasiriyah, Basrah, Baghdad, and many localities in between. This was partly by design, and partly the result of chance. The rolling transition from Phase III to Phase IV was expected, but the speed and suddenness of the regime's collapse had been breathtaking. The shift was perhaps clearest for the wing. From one day to the next, without a great deal of warning, the kill boxes (the targeting control measure in the air war) were simply "closed." This apparently happened on 11 April. There would still be calls for air support of various sorts, but it would no longer be a routine occurrence, and the wing could start thinking about drawing down in theater. On the ground, the violence also tapered off throughout the country, especially in the Marine area of operations in the southern Iraq—though the change for an infantryman or the driver of a light armored vehicle was a little less dramatic. He still went out on patrol, with his weapons loaded, and had to be prepared for a fight at any time.[10]

While the British division ran its own occupation—with some success, by all accounts—General Mattis's division set the pace for the occupation in the Marine governates. He already had a distinct vision for the way he wanted to implement the MEF order. Like MEF, Division would issue general guidelines. Each of its governates would be run by a reinforced infantry battalion. The reinforcements might consist of a governate support team, a psyops team, a human intelligence exploitation team, civil affairs elements, and sometimes engineer or SeaBee elements. The battalion commander would have a great deal of autonomy, but given the small size of his force, he would have no choice but to rely heavily on the international and nongovernmental organizations as well as whatever Iraqis he could mobilize. Interestingly, he would work not for his regiment but for Division itself; General Mattis's plan was for the regimental staffs to focus on the retrograde and on preparations for the next contingency, the "recocking" that figured in so many plans and talks. This would enable him to satisfy the twin mandates in the MEF order, not to mention the spirit of the order.

It was a dramatic move. General Mattis began the occupation by sending about fifteen thousand of his twenty-three thousand Marines home, along with all of his tanks and assault amphibious vehicles, his armored personnel carriers, but not his light armored vehicles, which remained very useful. This was one way to reinforce his message about how to occupy a country, both to his Marines and to the Iraqis. He still intended for the Marines to patrol on foot and for the two groups to become intimately familiar with each other, even to trust each other. But he did not want "a heavy boot print" or the "sense of oppression" that could come if "everywhere you looked you saw a Marine. If we needed more people, . . . I wanted to enlist the Iraqis [for] . . . our common cause."[11]

The division had three basic policies. The first was "Do no harm," expressed in the kind of Mattis aphorism that all Marines could understand: "If someone needs shooting, shoot him. If someone doesn't need shooting, protect him." The second was to win hearts and minds through good works. The third and final was to be ready at all times to win the ten-second gunfight.[12] The general's statements of policy branched into specific guidance. Because he wanted the Marines and the Iraqis to trust each other, he literally wanted them to look each other in the eye; in fact, one of his directives was for Marines to remove their sunglasses when speaking to Iraqis. Another piece of guidance followed from his commonsense observation that the Iraqis would cooperate more readily if the Marines helped their children, and he sent units into the local schools to clean them up and get them running again.

Again like MEF, Division began its work in each province with a survey, with a view to developing a campaign plan tailored to the needs of each province. Generally speaking, the routine was similar to the one that Division had followed in Baghdad before the MEF had published its order for Phase IV. Reestablishing security was paramount. Marines themselves did some of that work, but wanted to vet and train Iraqi police to take over from them as quickly as possible. The Iraqis joined Marine-led patrols with a view to gradually switch roles.

The division's various locations included Al Muthanna (2d Battalion, 5th Marines); Karbala (3d Battalion, 7th Marines); Al Qadisiyah (3d Battalion, 5th Marines); An Najaf (1st Battalion, 7th Marines); and Babil (1st Battalion, 4th Marines). The provinces of Wasit and Dhi Qar were added when 2d Battalion, 25th Marines; 3rd Battalion, 23d Marines; and the 4th Light Armored Reconnaissance Battalion came over to Division from Task Force Tarawa, which was rotating home at the end of May.

The 3d Battalion, 5th Marines (3/5) was blessed with an unusual Iraqi partner who became the local police chief, Brigadier General Fuad Hani Faris. A wounded veteran of the Iran-Iraq War, he was said to be critical of Saddam and appears to have been one of the many Iraqi soldiers who simply wrote their own travel orders when the war began. Faris moved himself from Hillah, where he had been assigned, to Ad Diwaniyah, where his wife's family lived. When the postwar looting began, he organized Iraqi soldiers into guard forces and protected some of the factories, ammunition supply points, and government buildings in the city until the U.S. Army appeared. He happily agreed to help rebuild the area and transferred his loyalties to the Marines when they replaced the Army in Ad Diwaniyah.[13]

The experiences of the Weapons Company 3/5 in Ad Diwaniyah in early May illustrate what it was like for junior Marines charged with policing a city. The company was quartered in town in a villa that had belonged to a recently departed strongman. Set in a large, pleasant, walled compound next to a stream and including both a vegetable garden and a more formal garden, the airy, two-story villa had been looted in early April—stripped even of doorframes and floor tiles. The Marines had to begin by cleaning it up and restoring it. The idea was to turn it into a police station, complete with armory and holding cells. Next the company put out the word that it would be paying local policemen, which quickly attracted them to the small base and allowed the Marines to begin the process of vetting, organizing, training, and equipping them. In the words of one observer:

> This afternoon the Marines were going to pay the Iraqi [policemen]—and issue weapons. . . . The Marines frisked the Iraqis as they came in [to the compound], confiscated (temporarily) their AK-47s (the small version with the folding stock . . .) but let them keep their pistols if they were unloaded. Marines in HMMWVs overwatched the process and armed Marines stood near the Iraqis as they formed themselves up. There were traffic police— dressed in white, with [peaked] hats like those worn by police all over the world—and security police—dressed in green outfits with the [black] Iraqi berets—all worn in different styles from the pillbox (which looks ridiculous) to the usual Iraqi mushroom shape (which is not that snappy either). No one looked hungry—unlike some of the people on the streets. A couple of the . . . [policemen] bordered on obesity. There were a few officers among them—[men with more braid who looked like] they were used to being in charge and leading (manipulating?) others. I watched one of them work his wiles on one of the translators used by the Marines. By and large, it seemed like a good-natured crowd. A few of them . . . [were] a little nervous as I took photos—but most smiled and waved at me.[14]

In the meantime Marines continued to patrol the streets, apprehend looters, and hold them for a day or two in a makeshift outdoor prison, performing various kinds of less than pleasant tasks around the compound, such as filling sandbags or burning waste in the latrines. (Whether the looters learned their lesson was doubtful. One of the looters claimed he was innocent because he had been *hired* to loot, saying the man the Marines should arrest was his employer.) One thing the Marines learned was that no one wanted to be a policeman in Ad Diwaniyah without a weapon—no one seemed to like policemen, who bore the double stigma of having worked for the former regime and now of collaborating with the occupiers—and so they quickly decided to allow the Iraqis to carry sidearms and AK-47 rifles.

While some Marines addressed security, others worked on the infrastructure. At the battalion command post, located on the grounds of a modern but unfinished medical school campus, there was a thriving S-5 (Civil Affairs) section and a chart showing the lines of operation, which included such entries as "Water/Sewage, Electrical, Medical, Education and Law, Fire, Public Transportation, Food and Distribution." An officer's name was written in next to each entry. For example, 2d Lt. Glen J. Bayliff, whose main qualification for the job was that he was the S-4, was responsible for public transportation, which meant conducting surveys, remaining abreast of developments, and helping to coordinate indigenous efforts with those of international or nongovernmental organizations. Sometimes Marine Reservists, described as the Corps' "hidden asset" by one grateful battalion commander, came to the rescue with their civilian skill sets as policemen, lawyers, or city managers. Many Marines found that neither ORHA nor the organization that replaced it, the Coalition Provisional Authority (CPA), had enough resources to weigh in at the day-to-day, working level. For the most part, they were left to their own devices.[15]

Some national events took place that did have repercussions on the local level. Before the war, President Bush is said to have approved a plan that would have put "several hundred thousand Iraqi soldiers on the U.S. payroll and kept them available" for various tasks from providing security to repairing roads. But in a surprise move on 23 May, Ambassador L. Paul Bremer, head of the CPA, issued a decree disbanding the army and canceling pensions.[16] Some three weeks later, on 15 June, CFLCC turned over responsibility for the occupation of Iraq to V Corps (while keeping its responsibilities for supporting the force). This was the last day of the amnesty period under the coalition decree, which limited the number and types of weapons Iraqis could possess. The predictable result of both policies was an upswing in violence against coalition forces, especially in the area west of Baghdad around Ar Ramadi and Fallujah, two names that would become all too familiar to Marines in 2004.

In 2003, this was not part of the MEF area of operations, but it was contiguous to it. Army convoys traveling from Kuwait to Ar Ramadi and Fallujah had to pass through northern Babil province, which did fall under the MEF. MEF's Future Operations staff "began studying and planning to defeat this threat." The result was a plan to set up an armored task force to patrol the area.[17]

Built around the Reservists of the 4th Armored Reconnaissance Battalion, under the spirited command of Lt. Col. Andrew Pappas, USMCR, the task force took the name "Scorpion" and was clearly undeterred either by the challenge or the marginal living conditions it faced. A visiting journalist, Pamela Hess of United Press International, captured the spirit of Camp Scorpion:

> Mad Max would turn up his nose. . . . There is nothing but garbage and dirt and sand as far as the eye can see. Marines live and sleep in the open air of a gravel parking lot, except for the few one-story concrete buildings that are air-conditioned on the rare occasions the generators can be coaxed to work. They have no chow hall . . . and until . . . recently . . . [sanitary] facilities were a plywood bench with four holes. . . . Powerful winds sweep the grounds, kicking up massive dust clouds that coat everything in dull brown powder several times a day. "This is the best we've had it!" laughs Master Gunnery Sergeant Paul D. Clark from Austin, the battalion's operations chief.[18]

The Marines used their imagination to defeat the enemy. They adopted a Trojan-horse approach, disguising their vehicles as Army supply trucks and then counter-ambushing the locals who had apparently been paid by Ba'athists to take potshots at the convoys. They experimented with various other ways to escort the convoys, training the Army truck drivers in convoy operations and molding Marines and soldiers into one team. Forced to seek cover some distance from the highway, the insurgents took to using increasingly sophisticated "improvised explosive devices"—the small but often deadly bombs that could be rigged to detonate when vehicles passed by. Division resisted advice to reply to attacks with heavy firepower, which its leaders felt might be counterproductive. Instead they decided to go to the source, that is, trying to neutralize the perpetrators before they struck. This they did by collecting intelligence about them and conducting raids, often on the compounds of the relatively wealthy. It was possible to leverage the various civil affairs initiatives to get information: locals grateful for a month or two of electricity or clean water might give the Marines tips about potential insurgents, and the result might be a productive raid at dawn, a time chosen by the division to minimize the risk of harm to bystanders. Success reinforced success. When locals saw the Marines arrest and remove one perpetrator, other Iraqis were emboldened to pass on a tip that would lead to the next raid. Lieutenant Colonel Pappas commented that even if one of the attackers got away after an ambush, often the locals would approach his Marines later on and tell them where to find him.[19] Colonel Pappas's S-2, Maj. Steven B. Manber, added that even though the task force was rich in technical collection assets, 90 percent of its successful operations stemmed from human intelligence.[20]

Similar approaches were applied to more exotic locales: guarding the border with Iran in desert forts that looked like the set for a modern-day movie about the French Foreign Legion; defusing tensions in the holy Shia cities of Najaf and Karbala; uncovering and processing mass graves that were filled with the victims of the Saddam regime; patrolling the border with Saudi Arabia. Looking for weapons of mass destruction remained high on the Marines' agenda, and on that of other coalition forces. The results were as frustrating as they were unexpected. General Conway commented that "in terms of . . . the weapons, we . . . certainly had our best guess . . . [based on what] the intelligence folks were giving us. We were simply wrong. . . . It remains a surprise to me now that we have not uncovered weapons. . . . It's not for lack of trying. We've been to virtually every ammunition supply point between the Kuwaiti border and Baghdad, and they're simply not there."[21]

The Enlisted Marine

In April and May 2003 there was almost universal praise for the young enlisted Marines who served in Kuwait and Iraq. The field historians who deployed from Washington to the field to conduct interviews during and after the war heard story after story praising the spirit, ingenuity, and "stick-to-itiveness" of the individual Marine, and they often experienced it themselves firsthand. It was the small acts that stood out, whether it was the Marines who sensed, rightly, that spare parts would be in short supply up the road in Iraq and stopped to strip them from wrecked vehicles as they moved north, or the AAV mechanics who repaired vehicles while they were moving under tow, or the Marines performing the lonely work of unwinding the hose reel in the desert, or the determination "to get there" of the driver of a seven-ton truck making his way through the sand at night, or rescuing children under fire. Whatever his assigned task, each of these Marines was also prepared to fight as a rifleman, revalidating one of the basic tenets of the Marine credo. What struck many MEF officers after the war was how well combat infantrymen adapted to the demands of occupation duty, switching from a "weapons free" to a "weapons tight" frame of mind. They marveled at the restraint that these young men and women were now showing. The praise for the enlisted Marine sometimes contrasted with what Marine officers said about one another, with the friction that often comes from having too many senior officers with strong personalities gathered in one command or staff.

By early summer, Babylon was the scene of turnover preparations. The location encompassed both the ancient city and the site of another sumptuous modern palace built by Saddam, on an artificial hill, where Marines could camp out. There being little electricity and no running water, but lots of big rooms with high ceilings and marble floors, it was a relatively cool and clean place to pitch a tent.

There was a certain satisfaction to it: Marines were now camping in Saddam's bed-room and ballroom. Both MEF and Division had their headquarters in Babylon, which was not far from CFLCC's forward headquarters in Baghdad. It was here that in late June they received the various parts of the Polish-led multinational division, which pitched their tents among the Marine units. There now began a process of turnovers, the first beginning in early July. Six more reliefs occurred in fairly rapid succession—not always smoothly. Division's General Kelly reported that it was "an understatement to say that the multinational soldiers were shocked at the unexpected level of danger . . . in [their] zones," to say nothing of the spar-tan living conditions and the 130-degree heat in midsummer—all of which the Marines sometimes seemed to revel in, even though there can be little doubt that many, if not most, were also ready to go home after months, and in a few cases two or three years, in theater.[22] (There has always been a strange dynamic in Marine deployments. On the one hand, most Marines want very badly to march to the sound of the guns. No one wants to be left behind when the unit goes to war. But as soon as the fight is over, almost everyone wants to go home.)

With the exception of the city of An Najaf, General Conway was able to turn over responsibility for the zone to the commander of the multinational division in a ceremony at Babylon on 3 September and send his troops south.[23] After the turnovers, there was a general sense of satisfaction among senior Marines with MEF and Division's accomplishments. Although some civilian experts noted per-sistent problems, particularly unemployment and inability to communicate with Iraqis, there were some undeniable statistics. For example, the number of attacks on convoys in northern Babil province was now dramatically lower, and there were no Marines killed in action during the occupation phase (although some were wounded and, tragically, others killed in various accidents). General Mattis made the claim that since early summer the Iraqis had been "running the things that are most important to people. Are the street lights on? Is the neighborhood safe? These kinds of things are already in their hands with the Marines very much in the background."[24]

What was left for the dwindling number of Marines in Iraq and Kuwait was to complete the retrograde process. Through most of the summer, 1st FSSG For-ward conducted redeployment operations from Kuwait while exercising com-mand and control over CSSG-11, which continued to support Division. Until mid-October, MEF Rear was still at Camp Commando, and CFLCC continued to lend its resources to support the Marines. With the assistance of the 377th Theater Support Command, Marines went through washdown and the loading onto various kinds of shipping and aircraft. The two amphibious task forces had preceded them, both setting sail in late May with heavy loads of troops and equipment, each going in a different direction. (ATF-West had taken the more

General Conway Sums Up

During the turnover to the multinational division at Camp Babylon on 3 September, General Conway summed up the past five months in a few words: "As we headed south out of Baghdad for these provinces, we did so with a certain amount of trepidation. Marines don't traditionally do nation-building or security operations. We have no doctrine for it. We weren't sure where the resources would come from. And we weren't sure how we would be received by the people of southern Iraq, who had seen American troops attack up through their governates. . . . [But] in some regards, a negative can become a positive. A lack of doctrine allowed us to pass some very simple rules to our Marines and soldiers. They were: treat others as you would like to be treated. Deal with the people with fairness and firmness and dignity. And among other things, we emphasized the children. They are the future of this country. It's hard to be angry with someone when he's doing good things for your children."*

*Sgt. Colin Wyers, "I MEF Transfers Authority for Southern Iraq to Polish-led Division," dated 3 Sept. 2003 (Story ID No. 200395144422 posted on MarineLink).

exotic route, stopping for liberty in Australia on the way.) Before flying home, other units left heavy equipment with the FSSG's "Regeneration Control Element," which in turn consolidated its holdings for turn-in to a special purpose MAGTF. By 31 October the MEF was completely gone from theater.[25]

The Marine Logistics Command morphed into the Special Purpose MAGTF under the new commanding general of 2d FSSG, Brig. Gen. Ronald S. Coleman, who came to Kuwait in June to replace Brigadier General Lehnert, who was bound for a new job at SouthCom. General Coleman took up residence in the bleak expanses of Tactical Assembly Area Fox. His original charter was to repatriate and repair the MPF equipment that had been used in Iraq, and the plan was for him to get it done by the spring of 2004. (MPF equipment was the Marine equipment that had been prepositioned on chartered ships that made up the Maritime Prepositioning Force.) But Coleman found a way to get the job done much faster. One of the threshold issues was whether it made more sense to do the maintenance and repairs in Kuwait and then reload the MPF shipping, or to ship the gear first to the CONUS and then have it repaired at home. Various factors, including cost and temperatures so high that much of the time his Marines were literally unable to touch anything that was made of metal, made it advisable to choose the second option, and General Coleman was able to get every piece of Marine equipment out of Kuwait—and his Marines home—in time for the Marine ball in November.[26]

General Coleman left TAA Fox more or less as it had been a year earlier. Now it was almost as if the Marines had never passed through Kuwait on their way to Iraq. But there were already inklings that they would return to theater. After his work was done, General Coleman remembered a meeting with General Mattis in the summer of 2003. The division commander was concerned about the gear that was now in the Special Purpose MAGTF's charge, because he thought he would be needing it again shortly.[27] He seemed to know there would not be much rest for his Marines.

12

Save Rounds, Alibis, and the Lessons-Learned Process

The MEF and the Law of War: How Marines Treated Iraqis

Before the MEF crossed the line of departure into Iraq on 20 March, every Marine received clear guidance: the enemy was the Iraqi regime, not the Iraqi people. Starting with General Conway, commanders went to considerable lengths to disseminate, down to the frontline Marine, the rules of engagement (ROE) and the CentCom mandate to limit collateral damage, along with their own views on avoiding "triumphalism" or disrespect for the people and customs of Iraq. Marines were to be liberators, not conquerors, and they were to obey the Law of War. This was not an afterthought—an addendum to other kinds of training—but a theme that ran throughout the MEF's preparations for war. It was especially true for Division, the major subordinate command most likely to encounter the enemy face to face.[1]

The MEF's legal office spent the months before the war working up the ROE and then preparing and disseminating presentations for the major subordinate commands. Following MEF's lead, General Mattis issued written, detailed guidance on the Law of War on at least two occasions, in addition to continuously repeating and explaining the division's motto, "No better friend, no worse enemy." In one prewar memorandum, he predicted that Marine "discipline will be severely tested by an unscrupulously led enemy who is likely to commit Law of War violations," and went on to outline eleven commonsense Law of War "principles."[2] To the same effect, in late 2002 as he sensed the approach of war, he urged his commanders to prepare their Marines for the probability of asymmetric attacks and, at the same time, reminded them that "both decisive force and chivalry will be critical to freeing Iraq."[3]

To drive the message home, General Mattis had his staff judge advocate, Lt. Col. John R. Ewers, and his deputy, Maj. Joseph Lore, deliver classes on the Law of War and rules of engagement to Division units both before and during the deployment; the general wanted the message to come from an independent expert on the subject, not the unit commander. Mattis went so far as to have Ewers create a team to travel around the battlefield and investigate allegations of wrongdoing before the smoke had cleared. Riding in a soft-skinned HumVee, Ewers was doing just that when he was wounded on 23 March 2003 near the town of Az Zubayr in southeastern Iraq. (The investigation involved a report that a media vehicle had been hit by fire from the 1st Tank Battalion.)[4]

It is fair to ask whether the Marines followed this guidance before and after combat. At this stage, the evidence, recorded in situation reports and through contact with Marine lawyers, is largely anecdotal and may never progress much beyond that. It appears that by and large most Marines did as they were told, sometimes even going the extra mile for Iraqis, but some Marines occasionally departed from the spirit or the letter of the law.

The best-known example of "nontriumphalism" was the incident at Firdos Square when Corporal Chin placed an American flag over Saddam's statue but quickly replaced it with an Iraqi flag and left it to the citizens of Baghdad to complete the work of destroying that symbol of the regime. Other, less well-known examples have to do with the care many Marines took not to kill civilians, even when there were legitimate targets nearby. In one case on 2 April, which illustrates the dilemmas that conscientious Marines faced in Iraq, Maj. Peter S. Blake, an AV-8B Harrier pilot, waited for a gap in the civilian traffic—which had, maddeningly, continued to flow in and around the battlefield all over the country— before launching his attack against an Iraqi multiple rocket launcher with a "guided" bomb. Within the next few seconds, a civilian truck came into view, and Blake decided to "slew" (or misguide) the bomb into the Tigris River to save innocent lives. He waited again for a break in the traffic before launching a second—and final—attack. Even though at the last moment another civilian truck appeared, he felt this time he had no choice, since 5th Marines was almost literally around the corner.[5] There are numerous other such examples, like the one in early April when Marines held their fire until they knew whether an approaching school bus was filled with enemy fighters or innocent civilians, which turned out to be the case.[6] In another, more personal example, on 29 March members of the 1st FSSG took the trouble to bury a two-year-old Iraqi boy who had stepped on a landmine and been medevacked to Charlie Surgical Support Company, then in the vicinity of Jalibah, where doctors tried in vain to save his life. The boy had come to the field hospital without identification or relatives, and the Marines and sailors who were present decided to give him a proper Muslim burial. They researched the subject carefully, then found three Muslims to perform the ceremony in the prescribed tradition, which included wrapping the body in a shroud and placing it in a grave with the child's face toward Mecca. The chief of staff of the FSSG, Col. Darrell L. Moore, took time out of his busy day to assist in the ceremony. This small act was one of decency, pure and simple; no journalists or angry townspeople were present to demand that the Marines "do the right thing."[7]

On the other side of the ledger, a few sources record cases where Marines overstepped the bounds of fire discipline or military law. In December 2003 the *Marine Corps Times* reported on the case of eight Marines charged in the death of a fifty-two-year-old Iraqi detainee who was found dead in his cell in An Nasiriyah in the spring of 2003. The charges included "willfully failing to properly safeguard the health" of those in custody, as well as assault and making false official statements.[8] According to the deputy staff judge advocate of 1st Marine Division, Major Lore, this was one of a handful of similar incidents that was investigated and resulted either in nonjudicial punishment or court-martial. In their book *The March Up*, Maj. Gen. Ray Smith and Bing West tell a story about the time when General Kelly, the assistant commander of 1st Marine Division, admonished an unnamed battalion commander on 26 March for letting his troops needlessly shoot at approaching civilians. The Marines had a legitimate concern about suicide bombers in civilian vehicles, but that did not mean every heedless civilian who came within half a mile of a Marine position had to be stopped with deadly force. Although Smith and West go on to discuss their impression that most Marines agonized over the decision to fire or not to fire, two journalists who spent time with different units during the combat phase of the war, Evan Wright and Peter Maas, convey the impression that some young Marines were all too ready to fire at civilians, and that their officers and noncommissioned officers did not always do a good job of restraining them. This was especially true after Marines learned about the fighting at An Nasiriyah, where the enemy had worn civilian clothes and Marine casualties were heavy. At that point, the enemy for many, if not most, Marines became any Iraqi with a gun.[9]

It is important to note that at least five such cases resulted in some form of disciplinary proceedings against the perpetrators. According to Major Lore, these proceedings ran the gamut from nonjudicial punishment to general court-martial. With the passage of time, there will be more clarity on these events. As of this writing, even basic statistics are difficult to come by. The I MEF staff judge advocate's command chronology for the first half of 2003 states that during Phase III of Operation Iraqi Freedom its primary focus was reporting and investigating violations of the laws of armed conflict. The same document shows that the MEF staff judge advocate was involved in some way in one general court-martial, eight special courts-martial, and one summary court-martial, but without delving into the individual cases it is difficult to interpret the significance of these statistics.

The bottom line? The MEF commander and his subordinates did the right thing. They told virtually every Marine what they expected, and they did so in some detail. During the war, the Marine leadership took measures to enforce the standards it had set. Most Marines appear to have met those standards, while a handful fell short and were disciplined when a case could be made against them.

A Few Observations on Command during the Information Age, as Exemplified in the Iraq War

At senior headquarters there has probably never been so much incoming information as there was during the Iraq War, whether it came from official sources or from unofficial sources such as CNN or Fox News. Putting more information into the hands of senior commanders looks, at first glance, like setting the conditions for micromanagement. But generally that did not happen. First, most seniors seemed to exercise restraint most of the time. General McKiernan, for one, understood he was there to shape the fight and then leave the details up to subordinate commanders. Second, even if he had wanted to micromanage, the pace of operations generally outstripped the pace of information, especially of good information. General McKiernan commented that since first reports were so often wrong, it was better not to act on them. Finally, even if a higher headquarters had good information and wanted to micromanage, it was often difficult to do so, especially if the subordinate command was moving or was at or below the digital divide. Communications with mobile units or units in built-up areas were just not that good.

Even routine management was difficult. The staffs who tried to stay ahead of the curve and "paper the war" often failed, at least between 20 March and 9 April. Events happened faster than anyone could write old-fashioned op orders, especially Fragmentary Orders, before they were overtaken by events. One of the operations officers at Division, Lt. Col. Paul J. Kennedy, commented that the ops tempo was such that he couldn't wait for the actual FragOs, but found it possible to work off the preliminary Warning Orders (WarnOs) put out by the MEF.[10] This was even true at lower levels. At RCT 5, Colonel Dunford found he could not control his command through any kind of systematic planning process after the Opening Gambit.[11] Interestingly, the special operations community appeared to have an unusually long planning cycle—up to ninety-six hours—which did not make for happy customers at MEF. As one senior commander commented, "If they can't plan and execute any faster, we are going to have a lot of highly trained guys doing flutter kicks in the rear during ops."[12] Along the same lines, comments were made about the process for generating CFACC sorties being far too slow.

The result was more and more instances of "healthy," straightforward command and control. Imaginative commanders brought "new" products on line to replace the older, barely manageable processes that looked in many ways like a return to the basics. Effects-based planning was one such product. When it worked as intended, General McKiernan's battle update assessment was another. Written or "audible," most operations orders in Operation Iraqi Freedom were about desired effects and reflected the commander's intent. Speaking for Division, the G-3 during OIF, Lt. Col. Clarke R. Lethin, made a pitch for communicating that intent: "How many times have we seen commander's intent developed by the staff, lethargically reviewed by the commander, and then delivered in a briefing without the least bit of emotion? [By contrast,] the division fought by [traditional] commander's intent—a statement of intent that reflected the commander's personality, intuition, sense of purpose, and then [was] delivered to every Marine and sailor in the division."[13]

Lethin could have been speaking for the MEF as a whole. General Conway and his subordinates made distinct efforts to communicate their intent, in person, to the extent possible, to every member of their commands. This was one reason for their series of "go-to-war" speeches. They did much the same after the MEF crossed the line of departure. Although General Conway could have commanded the MEF from Camp Commando in Kuwait, he believed it was necessary to stay forward, to see for himself what was going on, and to meet with his commanders face to face. He left the staff work—and the increasingly time-consuming CFLCC battle update assessments—to others and, as his forces advanced deeper into Iraq, moved the MEF Forward Command Post first to Jalibah on 24 March and then to An Numaniyah in early April. Just before the assault on Baghdad, Conway very nearly succeeded in his attempts to visit every unit in 1st and 7th Marines, which were about to engage in the difficult task of subduing the capital city. Almost like a commander in the U.S. Civil War, he wanted to see, and be seen by, his Marines before the battle.[14] In similar fashion, General Mattis kept his finger on the pulse of his division during the battle. He separated himself from the "noise" of staff work and, in search of a purer form of warfighting, set off on the battlefield with a tiny retinue and a cell phone. He prosecuted the war as much through personal contact with his commanders, either face to face or on the telephone, as through staff channels.

Those who did not meet personally with General Mattis could read his intents messages that were posted, sometimes daily, on the division Web site on the

SIPRnet for all with access to this classified network to see. These messages were short—one or two pages long—and written in plain English, outlining the situation as Mattis and his staff saw it and telling readers what the division intended to accomplish. The same was true of some of the slides presented at the battle update assessments and posted on the CFLCC Web site; the best slides were carefully drafted and approved by the commander himself. Some contained "balloons" clearly highlighting his intent. Many Marine officers began the day by reviewing what was posted on the CFLCC Web site and those of higher, adjacent, and subordinate commands. One staff officer, Col. Ronald J. Johnson, General Natonski's G-3, commented that posting information about Tarawa on the Web enabled MEF to keep track of the task force and simplified relations between the two commands.[15]

Transmitting products like the intents messages and the BUA slides, the SIPRnet web made this one of the most democratic wars in the nation's history in the sense that if you had access to a classified computer, as most staff officers and commanders did, you could be empowered by information that in the past was held only by a few officers. The availability of information could make operations that much more efficient: staffs with access to the same data could plan and operate at the same time without going through time-consuming coordination rituals. Gone were the days when planners had to work in isolation and then push products up their stovepipes for their commanders to approve before the commanders passed it to their counterparts. This usually far outweighed the downside, which was that now "an overeager command could monitor every potential contingency and plan for commitments that would never be levied—creating unnecessary confusion and fatigue."[16]

Data Collection and Formal Lessons Learned

Although history is not about lessons learned, even an overview of the first phase of the Iraq War would be incomplete without a few words about data collection and lessons learned. Not only did various teams collect a great deal of material that may be of use to future historians, but the process itself has an interesting history, not to mention some of the lessons learned themselves.

There was a time, especially after the combat phase, when it seemed that there was not enough tent space and computer terminals for all of the lessons-learned teams in theater. The senior lessons-learned team was from Joint Forces Command in Norfolk, tasked by the Pentagon to produce the official joint report. The Army had at least two lessons-learned groups in theater, including one whose officers produced the admirable preliminary Army history of OIF, titled *On Point* (published by the Combat Studies Institute Press at Fort Leavenworth in 2004).

The Marine Corps had the combat assessment team from the Marine Corps Combat Development Command (MCCDC) at Quantico. Then there were the various groups of field historians, embedded within "supported" commands. Once deployed, Marine historians worked closely with historians from other branches, especially their counterparts from the Army and the joint history staffs, as well as the Marine assessors and, to a lesser extent, those from other services. Though there was a distinct pecking order among these various groups, with historians generally coming from organizations with relatively little bureaucratic clout, most got along well. Data was usually shared freely across the board. There has probably never been so much available, retrievable, and useful historical data.[17]

The recent history of the Marine assessors goes back to Desert Storm, when battle assessment teams deployed from the MCCDC at Quantico to theater to conduct interviews and generally gather data to drive postwar analyses and complement the young Marine Corps Lessons Learned System (MCLLS), described as "a passive system," which relied on units to report their observations. Most of their interviews were anonymous, which limited their usefulness to historians. Their reports tended to go into established "channels"—that is, they did not necessarily turn into front-burner action items. Today, over 250 four-inch binders of Desert Storm material sit quietly on the shelves of the Grey Research Center at Quantico, and MCLLS is unknown to many parts of the Marine Corps public. After September 11, Lt. Gen. Edward Hanlon Jr., commanding MCCDC, ordered the creation of a combat assessment team that deployed to theater for Afghanistan to conduct data during, not after, combat operations and to turn it around quickly, in useful form, to the "advocates"—that is, representatives of the various communities of operators in the Marine Corps. Afghanistan was a useful opportunity to rediscover good and bad ways to learn lessons, and the result, less than a year later, was a sophisticated operation for the Iraq War led by Col. Philip J. Exner, a dynamic thinker and operator out of MCCDC's Studies and Analysis Division. He began by surveying the process:

> We . . . looked at past "lessons learned" efforts. Both authors and audiences were somewhat skeptical of the value of traditional approaches, which usually involved publication of a large tome or collection of documents. . . . One of the other services published an after-action for a more recent operation that consisted of a 5,000-page main report with an 800-page executive summary and nearly 100,000 pages of appendices. Such monumental efforts often miss the very change agents who are essential to converting lessons into lessons learned because the action officers and decision-makers are often overwhelmed with information and chronically short of time.[18]

With the support of the commandant, Exner worked to embed his assessors in the operating forces for the duration—in much the same way that journalists and historians were embedded—so that they could develop better access and understanding and collect better data. The data, in the form of interviews and surveys, went into a massive database in Quantico that was searchable and, to some extent, linked with data collected by historians working alongside the assessors. The assessment teams gave briefings to general officers, posted their findings on Web sites, and produced timely, reader-friendly reports for the advocates. For the more general Marine Corps public, MCCDC published the teams' findings in mercifully brief summary reports that initially were limited to official use but will no doubt find their ways into libraries and research centers before long.

This is not to say that the operators themselves neglected the after-action process. What was probably the first comprehensive "hot wash" took place in Bahrain at MarCent headquarters on 20 May 2003. The highlight was a blow-by-blow chronological review of the operation by the MEF G-3, Colonel Brown.[19] The next major evolution was sponsored by the Marine Corps Association at Quantico on 29 July 2003 and featured briefings by Generals Conway, Mattis, Amos, and Natonski.[20] General Conway's brief was a very good "executive summary" of the operation. Some of the specific lessons learned covered on that day were

> The utility of the medical surgical units at the front; the use of SAPI, or small arms protective inserts, for the flak jackets; the positive impact of the embedded media; the concept of combat maintenance being performed with units on the fly; and the merit in organizing large, flexible combat battalions. . . . Challenges [that is, problem areas] included . . . [having two] Marine Corps supply systems (ATLASS I and ATLASS II), integration with special operations forces, casualty reporting, combat identification to prevent fratricide, and the need to sharpen coalition intelligence sharing.[21]

A few weeks later, on 4 September 2003 there was another conference along the same lines, the Marine Corps Association–U.S. Naval Institute Forum 2003, which featured talks by General Mattis and General Zinni, who was not afraid to strike out on his own and offer some pithy comments about how he saw the situation in Iraq. On 4 September, and then again in May 2004, Zinni criticized the administration's policy in language a drill instructor might have used; he said he remembered the official "garbage and lies" of the Vietnam era and asked if it was happening again. Zinni also offered a thoughtful analysis of what had gone wrong—the "ten mistakes" that "history is going to record." He attacked the reasons for going to war, arguing that the United States had successfully contained Saddam and that it needed first to resolve the conflict between Israel and Palestine. "I couldn't believe what I was hearing about the benefits of this strategic move. That the road to Jerusalem led through Baghdad, when just the opposite is true." He went on to make a number of points about Phase IV, citing the inadequate planning at both the Pentagon and CentCom levels, the inadequate number of troops for occupation duties, and the—to him amazing—decision to disband the Iraqi army.[22]

Marines are likely to remember the observations about Phase III that emerged from these sessions. The first had to do with maneuver warfare and the MAGTF concept. There was general agreement that the Iraq War had revalidated Marine doctrine in at least two respects: speed and organization. The MEF was organized and equipped for speed. It had moved much faster than the enemy; the enemy never had time to visualize the outlines of our OODA loop, let alone get inside it. The MAW had remarkable new precision technologies (and new doctrines to go with them) to enable it to fight with unprecedented effectiveness. The wing and the FSSG had not just supported Division, which was itself organized into mobile, independent combat teams; they also had been maneuver elements in their own right, integrated into the overall scheme of maneuver. With the MLC's and the FSSG's contributions, and the wing's willingness to switch from the deep battle to close air support to cargo missions on short notice, the division had been able to go the distance, to project Marine power on the ground far from saltwater. This was another way of saying that Operation Iraqi Freedom had revalidated the concept of the "MEF single battle." I MEF had demonstrated, yet again, that the whole was greater than the sum of its parts, whether the issue was deep fires, rear area security, or keeping the supplies flowing to the front.[23]

Conclusions about Phase IV were more cautious. No one contradicted General Zinni and claimed there had been elaborate preparations for Phase IV. Nowhere in CentCom or CFLCC had there been a plan for Phase IV that was like the plan for Phase III, let alone all of the preparations that accompanied it, including the cross talk during its development, the many rehearsal of concept drills, and the exchange of liaison officers. There were the arguments, like General Zinni's, for bringing many more American troops to theater for occupation service. He wanted them to be on hand before anyone crossed the line of departure, available to stabilize the country as soon as the fighting ended. (A corollary advanced by some was that the coalition could have moved more slowly from Kuwait to Baghdad in order to secure the objectives that had just been seized.) Still, General Mattis repeated his assertion that he had had the right force mix on the ground in the summer of 2003—a battalion for each province, some aviation, and not much by way of mechanized assets. It was not necessarily how many troops there were on the ground, but what their skills were and what they were being told to do. That was why he had sent his mechanized Marines home in

May. The mostly infantry Marines who stayed through the summer quickly proved their ability to shift and learn on the fly, and they did a more than creditable job as interim occupiers in the southern half of Iraq during the relatively brief period between the end of combat operations and their return home. Along with General Mattis, at least one other senior MEF officer stressed that one of the keys to success was getting the timing right: the longer the occupiers stayed, the greater the challenges would become. The implication was that the Marines succeeded in the short term but that any occupier would face problems in the medium and long term.[24]

Generals Hailston, Conway, Mattis, and Zinni made one overarching point that will find favor with historians. It was that since the Iraqi military was comparatively weak, and since every contingency is unique in its own way, it is dangerous to overgeneralize from the Iraq War, to imagine that the next war will necessarily be like the last.

Appendix A

THE SECRETARY OF THE NAVY
WASHINGTON, D.C. 20350-1000
3 November 2003

The President of the United States takes pleasure in presenting the
PRESIDENTIAL UNIT CITATION to

I MARINE EXPEDITIONARY FORCE

for service as set forth in the following

CITATION:

For extraordinary heroism and outstanding performance in
action against enemy forces in support of Operation IRAQI FREEDOM
from 21 March to 24 April 2003. During this period, I Marine
Expeditionary Force (MEF) (REIN) conducted the longest sequence
of coordinated combined arms overland attacks in the history of
the Marine Corps. From the border between Kuwait and Iraq, to the
culmination of hostilities north of Baghdad, I MEF advanced
nearly 800 kilometers under sustained and heavy combat. Utilizing
the devastating combat power of organic aviation assets, coupled
with the awesome power resident in the ground combat elements,
and maintaining momentum through the herculean efforts of combat
service support elements, I MEF destroyed nine Iraqi Divisions.
This awesome display of combat power was accomplished while
simultaneously freeing the Iraqi people from more than 30 years
of oppression and reestablishing basic infrastructure in the
country. During the 33 days of combat, to the transition to
civil-military operations, I MEF sustained a tempo of operations
never before seen on the modern battlefield, conducting four
major river crossings, maintaining the initiative, and sustaining
forces. The ferocity and duration of the campaign was made
possible through the skills and determination of the Soldiers,
Sailors, Airmen, Marines, and Coalition Partners comprising I MEF
at all levels, all echelons, and in all occupational fields. By
their outstanding courage, aggressive fighting spirit, and
untiring devotion to duty, the officers and enlisted personnel of
I Marine Expeditionary Force (REIN) reflected great credit upon
themselves and upheld the highest traditions of the Marine Corps
and the United States Naval Service.

For the President,

Secretary of the Navy

The following narrative was prepared by the staffs of the subordinate elements of the MEF, then forwarded to MEF. The MEF staff collated the entires and submitted the result to Headquarters, Marine Corps, as part of the supporting documentation for the award. Written shortly after the combat phase of Operation Iraqi Freedom, it represents the participants' own impressions of their accomplishments at the time.

Summary of Action

Prepared by I MEF to support Presidential Unit Citation

I Marine Expeditionary Force (REIN) was composed of the I Marine Expeditionary Force Headquarters Group, 1st Marine Division (-) (REIN), 3d Marine Aircraft Wing (-) (REIN), 1st Force Service Support Group (-) (REIN), the I MEF Engineer Group, Task Force Tarawa (2d Marine Expeditionary Brigade), 15th Marine Expeditionary Unit (Special Operations Capable), 24th Marine Expeditionary Unit (Special Operations Capable), and the 1 Armoured Division of the United Kingdom. This task-organized Marine Air Ground Task Force (MAGTF) began deployment for combat operations in October 2002 and is most deserving of being awarded the Presidential Unit Citation for actions from 21 March to 24 April 2003. Operation IRAQI FREEDOM resulted in a number of firsts for the United States Marine Corps. Contained below is a summary of action from each Major Subordinate Command (MSC) and Major Subordinate Element (MSE) to support the award of the PUC.

I Marine Expeditionary Force Headquarters Group

Operation IRAQI FREEDOM was the first operational use of the MEF since Operation DESERT SHIELD/DESERT STORM twelve years earlier. I MHG provided the basic life support for the MEF Command Element, the largest Force Reconnaissance Company in the history of the Corps, a significantly reinforced Intelligence Battalion, two full Communications Battalions, and two complete ANGLICOs. I MHG developed and secured five separate MEF Command Post locations from which basic command and control of assigned forces was executed. Throughout the operation, I MEF Command Element, supported by I MHG, operated continuously with no less than three command and control nodes: I MEF, I MEF (Forward), and I MEF Camp Pendleton. Leveraging information technology to the fullest and using reach back capabilities to the fullest extent, I MEF was able to web-base the majority of its war fighting applications thereby giving all subordinate, adjacent, and higher units near real-time information on battlefield activities.

1st Marine Division

During the successful execution of Operation IRAQI FREEDOM, the 1st Marine Division conducted the longest sequence of coordinated overland attacks in Marine Corps history. From crossing the Line of Departure (LOD) on the border between Kuwait and Iraq, to the culmination of hostilities well north of Baghdad, the Division covered 808 kilometers in 17 days of sustained combat.

Preparation

On short notice, and prior to the commencement of hostilities, the Division was required to develop a deception plan to cover its movement to designated attack positions. This plan and its subsequent, complex night movement enabled the Division to tactically move 20,000 Marines and sailors from their Life Support Areas (LSAs) in Kuwait to their intermediate Attack Positions/Position Areas (Aps/Pas) immediately south of the Iraq/Kuwait border. The Division successfully completed this movement in less than 24 hours, without loss of life and without being detected by the enemy. Once in its Aps/Pas, the Division set conditions to cross the LOD on four hours' notice.

Initial Attack

On 19 March, intelligence sources indicated that enemy action was threatening to destroy the strategic Rumaylah oilfield previously identified in plans as Division Objective 3. In light of this information, Regimental Combat Team-5 (RCT-5) crossed the LOD nine and a half hours early and secured the mission-critical Gas and Oil Separation Plants (GOSPs). Despite the fact that two Iraqi Regular Army Brigades, supported by artillery, were defending the GOSPs, the Regiment was able to secure the objective in 16 hours of hard fighting while limiting damage, and suffering only one KIA and one WIA.

On the morning of 21 March, the remainder of Division units crossed the LOD and commenced their attack to secure Division Objective 2, which included the Az Zubayr Pumping Station (considered the key oil infrastructure node in southern Iraq). Despite a determined defense by the Iraqi 51st Mechanized Division, RCT-7 secured the objective 24 hours after crossing the LOD. By the morning of 22 March, the 1st Marine Division destroyed the 51st Mechanized Division, secured its first four objectives and transferred approximately 300 Enemy Prisoners of War (EPW) to British forces.

In the next 48 hours, the Division captured the area south of the Saddam River and transferred control of that area to the British during an efficiently executed 12-hour Relief in Place (RIP). This action succeeded in fixing in place three Iraqi Divisions and opened the way for the advance on Baghdad via the critical crossroads city of Al Kut. During this time, the Division captured Iraqi Lieutenant General Amir Hamudi Al-Sadi, the Regime's Presidential Advisor for Scientific and Technical Affairs. LtGen Al-Sadi was number 32 on the U.S. list of Most Wanted Iraqi Regime officials and was wanted for his knowledge of Iraq's WMD program, particularly his key part in the development of Iraq's nuclear weapons program. During this phase the Division suffered 14 casualties: one KIA and thirteen WIA.

Across the Euphrates

On 23 March, the Division began crossing the Euphrates River in the vicinity of An Nasiriyah using bridges to the east and west of the city. Within 12 hours, the Division passed 8,000 vehicles through this vital choke point and was then poised for operational maneuver on Baghdad.

The Division used a two-pronged attack from An Nasiriyah to the Tigris River crossings. RCT-1 advanced through the gauntlet of An Nasiriyah and north up Highway 7. This RCT battered through regular and irregular forces in Al Gharraf, Ash Shatrah, and Al Hayy to the vicinity of Al Kut, where it succeeded in fixing the Baghdad Division of the Iraqi Republican Guard, preventing it from threatening the Division's crossing of the Tigris River and, subsequently, the Division's flank and rear. The remaining two RCTs (RCT-5 and RCT-7) advanced north up Highway 1, successfully attacking through the vicinity of Ad Diwaniyah, where they captured an enormous 40-bunker ammunition supply point (ASP) of the Saddam Fedayeen and Al Quds militias. Also, the Division seized an operational Highway airstrip at Hantush in central Iraq. This movement posed a significant threat to southern Baghdad that could not be operationally ignored by the Iraqi high command.

In order to relieve the stress on its logistics throughput capabilities, and to provide the needed support for the planned crossing of the Tigris River and the impending assault on Baghdad, the Division opened an Highway airstrip to C-130 traffic within eight hours. This assault airstrip accepted and processed over 400 tons of supplies, including 180 tons of fuel and 300 pallets of MREs, in support of the planned assault.

Across the Tigris

On 2 April, the Division attacked across the Tigris River near An Numaniyah, seizing a key bridge and successfully conducted the second major river crossing in one week. The Division's attack effectively cut off the Baghdad Division of the Republican Guard from the capital and denied its escape route to reinforce defensive positions within Baghdad. The remainder of the Baghdad Division was destroyed in a simultaneous attack by RCT-1 and RCT-7 near Al Kut. Within 12 hours the Division had massed its combat power to the north of the Tigris and continued its attack on Baghdad, while also seizing a terrorist camp near Salmon Pak, and the Iraqi Nuclear Energy Commission Research Facility.

Into Baghdad

Keeping the enemy off balance and retaining its tactical momentum, the Division conducted an assault bridging operation while under fire to cross the Diyala River and enter Baghdad, a city of six million people, on April 7. This was the first assault bridge crossing conducted in the face of the enemy since World War II. The Division secured the eastern half of Baghdad in six days with a total of 76 casualties, four KIA and 72 WIA. The Division's fire discipline and judicious use of supporting arms in this densely populated area avoided a potentially catastrophic toll among the civilian population and minimized collateral damage.

During the fight for Baghdad, the Division seized key facilities, including the Rasheed Military Complex, the Atomic Energy Commission, the Baghdad University, Tariq Aziz's residence, the Ministry of Defense Complex, the Fedeyeen Headquarters, and the Directorate for General Security (DGS) Headquarters. Additionally, one RCT supported the employment of TF-20 in the successful capture of Abal Abbas, one of the key terrorist leaders associated with the 1985 Achille Lauro cruise ship attack. During the attack on the Al Azamiya Palace area, the Division received a verbal MEF FRAGO to contain a mosque suspected of holding Saddam Hussein. Division Marines displayed noteworthy valor in this mission, incurring one KIA and 22 WIA.

Upon achieving its objectives in eastern Baghdad, the Division initiated actions to create conditions for good order by leveraging the existing support infrastructure, i.e., public safety, food supply, health services, transportation, and utilities. Additionally, the Division supported three Task Force 20 raids searching for high-ranking Iraqi Regime officials and exploited documents and information from captured Iraqis via its embedded Human [Intelligence] Exploitation Teams (HETs).

North to Tikrit

On 10 April, at CFLCC and MEF direction, the Division formed an LAR-based task force, TF Tripoli, which, within 24 hours, attacked Tikrit, Saddam Hussein's birthplace and a significant regime bastion. TF Tripoli secured Tikrit within two days. Along the way, it opened a secure route for follow-on use by the U.S. Army's 4th Infantry Division, seized ammunition storage facilities that included Roland Surface-to-Air Missiles, SA-3 SAMs, and Abibil Surface-to-Surface Missiles. Acting on intelligence information, TF Tripoli entered Samara and rescued seven U.S. POWs without incurring casualties.

Leveraging goodwill among the tribal leaders in northern Iraq that was generated by Division Civil Military Operations personnel, TF Tripoli exploited the opportunity to secure the key northern city of Bayji without firing a shot. Within days the Division was able to pacify the Tikrit region and turn over significant operating responsibilities to the local inhabitants.

Stabilization Operations

In Baghdad, the Division established a Civil-Military Operations Center (CMOC) to work with key civil leaders and NGOs to restore services to Baghdad. This center quickly became a hub of stabilization and reconstruction activity, sending a positive message to the citizens of Baghdad concerning the U.S. presence. The Division and Civil Affairs (CA) personnel continued working with the International Committee of the Red Cross to make area hospitals operational again and initiated joint Marine-Iraqi Police patrols to restore order and confidence.

The Division transitioned from combat operations to Civil-Military Operations in Baghdad with no disruption—a significant event for any military force.

The Division's initiation and conduct of security and civil-military affairs in a city of six million inhabitants and, subsequently, to holy cities and areas of influence, are preceded in U.S. military history only by the United States' occupation forces facilitating rebuilding programs in post–WWII Europe and Japan. These accomplishments were all firsts for a Marine Division and are emblematic of the unprecedented valor, determination, and resolve among the individual Marines, soldiers, and sailors of 1st Marine Division.

3d Marine Aircraft Wing

3d Marine Air Wing (3d MAW) set new standards of achievement during its execution of both the deployment and combat phases of Operation Iraqi Freedom. Executing a massive deployment of troops and equipment in record time, 3d MAW then carried out an unparalleled campaign against Iraqi forces that resulted in the destruction of at least eight Iraqi Divisions and an air campaign that significantly removed the enemy's will to fight.

Deployment

Deployment Order 164 initiated 3d MAW participation. 3d MAW positioned a force of 135 Marines in Kuwait during November of 2002 to establish initial basing sites and orchestrate the flow of personnel and equipment. From this initial presence, 3d MAW provided key support of the offload of two complete Maritime Prepositioning Ships (MPS) squadrons (a total of 11 ships) with MAW and MEF equipment. This was followed by four fast sealift ships loaded with the aircraft of several helicopter squadrons. The offload of these ships was conducted on a 24-hour-a-day, seven-day-a-week basis and was completed in 45 days without a single injury to any Marine or Sailor. The result was the assembly of more equipment in one location than had been accomplished in Marine Corps history. Additionally, 3d MAW offloaded three ammunition ships that ultimately provided 29.1 million pounds of aviation ordnance for the pending operation and contributed to the establishment of the largest cache of aviation ordnance ever. Aircraft and personnel from the east and west coasts arrived aboard 17 amphibious ships (plus two T-AVB aviation logistics ships) and by the air ferrying of other aircraft to the theater of operations. At its peak, 3d MAW grew to 15,451 personnel. Augmentation was provided from the 1st, 2d, and 4th MAWs and a host of additional sources to meet the requirements of combat. This made the 3d MAW the largest Marine Air Wing deployed since Vietnam.

Basing

Establishing itself at two primary Air Bases in Kuwait (Al Jaber Air Base and Ali Al Salem Air Base), wing elements built compounds and improved operational areas. Third MAW set up 440 tents at Al Jaber and 400 tents and mess facilities at both sites. Seabees constructed concrete ramps at Al Jaber to accommodate the huge influx of aircraft, and additional ground preparation was made to lay AM-2 matting for additional ramp space. Additional detachments were also established at Prince Sultan Air Base, Saudi Arabia and at Sheik Isa Air Base, Bahrain. Ultimately, 3d MAW deployed 435 aircraft, making it the largest overseas deployment of Marine aviation assets since the height of the Vietnam War.

Shaping the Battlefield

During deployed operations leading up to Operation Iraqi Freedom, 3d MAW flew sorties between 15 February 2003 and 20 March 2003 into Iraq in support of Operation Southern Watch. Additional Unmanned Aerial Vehicle (UAV) missions were also flown into Iraq during this period. These missions provided key imagery intelligence of the enemy situation and allowed commanders at the highest level to shape the initial planning for the conduct of a ground offensive against Iraq.

Direct Support

Preparations for combat included a focus on best methods to support ground forces. 3d MAW units established unique direct support relationships at the Regimental Combat Team (RCT) level and above [which] allowed ground units to be supported with the full range of MAW assets, including Direct Air Support Centers (DASC), Air Support Elements (ASE), imagery liaison cells from VMU squadrons, dedicated Casualty Evacuation (CASEVAC), and Command and Control aircraft.

Forward Basing

3d MAW forces began combat and combat support actions immediately at the start of hostilities by moving over 4,000 Marines and sailors and over 900 vehicles from the Marine Air Control Group and Marine Wing Support Group with ground forces as they crossed the berm into Iraq in order to establish a chain of Forward Arming and Refueling Points (FARPs) and Forward Operating Bases (FOBs) that would allow MAW rotary and fixed wing assets to support ground combat elements at all times. This action resulted in the creation of 15 FARP and FOB sites that provided ordinance and fuel for hundreds of aircraft sorties during the campaign and covered over 500 miles as the ground forces advanced, an accomplishment unparalleled in Marine Corps history. Although designed to provide fuel and ammunition only to MAW aircraft, these forward sites provided fuel for tanks, light armored vehicles, and a variety of rolling stock from Marine ground combat elements at critical times in order to allow the ground attack to continue its aggressive forward momentum. These elements of 3d MAW were frequently at the forward most combat areas and sustained both Killed in Action (KIA) and Wounded in Action (WIA) casualties.

Strike Air

Marine fixed wing assets of MAG-11 provided over 4,000 sorties in close air support (CAS) and air interdiction missions, dropping over 3.8 million pounds of ordnance. Quickly adapting to the fluid nature of the battlefield, the fixed wing elements developed tactical innovations that allowed them to maximize the use of imagery intelligence in order to quickly attack mobile targets while this intelligence information was still current. The use of airborne "wolf packs," using F/A-18D Forward Air Controllers (FACs) to search for targets and channel aircraft to engage enemy armored assets, led to the successful attack of units such as the Baghdad Division and the Al Nida Division. These two Republican Guard Divisions were struck with such intensity that contemporary battle hit assessments rated them at less than 25 percent strength with remaining military equipment abandoned prior to ground attack by elements of 1st Marine Division. AV-8 aircraft were deployed with equal lethality and with the ability to provide all-weather CAS. Despite the challenges of an austere operating environment, elements of MAG-13 staged aircraft far forward into Iraq as part of the air campaign, dropping 939 precision guided munitions (PGM) and 814 non-guided bombs. They also provided imagery intelligence with the Litening II system that became valued not only at the tactical level, but also as a national level collection asset during the POW raid at the hospital compound in An Nasiriyah. Aircraft maintenance elements worked around the clock to maintain readiness throughout the force and to continue to provide constant aircraft support to ground units. Ultimately, the fixed wing assets of 3d MAW achieved these impressive results while suffering no combat aircraft losses or casualties.

Assault Support

Rotary wing assets from MAG-29, MAG-39, and MAG-16 were instrumental in providing effective support of the ground campaign. Close coordination with ground elements was again the hallmark of the success of these units. Helicopter crews consistently landed or staged at ground force areas to conduct face-to-face liaison in order deliver the full impact of the Marine Air-Ground Task Force (MAGTF) on the enemy. Assault support lift assets had conducted intense preparations to conduct the largest heliborne assault lift in history by moving Royal Marines of 42 Commando to the Al Faw Peninsula. Initial attack missions successfully destroyed numerous key Iraqi border outposts, while specialized lift missions inserted and extracted Marine Force Reconnaissance teams to support the advance of combined forces. Assault support aircraft played a key role in CASEVAC during intense fighting in An Nasiriyah. Helicopter crews repeatedly came under fire and advanced into "hot" Landing Zones (LZs) without regard to their own safety to quickly extract Marine casualties. Throughout the operation, these crews also routinely conducted CASEVAC missions to retrieve enemy prisoners of war (EPW) and Iraqi civilians who had been wounded in the fighting. Marine assault support aircraft provided hundreds of sorties to provide forward ground combat elements with food, water, and ammunition, as well as transportation of personnel. Elements of MAG-16 flew in support of the successful special operations POW snatch mission in An Nasiriyah and also for numerous ongoing reconnaissance inserts and extracts.

Rotary Wing CAS

Marine UH-1 gunships and AH-1 attack helicopters exemplified the aggressive spirit of 3d MAW in providing close-in attack of enemy positions immediately forward of friendly forces. These aircrews constantly exposed themselves to enemy fire performing road reconnaissance, CAS, and command and control missions. Attack helicopters destroyed numerous enemy armored vehicles, tanks, and enemy firing positions. They were particularly adept at engaging targets in the close spaces of urban areas, where they frequently used TOW missiles and 20mm guns to target enemy sniper positions while minimizing damage to adjacent areas. Road reconnaissance missions were executed with the distinct intention of drawing enemy fire and thereby determining enemy positions before ground forces were exposed to fire. 3d MAW HMLA squadrons received enemy fire on an ongoing basis; 22 AH-1 aircraft and 2 UH-1 aircraft sustained damage from enemy action, some sustaining hits again on additional missions.

Combat Resupply

3d MAW pooled the assets of both active and reserve KC-130 squadrons to form a KC-130 force of 24 aircraft that was key to the sustainment of forward operating forces. These aircraft flew over 1,011 sorties and transported thousands of pounds of fuel and supplies to unimproved Forward Operating Bases under dangerous flight conditions, frequently receiving antiaircraft fire. KC-130 aircraft were instrumental in moving key supplies forward when other ground convoy methods had become bottlenecked. This included the movement of MREs forward to 1st Division at a point when Division rations had been cut from 3 MREs per day/per man to 1 MRE per day/per man. They also moved 155mm artillery shells forward to fill a critical shortage in 11th Marines prior to the final push toward Baghdad. These actions were in addition to the ongoing lift of personnel and equipment to sustain the attack. Finally, they provided transport to seven U.S. POWs retrieved north of Baghdad.

Destruction of the Enemy

Employing 9,800 sorties of fixed and rotary wing aircraft to adeptly execute its mission, 3d MAW ruthlessly attacked enemy forces while minimizing the unnecessary loss of civilian lives and property. Constantly keeping the enemy "between a rock and a hard place" by forcing them to choose between destruction by moving, or destruction by remaining stationary, 3d MAW decimated the Iraqi 11th, 14th, 18th, and 51st Infantry Divisions, the 6th and 10th Armored Divisions, the Baghdad Republican Guard Infantry Division, and the Al Nida Republican Guard Armored Division. These formations were rendered combat ineffective through such focused and intense application of aerial firepower that most offered no resistance above the small-unit level once contact was made by Marine ground forces. The actions of 3d MAW were clearly instrumental in diminishing the enemy's "will to fight" and significantly shortened the ground campaign. The close coordination of the 3d MAW fight demonstrated the full combat power of the MAGTF team. The actions of the 3d MAW are of the highest order and rank with the greatest achievements of the U.S. Marine Corps.

1st Force Service Support Group

During Operation IRAQI FREEDOM, 1st FSSG Battalions played a critical role supporting all I MEF personnel.

6th Engineer Support Battalion

Upon activation and consolidation and follow-on relocation to Kuwait, 6th ESB was assigned the Bulk Liquids Mission, consisting of both fuel and water. Assigned the deployment of the Hose Reel System, this battalion constructed 60 miles of fuel hose, along with a 1.2 million-gallon fuel farm in order to push bulk quantities of fuel deep into Iraq. The system installed was six times larger than *any* other previously built system and was constructed in *one-half* the time allotted. The system installation continued during the worst sand storm in 20 years, enabling the timely providing of fuel to Wing and Division units engaged in the Battle for An Nasiriyah. Subsequently, the system was enlarged with another 30 miles of hose and an additional 600,000 gallons of fuel storage in order to become a theater level asset. In total, *7.9 million gallons of fuel* were pumped through the Hose Reel System. Five additional fuel sites were established and provided a total storage capacity of 4.8 million gallons of fuel.

8th Engineer Support Battalion

8th ESB was assigned the Assault Bridge mission in direct support of the 1st Marine Division and Task Force Tarawa. The battalion completed nine assault bridge crossings, and five of the crossings were opposed by direct enemy combat action. In 14 hours and during darkness on 29–30 March 2003, the battalion built a single lane across the Tigris River west of An Numaniyah, under enemy fire. Once established, the bridge enabled the Division to continue the attack toward Baghdad. Over a 36-hour period during 6–7 April 2003, the battalion built three bridges at separate sites and under enemy fire, across the Narh Diyala River east of Baghdad. The bridges directly facilitated the crossing of three regiments into Baghdad. The battalion then maintained the bridges to support logistics traffic in support of the attack, and after the city was secured, the bridges allowed for the normalization of civilian traffic into and out of the city.

7th Engineer Support Battalion

7th ESB was assigned the mobility, counter-mobility, survivability, and general engineering support mission in the I MEF zone. At the start of combat operations, the battalion cut breach lanes through the Kuwait-Iraq border, enabling 1st Marine Division and Task Force Tarawa's rapid attacks into Iraq. As the 1st Marine Division and Task Force Tarawa moved north into Iraq, the battalion improved dozens of kilometers of Route 1, the main supply route for I MEF's push forward to Baghdad. Additionally, as I MEF moved further forward into Iraq, the battalion constructed, maintained, and improved Support Areas Coyote, Viper, Anderson, Basilone, Chesty, and Edson. During combat operations, the battalion's engineers were operating simultaneously over 450 miles, enabling the movement of huge quantities of material. After the fall of the Iraqi regime, the battalion transitioned to the collection, movement, and destruction of captured ammunition and safely disposed of thousands and thousands of tons of captured enemy material, significantly reducing the threat such materials posed to the Iraqi people and coalition military forces. 7th ESB also provided potable water for I MEF forces. By the third day of the war, the first water site was established and produced 200,000 gallons of fresh water daily. Eight additional separate Reverse Osmosis Water Purification Unit (ROWPU) sites were established from southern Iraq to Baghdad, producing over 3 million gallons of fresh water at those sites.

Combat Service Support Battalion-10

CSSB-10 provided direct support to all 1st Marine Division units in the I MEF zone. The battalion's primary method of support was through the establishment of Repair and Replenishment Points (RRPs). During the combat phase of the operation, the battalion established 14 separate RRPs, covering hundreds of miles in span of control and rapid movement, mostly at night and often under enemy fire. The battalion also operated convoys in order to support those units unable to receive supplies at the designated RRPs. During the combat phase of the operation the battalion conducted over 400 such convoys, covering nearly 120,000 miles, in order to sustain the forward momentum of the 1st Marine Division in its attack toward Baghdad. The battalion distributed nearly 3,000 pallets of MREs, nearly 1,000,000 gallons of water, over 2,000,000 gallons of fuel, and over 2,000 tons of ammunition. The battalion also processed 1,453 EPWs [enemy prisoners of war] and handled 124 containers (the equivalent of 148,800 bags) of mail destined for I MEF Marines and sailors.

Combat Service Support Battalion-12

CSSB-12 provided general support to units in the I MEF zone. While in Kuwait, the battalion established the largest deployed ASP in Marine Corps history. The battalion established and operated five separate MEF support areas, traveling nearly 700 miles. During the 28 days of most intense operations, the battalion transported and distributed 3,452 pallets of MREs; received, stored and distributed 1,848,310 gallons of fuel; produced, stored, and distributed 752,988 gallons of water; and received 5,342 tons of ammunition. In particular, one emergency ammunition package involved the direct delivery re-supply of over 1000 artillery high explosive projectiles, powders, and fuses from Support Area Chesty forward 110 miles to 11th Marine Regiment firing positions 17 miles east of Baghdad. The battalion accomplished this critical re-supply support mission within six hours of the battalion's receipt of the mission tasking. The battalion also conducted 3d and 4th echelon maintenance on I MEF equipment, completing repairs on 4,262 principal end items of combat equipment. The battalion's medical treatment facility saw 493 patients during the most intense days of combat—345 US military, 81 EPWs, 64 foreign nationals, and 3 civilian reporters. Many of the procedures performed were major surgical (life-saving) procedures.

Fleet Hospital Three (FH-3)

This fleet hospital, personnel and equipment, was forward deployed to SA Viper in Iraq and became fully operational within five days of emplacement. This fleet hospital was the most medically and surgically advanced facility ever forward deployed in a combat zone. The hospital was able to provide 21 distinct surgical and medical specialties in a 116-bed fully transportable hospital setting. During combat operations, the hospital admitted 437 war casualties and performed 546 major surgical procedures.

Combat Service Support Battalion-18

CSSB-18 provided general support to units in the I MEF zone. Within hours of the inception of combat operations in Iraq, the battalion crossed into Iraq and rapidly established the first USMC support area inside Iraq. During combat operations, the battalion transported and distributed 5,270 pallets (253,000 cases) of MREs, coordinated the movement of nearly 7,000,000 gallons of fuel, and unloaded and issued nearly 15,000 short tons of ammunition.

1st Transportation Support Group

The Group's mission was to provide general support distribution to I MEF forces. The Group was organized into Convoy Control companies; Heavy, Light, and Bulk Liquids companies; Landing Support companies; and a Headquarters company. The Group was comprised of active duty elements from 1st Transportation Support Battalion, Marine Corps Reserve elements from 6th Motor Transport Battalion, and an activated Army Reserve unit, the 319th POL Company. The Group's convoys routinely numbered more than 60 vehicles per convoy and the convoys were often engaged by enemy forces attempting (unsuccessfully) to delay or disrupt the flow of needed material to the operating forces. The Group operated from Kuwait to Baghdad, traveling over 1.3 million road miles to successfully deliver thousands of tons of supplies and over 7,000,000 gallons of fuel to I MEF operating forces.

I Marine Expeditionary Force Engineer Group

U.S. Marines and Navy Seabees have had a special relationship since the Battle for Guadalcanal in 1942. In combat 63 years later, the closeness of this unique relationship continued to hold true in Kuwait and Iraq in the form of the MEF Engineer Group (MEG). The MEG was established by the I MEF CG, General Anthony C. Zinni, at Camp Pendleton in 1995. It was based upon the original USMC engineer regiments within each Marine division during WWII. Each of these was comprised of both Marine engineers and Seabees.

For Operation IRAQI FREEDOM, under the command of Admiral Charles Kubic, the MEG consisted of three distinct Task Forces: TF-Mike (Mobility), which had the mission of moving forward directly behind the MAGTF's GCE to provide Mabey-Johnson Bridging (non-standard replacements for USMC AVLB, MGB, and Ribbon Bridge); TF-Charlie (Construction), which would follow in trace of TF-M providing support through construction and maintenance of MSRs; and TF-Echo (Endurance), which would follow in trace of the others providing sustainment support. All three task forces were heavily Seabee in personnel, with a solid representation of Army units. The MEG headquarters consisted to a large degree of Seabees and Marines with some Army staffing. All told, the MEG had approximately 4,000 Seabees, soldiers, and Marines serving in it. Toward the end of the war, the MEG technically became a "CMEG" ("C" for combined) when a Republic of Korea engineer battalion was assigned to TF-Echo.

Major accomplishments of the MEG are significant and focused on the names of the task forces: mobility, construction, and endurance (sustainment). The main mobility support provided to the MEF was British-built Mabey-Johnson Bridging (very similar to the famous Bailey of WWII). The MEG had 1,120 meters of this and carefully planned to fully transport and employ it at key crossing sites on the Euphrates, Tigris, and Diyala Rivers of Iraq. Innovative use of moles, culverts, sheet pile, and other construction methods were incorporated so that this vital bridging could be used even in a worst-case scenario. This was planned against the potential for the enemy confronting I MEF with up to 1,800 meters of blown bridge gaps. Not only was the MEG able to fully transport itself (some 2,200 major pieces of civil engineer support equipment or CESE) over some 400 miles of advance from the Kuwaiti border to Baghdad, but it created new roads and maintained most of the MSRs for this entire distance. This equipment consisted of extensive earthmoving, line haul, construction, weight and material handling capabilities. And the MEG was able to do this in record time from the attack of 19 March through the handover of the USMC portion of Baghdad to the Army on 20 April 2003.

The eyes and ears of the MEG were provided by specially developed SERTs (Seabee Engineer Reconnaissance Teams). These squad-sized units were extremely mobile and well-protected crews with a wide range of civil engineer estimate capabilities. Their early and advance assessment of countermobility situations allowed Seabee expeditionary logistics to be highly utilized across the entire battle space in close support of the MAGTF.

The Seabee motto of "Can Do" best exemplifies the fact that the MEG did all of this by convoying its own troops, vehicles, construction materials, camps and bridges, while all the time staying focused and attuned to the needs of the Marines it supported. This devotion to 1st Marine Division (as it was on Guadalcanal) can in no better way be exemplified than during the Battle for Baghdad. At the height of this struggle in the eastern sector of the city, when Marines found themselves desperately short of MREs and ammo, Seabees used their considerable line haul to improvise lift and physically distribute these badly needed commodities to their Marine buddies.

The MEG has earned an honored position as a major subordinate command within I MEF. Seabees have proven again in combat that they can be counted upon to go into battle alongside their Marine "band of brothers." This solid teamwork, positive interaction, accomplishments, and speed of execution throughout the past month of combat have made a unique statement in U.S. and world military history. I MEF in under 4 weeks covered the same distance it took Britain to cover in 4 years in WWI. Engineers made an important difference here within a winning, task organized, MAGTF configuration. Speed, agility, shock, and combat leadership proved decisive. The MEG concept is now combat proven as an important MEF "arrow in the quiver" of Marine infantry.

Task Force Tarawa (2d Marine Expeditionary Brigade)

Task Force Tarawa (TF Tarawa) with its headquarters as the 2d Marine Expeditionary Brigade (2d MEB) stood up on 6 Jan 2003 and departed North Carolina aboard amphibious shipping on 16 Jan arriving in Kuwait on 15 Feb 2003. TF Tarawa engaged in planning and training with I MEF, then on order moved to its attack position in Assembly Area Hawkins for the attack into Iraq.

TF Tarawa occupied a critical position on left flank of I MEF adjacent to V Corps' 3d Infantry Division (3d ID), assigned to attack in zone and conduct a relief in place (RIP) with 3d ID forces, thus enabling 3d ID to continue their attack to the west and north toward Baghdad. Subsequently, TF Tarawa was to facilitate the movement of 1st MARDIV forces west and north along Highways 1 and 7 by seizing and securing key choke points in zone and enabling the free flow of traffic along those routes.

On 21 March, TF Tarawa attacked into Iraq through four breach lanes in the Kuwaiti and Iraqi berms. One of the lanes created by TF Tarawa was ASR ASPEN, which would be utilized throughout the war as a key supply route. Moving cross-country to free up roads for heavy wheeled traffic, TF Tarawa occupied defensive positions east of Jalibah to protect the right flank of 3d ID, allowing them to focus on seizing a bridge over the Euphrates River, west of An Nasiriyah. Due to the swift advance of coalition forces, TF Tarawa altered its timeline and conducted RIP with 3d ID on evening of 22 March, and prepared to secure Hwy 1 crossing of the Euphrates River, a critical juncture on what turned out to be the major supply route for coalition forces through much of the war. The early RIP enabled the 3d ID to maintain momentum and cross the Euphrates ahead of schedule.

On 22 March, TF Tarawa attacked to seize and secure the eastern bridges across the Euphrates within the city of An Nasiriyah, in order to allow 1st MARDIV forces to utilize Hwy 7 as an avenue of approach into northern Iraq. This initiated the battle for An Nasiriyah, which unfolded over an eight-day period, during which TF Tarawa seized and secured the bridges and liberated the city.

On morning of 23 March, TF Tarawa attacked toward the bridges with Regimental Combat Team 2 (RCT-2) and 1st Battalion, 2d Marines (1/2) in the lead. 1/2 encountered resistance from enemy forces in civilian clothes armed with heavy machineguns, small arms, and mortars on the outskirts of An Nasiriyah. Attacking forward 1/2 encountered vehicles and personnel from an Army convoy of the 507th Maintenance Company of the 5-52 Air Defense Artillery Battalion. Securing the site around the Army vehicles, 1/2 recovered 14 soldiers of which four were wounded. After arranging CASEVAC for the wounded TF Tarawa discovered that these soldiers represented only part of a convoy that had mistakenly driven into An Nasiriyah the night previously and had been ambushed by enemy forces. Quickly 1/2 continued the attack into An Nasiriyah to attempt to rescue any remaining Army personnel and to secure the assigned bridges. Encountering stiff resistance from enemy forces occupying urban terrain, RCT-2 and TF Tarawa utilized supporting fires from air and artillery to advance and seize the southernmost of the two eastern bridges, in the process destroying eight enemy tanks and inflicting over 100 enemy dead. At this point RCT-2 moved 2d battalion 8th Marines (2/8) forward to secure the bridge seized by 1/2 and continued the assault with 1/2 toward the northernmost bridge. 1/2 seized the northern bridge utilizing tanks, assault amphibian vehicles (AAVs), and infantry along with supporting arms against significant resistance. Enemy forces conducted counterattacks, rushing from buildings to close with 1/2 vehicles to lob grenades and fire rocket-propelled grenades (RPGs). Several AAVs and a Tank Recovery vehicle were destroyed in this manner. RCT-2 maintained its hold on the bridges despite continued attacks.

On 24 March the fighting around the bridges continued as TF Tarawa cleared the enemy from the route through An Nasiriyah. Significant indirect fire was directed at TF Tarawa throughout the day and 1st Battalion, 10th Marines (1/10) conducted 14 separate counter-battery fire missions, which covered a 360-degree arc in and around the city.

On 25 March, TF Tarawa had secured the route across the bridges through the city and RCT-1 conducted a passage of lines along the route to continue the attack north along Highway 7. Additionally, RCT-7 and RCT-5 of the 1st MARDIV passed through TF Tarawa at the bridge over the Euphrates on Highway 1 in order to continue their advance north. TF Tarawa also began to expand its control of the city by attacking with 2/8 to seize an enemy strongpoint at the Tykar Hospital in eastern An Nasiriyah. Upon seizing the hospital, TF Tarawa discovered 3,000 NBC suits, large caches of weapons and ammunition, and evidence relating to the capture of members of the 507th Maintenance Company. Evidence obtained at the hospital confirmed that it was being used as an enemy strongpoint/command post in defiance of Geneva Convention restrictions. At the same time as 2/8 attacked in the east, 3/2 attacked in the west of the city to clear enemy opposition. Moving quickly 3/2 captured two busloads of enemy reinforcements approaching the city. Throughout the day TF Tarawa took over 500 enemy prisoners of war.

On 26 March, TF Tarawa continued operations to clear An Nasiriyah. Fighting house to house and utilizing supporting arms TF Tarawa expanded the area under its control within the city. Meanwhile enemy forces intent on counterattacking to regain the bridge sites gathered at a train station to the south of the city. The estimated strength was over 1,000 enemy fighters. ODA forces verified the enemy rally point at the station and TF Tarawa engaged with artillery to destroy and disperse the enemy. Later intelligence estimated 200 enemy dead in this engagement. Despite the effectiveness of the artillery fire, enemy forces conducted counterattacks against the TF throughout the night. Due to poor weather conditions air support was unavailable and TF Tarawa responded with organic assets against these attacks directed toward every sector. Throughout the night ground CASEVACs were organized from the TF HQ to evacuate friendly and enemy wounded.

On 27 and 28 March, TF Tarawa forces began to expand their control over An Nasiriyah, pushing forces east and west of the crossing sites and clearing out pockets of enemy resistance. An additional 100 EPW/detainees were captured. Using the intelligence from our ODA/OGA teams, TF Tarawa identified specific military targets that were being used by the paramilitary forces. Again using coalition air and PGMs, targets were struck with minimal or no damage to civilian structures. These surgical air strikes on military targets in the area further diminished the enemy's combat power and will to fight. Using members of Seal Team Six attached to TF Tarawa and based on intelligence gathered from our ODA teams, the city of Suk Ash Shuykah southeast of An Nasiriyah was identified as a marshalling place for enemy forces. Redirecting ISR assets, and using SEAL Team Six, TF Tarawa again directed precision air strikes against military targets in the city, resulting in numerous secondary explosions and unconfirmed reports of numerous enemy casualties, including some Ba'ath party leadership members.

As TF Tarawa continued its push to secure the city of An Nasiriyah, the ODA/OGA teams in support gained information from a local family that PFC Jessica Lynch, 507th Maintenance Co, was in the Saddam Hospital in eastern An Nasiriyah and had been severely injured in the initial ambush of the convoy. With the information deemed solid TF Tarawa began planning with TF-20 to conduct an operation to rescue PFC Lynch. Working together, TF-20 and TF Tarawa created a plan utilizing TF-20 forces to assault the hospital while TF Tarawa forces provided LZ control, counter sniper support, and supporting air and ground fire along with deception attacks by ground forces. In addition TF

Tarawa provided a reaction force to extract TF-20 should significant opposition be encountered. To control the operation TF-20 co-located their CP within TF Tarawa's Current Operations Center. The mission was executed on 1 Apr as planned and succeeded in recovering PFC Lynch alive along with the bodies of several missing members of the 507th. This was the first successful rescue of an American POW since WWII.

On 3 April, the big move to seize Baghdad began. TF Tarawa was immediately redirected to provide security along the major supply routes of Highway 1 and Highway 7 while maintaining forces to bring stability to An Nasiriyah. Augmented with forces from 15th MEU (SOC) and later 24th MEU (SOC), the area covered equaled that of the state of South Carolina. TF Tarawa's new zone covered a large area that included some cities and towns bypassed by previous coalition forces. In the western sector, in cities such as Ad Diwaydiah, enemy forces continued to operate and posed a threat to traffic on Highway 1. Making utmost use of its ODA assets, TF Tarawa identified enemy military targets in the city and struck them with precision munitions while cordoning off the city to reduce the threat. Al Hamsha, a city south of Ad Diwaydiah, was also targeted by TF Tarawa based on information gathered from ODA forces. The air strikes resulted in the death of the leading Ba'ath party official. The next day, the citizens who supported the U.S. attack against the Saddam regime took over the city. Along Highway 7, Marines from 24th MEU began clearing out several cities along the route that included Ash Shutra, An Nasr, Ar Rifa and Al Hayy. During a reconnaissance in force mission to Ash Shutra, 24 MEU (SOC) captured several Fedayeen soldiers and found the body of a Marine from 1st MARDIV who had been reported as missing in that area a week earlier. In the city of Suk Ash Shuykah, southwest of An Nasiriyah where earlier TF Tarawa had engaged enemy forces with precision air strikes, Marines from 15th MEU supported a direct action mission from SEAL Team Six with aviation assets and a Quick Reaction Force. The mission was successful in destroying numerous air defense pieces, and destroying several large cache sites. Throughout the area, TF Tarawa forces maintained secure supply lines. During the period from 3 April to 22 April, only three convoys reported being sniped at, and not one single convoy was ambushed, allowing important supplies to get through to support the attack on Baghdad.

With the main effort being the attack on Baghdad by both the V Corps and 1st MARDIV, the CFLCC commander became concerned with the threat represented by enemy forces still existing in the eastern portion of the country. The 10th Armored Division (10th AD) was known to be located in the vicinity of Al Amarah and had not been struck since the first days of the war. With all other major combat forces engaged in Baghdad the mission to eliminate the 10th AD fell to TF Tarawa. With no additional forces available, and having to retain its current missions and extensive battle space, TF Tarawa restructured its forces to accomplish the new mission. Consideration of the space involved and span of control required forced TF Tarawa to split its control capabilities for an extended period in order to accomplish all the missions assigned. On 8 April, as the forces assembled, TF Tarawa conducted coordinated coalition air strikes on the remaining elements of the 10th AD. Assessing these strikes and determining that the 10th AD was no longer a viable force, TF Tarawa elements moved quickly to seize key areas in the vicinity of the city. Gaining information that one of the air strikes had killed the commander of the 10th AD, and that Iraqis who supported the Coalition's war against the Saddam regime were rising up, TF Tarawa entered Al Amarah. This eliminated any possible threat to the eastern flank of the main attack on Baghdad.

With the success of the Al Amarah operation TF Tarawa was able to conduct a RIP with British forces on 12 April and return west. As TF Tarawa forces were relocating to Qalat Sikar following the Al Amarah operation, orders came down to attack and seize Al Kut to open up the Highway 7/Highway 6 route of supply.

Al Kut was reported to have from 500 to 2,000 enemy forces that included Fedayeen, militant Islamic terrorist groups, and remnants of Republican Guard forces. Working with ODA forces in direct support, and making extensive use of Force Reconnaissance assets, initial assessments were made concerning the city. Reports came back that Al Kut no longer had significant enemy forces present and that local resistance had control of the city. Consequently, TF Tarawa quickly moved on the city with the forces in hand and entered the city on the 12th of April. Assessing that no major threat remained in the area, coordination was quickly made and on 13 April the first convoy from 1st FSSG went through the city without incident.

After 13 April, TF Tarawa forces maintained security from An Nasiriyah along Highway 1 and Highway 7. Civil Affairs operations began in the major cities of An Nasiriyah, An Numaniyah, and Al Kut along with several other minor cities in the region. An Nasiriyah was declared a permissive environment for NGO support on 16 April, with Civil-Military Operations Centers (CMOCs) established at An Nasiriyah and Al Kut. TF Tarawa continued to conduct security operations in zone, which included Highway 6 from Al Kut to An Numaniyah.

During combat operations TF Tarawa was involved in some of the heaviest fighting in the war during the Battle of An Nasiriyah, taking 19 KIA and 57 WIA. These lives were not lost in vain. Through the sacrifices of TF Tarawa Marines the towns of An Nasiriyah, Al Amarah, and Al Kut were captured and secured. The maintaining of the main supply routes to support the V Corps and 1st MARDIV attacks on An Naraj, Karbala, Baghdad, and Tikrit was critical to their success. An estimated 2,000 plus enemy were killed in action from direct combat and air directed missions, an enormous amount of enemy tanks, artillery and air defense equipment was destroyed, as well as 700 EPWs taken. An enemy officer captured in An Nasiriyah stated that they were sure that if they put up a strong fight the U.S. soldiers would retreat. When, after repeated attacks, the Marines fought on, many of his soldiers lost their will to fight.

Although An Nasiriyah was the scene of some of the most difficult fighting throughout the war it was the first city to be declared by the UN as secured allowing the introduction of IO and NGOs. The UN declaration of the securing of An Nasiriyah is a testament to the abilities of TF Tarawa to excel in their performance of duty throughout the spectrum of warfare from all-out hostilities to civil affairs operations.

15th Marine Expeditionary Unit (Special Operations Capable)

On 16 February, 15th Marine Expeditionary Unit (Special Operations Capable)—15th MEU(SOC)—reported TACON to 3 UK Commando Brigade (3 Cdo Bde) of the British Royal Marines, commanded by Brigadier John Dutton. The Brigade Commander and selected subordinates and staffers from 3 Cdo Bde flew to the USS *Tarawa* to conduct working groups for Operation TELIC. Operation TELIC was the code name for coalition operations to seize the Al Faw Peninsula, its key Oil Infrastructure and the 15th MEU's subsequent attack to secure Umm Qasr port for Humanitarian Relief.

The 15th MEU(SOC), the supporting effort for the attack, attached Sierra Battery to 29 Commando for long-range prep fires for the main effort's attack; once released from that role, the battery returned to direct support of BLT 2/1. D Battery, 7 Royal Horse Artillery and 17/16 Battery, 3 Royal Horse Artillery fired in direct support of the 15th MEU's supporting attack on Umm Qasr. The BLT coordinated continuously to ensure maximum response for fires and counterfires from UK batteries.

Prior to crossing the line of departure, 15th MEU received TACON of Sensitive Site Exploitation Team (SST #2). SST #2 was a joint unit of soldiers, sailors, and airmen. They integrated with the 15th MEU S-3's E-NBCD Section. During the campaign, SST #2 and the MEU exploited 17 sensitive sites. Among the items recovered were evidence of war crimes against U.S. POWs, U.S. remains, and U.S. personal effects from POWs and casualties.

The Intelligence Section of the 15th MEU(SOC) Command Element integrated its Human Exploitation Team and Radio Bn detachment with those of the British forces. Combined US/UK teams uncovered information and provided actionable intelligence to missions in progress in Umm Qasr, facilitating the rapid opening of the port so that Humanitarian Assistance could flow into Iraq even as hostilities continued.

CTF 56, an EOD task force, also fell under control of the 15th MEU in Umm Qasr. Once the port was declared secured, 15th MEU(SOC) coordinated their efforts to rid the port of waterborne mines and UXO, enabling humanitarian shipping to arrive unimpeded into Iraq.

After just two days of fierce fighting the majority of Iraqi conventional forces in the Umm Qasr area were defeated, with the port facilities remaining intact to expedite follow-on Humanitarian Assistance efforts in theater. 15th MEU's BLT 2/1 defeated the 45th Bde of 11th ID, two platoons of 82mm mortars, four D-30 batteries, and a mechanized company in the first two days of fighting. The MEU took over 600 Iraqi POWs. Sporadic fighting against Saddam Fedayeen and other paramilitaries continued for three more days in the urban areas of Umm Qasr and Khor az Zubayhr against forces of up to company size.

While the MEU fought in Umm Qasr, a task-organized formation secured crossing points over the waterways connecting the mainland to the Al Faw Peninsula. This force of BLT recon and CAAT vehicles screened the flank of the Royal Marines on the peninsula, reducing bunkers overlooking the waterways and capturing Iraqi Army regulars.

Upon consolidating Khor az Zubayhr, a MEU convoy moved to link up with Task Force Tarawa, and transferred 200 EPWs from An Nasiriyah to HA Freddy—a trip of 320 km.

15th MEU(SOC) provided a security force to run a 200-vehicle convoy through An Nasiriyah to Qalat Sikar in support of 1st MARDIV. While enroute, the LAR company escorting the convoy encountered heavy resistance and defeated deliberate ambushes along Hwy 7. The convoy was delivered to Qalat Sikr with minimal losses to personnel and equipment.

The 15th MEU(SOC) then chopped to Task Force Tarawa. Reinforced with a NSWTU, ODA, OGA, 4th CAG, and a PSYOP det, the MEU relieved RCT-2 in place in An Nasiriyah. The MEU secured previously unoccupied areas of the city and quickly turned to assisting in the restoring city services, including health services, water distribution, police, and city government.

MEU forces coordinated a SEAL Direct Action mission in Suk Ash Shuyukh to destroy an anti-air weapons cache. Force Recon, a MEU QRF, and MEU aviation supported the raid, which destroyed the cache and associated facilities.

The 15th MEU contributed a supporting effort to a joint mission by TF-20 and TF Tarawa to recover U.S. Army POW PFC Jessica Lynch and the remains of other American soldiers previously listed as missing in action. During that action, the MEU's Maritime Special Purpose Force (MSPF), supported by BLT tanks and LAR, conducted a feint across the Euphrates River in order to allow

TF-20 to enter the Saddam General Hospital of Nasiriyah unhindered and accomplish their mission.

After the movement North of TF Tarawa the 15th MEU inherited over 2,400 square kilometers of terrain. MEU forces helped ensure the safety of convoys moving north in support of the MEF main effort. Not a single vehicle was lost transiting An Nasiriyah after 15th MEU(SOC) took over. The MEU eventually effected and maintained stability in the 13,400 square kilometers of Dhi Gar Province.

During stability operations, the MEU took tactical control of SeaBees from TF Echo, additional Psyop augments and coordinated the efforts of HA forces from the MEF and theater. MEU forces restored key infrastructure such as hospitals, courthouses, police stations, power, and water facilities and provided humanitarian assistance to orphanages and pediatric clinics.

Reachback Operations

Throughout Operation IRAQI FREEDOM (OIF) the Command Element of I MEF (REIN), supported by I MHG, and the Headquarters Elements of I MEF MSCs maintained and utilized an unprecedented level of reachback operations and capabilities, reducing the human and equipment footprints in theater and leveraging national, joint, and service assets and capabilities to the maximum extent possible, a complex process involving all staff sections and requiring constant interface between all command and control nodes.

I MEF G-2 integrated new, cutting-edge Intelligence, Surveillance, and Reconnaissance (ISR) technologies and resources never before leveraged in MEF-level operations, including P-3 Aerial Imagery Platform (AIP); Hunter Unmanned Aerial Vehicle (UAV); Predator UAV; Tactical Exploitation System; JSTARS; U-2; United Kingdom Tactical Signals Intelligence (SIGINT); and Critical Source (National Security Agency). Working in concert, the G-2 sections devised and implemented an integrated Coalition ISR Concept of Operations (CONOPS) for employment of UK-proprietary signals and imagery intelligence resources; and accomplished an unprecedented degree of ISR push-down to Regimental level, significantly enhancing the sensor-to-shooter process.

Working in concert from all disparate and widely separated nodes throughout OIF, I MEF G-1, G-3, G-4, and G-5 sections worked tirelessly, ensuring a constant flow of personnel, equipment, and all classes of supply when and as needed; ensuring accurate reporting at all levels; and ensuring accurate and timely Casualty Reporting, Evacuation, and Assistance. I MEF's Deployment Operations Team (DOT) provided direct coordination with deploying units, coordinating Time Phased Force Deployment Data (TPFDD) for 39,517 Marines and Sailors and 14,328 Short Tons of cargo and providing the massive amount of critical transportation data required by higher commands.

I MEF G-6 developed and maintained an unprecedented level of continuous and redundant communications between all command and control nodes, including reliance on Video Teleconferences (VTC) for vital and continuous communication between deployed force and I MEF Camp Pendleton. Noteworthy actions included preparation, submission, approval, and fielding of numerous Universal Need Statements (UNS) for critical communications equipment acquisition. Efforts resulted in acquisition of mission-essential equipment including: PRC-150 and 148 radios for reconnaissance units, ruggedized computers for FSSG CSS elements, Intel Analysis Workstations for I MEF G-2 and Intelligence Battalion, Tactical Data Network router upgrades, OS-302 SATCOM Antennas to allow for long-range voice and data communications for units on the move, and TQG-804A generators to increase power generation capabilities throughout the MEF.

Deployed forces at all levels benefited from extensive reachback capabilities established by I MEF and MSCs. I MEF Comptroller provided a specific example of the success of these efforts. Throughout OIF the I MEF Comptroller Section accomplished the complex and critical functions of Financial Management (FM) solely through reachback to I MEF Camp Pendleton, maintaining only a small cell forward. During the period mid-November 2002 through mid-July 2003 I MEF Comptroller Section executed and maintained accountability for approximately $750 million, 725 percent of a normal 12-month funding level.

Summary

The success of I Marine Expeditionary Force (REIN) in Operation Iraqi Freedom was a result of superb efforts on the part of all the Marines, Soldiers, and Sailors of I MEF at all levels, in all occupational fields, and in all of its diverse nodes, reflecting great credit upon each individual member, upholding the highest traditions of the United States Armed Forces.

Appendix B

Chronology of Events

2001

11 September   Al Qaeda terrorists attack the World Trade Center and the Pentagon.

25 November   Marines of Task Force 58 land in Afghanistan as part of the operation to deprive Al Qaeda of its base in that country.

2002

January   Marine Forces, Pacific orders I Marine Expeditionary Force (MEF) to focus on preparing for contingencies in the Cent-Com theater; MEF planners begin over a year of work on plans to invade Iraq.

2 August   Maj. Gen. James N. Mattis becomes Commanding General, 1st Marine Division, and puts the division on a virtual war footing.

11 October   The Pentagon orders I MEF to deploy its headquarters staff to Kuwait for service with Coalition Forces Land Component (CFLCC) under Army Lt. Gen. David D. McKiernan.

15 November   I MEF headquarters deploys to Kuwait; newly appointed I MEF commander Lt. Gen. James T. Conway deploys with his headquarters.

16 November   3d Marine Air Wing (MAW) forward command post, under the command of Maj. Gen. James F. Amos, arrives in Kuwait.

18 November	1st Marine Division forward command post arrives in Kuwait.
24 November	CFLCC exercise to test command and control links with MEF and other commands, "Lucky Warrior 03-1," begins.
9 December	CentCom exercise "Internal Look," based on the current version of the plan for the invasion of Iraq, begins.

2003

January	Intense preparations to integrate 1(United Kingdom) Armoured Division into the MEF occur; this division assumes responsibility for securing southeast Iraq.
2 January	Pentagon issues Deployment Order 177A, soon to be followed by 177B, which orders the wholesale deployment of MEF forces to theater.
6 January	Rehearsal of Concept (ROC) drill occurs at MAW in Miramar, California; many ROC drills at various levels follow in the coming weeks.
13 January	Gen. Michael W. Hagee becomes the 33d Commandant of the Marine Corps.
15 January	Amphibious Task Force (ATF) East departs Morehead City, North Carolina, for Kuwait with 2nd MEB onboard.
17 January	Amphibious Task Force (ATF) West departs San Diego, California, for Kuwait carrying elements of I MEF.
8 February	With MEF participation, CFLCC exercise "Lucky Warrior 03-2," labeled "a dress rehearsal" for war, begins.
16 February	2nd MEB begins to go ashore in Kuwait to reinforce I MEF; its aviation elements transfer to 3d MAW control and the ground elements are redesignated Task Force Tarawa.
24 February	ATF West begins offloading its West Coast Marine units in Kuwait; most other Marines follow by air.
9 March	First leaflets dropped in Baghdad urging noninterference with coalition operations and soliciting support from Iraqi people.

17 March	President Bush issues an ultimatum to Saddam Hussein to leave Iraq within forty-eight hours.
18 March	Operation Southern Watch aircraft conduct air strikes against Iraqi early warning radars and command-and-control capabilities; Marine forces are ordered to staging areas.
Night of 19–20 March	U.S. Air Force aircraft and Navy vessels conduct unplanned attack against Saddam Hussein and other Iraqi leadership targets in what becomes popularly known as the "decapitation strike." It does not succeed but does initiate hostilities.
20 March	Iraq retaliates by firing surface-to-surface missiles against coalition troops in Kuwait; ground combat operations begin in the night; MEF is supporting attack to Army's V Corps; Regimental Combat Team 5 is leading Marine unit.
21 March	Marines capture the Rumaylah oil fields, a key CentCom objective; Marines and British forces secure the port of Umm Qasr before moving on the city of Basrah, the most important British objective.
23 March	Task Force Tarawa begins to secure the city of An Nasiriyah and its key bridges over the Euphrates River and the Saddam Canal; heavy fighting ensues; friendly fire incident occurs at bridge over canal. II MEF commander Maj. Gen. Henry P. Osman deploys to northern Iraq to establish the Military Coordination and Liaison Command (MCLC) under operational control of CentCom in order to maintain political stability.
Night of 24–25 March	"Mother of all sandstorms" begins, slowing operations' tempo for approximately two days.
24–27 March	1st Marine Division continues to advance up Routes 1 and 7 toward Baghdad.
27 March	"Operational pause" begins to consolidate supply lines and address threats by irregular Iraqi formations on the ground; MAW air offensive continues unimpeded, rendering many Iraqi units combat ineffective.
1 April	Division resumes progress toward Baghdad; FSSG performs Herculean feats of resupply with cooperation of Wing and Marine Logistics Command.

3 April	U.S. Army troops move on Saddam International Airport, key terrain outside Baghdad.
5 April	U.S. Army conducts first "Thunder Run" armored raid, into Baghdad.
6 April	Most of Basrah, Iraq's "second city," is in British hands.
7 April	RCT 7 crosses the Diyala River and moves on outskirts of Baghdad from the east; Army conducts second "Thunder Run" into capital.
9 April	Marines of 3d Battalion, 4th Marine Regiment, part of RCT 7, assist Iraqi civilians in toppling a large statue of Saddam Hussein in Firdos Square in the Marine AO, Eastern Baghdad.
10 April	RCT 5 is engaged in heavy fighting at Al Azimiyah Palace and Abu Hanifah mosque in Baghdad; looting begins as fighting tapers off; Marines begin postcombat operations.
11–12 April	After the collapse of Iraqi authority in northern cities of Mosul and Kirkuk, Kurdish forces occupy the resulting power vacuum, followed by U.S. forces over succeeding days, including Marines from 26th MEU(SOC).
13–14 April	Task Force Tripoli, out of 1st Marine Division, takes control of Tikrit, Saddam Hussein's hometown.
20 April	The relief in place with U.S. Army in Eastern Baghdad is complete; MEF redeploys its forces to the southern third of Iraq; the mission is now security, humanitarian assistance, and reconstruction; focus of effort is seven infantry battalions from 1st Marine Division in seven governates (or districts).
22 April	24th MEU(SOC), which had supported TF Tarawa, begins redeploying to its ships; other Marine units soon follow suit as part of draw-down to reduced manning levels that are maintained through the summer.
1 May	Under a banner reading "Mission Accomplished," President Bush announces that major combat operations are over; 26th MEU(SOC) departs Mosul and returns to its ships in the Mediterranean.

12 May   Ambassador L. Paul Bremer takes over as civil administrator in Iraq, replacing Jay M. Garner; Bremer's Coalition Provisional Authority soon replaces Garner's Office of Reconstruction and Humanitarian Assistance.

22 July   Saddam Hussein's sons, Uday and Qusay, are killed in a firefight with U.S. Army in Mosul.

19 August   A truck bomb explodes at the UN headquarters in Baghdad, killing twenty people, including the UN High Commissioner for Human Rights.

3 September   In Babylon, MEF conducts a transfer of authority to a Polish-led international coalition force; most remaining Marines return to CONUS.

10 November   Marines of Special Purpose MAGTF celebrate the Marine Corps birthday in CONUS after completing the work of repatriating all Marine Corps equipment from theater.

This chronology reflects the work of Capt. Christopher M. Kennedy and interns assigned to the Historical Division, who contributed many of these entries.

Appendix C

Troop List: USMarCent in Operation Iraqi Freedom, March–November 2003

U.S. Marine Corps, Central Command (USMarCent)

Command Element

Combined/Joint Task Force–Consequence Management

Marine Logistics Command

Special Purpose MAGTF

I Marine Expeditionary Force (Rein)

A. Command Element

15th Marine Expeditionary Unit (SOC)
Command Element
Battalion Landing Team 2d Battalion, 1st Marines
Marine Medium Helicopter Squadron-161 (Rein)
Marine Expeditionary Unit Service Support Group-15

24th Marine Expeditionary Unit (SOC)
Command Element
Battalion Landing Team 2d Battalion, 2d Marines
Marine Medium Helicopter Squadron-263 (Rein)
Marine Expeditionary Unit Service Support Group-24

Task Force Yankee
11th Marine Expeditionary Unit, Command Element (-)
  2d Battalion, 6th Marines (-) (Rein)
  Sensitive Site Team #3, U.S. Army
  75th Exploitation Task Force, U.S. Army
  Company C, 478th Engineer Battalion, U.S. Army

I Marine Expeditionary Force Headquarters Group
6th Communications Battalion (-)
9th Communications Battalion (-)
1st Radio Battalion (-)(Rein)
1st Intelligence Battalion (-)(Rein)
1st Force Reconnaissance Company (-)(Rein)
I Marine Expeditionary Force Liaison Element
3d Air Naval Gunfire Liaison Company
4th Air Naval Gunfire Liaison Company
3d Civil Affairs Group
4th Civil Affairs Group

B. Marine Ground Combat Element

1st Marine Division (Rein)
Headquarters Battalion
1st Marine Regiment (-)(Rein) (Regimental Combat Team 1)
  Headquarters Company
  3d Battalion, 1st Marines
  1st Battalion, 4th Marines
  2d Battalion, 23d Marines
  2d Light Armored Reconnaissance Battalion (-)
5th Marine Regiment (-)(Rein) (Regimental Combat Team 5)
  Headquarters Company
  1st Battalion, 5th Marines
  2d Battalion, 5th Marines
  3d Battalion, 5th Marines
  2d Tank Battalion (-)(Rein)
  1st Light Armored Reconnaissance Battalion (-)
  Company C, 4th Combat Engineer Battalion
7th Marine Regiment (-)(Rein) (Regimental Combat Team 7)
  Headquarters Company
  1st Battalion, 7th Marines

3d Battalion, 7th Marines
3d Battalion, 4th Marines
1st Tank Battalion (-)(Rein)
3d Light Armored Reconnaissance Bn(-)(Rein)
11th Marine Regiment (-)(Rein)
  Headquarters Battery (-)
  Detachment Headquarters Battery, 10th Marine Regiment
  1st Battalion, 11th Marines (-)
  2d Battalion, 11th Marines (-)
  3d Battalion, 11th Marines (-)
  5th Battalion, 11th Marines (-)
1st Combat Engineer Battalion (-)(Rein)
2d Combat Engineer Battalion (-)(Rein)
1st Reconnaissance Battalion (-)(Rein)
2d Assault Amphibian Battalion (-)(Rein)
3d Assault Amphibian Battalion (-)(Rein)
4th Assault Amphibian Battalion
2d Radio Battalion
Military Police Company, 4th Marine Division
Communications Company, 4th Marine Division
Battery I, 3d Battalion, 10th Marines
Battery R, 5th Battalion, 10th Marines

2d Marine Expeditionary Brigade (*Task Force Tarawa*)
Command Element
  Det, II Marine Expeditionary Force Headquarters Group
  II Marine Expeditionary Force Liaison Element
  Company C, 4th Reconnaissance Battalion
  2d Battalion, 6th Marines (Originally with TF Yankee)
  2d Force Reconnaissance Company
  2d Intelligence Battalion (-)
2d Marine Regiment (-)(Rein) (Regimental Combat Team 2)
  Headquarters Company
  1st Battalion, 2d Marines
  3d Battalion, 2d Marines
  2d Battalion, 8th Marines
  1st Battalion, 10th Marines
    Battery F, 2d Battalion, 10th Marines
  Company A, 2d Combat Engineer Battalion
  Company A, 8th Tank Battalion

Company C, 2d Light Armored Reconnaissance Battalion
Company A, 2d Assault Amphibious Battalion
Company A, 2d Reconnaissance Battalion (Rein)

C. Marine Aviation Combat Element/3d Marine Aircraft Wing
Marine Wing Headquarters Squadron-3
Detachment, Marine Wing Headquarters Squadron-2

Marine Aircraft Group-11 (-)(Rein)
Marine Aviation Logistics Squadron-11 (-)(Rein)
Marine Aviation Logistics Squadron-14 (-)
    Detachment, Marine Aviation Logistics Squadron-31
Marine Aerial Refueler Transport Squadron-352 (-) (Rein)
    Det, Marine Aerial Refueler Transport Squadron-234
    Det, Marine Aerial Refueler Transport Squadron-452
Marine Fighter Attack Squadron-232
Marine Fighter Attack Squadron-251
Marine Fighter Attack Squadron (All Weather)-121
Marine Fighter Attack Squadron (All Weather)-225
Marine Fighter Attack Squadron (All Weather)-533
Marine Tactical Electronic Warfare Squadron-1
Marine Tactical Electronic Warfare Squadron-2

Marine Aircraft Group-13 (-)(Rein)
Marine Aviation Logistics Squadron-13 (-)
Marine Attack Squadron-211 (-)
Marine Attack Squadron-214
Marine Attack Squadron-223 (-)
Marine Attack Squadron-311
Marine Attack Squadron-542

Marine Aircraft Group-16 (-)(Rein)
Marine Aviation Logistics Squadron-16 (-)
Det, Marine Aviation Logistics Squadron-26
Marine Medium Helicopter Squadron-165
Marine Heavy Helicopter Squadron-462
Marine Heavy Helicopter Squadron-465

Marine Aircraft Group-29 (-)(Rein)
Marine Aviation Logistics Squadron-29 (-)
Marine Medium Helicopter Squadron-162

Marine Medium Helicopter Squadron-365 (-)
Marine Heavy Helicopter Squadron-464
Marine Light Attack Helicopter Squadron-269

Marine Wing Support Group-37 (-)(*Rein*)
Marine Wing Support Squadron-271
Marine Wing Support Squadron-272
Marine Wing Support Squadron-371
Marine Wing Support Squadron-372
Marine Wing Support Squadron-373
Company C,`1st Battalion, 24th Marines
4th Marine Air Wing, Military Police Detachment

Marine Air Control Group-38 (-)(*Rein*)
Marine Tactical Air Control Squadron-2, ATC Detachment B
Marine Air Control Squadron-1 (Rein)
Det, Marine Air Control Squadron-2
Marine Wing Communications Squadron-28 (-)
Marine Wing Communications Squadron-38 (Rein)
Marine Tactical Air Control Squadron-28 Detachment
Marine Tactical Air Control Squadron-38 (Rein)
Marine Tactical Air Control Squadron-48 Detachment
Marine Air Support Squadron-1
Marine Air Support Squadron-3 (Rein)
    Battery B, 2d Low Altitude Air Defense Battalion
    3d Low Altitude Air Defense Battalion
Marine Air Support Squadron-6 Detachments (CA and MA)
Marine Unmanned Aerial Vehicle Squadron-1
Marine Unmanned Aerial Vehicle Squadron-2

Marine Aircraft Group-39 (-)(*Rein*)
Marine Aviation Logistics Squadron-39 (-)
Marine Light Attack Helicopter Squadron-169
Marine Light Attack Helicopter Squadron-267
Marine Medium Helicopter Squadron-268
Marine Medium Helicopter Squadron-364
Marine Light Attack Helicopter Squadron-369

Atlantic Ordnance, Command Expeditionary Force

C-12 Det, Headquarters & Headquarters Squadron, MCAS, Miramar, CA

D. Marine Combat Service Support Element/1st Force Service Support Group

Detachment, Headquarters and Service Battalion*

Combat Service Support Group 11 (BSSG-1)
Headquarters
Combat Service Support Battalion 10 (CSSG-1)
Combat Service Support Company 111
Combat Service Support Company 115
Combat Service Support Company 117

Combat Service Support Group 13 (4th Landing Support Battalion)
Headquarters, 4th Landing Support Battalion
Combat Service Support Company 133
Combat Service Support Company 134
Combat Service Support Company 135

Combat Service Support Group 14 (4th Supply Battalion)
4th Supply Battalion (-)

Combat Service Support Group 15 (1st Supply Battalion)
1st Supply Battalion (-)
Combat Service Support Battalion 12 (1st Maintenance Battalion)
Combat Service Support Battalion 18 (H&S Bn, 1st FSSG)
Combat Service Support Battalion 22
Combat Service Support Company 151

Transportation Support Group
1st Transportation Support Battalion (-)
6th Motor Transport Battalion

7th Engineer Support Battalion (-)(Rein)

6th Engineer Support Battalion (-)(Rein)

---

*FSSG headquarters elements were reorganized into Combat Service Support Group 16 in April 2003.

8th Engineer Support Battalion (-)(Rein)

Communications Company, Headquarters and Service Battalion, 4th Force Service Support Group

Mortuary Affairs Company, Headquarters and Service Battalion, 4th Force Service Support Group

Military Police Company A, Headquarters and Service Battalion, 4th Force Service Support Group

Military Police Company B, Headquarters and Service Battalion, 4th Force Service Support Group

Military Police Company C, Headquarters and Service Battalion, 4th Force Service Support Group

Combat Service Support Battalion-16 (Combat Service Support Detachment-16)

Combat Service Support Battalion-19 (Marine Expeditionary Service Support Group-11)

1st Dental Battalion (-)

Fleet Hospital Three (FH-3)

Fleet Hospital Fifteen (FH-15)

PM-MMART-5 (Preventive Medicine Unit), Navy Environmental Health Center

PM-MMART-2 (Preventive Medicine Unit), Navy Environmental Health Center

Health Services Battalion (1st Medical Battalion)
    Company A
    Company B
    Company C

Company E
Company F

E. I Marine Expeditionary Force Engineer Group

Command Element

30th Naval Construction Regiment
Naval Mobile Construction Battalion 5
Naval Mobile Construction Battalion 7
Naval Mobile Construction Battalion 74
Naval Mobile Construction Battalion 133
Naval Mobile Construction Battalion 4
Naval Construction Force Support Unit 2 (-)
Underwater Construction Team 2 Air Detachment

22d Naval Construction Regiment

Naval Mobile Construction Battalion 15 Air Detachment

Naval Mobile Construction Battalion 21 Air Detachment

Naval Mobile Construction Battalion 25 Air Detachment

Construction Battalion Maintenance Unit 303 Detachment

F. 1 (UK) Armoured Division (-)(Rein)

7 Armored Brigade (British Army)
1st Battalion, The Black Watch
1st Battalion, The Royal Regiment of Fusiliers
The Royal Scots Dragoon Guards
2d Royal Tank Regiment
3d Regiment, Royal Horse Artillery
32 Engineer Regiment

16 Air Assault Brigade (British Army)
1st Battalion, The Parachute Regiment
3d Battalion, The Parachute Regiment

1st Battalion, The Royal Irish Regiment
7th Parachute Regiment, Royal Horse Artillery

3 Commando Brigade (-) (*Royal Marines*)
40 Commando Group
42 Commando Group
29 Commando Regiment, Royal Artillery

G. Reinforcing U.S. Army Units
Detachment, 9th Psychological Operations Battalion
354th Public Affairs Detachment
Det, Headquarters & Headquarters Command, 468th Chemical Battalion
U.S. Army Space Support Team
86th Signal Battalion
208th Signal Company
Company C, 40th Signal Battalion
3d Battalion, 27th Field Artillery
1st Field Artillery Detachment
498th Medical Company
H&H Battery, 108th Air Defense Artillery Brigade
2nd Battalion, 43rd Air Defense Artillery
3d Battalion, 124th Infantry
555th Maintenance Company
Det, Headquarters and Headquarters Company, 378th Support Battalion
777th Maintenance Company
727th Transportation Company
319th Transportation Company
319th Transportation Detachment
299th Engineer Company
459th Engineer Company
Det, Headquarters and Headquarters Co., 716th Military Police Battalion
Headquarters and Headquarters Company, 265th Engineer Group
130th Engineer Battalion
478th Engineer Battalion
Headquarters and Headquarters Company, 358th Civil Affairs Brigade
304th Civil Affairs Brigade
402d Civil Affairs Brigade
432d Civil Affairs Battalion
367th Mobile Public Affairs Detachment

305th Tactical Psychological Operations Company
307th Tactical Psychological Operations Company
312th Tactical Psychological Operations Company
1092d Engineer Battalion (Wheel)

H. Marine Follow-on Forces

3d Battalion, 23d Marines
4th Combat Engineer Battalion (-)
4th Light Armored Reconnaissance Battalion (-)
2d Battalion 25th Marines
Truck Co., 4th Marine Division

Sources for this appendix are: MarAdmin 507/03, various versions, October–December 2003, with CG, I MEF, "Modifications to the I MEF Presidential Unit Citation Unit Listing" (date illegible), with additions/corrections by Annette Amerman, Historian, Reference Section, HD. 9/04. 1st FSSG was reorganized shortly before deployment; previous unit designations are shown in parentheses after the unit's designation in OIF.

Appendix D

*Command List: USMarCent in Operation Iraqi Freedom, March–November 2003**

U.S. Marine Corps, Central Command (USMarCent)

  Commanding General: Lt. Gen. Earl B. Hailston
    Chief of Staff: Col. Peter Miller
    G-1: Col. Richard B. Harris
    G-2: Col. William E. Rizzio
    G-3: Col. Timothy C. Wells
    G-4: Col. Philip N. Yff
    G-5: Col. Timothy L. Hunter
    G-6: Col. Kevin B. Jordan
    SJA: Lt. Col. Robert E. Pinder
    Comptroller: Col. Robert J. Herkenham

  Combined/Joint Task Force–Consequence Management
    Commanding General: Brig. Gen. Cornell A. Wilson, USMCR

---

*Includes billets in units that served in theater for part but not all of the period covered. Basic sources are MarAdmin 507/03, various versions, October–December 2003, with CG, I MEF, "Modifications to the I MEF Presidential Unit Citation Unit Listing" (date illegible), with additions/corrections, and Command Chronologies. The FSSG was reorganized shortly before deployment, making it difficult to track organizational data. For additional detail on units, consult appended Troop List.

Marine Logistics Command
  Commanding General: Brig. Gen. Michael R. Lehnert

Special Purpose MAGTF
  Commanding General: Brig. Gen. Ronald S. Coleman

I Marine Expeditionary Force (Rein)

A. Command Element
  Commanding General: Lt. Gen. James T. Conway
  Deputy: Maj. Gen. Keith J. Stalder

    Chief of Staff: Col. John C. Coleman
    G-1: Col. William J. Hartig
    G-2: Col. Alan R. Baldwin (to July)
       Col. James R. Howcroft (from July)
    G-3: Col. Larry K. Brown
    G-4: Col. Matthew W. Blackledge
    G-5: Col. Christopher J. Gunther (to summer)
       Col. Anthony L. Jackson (from summer)
    G-6: Col. George J. Allen (to 15 June)
       Col. Marshall I. Considine (after 30 June)
    SJA: Col. William D. Durrett
    Surgeon: Capt. Joel A. Lees, USN
    Chaplain: Capt. John S. Gwudz, USN
    I MEF Headquarters Group: Col. John T. Cunnings

    15th Marine Expeditionary Unit (SOC)
      Commanding Officer: Col. Thomas D. Waldhauser

    24th Marine Expeditionary Unit (SOC)
      Commanding Officer: Col. Richard P. Mills (to 6 June)
         Col. Ronald J. Johnson (after 6 June)

    11th Marine Expeditionary Unit, Command Element (-)
      Commanding Officer: Col. Anthony M. Haslam

B. Marine Ground Combat Element
  1. 1st Marine Division (Rein)
     Commanding General: Maj. Gen. James N. Mattis

Assistant Division Commander: Brig. Gen. John F. Kelly
Chief of Staff: Col. Bennett W. Saylor (to late spring)
   Col. Joseph F. Dunford (from late spring)

1st Marine Regiment (-)(Rein) (Regimental Combat Team 1)
   Commanding Officer: Col. Joseph D. Dowdy (to 4 April)
      Col. John A. Toolan (after 4 April)

5th Marine Regiment (-)(Rein) (Regimental Combat Team 5)
   Commanding Officer: Col. Joseph F. Dunford (to 23 May)

7th Marine Regiment (-)(Rein) (Regimental Combat Team 7)
   Commanding Officer: Col. Steven A. Hummer

11th Marine Regiment (-)(Rein)
   Commanding Officer: Col. Michael P. Marletto

2. 2d Marine Expeditionary Brigade (Task Force Tarawa)
   Commanding General: Brig. Gen. Richard F. Natonski
   Chief of Staff: Col. James Smoots

2d Marine Regiment (-)(Rein) (Regimental Combat Team 2)
   Commanding Officer: Col. Ronald L. Bailey

C. Marine Aviation Combat Element/3d Marine Aircraft Wing
Commanding General: Maj. Gen. James F. Amos
Assistant Wing Commander: Brig. Gen. Terry G. Robling
Chief of Staff: Col. Gerald A. Yingling Jr.

Marine Aircraft Group-11 (-)(Rein)
   Commanding Officer: Col. Randolph D. Alles

Marine Aircraft Group-13 (-)(Rein)
   Commanding Officer: Col. Mark R. Saverese

Marine Aircraft Group-16 (-)(Rein)
   Commanding Officer: Col. Stuart L. Knoll

Marine Aircraft Group-29 (-)(Rein)
   Commanding Officer: Col. Robert E. Milstead Jr.

Marine Wing Support Group-37 (-)(Rein)
    Commanding Officer: Col. Michael C. Anderson

Marine Air Control Group-38 (-)(Rein)
    Commanding Officer: Col. Ronnell R. McFarland

Marine Aircraft Group-39 (-)(Rein)
    Commanding Officer: Col. Richard W. Spender (to 5 June)
    Col. Kenneth P. Gardiner (after 5 June)

D. Marine Combat Service Support Element/ 1st Force Service Support Group
Commanding General: Brig. Gen. Edward G. Usher III (to 10 July)
    Brig. Gen. Richard S. Kramlich (from 10 July)
Deputy Commander: Col. John L. Sweeney
Chief of Staff: Col. Darrell L. Moore

Combat Service Support Group 16 (Headquarters Elements)
    Commanding Officer: Lt. Col. Michael J. Taylor

Combat Service Support Group 11 (BSSG-1)
    Commanding Officer: Col. John J. Pomfret (to summer)
    Col. Charles L. Hudson (from summer)

Combat Service Support Battalion 13 (4th Landing Support Battalion)
    Commanding Officer: Lt. Col. Michael D. Malone

Combat Service Support Group 14 (4th Supply Battalion)
    Commanding Officer: Col. John T. Larson

Combat Service Support Group 15 (1st Supply Battalion)
    Commanding Officer: Col. Bruce E. Bissett

Transportation Support Group
    Commanding Officer: Col. David G. Reist

E. I Marine Expeditionary Force Engineer Group
Commanding Officer: Rear Adm. (UH) Charles R. Kubic, USN

F. 1 (UK) *Armoured Division* (-)(*Rein*)
Commanding General: Maj. Gen. Robin V. Brims
Chief of Staff: Col. Patrick C. Marriott

7 Armored Brigade (British Army)
Commanding Officer: Brig. Graham J. Binns

16 Air Assault Brigade (British Army)
Commanding Officer: Brig. Jacko Page

3 Commando Brigade (-) (Royal Marines)
Commanding Officer: Brig. Jim Dutton

Appendix E

Abbreviations and Other Terms

AAV: assault amphibious vehicle

ACE: aviation combat element (usually of a MAGTF)

A-Day: the day the main CFACC air attack was to begin

ANGLICO: air-naval gunfire liaison company (an especially useful element for coordinating joint and combined operations, reintroduced into the Marine Corps under the commandancy of General J. L. Jones Jr.)

Aps/Pas: attack positions/position areas

AO: area of operations

AOR: area of responsibility

ArCent: U.S. Army Forces, Central Command

ARG: amphibious ready group (of U.S. Navy ships, typically loaded with a MAGTF)

ASE: aviation support element

ATF: amphibious task force

ATLASS: asset tracking logistics and supply system (used by FSSG)

ATO: air tasking order (the "plan of the day" for CFACC, the master daily air scheduling document created by CFACC)

BCT: brigade combat team, a U.S. Army designation

BFT: Blue Force Tracker (a satellite system that allows commanders to see the locations of friendly units on a computer screen)

BUA: battle update assessment, term used by CFLCC for its main daily wartime brief

CAAT: combined antiarmor team (found in Marine infantry battalions)

CAP: combat air patrol

CAS: close air support

CAX: combined arms exercise (usually live fire, integrating infantry, artillery, and air)

CE: command element

CentAF: U.S. Air Forces, Central Command

CentCom: U.S. Central Command, the joint (and sometimes combined) command responsible for the Middle East, headed by the combatant commander (formerly known as a regional commander in chief)

CFACC: Coalition Forces Air Component Commander, a functional command under the combatant commander

CFLCC: Coalition Forces Land Component Command, a functional command under the combatant commander

CFMCC: Coalition Forces Maritime Component Command, a functional command under the combatant commander

CG: Commanding General

Civil Affairs: military interface with civilian organizations during/after military operations

CJTF: Commander, Joint Task Force or Combined/Joint Task Force

C/JTF-CM: Combined/Joint Task Force–Consequence Management

CMO: civil-military operations

CNA: Center for Naval Analyses, a naval think tank

ComUSMarCent: Commander, Marine Corps Forces, Central Command, the Marine service component command under the combatant commander in the CentCom AOR

ComUSNavCent: Commander, U.S. Naval Forces, Central Command, the Navy service component commander under the combatant commander in the CentCom AOR

CONUS: continental United States

CP: command post

CSSE: combat service support element (usually of a MAGTF)

CTF-58: Commander, Task Force 58, a designation used in Operation Enduring Freedom

DASC: direct air support center

DS/DS: Desert Shield/Desert Storm

EAF: expeditionary air field

EFCAT: Enduring Freedom Combat Assessment Team, later Expeditionary Forces Combat Assessment Team

EPW: enemy prisoner of war

EuCom: U.S. European Command

Expeditionary Maneuver Warfare: official USMC doctrine for warfighting

FAC(A): Forward Air Controller (Airborne)

FARP: forward arming and replenishment point

Fedayeen: Arabic word meaning "men of sacrifice"; in OIF referring to irregular fighters for Saddam Hussein

FPOL: forward passage of lines, which occurs when one unit passes through another, distinct from a RIP, or relief in place (see below)

FOB: forward operating base

FRSS: forward resuscitative surgery system

FSSG: force service support group

Functional Component Commander: joint commander of forces from two or more military departments, usually of a similar type (e.g., land, air, or sea), for a specific operation or period of time

GCE: Ground Combat Element (usually of a MAGTF)

G-Day: ground day (the day the ground attack was to begin)

GOSP: gas and oil separation plant

HET: human intelligence exploitation team

Hot Refueling: to refuel an aircraft with the engines still running

HQMC: Headquarters Marine Corps

Humint: human intelligence (intelligence from a human source)

HumVee: high-mobility, multipurpose, wheeled vehicle (the jeep of this war)

IL: "Internal Look," a CentCom exercise

IMA: individual mobilization augmentee (a USMCR category)

IO: information operations (action taken to affect enemy information systems or perceptions, related to PsyOps; sometimes used to refer to operations against enemy computer systems)

IOs/NGOs: international organizations/nongovernmental organizations

IPB: intelligence preparation of the battlefield (collecting and analyzing data about a future battlefield)

IRR: individual ready reserve (a USMCR category)

IVO: "in the vicinity of"

IZ: Iraq or Iraqi

JDAM: joint direct attack munition (a type of precision ordinance, delivered by air)

JSOTF: Joint Special Operations Task Force

JSTARS: Joint Surveillance Target Attack Radar System

Kill box: a geographical zone, typically square or rectangular, used by the Air Force to direct sorties against targets. Iraq was divided into kill boxes, which were said to be "open" or "closed."

LAR: light armored reconnaissance

LAV: light armored vehicle

LNO: liaison officer

LOC: line(s) of communication (as in, supply lines)

LOO: lines of operation (as in "multiple lines of operation," officially defined as "lines which . . . connect the force with its base of operations and its objectives"); in OIF, expanded to refer to synchronized operational initiatives.

LRPE: long-range planning element

LSA: life support area

LZ: landing zone

MACCS: Marine Air Command and Control System

MAGTF: Marine Air-Ground Task Force (the basic organization for committing Marines to combat, with command, air, ground, and support elements)

MANPADS: man-portable air defense system (antiaircraft rockets)

MarCent: Marine Corps Forces Central Command

MarForEur: Marine Forces Europe

MarForPac: Marine Forces Pacific

MAW: Marine Air Wing (rough equivalent of a ground division in size)

MCCDC: Marine Corps Combat Development Command

MCLC: Military Coordination and Liaison Command (in northern Iraq in March and April 2003)

MCLLS: Marine Corps Lessons Learned System

MEB: Marine Expeditionary Brigade (a detachable part of the MEF)

MEF: Marine Expeditionary Force (a corps-level MAGTF)

MEU(SOC):   Marine Expeditionary Unit (Special Operations Capable), a small MAGTF built around a battalion landing team

MLC: Marine Logistics Command (a theater-level component subordinate to MarCent)

MOPP: Mission-Oriented Protective Posture (a state of readiness with respect to the threat of an NBC attack; levels run from 0 to IV and correspond to the amount of protective clothing, boots, and mask worn)

MPF:	Maritime Prepositioning Force (made up of MPS)
MPS:	Maritime Prepositioning Ships (staged in strategic locations, carrying equipment for use in wartime contingencies)
MRE:	meals ready-to-eat
MSC:	Major Subordinate Command (Division, Wing, and FSSG are MSCs of a MEF)
MSR:	main supply route
NavCent:	Naval Forces, Central Command
NBC:	nuclear, biological, chemical (as in the "threat of an NBC attack" or "NBC protective gear")
NIPRNET:	non-secure Internet Protocol Router Network (the U.S. military's unclassified e-mail system)
NSA:	naval support activity (as in NSA Bahrain, a small naval base)
OEF:	Operation Enduring Freedom
OGA:	other government agencies
OIF:	Operation Iraqi Freedom
OODA Loop:	A theory propounded by Air Force Col. John Boyd and embraced by many Marines. "OODA" stands for the sequence of "observation, orientation, decision, action." Boyd's argument was that the warrior (originally the fighter pilot) who can go through the "loop"—the four steps—faster will win.
OpCon:	operational control; command authority that is inherent in combatant command authority (which is exercised by the combatant commander) and may be delegated. It is the authority to perform functions of organizing and employing subordinate commands. Compare with TaCon.
OPlan:	operation plan
OpOrd:	operation order
OpSec:	operational security, protecting information about status/ plans of force
OPT:	operational planning team (term used for an ad hoc planning group, also seen as OPG)

ORHA: Office for Reconstruction and Humanitarian Assistance, created by the Pentagon in early 2003 to oversee the immediate postwar period in Iraq

PGM: Precision Guided Munition, or "smart bomb"

Prep Fires: short-term "shaping," as in to prepare an objective for attack

Psyops: psychological operations

R2P2:   Rapid Response Planning Program

RCT: Regimental Combat Team

RFF: request for forces

RIP: relief in place (when one unit replaces another in a given area)

ROE: rules of engagement

RPG: rocket-propelled grenade

RRPs: repair and replenishment points

RSOI: reception, staging, onward movement, integration (the phases that units pass through upon reaching a combat theater between disembarking from a ship or airplane and being integrated into combat units)

SA: situation(al) awareness, as in "to have SA" or to "spin up SA," meaning to know what is going on

SacEur: Supreme Allied Commander, Europe

SATCOM: satellite communications

SAW: School of Advanced Warfighting, part of Marine Corps University; also Squad Automatic Weapon

SeaBee: Navy engineer, from "CB," or "Construction Battalion"

SEAL: Sea-Air-Land (Team), Navy special forces

SERT: SeaBee Engineer Reconnaissance Team

Shape: to prepare, as in "to shape a battlefield or enemy unit," usually through air strikes and before a ground attack

SIPRnet: Secret Internet Protocol Router Network (the secure military Internet system)

SJA: Staff Judge Advocate

Slingshot: code word for "We are being overrun."

SMCR: Selected Marine Corps Reserve (the drilling Reserves, usually organized into units)

SoCom: Special Operations Command

SOF: Special Operations Forces

SSE: Sensitive Site Exploitation; in Iraq, a word used for searching for WMD (see below)

STOM: Ship to Objective Maneuver (Marine Corps doctrine for deep operations, a subset of Expeditionary Maneuver Warfare)

Synchronization: The process of coordinating and focusing forces and activities in time and space to produce maximum effect on the enemy at a given point.

TaCon: Tactical Control (detailed and local control of units, inherent in OpCon but may be delegated)

TF: Task Force

TPFDD: Time Phased Force and Deployment Data

TPFDL: Time Phased Force and Deployment List

TransCom: U.S. Transportation Command (responsible for military transportation)

TSC: Theater Support Command

UAV: unmanned aerial vehicle

UCAX: urban combined arms exercise

USCINCCENT: U.S. Commander in Chief, Central Command; the title used for the CentCom commander before Secretary Rumsfeld took office

VTC: video teleconference

WMD: weapons of mass destruction (nuclear, chemical, or biological weapons)

Notes

Chapter 1

1. Col. John A. Tempone, e-mail to author, 16 Jan. 2004 (Reynolds Working Papers, Marine Corps Historical Center [MCHC], Washington, D.C.).
2. See, for example, Jay E. Hines, "Operation Enduring Freedom," *21st Century Defense: U.S. Joint Command* (Clearwater, Fla.: Belmont International, 2002), pp. 38–46. This is an excellent overview of the operation from the CentCom point of view by that command's historian.
3. For a discussion of the historical context, see Williamson Murray and Maj. Gen. Robert H. Scales Jr., *The Iraq War* (Cambridge, Mass.: Harvard UP, 2003), pp. 48–59.
4. Interview with Brig. Gen. Christian B. Cowdrey, 26 April 2003 (MCHC, Washington, D.C.). A draft of "The Informal History of MarCent" states: "as operations developed, ComUSMarCent was tasked by the Secretary of Defense, and the chairman [of the] Joint Chiefs of Staff and Commander, Central Command to: (1) establish . . . C/JTF-CM [and] (2) support coalition . . . [forces] with two Marine MEUs under the command of a Marine General Officer . . . [while] deploying MarCent headquarters to Bahrain" (Copy in Reynolds Working Papers, MCHC, Washington, D.C.). For a snapshot of Marine operations on and after September 11, see U.S. Marine Corps, *Operation Enduring Freedom Combat Assessment Team Summary Report* (Quantico, Va.: Marine Corps Combat Development Command, 2003), pp. 47–50, hereafter MCCDC, *OEF Summary Report.* This report, by Marines assigned to MCCDC's Studies and Analysis Division, is a very useful all-around source, as are the thousands of documents and interviews that they collected.
5. Interview with Gen. James L. Jones Jr., 14 June 2004 (MCHC, Washington, D.C.). General Jones contrasted the utility of a MEB with that of a MEF-Forward, which he saw as less useful in the joint/combined arena. The MEB has a checkered history. It was coming back into favor in the early part of the twenty-first century. See, for example, interview with Gen. Anthony C. Zinni, 7 Jan. 2004 (MCHC, Washington, D.C.). Zinni describes the continuing struggle between the "MEFers," who believe that the Marine Corps should focus its energies at the MEF level, and the "MEBers," who believe the same of the MEB.
6. There are numerous sources on the history of C/JTF-CM. The Cowdrey interview is a good firsthand description of the first few months of its existence. C/JTF-CM also filed an excellent set of command chronologies with the archives of the Marine Corps Historical Center in Washington, D.C.
7. Some picked up the rhythm more quickly than others. This was true of the retired officers, some with CentCom experience, and the IMAs, who were trained for specific wartime jobs, but tended to be less true of the IRRs, who came from a large pool of less active Reservists. Although MarForPac had an IMA detachment, quickly

mobilized to augment its staff to take on the increased responsibilities of two fronts, the small liaison element at MarCent did not. The Marine Corps' Enduring Freedom Combat Assessment Team suggested that the lesson learned here was: if you don't have your own IMAs you have shaped to your needs, the Marine Corps' personnel system is unlikely to give you what you want in times of crisis—and you should not be surprised when that happens. MCCDC, *OEF Summary Report,* p. 73.

8. MCCDC, *OEF Summary Report,* p. 63: "Brigadier General Mattis, originally designated COMMARCENT (Forward) . . . assumed significant responsibilities as the Marine Service component commander forward in the AO for ensuring the proper employment, administration, and sustainment of Marine Corps Operating Forces in theater."

9. Task Force 58 Command Chronology, 27 Oct. 2001–26 Feb. 2002 (MCHC, Washington, D.C.), p. 4; hereafter TF 58 ComdC. Although it contains some idiosyncrasies, this is an unusually well-written command chronology and gives the reader an excellent picture of Marine Corps operations against the Taliban.

10. Maj. Gen. James N. Mattis, "The Professional Edge," *Marine Corps Gazette,* Feb. 2004, p. 19; Bruce Catton, *Grant Takes Command* (Boston: Little, Brown, 1969).

11. See, for example, Murray and Scales, *Iraq War,* p. 116f.

12. MCCDC, *OEF Summary Report,* p. 62.

13. TF 58 ComdC, p. 14.

14. Ibid., p. 9. The Combat Assessment Team surmised that this "staff lite" arrangement worked because it included the two traditional MEU staffs; "staff lite" by itself might not have been as successful. MCCDC, *OEF Summary Report,* p. 64.

15. TF 58 ComdC, p. 10.

16. Ibid., pp. 9, 16.

17. Ibid. Some journalists reported the remark as, "The Marines have landed and we now own a piece of Afghanistan," which the Pentagon apparently "scrambled to disavow." See, for example, Christopher Cooper, "How a Marine Lost His Command in the Race to Baghdad," *Wall Street Journal,* 5 April 2004, p. 1.

18. Lt. Col. Frank G. Hoffman, USMCR, "The U.S. Marine Corps in Review," U.S. Naval Institute *Proceedings,* May 2002, p. 84. Other articles about this operation include Brig. Gen. Michael E. Ennis, "A New Operating Environment," *Marine Corps Gazette,* Aug. 2002, p. 46f, and Capt. Jay M. Holtermann, "The 15th Marine Expeditionary Unit's Seizure of Camp Rhino," *Marine Corps Gazette,* June 2002, pp. 41–43.

19. Interview with Brig. Gen. James N. Mattis, 20 Jan. 2002 (Naval Historical Center, Washington, D.C.); hereafter Mattis interview no. 1. For background, see U.S. Marine Corps, "Expeditionary Maneuver Warfare," *Marine Corps Gazette,* Feb. 2002, pp. A-1–A-10: "Seabasing enables forces to move directly from ship to objectives deep inland and represents a significant advance from traditional, phased amphibious operations."

20. Interview with Col. Timothy C. Wells, 27 Feb. 2003 (MCHC, Washington, D.C.). See also MarForPac ComdC July–Dec. 2001 (MCHC, Washington, D.C.).

21. MarForPac ComdC July–Dec. 2001 (MCHC, Washington, D.C.).

22. Interview with Lt. Gen. Earl B. Hailston, 19 May 2003 (MCHC, Washington, D.C.); Wells interview.

23. Col. Nicholas E. Reynolds, "OIF Field History Journal," 2003 (Archive, MCHC, Washington, D.C.), entry for 10 April 2003; hereafter Reynolds journal.

24. Between 2001 and 2003, the words "combined" and "coalition" were both used in the titles of these organizations to mean the same thing. While "joint" refers to U.S. commands with more than one service, "combined" or "coalition" refers to commands that also include foreign elements. For the sake of simplicity and consistency, I will use "coalition."

25. TF 58 ComdC, p. 32.

26. For a discussion of this topic, see Charles J. Quilter II, *With the I Marine Expeditionary Force in Desert Shield and Desert Storm* (Washington, D.C.: History and Museums Division, U.S. Marine Corps, 1993), pp. 8–11. There was always a lively exchange of views and data between the CentCom theater and HQMC, especially the office of the Deputy Commandant for Plans, Policies, and Operations (PP&O). During 2002 and 2003, General Hailston and Lt. Gen. Emil R. Bedard of PP&O were in close contact, discussing and coordinating plans virtually on a daily basis. See, for example, Jones interview and chaper 2, p. 20, of this text.

27. Zinni interview.

28. Interview with Col. Stephen W. Baird, 31 May 2003 (MCHC, Washington, D.C.).

29. General Hailston agreed with this point of view. See Lt. Col. Jeffrey Acosta, "OIF Field History Journal," 2003 (MCHC, Washington, D.C.), entry for 31 March 2003; hereafter Acosta journal. See also Wells and Hailston interviews.

30. Interview with Lt. Gen. James T. Conway, 7 Dec. 2003 (MCHC, Washington, D.C.).

31. See, for example, MCCDC, *OEF Summary Report,* p. 63. Various Marines made such comments to the author during a visit to Tampa in December 2001.

32. MCCDC, *OEF Summary Report,* p. 57.

33. See, for example, MCCDC, *OEF Summary Report,* pp. 9–15, which argues that the operation did not fully validate expeditionary maneuver warfare but showed the utility of some of its tenets.

34. Interview with Lt. Gen. David D. McKiernan, 30 June 2003 (U.S. Army Center of Military History, Washington, D.C.), hereafter McKiernan interview no. 4. To cite other examples: General Hailston also commented on his good relations with General Franks; General Mattis repeatedly stressed the value of establishing good relations with neighboring commanders of all services—both joint and combined. (Hailston interview; Mattis interview no. 1; TF 58 ComdC.) See also Reynolds journal, entry for 10 Nov. 2003, describing a talk by Williamson Murray and Maj. Gen. Robert H. Scales Jr., during which they contrasted the personalities—and their relationships—in the two wars.

35. See, for example, Zinni interview.

36. Murray and Scales, *Iraq War,* p. 47f.

37. See, for example, Bing West and Maj. Gen. Ray L. Smith, USMC (Ret.), *The March Up* (New York: Putnam, 2003), p. 221. The current edition of FMFM 1 is known as MCDP 1. The original edition appeared in 1989.
38. McKiernan interview no. 4.
39. Ibid. Franks described himself as a maverick. Tommy Franks, *American Soldier* (New York: Regan Books, 2004), p. 367. For a critical appraisal of General Franks, see Andrew Bacevich, "A Modern Major General," *New Left Review,* Sept.–Oct. 2004, pp. 123–34.
40. Zinni interview.
41. Acosta journal.
42. Murray and Scales, *Iraq War,* p. 60.
43. Kevin Peraino, "Low-Key Leader/Lt. Gen. David McKiernan Is the Soft-spoken Soldier with the Hard Job of Commanding U.S. Ground Forces in Iraq," *Newsweek* Web Exclusive, 19 March 2003.
44. Conway interview. When asked how the "right" Marines—a virtual dream team— had come to serve in key billets in the CentCom AO in 2002 and 2003, the commandant said it had been as much a matter of good long-term personnel policies as of any specific, short-term assignments. Jones interview.
45. Murray and Scales, *Iraq War,* p. 65.
46. See, for example, interview with Col. Christopher G. Wright, 4 Dec. 2003 (MCHC, Washington, D.C.).
47. Reynolds journal, entry for 10 May 2003.
48. Conway interview.
49. Maj. Theodore R. McKeldin, III, "OIF Field History Journal," 2003, entry for 2 April 2003; hereafter McKeldin journal.

Chapter 2

1. For a history of the war based largely on reporting by the *New York Times* and including coverage of political events, see, for example, Todd S. Purdum, *A Time of Our Choosing: America's War in Iraq* (New York: Henry Holt, 2003), p. 20. Two other, somewhat more controversial books that cover the political background to the war are Bob Woodward, *Plan of Attack* (New York: Simon and Schuster, 2004) and Richard A. Clarke, *Against All Enemies* (New York: Free Press, 2004). Franks, *American Soldier,* esp. pp. 315, 328–33, describe the initial taskings and briefings in late 2001.
2. Gregory Fontenot, E. J. Degen, and David Tohn, *On Point: The United States Army in Operation Iraqi Freedom* (Fort Leavenworth, Kan.: Combat Studies Institute Press, 2004), p. 31. This is a very useful and detailed early work on the conflict. On directives in 2001 to prepare for a possible war with Iraq, see, for example, Purdum, *Time of Our Choosing,* p. 20. For the point of view of a Marine planner at HQMC in 2001, see, for example, interview with Lt. Col. James L. Western, 30 Dec. 2003 (MCHC, Washington, D.C.).

3. I MEF ComdC, Jan.–June 2002 (MCHC, Washington, D.C.), section 2, p. 16.

4. For all of the quotations in this paragraph, ibid., pp. 28–29, 59.

5. Interview with Lt. Col. George W. Smith Jr., 8 June 2004 (MCHC, Washington, D.C.), hereafter G. W. Smith interview no. 2. For general background on the planning process, see also interviews with Col. Christopher J. Gunther, 24/25 May 2003 (MCHC, Washington, D.C.), and Lt. Col. Gregory M. Douquet, 29 April 2003 (MCHC, Washington, D.C.). Although he did not become the MEF G-5 until the middle of 2002, Colonel Gunther describes how the planning for Iraq evolved from February 2002 onward. Lt. Col. Douquet was the senior MAW planner, serving with MEF G-3 Future Operations from February 2002 to April 2003.

6. Murray and Scales, *Iraq War,* p. 92.

7. Zinni interview.

8. Murray and Scales, *Iraq War,* p. 54.

9. Ibid.

10. G. W. Smith interview no. 2. Franks, *American Soldier,* pp. 382–431, describes the evolution of the various plans in 2002 from his point of view, especially his broad-brush briefings to the president and the secretary of defense, which led to general guidance for the planners.

11. Interview with Lt. Col. G. W. Smith, 18 March 2003 (MCHC, Washington, D.C.), hereafter G. W. Smith interview no. 1.

12. G. W. Smith interview no. 2.

13. Reynolds journal, entry for 1 July 2004, based on a conversation with former PP&O Current Operations officer Col. Ronald J. Johnson.

14. G. W. Smith interview no. 2. While in Tampa, Smith was able to hold a secure telephone conversation with General Hagee virtually every day, briefing him on developments and receiving his guidance.

15. This was one of the fundamentals of the Marine Corps planning process: "continuous planning requires continuous coordination laterally and between echelons as plans are adjusted and refined over time." See U.S. Marine Corps, *Planning* (Marine Corps Doctrinal Publication) (Washington, D.C.: Department of Navy, 1997), p. 83.

16. G. W. Smith interview no. 2; I MEF ComdC Jan.–July 2002 (MCHC, Washington, D.C.), passim.

17. MCCDC, *OEF Summary Report,* p. 54; Fontenot et al., *On Point,* p. 42.

18. McKiernan interview no. 4.

19. Conway interview; Hailston interview.

20. See, for example, interview with Maj. Gen. Robert R. Blackman, 31 May 2003 (MCHC, Washington, D.C.); G. W. Smith interview no. 2. On General McKiernan's approach to joint operations from a Marine point of view, see interview with Col. Marc A. Workman, 30 Nov. 2002 (MCHC, Washington, D.C.).

21. McKiernan interview no. 4.

22. See, for example, the comment on this subject in Zinni interview.

23. Fontenot et al., *On Point,* p. 45. This conclusion assumes that the subordinate commands had the requisite clearances to access highly classified files.

24. Tom Clancy with General Tony Zinni (Ret.) and Tony Koltz, *Battle Ready* (New York: G. P. Putnam's Sons, 2004), p. 315.
25. Zinni interview.
26. MCCDC, *Operation Iraqi Freedom Combat Assessment Team Summary Report,* Spring 2004 Studies and Analysis Division, Working Draft), p. 40, hereafter MCCDC, *OIF Summary Report.*
27. There was a complicated set of agreements about this, which are examined in detail in LeRoy D. Stearns, *The 3rd Marine Aircraft Wing in Desert Shield and Desert Storm* (Washington, D.C.: U.S. Marine Corps History and Museums Division, 1999), esp. pp. 45–49. See also Michael R. Gordon and General Bernard E. Trainor, *The Generals' War* (Boston: Little, Brown, 1995), p. 311. This is a basic source on Desert Shield/Desert Storm.
28. Interview with Maj. Gen. James F. Amos, 16 May 2003 (MCHC, Washington, D.C.); Hailston interview.
29. Stearns, *3rd Marine Aircraft Wing,* p. 47.
30. See G. W. Smith interview no. 2, and Reynolds journal, entry for 29 July 2003, describing a postwar briefing by the general officers that commanded the MEF's major subordinate commands. Excess CFACC sorties often "volunteered" to fly Marine missions; they seemed to enjoy working within the Marine air control system. Interview with Capt. Ryan M. Walker, 22 April 2003 (MCHC, Washington, D.C.). By and large, once the war started, the system worked. See MCCDC, *OIF Summary Report,* p. 40.
31. Fontenot et al., *On Point,* p 13.
32. Murray and Scales, *Iraq War,* pp. 154–83. For a comment on Iraqi exiles in general, see, for example, Clancy, *Battle Ready,* p. 345.
33. G. W. Smith interview no. 2.
34. The issue of synchronicity is addressed in, among other sources, interview with Lt. Col. Richard T. Johnson, 26 April 2003 (MCHC, Washington, D.C.); McKeldin journal, entry for 28 Feb. 2003; and interview with Lt. Col. Paul J. Kennedy, 6 Nov. 2003 (MCHC, Washington, D.C.). Lieutenant Colonel Kennedy is right insofar as General Mattis was a very effective advocate for his ideas. However, it appears that others at MEF and CentCom had reached the same conclusion on their own. See, for example, G. W. Smith interview no. 2, and Douquet interview.
35. There are numerous sources on this topic. G. W. Smith interview no. 2 contains details of meetings on the subject, including a meeting between Generals McKiernan and Conway on 29 January 2003 when they discussed, and agreed on, this subject.
36. Quoted in House of Commons Defence Committee, *Lessons of Iraq* (London: Stationery Office, 2004), Vol. 1, pp. 34–35. This is a useful source with many lengthy— and candid—quotations by British officers. It appears to be more candid than the Ministry of Defence's "lessons learned" publications on the war, which are described at greater length in chapter 10, on the British forces.
37. Fontenot et al., *On Point,* pp. 93–94; interview with Terry Moran, 23 Aug. 2003 (U.S. Army Center of Military History, Washington, D.C.). On 1 March, General

Conway commented that the air campaign was likely to be brief in order to achieve surprise, which implies a very brief separation between A-Day and G-Day. Col. Reed R. Bonadonna, "Notes from Address by Lt. Gen. Conway, CG I MEF to Officers of Task Force Tarawa," 1 March 2003 (Copy in Reynolds Working Papers, MCHC, Washington, D.C.). This is consistent with the scenario for the 10 March 2003 MEF ROC drill, when General Conway reminded his staff not to "expect a return of A and G separated by multiple days." I MEF ComdC, Jan.–June 2003 (MCHC, Washington, D.C.), "FutOps" (Documents), "I MEF ROC Drill, 10 Mar 03."

38. G. W. Smith interview no. 2. See also Gunther interview. The OODA loop is a concept pioneered by USAF Col. John Boyd. It stands for "observation/orientation/decision/action." Boyd's argument was that if you want to win an aerial dogfight, you will go through this loop faster than your enemy—that is, you will get inside his OODA loop.

39. Fontenot et al., *On Point,* p. 74.

40. G. W. Smith interview no. 1.

41. Interview with Maj. Evan A. Huelfer, 16 March 2003 (U.S. Army Center of Military History, Washington, D.C.); G. W. Smith interview no 2; Fontenot et al., *On Point,* p. 45. Major Huelfer was CFLCC's lead planner and a great source for historical data. He and Lieutenant Colonel Smith, MEF's lead planner, used almost identical wording in discussing this phenomenon. The prominent academic Edward Tufte has developed similar ideas about how PowerPoint can have the effect of "dumbing down" debates. See, for example, his whimsically titled but quite serious article "PowerPoint Is Evil" in the September 2003 issue of *Wired* magazine.

42. On the neoconservative movement, see James Mann, *Rise of the Vulcans: The History of Bush's War Cabinet* (New York: Viking, 2004). On some of the neoconservative plans that were presented to Franks, see Franks, *American Soldier,* p. 373. For a general source on the planning process, see Woodward, *Plan of Attack.* Although Woodward and Franks cover much of the same ground, Woodward describes a slightly different dynamic from Franks, suggesting that the Pentagon, and not CentCom, generally took the lead in proposing various plans. For a more critical view of the development of the administration's policy on Iraq, see W. Patrick Lang, "Drinking the Kool-Aid," *Middle East Policy,* Summer 2004, pp. 39–60.

43. Although Franks said he had a productive relationship with Rumsfeld and liked working with the secretary, he also expressed reservations about his "centralized management style." See Franks, *American Soldier,* pp. 313, 333, 362, 373, and 545. Col. Kevin Benson, the senior CFLCC planner, reported similar frustrations with the Pentagon during the planning stage. Col. Kevin Benson, "Brief at Naval War College," 25 Aug. 2004 (Copy in Reynolds Working Papers, MCHS, Washington, D.C.). See also Anthony H. Cordesman, *The Iraq War: Strategy, Tactics, and Military Lessons* (Washington, D.C.: CSIS, 2003), p. 150, and questions about "alleged meddling . . . by the Office of the Secretary of Defense—especially in the planning process" down to the CFLCC/MEF level, in U.S. Naval Institute, "Interview: Lieutenant General James T. Conway, USMC," U.S. Naval Institute *Proceedings* (November 2003).

Some have suggested that war planning for Iraq needs to be understood in the context of relations between the secretary and the military starting in 2000. See, for example, Elaine M. Grossman, "To Understand Insurgency in Iraq: Read Something Old, Something New," *Insider,* 2 Dec. 2004, containing a comment by Lt. Gen. Gregory Newbold, USMC (Ret.), who retired in 2002 from a senior position in the J-3 at the Pentagon, that a cautionary tale about the Pentagon during the Vietnam years "contains remarkable parallels with today's environment." The book is H. R. McMaster, *Dereliction of Duty* (New York: Harper Collins, 1997). It will be a number of years before the sources are available for anyone to analyze the Iraq War in the same way.

44. Zinni interview; Jones interview.
45. See, for example, Lt. Col. Ronald J. Brown, *With Marines in Operation Provide Comfort: Humanitarian Operations in Northern Iraq* (Washington, D.C.: USMC History and Museums Division, 1995); Gordon and Trainor, *Generals' War,* p. 459.
46. G. W. Smith interview no. 2; Huelfer interview; Moran interview. Moran, a retired Army lieutenant colonel, was General McKiernan's special assistant, privy to a great deal of information about the plan for the war.
47. Huelfer interview; Benson, "Brief at Naval War College." Benson and Huelfer cover much the same ground.
48. Huelfer interview.
49. G. W. Smith interview no. 2.
50. There is an excellent discussion of this topic in Fontenot et al., *On Point,* pp. 44–47. Once again, Huelfer and Smith also offer excellent descriptions of the process from the planner's perspective. Huelfer interview, G. W. Smith interview nos. 1 and 2.
51. Huelfer interview; G. W. Smith interview no. 2.
52. Huelfer interview.
53. G. W. Smith interview no. 2.
54. G. W. Smith interview no. 2. As described below, both the MEF and V Corps planned extensively for the fight even after CFLCC decided in September that Baghdad planning would fall to V Corps.
55. G. W. Smith interview no. 2; interview with Lt. Col. Yanni Marok, Royal Marines, 14 April 2003 (MCHC, Washington, D.C.). Marok joined the MEF G-3 Future Operations staff in September and developed an excellent relationship with other planners, including Smith. His interview is particularly useful for the data it contains on Al Faw.
56. Marok interview. This occurred in the 12–13 Dec. time frame at a conference in Bahrain. Colonel Gunther was acting with the knowledge and approval of his superiors.
57. G. W. Smith interview no. 2. Franks, *American Soldier,* p. 396, contains his schematic of the various lines of operation.
58. I MEF ComdC, July–Dec. 2002 (MCHC, Washington, D.C.); interview with Col. George F. Milburn, 1 March 2003 (MCHC, Washington, D.C.); P. J. Kennedy interview.
59. Reynolds journal, entry for 19 July 2004, quoting from journal kept by one of the officers present.

60. Reynolds journal, entry for 18 July 2004.
61. Interview with Lt. Gen. David D. McKiernan, 20 June 2003 (U.S. Army Center of Military History, Washington, D.C.), hereafter McKiernan interview no. 3. See also Blackman interview, Workman interview, and the television documentary about CFLCC by CNN, "The Warroom" (Atlanta: CNN, 2003).
62. There are numerous sources about this approach, defined as "a methodology for planning, executing, and assessing operations . . . to attain the effects required to achieve desired . . . outcomes." Edward C. Mann III, Gary Endersby, Thomas R. Searle, *Thinking Effects: Effects-Based Methodology for Joint Operations* (Maxwell Air Force Base, Ala.: Air University Press, 2002), p. 2.
63. Interview with Col. Gregory J. Plush, 15 April 2003 (MCHC, Washington, D.C.); and Workman interview.
64. Fontenot et al., *On Point,* p. 43; Blackman interview; CNN, "The Warroom."
65. Interview with Col. Patrick J. Burger, 16 April 2003 (MCHC, Washington, D.C.). There were approximately twelve Marine LNOs at CFLCC.
66. To similar effect, see MCCDC, *OEF Summary Report,* p. 11, reporting its finding that providing adequate numbers of staff officers for such components was a challenge for the Marine Corps.
67. Blackman interview. See also Workman and Cowdrey interviews. Brigadier General Cowdrey was one of the "January" augmentees. In February 2003 there were some thirteen hundred members of the CFFLC staff. Interview with Lt. Col. Terrance J. Johns and Maj. Robert F. McTague II, 22 Feb. 2003 (CFLCC Military History Group interview, pp. 322–32).
68. Huelfer interview. Both General McKiernan and his special assistant, Terry Moran, remembered a version of the plan in the fall of 2003 around the time of their arrival at Camp Doha. The general termed it "a very small force . . . a brigade combat team from the 3rd ID and a MEU from the Marines." McKiernan interview no. 4. Moran used more or less the same terms: "Early on, there was some discussion of that start force being no more than a brigade of the 3rd ID, reinforced out of the MEU . . . so the thought was that we would cross the LD with that very small force, and it would be rapidly reinforced by the MEF and by the V Corps. That was probably a bit . . . imprudent." Moran interview.
69. See, for example, Fontenot et al., *On Point,* p. 41.
70. Jones interview.
71. The history of this idea goes back to the spring of 2002, when General Mikolashek proposed it to General Franks, who accepted it. However, it was not actively pursued until the summer of 2002, when it was briefed to the British, who were very enthusiastic about the idea and played a key role in resurrecting it. Huelfer interview. British sources are consistent with Huelfer's memory. See House of Commons, *Lessons of Iraq,* Vol. 1, p. 45.
72. Blackman interview. This tracks with the comments by General McKiernan and Moran with respect to the plans that were under discussion in the fall of 2003 but diverges somewhat from two of the lead planners' comments. G. W. Smith interview

no. 2; R. T. Johnson interview; I MEF ComdC July–Aug. 2002 (MCHC, Washington, D.C.), esp. section 2 narrative summaries for G-3 Future Operations and G-5 Plans. Fontenot et al., *On Point*, p. 53, offer an excellent description of the exercise as "McKiernan's first opportunity to . . . conduct operations with his new staff and new general officers and to exercise the new [CFLCC] organization . . . [as well as] the first opportunity for CFLCC's major subordinate elements . . . to practice operations under . . . CFLCC. Much of the exercise focused on team building and establishing [joint] standard operating procedures." For a more general discussion of planning issues at this time, see Cordesman, *Iraq War*, especially pp. 149–59.

73. Interview with Lt. Gen. David D. McKiernan, 19 Dec. 2002 (U.S. Army Center of Military History, Washington, D.C.), hereafter McKiernan interview no. 1. See also R. T. Johnson interview.

74. Interview with Lt. Gen. David D. McKiernan, 1 May 2003 (Copy in Reynolds Working Papers [MCHC, Washington, D.C.]), hereafter McKiernan interview no. 2. This was a group interview with officers representing both the Military History Group at Camp Doha and various Army lessons-learned initiatives. Much of the same ground is also covered in McKiernan interview no. 1.

75. Huelfer interview.

76. Moran interview.

77. I MEF ComdC, Jan.–June 2003 (MCHC, Washington, D.C.), especially "Command Element," p. 41; Blackman interview.

78. Part of the explanation for the selection of 2d MEB as opposed to 2d Marine Division may have been that much of the division staff was already committed to an ongoing CentCom operation in the Horn of Africa and was simply not available. The 7,100 Marines would include the three infantry battalions of Regimental Combat Team 2 (RCT 2), something less than 1,000 Marines in the MEB headquarters, a combat service support element, and 81 aircraft. Apart from the units that were organic to 2d Marines, the larger units earmarked for deployment with the MEB were: 2d Battalion, 8th Marines, which replaced the already deployed 2d Battalion, 2d Marines; 1st Battalion, 10th Marines; 2d Force Recon Company; Company A, 8th Tanks; Company A, 2d Assault Amphibious Battalion; and Company C, 2d Light Armored Reconnaissance Battalion. Upon arrival in Kuwait, the aviation and support elements would out-chop to the MAW and the FSSG, but later on, other units came under Tarawa's control, such as 15th MEU, enabling it to reach a maximum strength of some 15,000 Marines and sailors.

79. Reynolds journal, entry for 1 July 2004.

80. Zinni interview.

81. I MEF ComdC, 1 Jan. 2003–30 June 2003 (MCHC, Washington, D.C.), especially FutOps Folder, "Chg 1 to I MEF OPLAN 1003V," 16 March 2003.

82. McKiernan interview no. 4; G. W. Smith interview no. 2. This is one of the few instances when there was a whiff of service politics in General McKiernan's basic policy decisions. There was no compelling reason to assign Baghdad exclusively to V Corps.

83. It would not become clear until mid-March 2003 that the 4th was not welcome in Turkey either. By then the U.S. Army's 4th Infantry Division and its equipment were in ships floating off the coast of Turkey. But this was not all bad. It enabled General Franks to bolster a deception plan that pointed to an attack from the north, which may have found its mark. Franks, *American Soldier,* p. 429.
84. G. W. Smith interview no. 2.
85. R. T. Johnson interview. Johnson notes that in December 2002 the senior British adviser at CFLCC, Brig. Gen. Albert Whitley, met with General Conway to discuss whether and how the British Army and the MEF could work together.
86. G. W. Smith interview no. 2.
87. Interview with Brig. Gen. Richard F. Natonski, 26 March 2004 (MCHC, Washington, D.C.), hereafter Natonski interview no. 2.
88. See, for example, Huelfer interview.
89. McKiernan interview no. 1.
90. Ibid. The phases are nicely laid out in Fontenot et al., *On Point,* p. xxiii.
91. One senior Marine operations officer put it very forcefully: before the war, there was "absolutely no plan for Phase IV. None. Zero. No guidance." This was an overstatement—there was always a plan of sorts—but if the word was not passed, perception was reality.
92. G. W. Smith interview no. 1; P. J. Kennedy interview. The Conway quote is from a 7 August 2003 interview published in the U.S. Naval Institute *Proceedings* (November 2003), which also appeared on the World Wide Web at *www.usni.org/proceedings/articles03.* See also Reynolds journal, entry for 1 July 2004.
93. Interview with Lt. Col. Jim Hutton, Royal Marines, 4 May 2003 (MCHC, Washington, D.C.).
94. Interview with Col. George F. Milburn, 3 Aug. 2003 (MCHC, Washington, D.C.); hereafter Milburn interview no. 2. This is another topic for a future researcher who could compare Marine, Army, and British plans and orders in this conflict and consider questions like: Had the British adapted to the information age, or were they simply applying lessons long since learned? How has American planning adapted to the information age? In a war of "shock and awe," when do planners reach the point of diminishing returns? Compare Malcolm Gladwell, *Blink* (New York: Little, Brown, 2005).
95. Rick Atkinson, *In the Company of Soldiers* (New York: Henry Holt, 2004), p. 26. This is, in my view, one of the best books about the war by an embedded journalist—or by anyone else. Atkinson does an excellent job of portraying the frame of mind of the staff of the 101st Airborne Division and of putting its accomplishments in context.
96. Bonadonna, "Notes from Address by LtGen Conway."
97. McKiernan interview no. 4.
98. Huelfer interview.
99. See, for example, Atkinson, *In the Company of Soldiers,* p. 107.
100. McKiernan interview no. 2, 1 May 2003 (Group Interview at Camp Doha, KU, copy on hand at MCHC, Washington, D.C.). Atkinson, *In the Company of Soldiers,* p. 105, reports a U.S. Army estimate of some 350,000 soldiers in the regular Iraqi

army and some 80,000 in the Republican Guard. Fontenot et al., *On Point,* pp. 99–102, offers a summary of the enemy order of battle as it appeared before the campaign. See also I MEF ComdC, Jan.–June 2003 (MCHC, Washington, D.C.), especially "FutOps" folder containing "Chg 1 to MEF OPLAN 1003V," dated 16 March 2003, and containing an assessment of enemy capabilities.

101. Reynolds journal, entry for 1 July 2004.
102. Interview with Maj. Gen. James N. Mattis, 23 Jan. 2004 (MCHC, Washington, D.C.); Wright interview.
103. Bonadonna, "Notes from Address by LtGen Conway." See also Atkinson, *In the Company of Soldiers,* p. 106, and Reynolds journal, entry for 4 Nov. 2003, on a talk by historians Williamson Murray and Robert Scales. They reported that three U.S. Army generals commented that they were astounded by the depth of control the regime had over the people, and that another command was astounded by the tenacity of the individual paramilitary fighters. It is their contention that the various U.S. intelligence agencies should have been able to develop, highlight, and present this kind of information, much of which was freely available on the Internet. See also note 105 below.
104. Steve Coll, "Hussein Was Sure of Own Survival; Aide Says Confusion Reigned on Eve of War," *Washington Post,* 3 Nov. 2003, p. A-1. This would certainly not have been out of character for Saddam Hussein, many of whose past decisions were not thought through, to put it mildly. See also Franks, *American Soldier,* p. 558, for a comment on the work of a Joint Forces Command lessons-learned team that debriefed Iraqi officers after the war. The team found that while some Iraqi units were well prepared, Iraqi command and control, especially at senior levels, was next to nonexistent. Finally, see various sources on a CIA report made public in 2004, including Douglas Jehl, "Inspector's Report Says Hussein Expected Guerrilla War," *New York Times,* 8 Oct. 2004, p. A-6.
105. These issues surfaced repeatedly in oral history interviews. See, for example, Blackman interview; Reynolds journal, entry for 1 July 2004; G. W. Smith interview no. 2; Zinni interview; and Clancy, *Battle Ready,* pp. 19–20. Some of this information existed inside CentCom and at other agencies inside the Washington Beltway. General Zinni had organized an interagency war game in 1999 to explore the challenges of rebuilding Iraq if Saddam Hussein were killed or deposed. For various reasons beyond the scope of this study, the topic was not a priority either for Pentagon or, by extension, CentCom planners at any time before March 2003. This issue is explored further in chapter 11.

Chapter 3

1. Conway interview.
2. Captain Lara A. Bennett et al., *No Better Friend, No Worse Enemy* (Camp Pendleton, Cal.: 1st Marine Division, 2004), pp. 6, 8. This book has pictures and text about the division in Operation Iraqi Freedom and was distributed by the Marine Corps Association.

3. Wright interview; interview with Col. John A. Toolan, 10 Dec. 2003 (MCHC, Washington, D.C.).

4. 1stMarDiv ComdC Jan.–July 2003 (MCHC, Washington, D.C.), section 2, chapter 3, p. 21. There are numerous other sources on the division's preparations for war, including Toolan interview; Wright interview; and interview with Col. Joseph F. Dunford, 2 May 2003 (MCHC, Washington, D.C.).

5. Jones interview.

6. Interview with Brig. Gen. Edward G. Usher III, 19 March 2003 (MCHC, Washington, D.C.), hereafter Usher interview no. 1; the Commanders and Staff of 1st FSSG, "Brute Force Logistics," *Marine Corps Gazette*, Aug. 2003, pp. 34–39. A field historian was attached to 1st FSSG during OIF. She was Maj. Melissa D. Kuo, who is preparing a monograph on combat service support in OIF I. I am indebted to her for reviewing my remarks on logistics and making suggestions.

7. Hailston interview; Usher interview no. 1; Lt. Col. M. D. Visconage, "OIF Field History Journal," 2003 (MCHC, Washington, D.C.), entry for 15 March 2003, hereafter Visconage journal; interview with Brig. Gen. Michael R. Lehnert, 8 May 2003 (MCHC, Washington, D.C.). One of the Marine field historians assigned to cover OIF I, CWO-2 William E. Hutson, conducted numerous interviews at the MLC that are available at the MCHC. By joint doctrine, each service is responsible for supplying itself, especially with respect to service-specific items. However, the combatant commander has the authority to create his own logistics structure, in particular to designate theater support mechanisms, typically for "common-user" items.

8. Reynolds journal, entry for 29 July 2003. This entry contains detailed notes on a set of briefings given by the OIF commanders, including Generals Conway, Mattis, and Amos, at Quantico. The author worked for General Amos at the Basic School.

9. This is a topic that the U.S. Air Force has explored over the years. See, for example, Robert P. Givens, *Turning the Vertical Flank* (Maxwell Air Force Base, Ala.: Air University Press, 2002). Colonel Givens outlines the criteria for thinking of air as a maneuver force, able to exert influence over enemy units and terrain on its own.

10. These topics are addressed in two excellent interviews with the MAW G-3, Col. Jonathan G. Miclot, on 20 March 2003 and 19 April 2003 (MCHC, Washington, D.C.).

11. 3d MAW ComdC Jan.–July 2003 (MCHC, Washington, D.C.), section 2, p. 6.

12. See, generally, ibid., and, for a discussion of FARPs, interview with Lt. Col. David P. Lobik, 24 April 2003 (MCHC, Washington, D.C.).

13. 3d MAW ComdC, Jan.–July 2003 (MCHC, Washington, D.C.), section 2, "G-5 Plans and Exercises."

14. Reynolds journal, entry for 29 July 2003.

15. MCCDC, *OIF Summary Report*, p. 18. This is a quote from a video teleconference; members of the Combat Assessment Team routinely attended these VTCs and made shorthand notes.

16. R. T. Johnson interview; I MEF ComdC Jan.–June 2003 (MCHC, Washington, D.C.), section 2, p. 6.

17. See, for example, MCCDC, *OIF Summary Report,* pp. 20–21.

18. Interview with Lt. Col. James W. Western, 20 Dec. 2003 (MCHC, Washington, D.C.).

19. Peraino, "Low-Key Leader." There are other representative discussions of this issue in Mattis interview no. 1; Lehnert interview; and Moran interview.

20. 2d MEBComdC, Jan.–June 2003 (MCHC, Washington, D.C.), section 3, "Significant Events."

21. 1stMarDivComdC, Jan.–June 2003 (MCHC, Washington, D.C.), section 2, chapter 2, p. 28.

22. The offload took about sixteen days, a few days less than the allotted time. MCCDC, *OIF Summary Report,* p. 55.

23. Ibid., p. 20. See also Milburn interview no. 2 for comments by the MEF G-5 on the process.

24. For a discussion of this topic, see Plush interview.

25. Maj. Grant A. Williams, "A Marine's Eye View of Kuwait," Milinet (an Internet service provider that posted news about the military on the Web), 27 Feb. 2003. This excerpt is from a report originally dated 19 Feb. 2003 (Copy in Reynolds Working Papers, MCHC, Washington, D.C.).

26. Peter Baker, "In War, Plans Yield to Improvisation," *Washington Post,* 24 March 2003, p. A-16.

27. Ibid. "MEF Forward" was the term used when the CG left MEF Main and went even farther forward with a very small staff. The Bug's footprint—just for its satellite dishes and related gear—was estimated at a mind-boggling one kilometer by one kilometer, and there were questions about why the MEF even needed the Bug, since the communications suite in Kuwait was so good, as good or better than the Bug's. The answer was that General Conway placed considerable emphasis on being physically close to his Marines. Reynolds journal, entries for 10 May 2003 and 19 July 2004, quoting MEF staff officers.

28. Interview with Col. Steven A. Hummer, 13 Feb. 2004 (MCHC, Washington, D.C.). See also McKeldin journal, esp. entry for 7 Feb. 2003.

29. Interviews with Brig. Gen. Cornell A. Wilson, 6 March 2003, 3 April 2003, and 17 May 2003 (MCHC, Washington, D.C.). The MCHC holds a number of other interviews on CM, along with CM's command chronology.

30. Reynolds journal, entry for 8 April 2003.

31. General James N. Mattis, "Memorandum for All Commanders," 20 Dec. 2002 (Copy in Reynolds Working Papers, MCHC, Washington, D.C.).

32. The division cruise book would state that during this period the division was "careful not to be wedded to a base plan. The tactical, physical, and moral readiness of the individual Marine was to . . . determine . . . success or failure, not reliance on a scripted plan." Bennett et al., *No Better Friend,* p. 13.

33. McKeldin journal, entry for 7 Feb. 2003.

34. For additional details see: I MEF ComdC, Jan.–June 2003 (MCHC, Washington, D.C.), section 2, "FutOps Narrative Summary"; McKeldin journal; CWO-2

William E. Hutson, "OIF Field History Journal," (MCHC, Washington, D.C.), entry for 4 Feb. 2003; hereafter Hutson journal. There is a discussion of this phase in the interview of the MEF's Current Operations officer, who pointed out all of the work involved in bringing the MEF staff together and producing the plan. Interviews with Col. Dennis Judge, 11 Aug. 2003 and 4 Nov. 2003 (MCHC, Washington, D.C.), hereafter Judge interviews no. 1 and no. 2.

35. I MEF ComdC, Jan.–June 2003 (MCHC, Washington, D.C.), FutOps Doc Folder, "I MEF ROC Drill, 10 Mar 03"; McKeldin journal, entries for 27 Feb. 2003 and 10 March 2003. For TF Tarawa, see Col. Reed R. Bonadonna, "Field Historian Journal" (MCHC, Washington, D.C.), entries for 2 and 10 March 2003; hereafter Bonadonna journal. This journal is very well written and gives the reader a good sense of what it was like to participate in OIF as a member of Task Force Tarawa. I recommend it highly both to the general reader and the reader who wants to learn more about Task Force Tarawa. In the run-up to combat operations, subordinate commanders down to the division level would use the terrain model at Doha again to brief General McKiernan and his staff on their plans. Interview with Maj. Gen. James D. Thurman, 27 May 2003 (Copy in Reynolds Working Papers, MCHC, Washington, D.C.).

36. Mattis interview no. 1; Hutson journal, entry for 27 Feb. 2003. See also 1stMarDiv ComdC, Jan.–June 2003 (MCHC, Washington, D.C.), section 2, "Narrative Summary," chapter 3. Division has written an unusually comprehensive narrative summary from its point of view.

37. For example, Colonel Judge, the MEF's Current Operations officer, stated he did not feel sure there would be a shooting war until the beginning of March, unlike General Mattis, who seemed to have "known" all along that there would be war. Judge interview no. 1.

38. Bonadonna journal, entry for 1 March 2003; Conway interview.

39. Bonadonna, "Notes from Address by LtGen Conway."

40. Mark Mazetti, "Fighting Words: A Marine Commander Readies His Troops for Combat," *U.S. News and World Report* Web Exclusive, 17 March 2003; McKeldin journal entry for 16 March 2003.

41. Conway interview; Murray and Scales, *Iraq War,* p. 65.

42. Conway interview; Nick Parker, "Countdown to Conflict," *The Mirror,* 15 March 2003, pp. 6–7; Vanessa Allen, "'Great to Have You Aboard' U.S. General Tells Brits," The Press Association (Web-based wire service), 14 March 2003.

43. Hutson journal, entry for 27 Feb. 2003.

44. Bonadonna journal, entry for 27 Feb. 2003.

45. Bennett et al., *No Better Friend,* p. 5.

46. Mattis interview no. 1.

47. Visconage journal, entry for 4 March 2003.

48. Maj. Gen. James F. Amos e-mail to multiple addressees, "Message from the Wing CG," 20 March 2003, on Col. Charles J. Quilter II CD-ROM in Reynolds Working Papers (MCHC, Washington, D.C.). General Natonski of Task Force Tarawa and the 1st FSSG's deputy commander and sergeant major also made the rounds of their

subordinate units, making final coordination and delivering words of encouragement. The limitations of space preclude including the details of their talks. See, for
example, Bonadonna journal, *passim*, and Maj. Melissa D. Kuo, Field History Journal (MCHC, Washington, D.C.), especially entry for 18 March 2003; hereafter Kuo
journal.

49. Sarah Oliver, "Not the Beginning, It's the End: The Words of Lieutenant Colonel
Tim Collins," *Mail on Sunday,* 16 March 2003, pp. 6–7.

50. One of the ironies of the war is that two months later the press also reported that
Collins was under investigation for mistreating prisoners. Maj. Re Biastre, a U.S.
Army civil affairs officer attached to Collins's battalion, lodged a formal complaint
against Collins that contained a number of charges. It soon emerged that on the streets
of occupied Rumaylah, Biastre had challenged Collins's authority in the presence of
Brigadier Jacko Page, Collins's immediate superior. Collins had reacted angrily, ordering Biastre's arrest for insubordination and then banishing him from the area. Biastre
in turn prepared a 2,400-word statement including specific charges against Collins
along with the observation that many British officers had expressed their resentment
of Americans. The charges were mistakenly attributed to Maj. Stan Coerr, an
ANGLICO Marine who was also attached to the battalion but outraged by the mistake, since he held Collins in high regard. In the end, after considerable press play in
the United Kingdom, the Ministry of Defence announced that the charges had been
dropped. The incident became a footnote to history that sheds light on the nature of
British-American relations during the war. Biastre's complaint was not entirely mis-
placed. Occasionally undercurrents of tension between the United States and the
British in Iraq would surface, which was natural since the British public was opposed
to the war and since the culture of the long-serving British military was so different
from that of the short-serving American military. Some British officers appeared more
likely to stand on their authority than their less formal American counterparts. But on
the whole, the United States Marines and the British soldiers and Royal Marines
worked together with less friction than American sister services in past conflicts, and
happily drank together at the end of Phase III. Anon., "Ministry Clears RIR Iraq
Hero," *Belfast News Letter,* 2 Sept. 2003, p. 6. Representative of other articles in the
British press about the affair are Jack Grimston and John Elliott, "First Picture of Man
Who Denounced Tim Collins," *Sunday Times* (London), 25 May 2003, page 1; and
Anon., "Colonel Tim: The Making of a Modern Hero," *Independent on Sunday* (Lon-
don), 25 May 2003, Features Section. Even though somewhat condescending to
Americans and Reservists, the last article is a thoughtful analysis of Collins's participa-
tion in the war, from his prewar speech through the investigation.

51. Anon., "The Smearing of Colonel Tim; The Eve of Battle Speech," *Daily Mail*
(London), 22 May 2003, p. 9.

52. See, for example, McKeldin journal, entries for 5 and 6 March 2003, and Reynolds
journal, entry for 1 July 2004, reporting on a talk with the G-3 of Task Force
Tarawa.

53. McKeldin journal, entry for 18 March 2003.

Chapter 4

1. McKiernan interview no. 1.
2. Bonadonna, "Notes from Address by LtGen Conway."
3. Ibid.
4. I MEF Sitrep [situation report] 181800Z to 191759ZMar03 (Copy in Reynolds Working Papers, MCHC, Washington, D.C.).
5. Fontenot et al., *On Point,* p. 93; I MEF Sitrep 171800Z to 181759ZMar03 (Copy in Reynolds Working Papers, MCHC, Washington, D.C.); McKeldin journal, entry for 18 March 2003; I MEF ComdC Jan.–June 2003 (MCHC, Washington, D.C.), especially Command Element, section 2, Current Ops Narrative.
6. See, for examples, interviews with Maj. Phillip N. Frietze, 14 May 2003 (MCHC, Washington, D.C.), and Maj. Daniel E. Longwell, 1 May 2003 (MCHC, Washington, D.C.); I MEF ComdC, Jan.–June 2003 (MCHC, Washington, D.C.), FutOps Command Chronology, section 2.
7. I MEF Sitrep 181800Z to 1981759ZMar03 (Copy in Reynolds Working Papers, MCHC, Washington, D.C.).
8. I MEF Sitrep 191800Z to 201759ZMar03 (Copy in Reynolds Working Papers, MCHC, Washington, D.C.).
9. See, for example, Kuo journal, entry for 20 March 2003.
10. Col. John C. Coleman interview, 11 Dec. 2003 (MCHC, Washington, D.C.). MEF Rear continued to function during the attack. As a result of the attack, MEF Forward accelerated its preparations to move away from Commando and, ultimately, into Iraq.
11. McKeldin journal, entry for 20 March; Kuo journal, entry for 20 March. Another description of the day can be found in Peter Baker, "Overtaken by Events, the Battle Plans Are Tossed Aside," *Washington Post,* 21 March 2003, p. A-20. The missile was most likely a Seersucker antiship missile, which literally flew under the air and missile defense radar, which is why there was no warning before the attack. It is not clear whether the warhead detonated; sources differ on this point. A Patriot antimissile battery brought down at least one other missile on 20 March. I MEF Sitrep 191800Z to 201759ZMar03 (Copy in Reynolds Working Papers, MCHC, Washington, D.C.).
12. I MEF Sitrep 191800Z to 201759ZMar03 (Copy in Reynolds Working Papers, MCHC, Washington, D.C.); McKeldin journal, entry for 20 March 2003. In General Conway's words, included in the 20 March sitrep, on account of "intel indicators that Iraqis had begun to destroy oil infrastructure, I MEF attacked into Iraq early."
13. Dunford interview.
14. I MEF Sitrep 191800Z to 201759ZMar03 (Copy in Reynolds Working Papers, MCHC, Washington, D.C.). A related stimulus was an erroneous CIA report that the Iraqis had moved a brigade of T-72 tanks into place near Safwan, just north of the border. This caused Division to make an additional shift in its plans to accommodate the heightened threat of enemy armor. I MEF Sitrep 201800Z to 211759ZMar03 (Copy in Reynolds Working Papers, MCHC, Washington, D.C.; General Mattis's comment is in the 20–21 March sitrep.)

15. I MEF Sitrep 181800ZMar03 to 191759Mar03 (Copy in Reynolds Working Papers at MCHC, Washington, D.C.). On the issue of synchronicity, see 1stMarDiv ComdC, Jan.–June 2003 (MCHC, Washington, D.C.), section 2, chapter 2, p. 12, and chapter 3, p. 6. Division planners considered the air war and shaping in the MEF AO to be two separate issues. For the most part, the targets in the "shock and awe" air war were far from that AO.

16. 3d MAW ComdC, Jan.–June 2003, section 3, "Sequential Listing of Significant Events." See also Acosta journal, entry for 20 May 2003, containing an excellent overview of the war from the standpoint of the MEF G-3, Col. Larry Brown.

17. See, for example, 3d MAW ComdC Jan.–June 2003 (MCHC, Washington, D.C.), section 2, p. 6, and Lobik interview.

18. Interview with Gy. Sgt. Melba L. Garza, 26 May 2003 (MCHC, Washington, D.C.).

19. Lt. Col. Gary Smythe, USA, "1st Marine Division Fire Support Coordination during Operation Iraqi Freedom," *Marine Corps Gazette,* June 2004, p. 31. In this war, many artillery missions, like counter-battery fire, were largely computerized and completed in a matter of seconds.

20. I MEF Sitrep 201800Z to 211759ZMar03 (Copy in Reynolds Working Papers, MCHC, Washington, D.C.).

21. This was later touted at a CFLCC briefing attended by the author in late March.

22. I MEF Sitreps 201800Z20Mar03 to 211759ZMar03; 211800ZMar03 to 221759ZMar03; and 221800ZMar03 to 231759ZMar03 (Copies in Reynolds Working Papers, MCHC, Washington, D.C.). See also 1stMarDiv ComdC Jan.–June 2003 (MCHC, Washington, D.C.), section 2, chapter 4.

Chapter 5

1. C. Cooper, "How a Marine Lost His Command."

2. Interview with Capt. Daniel J. Wittnam, 1 May 2003 (MCHC, Washington, D.C.); Bonadonna journal, entries for 2 and 10 March 2003; 2d MEB ComdC, Jan.–June 2003 (MCHC, Washington, D.C.), section 2.

3. Interviews with Maj. Daniel T. Canfield, 12 Dec. 2003; Lt. Col. Rickey L. Grabowski, 6 April 2003; Lt. Col. Royal P. Mortenson, 7 Nov. 2003; and Col. Ronald L. Bailey, 8 May 2003 (hereafter Bailey interview) (all at MCHC, Washington, D.C.).

4. I MEF Sitrep 211800ZMar03 to 221759ZMar03 Mar (Copy in Reynolds Working Papers, MCHC, Washington, D.C.), p. 125.

5. I MEF Sitrep 221800ZMar03 to 231759ZMar03 (Copy in Reynolds Working Papers, MCHC, Washington, D.C.).

6. See, generally, West and Smith, *March Up,* pp. 41, 59; the Company Commanders, 1st Battalion, 2d Marines, "The Battle of An Nasiriyah," *Marine Corps Gazette,* Sept. 2003, pp. 40–46. This is a good general source on the battle.

7. Bailey interview.

8. Reacting to a question about boundaries, General McKiernan commented that the events in An Nasiriyah did "not equate to any seam or any joint problem. There were

on-order boundaries, that were placed in effect both south and north of An Nasiriyah, between V Corps and I MEF, which made sense [and] which were triggered at the right time . . . I don't think the boundary shift could have gone much better." McKiernan interview no. 4. See generally 2d MEB ComdC, Jan.–June 2003 (MCHC, Washington, D.C.), section 2.

9. Natonski interview no. 2, and interview with Brig. Gen. Richard F. Natonski, 25 April 2003 (MCHC, Washington, D.C.); hereafter Natonski interview no. 1; Bailey interview.

10. An additional consideration General Natonski mentioned in a postwar interview was that the cluster of American forces south of An Nasiriyah made an excellent target for Iraqi weapons of mass destruction—a threat that was still very much on everyone's mind at the time. It is not clear whether he mentioned that point to Colonel Bailey on 23 March. Natonski interview no. 2.

11. To be sure, Marine recon elements close to the western bridge were working their way back toward Task Force Tarawa, and U.S. Army Special Forces were operating in the area on each side of the river, but this did not equate to a reconnaissance of the city itself. Reynolds journal, entry for 1 July 2004 (recording a conversation with Tarawa's G-3); Natonski interview no. 2.

12. See Maj. Walker M. Field, "Marine Artillery in the Battle of An Nasiriyah," *Marine Corps Gazette,* June 2004, pp. 26–30. General Natonski later praised 1st Battalion, 10th Marines for providing "invaluable" counter-battery fire during the battle, in addition to responding for calls for fire from Marines under attack. Natonski interview no. 2. The Bonadonna journal entries for 31 March 2003 and 30 April 2003 discuss his conclusion that the "big problems" were scant intelligence and fire support. See also Gary Livingston, *An Nasiriyah: The Fight for the Bridges* (Vernon, N.Y.: Caisson Press, 2004), pp. 172–73. This is a useful book with a number of oral histories.

13. Bailey interview. Colonel Bailey elaborated on this interview in a conversation with Colonel Bonadonna, which was subsequently relayed to the author.

14. Livingston, *An Nasiriyah,* p. 70. This may have been *sobka,* a geological phenomenon peculiar to the Middle East, which was encountered elsewhere in Iraq and mired other Marine vehicles. It may also just have been sewage, with the top layer baked into a crust.

15. Company Commanders, "Battle of An Nasiriyah"; Bonadonna journal, entry for 30 April 2003.

16. Staff Sgt. Lonnie O. Parker interview, 29 March 2003 (MCHC, Washington, D.C.).

17. Livingston, *An Nasiriyah,* p. 91; Wittnam interview, Natonski interview no. 2. Staff Sgt. Parker remembered that the RPG and small arms fire soon tapered off. Parker interview.

18. Interview with 1st Lt. Michael S. Seely, 3 May 2003 (MCHC, Washington, D.C.).

19. Wittnam interview.

20. Ibid.

21. Livingston, *An Nasiriyah,* p. 101.

22. Parker interview.

23. Col. Reed R. Bonadonna, "A Short History of Task Force Tarawa," unpublished manuscript included with Task Force Tarawa ComdC, Jan.–June 2003 (MCHC, Washington, D.C.).

24. Natonski interview no. 2. This was representative of cooperation with various special forces in the entire Marine AO, though General Mattis and General Conway eventually came to the conclusion that these operators were better at some tasks than others. In particular, they complained it could take them too long to plan a mission to take advantage of a rapidly breaking situation. See, for example, U.S. Naval Institute, "Interview: Lieutenant General James T. Conway, USMC," and chapter 12 notes below.

25. I MEF Sitrep 241800ZMar03 to 25175ZMar03 (Copy in Reynolds Working Papers, MCHC, Washington, D.C.).

26. See, for examples, Reynolds journal, entries for 1 April 2003 and 3 April 2003; Cordesman, *Iraq War,* p. 390, quoting a report: "Nasiriyah saw the culmination of this confusion over MOUT. Commanders were not prepared to go in and clear a town no bigger than Victorville"; Helene Cooper, "U.S. Troops Bypass Cities to Avoid Urban Warfare," *Wall Street Journal,* 28 March 2003; Bonadonna journal, entries for 28 March 2003 and 31 March 2003.

27. Natonski interview no. 2; Maj. [first name unknown] Bierman, "Summary of comments made by Col Johnson, G-3 Task Force Tarawa," as posted on CFLCC J-2 Web site 3 April 2003 (Copy in Reynolds Working Papers, MCHC, Washington, D.C.). As noted previously, without a doubt, there was supporting air on station and artillery on call throughout the period; the issue is whether there was an adequate amount of "prep fire."

28. McKiernan interview no. 4. See also West and Smith, *March Up,* pp. 35, 41–48, and C. Cooper, "How a Marine Lost His Command." Cooper discusses Dowdy's thought process.

29. As noted, many Marines had found that line-of-sight communication inside the city limits was terrible. For more on this controversy, see Natonski interview no. 2; Reynolds journal, entry for 1 April 2004; Wittnam interview; CentCom, "News Release 04-03-51: A-10 Friendly Fire Investigation Completed," 29 March 2004, hereafter CentCom News Release. See also Hector Becerra, Robert J. Lopez, and Rich Connell, "Report Details 'Friendly Fire' Casualties in Deadly Battle," *Los Angeles Times,* 28 March 2004. The report itself was placed online by Globalsecurity.org. Its title is M.S. Central Command, "Investigation of Suspected Friendly Fire Incident Near An Nasiriyah, Iraq, 23 March 03," dated 6 March 2004. For a thoughtful overview of friendly fire incidents during OIF-I, see Peter Pae, "'Friendly Fire' Still a Problem," *Los Angeles Times,* 16 May 2003.

30. Bonadonna, "Short History"; Bonadonna journal, entry for 23 and 24 March 2003; West and Smith, *March Up,* pp. 47, 52.

31. CentCom News Release.

32. *March Up,* p. 47; Lt. Col. Willard A. Buhl interview, 4 Nov. 2003 (MCHC, Washington, D.C.); Bonadonna journal, entry for 23 March: "The traffic was really snarled around an intersection of 2 major roads" to the south of An Nasiriyah. This

was almost certainly a reference to the point where the road from the south branched, with one branch leading to An Nasiriyah and the other to the western bridge, which meant the traffic jam was miles long.

33. Conway interview; Buhl interview; Natonski interview no. 2; West and Smith, *March Up,* p. 45.
34. Bonadonna journal, entry for 23 March 2003. For additional impressions of an officer in theater, see Kuo journal, entries for 23 and 24 March. For a relatively mild example of press commentary, see Peter Baker, "In War, Plans Yield to Improvisation," *Washington Post,* 24 March 2003, p. A-16.
35. McKiernan interview no. 4.
36. McKiernan journal, entry for 23 March 2003.
37. McKiernan interview no. 4.
38. Quoted in Bennett et al., *No Better Friend,* p. 51. What appears to be the original quote appears in Peter Baker, "Arab Volunteers Draw U.S. Scrutiny; Marine Commander Outraged by Willingness to 'Hide Behind Women,'" *Washington Post,* 9 April 2003, p. A-31.
39. Amos interview.
40. Mattis interview no. 1; I MEF Sitrep 241800ZMar03 to 251759ZMar03 (Copy in Reynolds Working Papers, MCHC, Washington, D.C.).
41. Brig. Gen. Edward G. Usher III interview, 11 May 2003 (MCHC, Washington, D.C.); hereafter Usher interview no. 2.
42. 1stMarDiv ComdC, Jan.–June 2003, section 2, chapter 5.
43. Bonadonna journal, entry for 25 March 2003.
44. Hummer interview.
45. Judge interview no. 1.
46. Reynolds journal, entry for 26 March 2003; I MEF Sitrep 261800ZMar03 to 271759ZMar03 (Copy in Reynolds Working Papers in MCHC, Washington, D.C.), which contains a reference to the suspension of air ops at the Jalibah airfield until 0300Z on that day. Atkinson, *In the Company of Soldiers,* reports that the skies finally cleared on the morning of 27 March.
47. Atkinson, *In the Company of Soldiers,* pp. 171–72.
48. McKiernan interview no. 3.

Chapter 6

1. Text of Navy Cross citation, approximate date March 2004. See Cpl. Jeremy Vought, "Rochester, N.Y., Marine Receives Navy Cross," 6 May 2004. Available at http://www.usmc.mil/marinelink/mcn2000.nsf/lookupstoryref/200456162723. See also interview with 1st Lt. Brian R. Chontosh, 4 May 2003 (MCHC, Washington, D.C.).
2. Mattis interview no. 1.
3. 1stMarDiv ComdC, Jan.–June 2003 (MCHC, Washington, D.C.), section 2, Executive Summary, p. 2.

4. Kuo journal, entry for 24 March 2003.

5. Usher interview no. 2; I MEF Sitrep 241800ZMar03 to 251759ZMar03 (Copy in Reynolds Working Papers, MCHC, Washington, D.C.).

6. Brig. Gen. Michael R. Lehnert and Col. John E. Wissler, "Marine Logistics Command, Sustaining Tempo on the 21st Century Battlefield," *Marine Corps Gazette,* Aug. 2003, pp. 30–33.

7. Interview with Brig. Gen. Michael R. Lehnert, 7 May 2003 (MCHC, Washington, D.C.). The Division G-3 commented on shortages from his perspective in an interview with Lt. Col. Clarke R. Lethin, 6 Nov. 2003 (MCHC, Washington, D.C.). For a frank discussion of the MLC and praise for General Lehnert's innovative leadership, see Hutson journal, entry for 25 April 2003.

8. Usher interview no. 2.

9. Commanders and Staff of 1st FSSG, "Brute Force Combat Service Support: 1st Force Service Support Group in Operation Iraqi Freedom," *Marine Corps Gazette,* Aug. 2003, p. 37.

10. Mattis interview no. 1. A related issue was that he wanted the Iraqis to continue to think he intended to come at Baghdad from Route 1. If they focused on Hantush, they might realize he was planning a lateral move before threatening the capital from the east. The stop order is reported in I MEF Sitrep 261800ZMar03 to 271759ZMar03 (Copy in Reynolds Working Papers, MCHC, Washington, D.C.).

11. See, for example, comments by the MEF G-3, Col. Larry K. Brown, in Acosta journal, entry for 20 May 2003 (describing a postwar symposium in Bahrain and Brown's comment to the effect that the Army had wanted a thirty-day pause), and G. W. Smith interview no. 2. Atkinson, *In the Company of Soldiers,* pp. 168, 171, 177, offers a good reflection of thinking by some senior army officers. They had a combination of concerns over supply shortages and the fedayeen, leading to a natural inclination to wait on reinforcements.

12. I MEF ComdC, Jan.–June 2003 (MCHC, Washington, D.C.), FutOps Document Folder, "CG Guidance/discussion with OPT 25 March 03." See also Elaine Grossman, "Marine General: Iraq War Pause 'Could Not Have Come at Worse Time,'" *Inside the Pentagon,* 2 Oct. 2003; Conway interview. The Marine general speaking out against the pause was General Mattis. General Conway also discussed the issue during an interview for the History Channel series on the Iraq War (released in 2003), saying he had welcomed the opportunity to do some consolidating and resupplying. The *Washington Post* reported a video teleconference on 25 March among Generals McKiernan, Wallace, and Conway, with McKiernan soliciting recommendations, Wallace expressing concerns, and Conway wanting to continue on to Baghdad. The source for this information is not clear. Rick Atkinson, Peter Baker, and Thomas E. Ricks, "Confused Start, Decisive End," *Washington Post,* 13 April 2003, p. A-1. Finally, there is a lengthy discussion of the "pause" in West and Smith, *March Up,* pp. 73–84, which conveys a picture of hard-charging Marines being held back because the Army was worried about its supply lines. That is one way to look at the situation, but there is another side, with different nuances, to this particular story.

13. Fontenot et al., *On Point*, p. 245, relies on two basic kinds of sources: Army note takers who were present at the meeting, and his interview with General McKiernan on 8 December 2003. The note takers' records are the only firsthand, contemporary—and currently available—source on the meeting.

14. Quoted in Fontenot et al., *On Point*, p. 245; see also Conway interview.

15. McKeldin journal, entry for 28 March 2003. The source for the "several days" quote is "CFLCC Update, 26 Mar 03" (OIF CD No. 65, MCHC, Washington, D.C.).

16. I MEF Sitrep 271800ZMar03 to 281759ZMar03 (Copy in Reynolds Working Papers, MCHC, Washington, D.C.).

17. McKeldin journal, entry for 29 March 2003.

18. "Lt Gen J Conway Holds Defense News Briefing via Teleconference from Iraq," Federal Document Clearing House Political Transcript of Interview, 30 May 2003.

19. I MEF Sitrep 271800ZMar03 to 281759ZMar03 (Copy in Reynolds Working Papers, MCHC, Washington, D.C.).

20. I MEF Sitrep 281800ZMar03 to 291759ZMar03 (Copy in Reynolds Working Papers, MCHC, Washington, D.C.).

21. "Lt Gen J Conway Holds Defense News Briefing."

22. I MEF Sitrep 271800ZMar03 to 281759ZMar03 (Copy in Reynolds Working Papers, MCHC, Washington, D.C.). See also 1stMarDiv ComdC, Jan.–June 2003 (MCHC, Washington, D.C.), section 2, chapter 6.

23. 2d MEB ComdC, Jan.–June 2003 (MCHC, Washington, D.C.).

24. Mattis interview no. 1.

25. Col. Charles J. Quilter II, e-mail to author, 19 Feb. 2004 (Copy in Reynolds Working Papers, MCHC, Washington, D.C.). See also I MEF Sitrep 301800ZMar03 to 311759Z Mar03 (Copy in Reynolds Working Papers, MCHC, Washington, D.C.), containing a brief account of the Amos-Mattis meeting: "True to form, 3rd MAW pledged its utmost support to the Div's planned scheme of maneuver against the Baghdad Div, to include addressing critical resupply needs."

26. Col. Charles J. Quilter e-mail to author, 21 Feb. 2004 (Copy in Reynolds Working Papers, MCHC, Washington, D.C.); Stu Saffer, "Colonel Charlie Quilter, USMC, The Oldest Marine in Iraq," *Laguna Life and People* (Laguna Beach, CA), March 2004, p. 18.

27. The concept of operations is clearly outlined in I MEF Sitrep 01800ZMar03 to 311759ZMar03 (Copy in Reynolds Working Papers, MCHC, Washington, D.C.). See also 1stMarDiv ComdC, Jan.–June 2003 (MCHC, Washington, D.C.), section 2, chapter 5.

28. Mattis interview no. 1.

29. Ibid.; Toolan interview. Generals Conway and Mattis discussed the relief before it occurred. Conway interview. It was reported in the press at the time. See, for example, Tony Perry, "Marine Commander Relieved of Duties," *Los Angeles Times*, 5 April 2003, p. A-15. A later article offers a comprehensive picture of the affair: C. Cooper, "How a Marine Lost His Command." The MCHC conducted an interview with Colonel Dowdy in December 2003 that is currently being accessioned.

Chapter 7

1. Fontenot et al., *On Point,* pp. 49–50, provides an excellent discussion of this topic, which is the basis for this paragraph.
2. See Blackman interview; 1stMarDiv ComdC, Jan.–June 2003 (MCHC, Washington, D.C.), section 2, chapter 3.
3. McKiernan interview no. 1. For further discussion, see for examples, 1stMarDiv ComdC, Jan.–June 2003 (MCHC, Washington, D.C.), esp. chapter 3, p. 13, and Atkinson, *In the Company of Soldiers,* p. 26, quoting Army Brig. Gen. Benjamin C. Freakley, the assistant division commander for operations of the 101st Airborne Division. Atkinson notes on p. 218 that this is a departure from the Army's reluctance to commit armor to an urban area, and on pp. 185–86 he notes General Wallace's preference for staying out of the cities and defeating the Iraqi army and the regime on other ground. This was obviously a minority opinion. Atkinson, on pages 287–88, comments that some Army planners believed the in-and-out raids could take weeks. West and Smith, *March Up,* p. 186, also discuss urban tactics.
4. See Reynolds journal, entries for 3 and 4 April 2003; interview with Col. Thomas C. Latsko, 22 April 2003 (MCHC, Washington, D.C.).
5. Paul Martin, "British Tactics in Basra Praised," *Washington Times,* 3 April 2003, p. 1; Peter Baker, "Tactics Turn Unconventional; Commanders Draw Lessons of Belfast in Countering Attacks," *Washington Post,* 20 March 2003, p. A-23.
6. 1stMarDiv ComdC, Jan.–June 2003 (MCHC, Washington, D.C.), section 2, chapter 3, pp. 19–20. For information on Urban Warrior, see interview with Randolph Gangle, 18 Oct. 2002 (MCHC, Washington, D.C.).
7. Gangle interview.
8. Mattis interview no. 1. This was not only Division policy, but it was also the conviction of at least one regimental commander, Col. Steven Hummer of 7th Marines, who did not want to withdraw from hard-won gains. Hummer interview.
9. 1stMarDiv ComdC, Jan.–June 2003 (MCHC, Washington, D.C.), section 2, chapter 6; West and Smith, *March Up,* p. 207.
10. McKiernan interviews no. 1 and no. 4; interview with Capt. Matthew H. Bazarian, 12 April 2003 (MCHC, Washington, D.C.), containing the comment that during Internal Look General McKiernan made it clear he did not want to have two commands splitting Baghdad.
11. I MEF ComdC, Jan.–June 2003 (MCHC, Washington, D.C.), section 2, "FutOps Command Chronology" and FutOps Documents Folder, "CG Guidance/discussion with OPT 25 Mar 03"; Buhl interview.
12. McKiernan interview no. 4.
13. McKiernan interview no. 1. For a slightly different view, see Acosta journal, entry for 20 May 2003, reporting a briefing by the MEF G-3 and his statement that "about a week before the war began, COMCFLCC gave I MEF the mission to secure eastern Baghdad." This is probably a slightly garbled reference to the branch plan.

14. I MEF ComdC, Jan.–June 2003 (MCHC, Washington, D.C.) section 2, "Future Ops"; Fontenot et al., *On Point*, p. 331. Fontenot makes the point that flexibility was intentionally built into the plan.

15. "CFLCC Update for 3 Apr 03" (Disk 65, OIF-I Document Collection, MCHC, Washington, D.C.); CFLCC Briefings (Disks 55 and 56, OIF-I Document Collection, MCHC, Washington, D.C.), entries for 3 and 4 April 2003.

16. Amos interview.

17. 1stMarDiv ComdC, Jan.–June 2003 (MCHC, Washington, D.C.), section 2, chapter 6.

18. The "digital divide" is explored in some detail in MCCDC, *OIF Summary Report*.

19. Milburn interview no. 2.

20. The general procedure at CFLCC and other major commands was for operational planning teams (OPTs), or other groups of specialists drawn from various disciplines, to study problems, propose solutions, and for senior officers to make decisions in small groups. For an excellent discussion of the BUA, see interview with Maj. Robert K. Casey, 27 April 2003 (MCHC, Washington, D.C.). There is an equally good description of how the CFLCC staff worked in the R. T. Johnson interview. The author attended numerous BUAs in March and April 2003 and heard Generals McKiernan and Blackman talk about how they wanted them to work. See also Blackman interview.

21. Judge interviews no. 1 and 2.

22. There are already numerous books and articles that address the subject of embedding. An excellent example is Atkinson, *In the Company of Soldiers*. On the Marine Corps side, there's Capt. Dan McSweeney, "Clowns to the Left of Me," U.S. Naval Institute *Proceedings*, Nov. 2003, pp. 46–48. By and large, the results of embedding were favorable all around; the reporting had more depth than it otherwise might have, and many journalists seemed more sympathetic to their subjects than they had been in previous conflicts.

23. I MEF Sitrep 051800ZApr03 to 061759ZApr03 (Copy in Reynolds Working Papers, MCHC, Washington, D.C.).

24. West and Smith, *March Up*, p. 207. This was certainly consistent with General McKiernan's command style, which was to tell commanders what he wanted them to do and then leave the rest up to them.

25. McKiernan interview no. 4 and Fontenot et al., *On Point*, chapter 6, offer a detailed discussion of the Army's movements.

26. P. J. Kennedy interview.

27. I MEF Sitrep 051800ZApr03 to 061759ZApr03 (Copy in Reynolds Working Papers, MCHC, Washington, D.C.).

28. I MEF Sitrep 061800ZApr03 to 071759ZApr03 (Copy in Reynolds Working Papers, MCHC, Washington, D.C.).

29. I MEF Sitrep 071800ZApr03 to 081759ZApr03 (Copy in Reynolds Working Papers, MCHC, Washington, D.C.).

30. 1stMarDiv ComdC, Jan.–June 2003 (MCHC, Washington, D.C.), section 2, chapter 6, p. 41.

31. Ibid. According to West and Smith, *March Up,* pp. 233–34, Colonel Hummer "forgot" to issue a withdrawal plan for this raid. This is consistent with Hummer interview. The cordon would not be fully complete until 0215Z on 9 April, when the division reported that RCT 5 had cut Highway 2, which ran to the northwest out of Baghdad, and that it had elements of the U.S. Army's V Corps in sight. I MEF Sitrep 081800ZApr03 to 091759ZApr03 (Copy in Reynolds Working Papers, MCHC, Washington, D.C.).

32. McKeldin journal, entry for 6 April 2003; Judge interview no. 1; Hummer interview.

33. 1stMarDiv ComdC, Jan.–June 2003 (MCHC, Washington, D.C.), section 2, chapter 6, p. 49; I MEF Sitrep 061800ZApr03 to 071759ZApr03 (Copy in Reynolds Working Papers, MCHC, Washington, D.C.).

34. I MEF Sitrep 071800ZApr03 to 081759ZApr03 (Copy in Reynolds Working Papers, MCHC, Washington, D.C.).

35. 1stMarDiv ComdC, Jan.–June 2003 (MCHC, Washington, D.C.), section 2, chapter 6, page 51.

36. McKeldin journal, entry for 9 April 2003.

37. Peter Baker, "Marines' Orders: Ready, Set, Switch," *Washington Post,* 10 April 2003, p. A-35. Baker's report tracks closely with the I MEF sitrep for the same time period.

38. McKeldin journal, entry for 9 April 2003.

39. 1stMarDiv ComdC, Jan.–June 2003 (MCHC, Washington, D.C.), section 2, chapter 6, p. 50.

40. Interview with Capt. Brian B. Smalley, 3 May 2003 (MCHC, Washington, D.C.).

41. Quoted in Mark Mazzetti, "Lt. Gen. James Conway, Commander of the 1st Marine Expeditionary Force," *U.S. News and World Report* Web Exclusive, 9 April 2003, p. 1.

42. Baker, "Marines' Orders." General Mattis commented later that the division had "full cooperation" from General Conway in his attack on Baghdad. As noted above, General McKiernan permitted his subordinate commanders a wide range of latitude in tactical decisions.

43. Ibid.; Conway interview; West and Smith, *March Up,* pp. 226–27, 233–34. The 1stMarDiv command chronology (section 2, chapter 6, page 50) mentions another plan that was supposedly under consideration on 9 April at "higher headquarters." This was for a second operational pause, to give the centralized authority in Baghdad a chance to turn over the city peacefully. Division and the MEF are said to have opposed the plan on the grounds that there was no longer any such authority. It is not clear how Division learned of this plan. Fontenot et al., *On Point,* chapter 6, does not report any such plan. Atkinson, *In the Company of Soldiers,* pp. 287–88, made the related point that "Army planners had anticipated that it could take weeks to reduce Baghdad through . . . raids, . . . allowing more time to bring forward military police, civil affairs, and other units required to keep order."

44. I MEF Sitrep 081800ZApr03 to 091759ZApr03 (Copy in Reynolds Working Papers, MCHC, Washington, D.C.); Hummer interview.

45. 1stMarDiv ComdC, Jan.–June 2003 (MCHC, Washington, D.C.), section 2, chapter 6, p. 53; McKeldin journal, entry for 9 April 2003. Fontenot et al., *On Point*, pp. 337–38, quotes a good firsthand account.
46. Reynolds journal, entry for 9 April 2003.
47. Dunford interview; 1stMarDiv ComdC, Jan.–June 2003 (MCHC, Washington, D.C.), section 2, chapter 6.
48. McKiernan interview no. 4. See also G. W. Smith interview no. 1, especially the comment that the coalition spent a lot of time and effort working out how it would break things but not a lot on how it would put things back together. This subject is addressed in greater detail in chapter 11 below.
49. Mazetti, "Lt. Gen. James Conway." See also Atkinson, *In the Company of Soldiers*, p. 287.
50. William Branigin and Anthony Shadid, "Authority Melts in Baghdad," *Washington Post*, 9 April 2003, p. A-1.
51. McKeldin journal, entry for 10 April 2003; I MEF Sitrep 091800ZApr03 to 101759ZApr03 (Copy in Reynolds Working Papers, MCHC, Washington, D.C.).
52. 1stMarDiv ComdC, Jan.–June 2003 (MCHC, Washington, D.C.), section 2, chapter 6, p. 65.
53. I MEF Sitrep 091800ZApr03 to 101759ZApr03 (Copy in Reynolds Working Papers, MCHC, Washington, D.C.).
54. 1stMarDiv ComdC, Jan.–July 2003 (MCHC, Washington, D.C.), section 2, chapter 6, p. 65.
55. See, for example, Jehl, "Inspector's Report Says Hussein Expected Guerrilla War." This does not mean a guerrilla war was carefully planned.
56. 2dMEB ComdC, Jan.–June 2003 (MCHC, Washington, D.C.), section 2; Text of Commander, MarForPac, "I MEF (Rein) United Award Recommendation for Presidential Unit Citation," covering the period 21 March–24 April 2003 (included as an appendix to this history).

Chapter 8

1. Mazetti, "Lt. Gen. James Conway." See also Conway interview for a report of his discussions with CFLCC on the north. For an excellent discussion of the strategic dimension, see McKiernan interview no. 1.
2. McKeldin journal, entry for 14 April 2003.
3. McKeldin journal, entry for 10 April 2003; I MEF Sitreps 081800ZApr03 to 091759ZApr03 and 091800ZApr03 to 101759ZApr03 (Copies in Reynolds Working Papers, MCHC, Washington, D.C.).
4. I MEF Sitrep 071800ZApr03 to 081759ZApr03 (Copy in Reynolds Working Papers, MCHC, Washington, D.C.).
5. West and Smith, *March Up*, p. 247, report that in September 2002, General Mattis ordered a contingency plan for a quick-moving task force to assist the Kurds if Turkey did not agree to open a northern front.

6. I MEF Sitrep 091800ZApr03 to 101759ZApr03 (Copy in Reynolds Working Papers, MCHC, Washington, D.C.), and 1stMarDiv ComdC, Jan.–June 2003 (MCHC, Washington, D.C.), section 2, chapter 7. Except where indicated, the rest of this chapter is based on these two sources. The oral histories at MCHC offer additional detail, such as that of Capt. Brian B. Smalley on 3 May 2003, who provides a vivid description of this operation from a company commander's point of view.
7. Amos interview.
8. McKeldin journal, entry for 12 April 2003; Conway interview.
9. I MEF Sitrep 121800ZApr03 to 131759ZApr03 (Copy in Reynolds Working Papers, MCHC, Washington, D.C.).
10. 1stMarDiv ComdC, Jan.–June 2003 (MCHC, Washington, D.C.), section 2, chapter 7, p. 21.
11. McKeldin journal, entry for 12 April 2003.
12. I MEF Sitreps 121800ZApr03 to 131759ZApr03 and 141800ZApr03 to 151759ZApr03 (Copies in Reynolds Working Papers, MCHC, Washington, D.C.).
13. I MEF Sitrep 181800ZApr03 to 191759ZApr03 (Copy in Reynolds Working Papers, MCHC, Washington, D.C.).
14. 1stMarDiv ComdC, Jan.–June 2003 (MCHC, Washington, D.C.), section 2, chapter 8, especially pp. 4–6, discuss this phase of the operation.
15. Ibid.; and Reynolds journal, entry for 4 May 2003. Col. Christopher C. Conlin came to much the same conclusion in his article, "What do you do for an encore?" *Marine Corps Gazette,* Sept. 2004, pp. 74–80.
16. 1stMarDiv ComdC, Jan.–June 2003 (MCHC, Washington, D.C.), section 2, chapter 8, p. 6.
17. Taken from the I MEF Casualty Report as of 14 May 2003, reported in Acosta journal, entry for 20 May 2003. These statistics include the casualties from the British division (20 KIA, 36 WIA). For the other MSCs, the breakdown was Division (22 KIA, 188 WIA); FSSG (2 KIA, 2 WIA); MAW (11 KIA, 8 WIA); Task Force Tarawa (19 KIA, 58 WIA).

Chapter 9

1. Karl Vick and Daniel Williams, "U.S. Troops Arrive in Kurd Area to Open Front," *Washington Post,* 24 March 2003, p. A-15.
2. Interview with Maj. Gen. Henry P. Osman, 19 Nov. 2003 (MCHC, Washington, D.C.).
3. Ibid.; Murray and Scales, *Iraq War,* pp. 186–95, is an excellent concise history of this operation within an operation. For information on Provide Comfort, as well as general background, see Lt. Col. Ronald J. Brown, *Humanitarian Operations in Northern Iraq, With Marines in Operation Provide Comfort* (Washington, D.C.: HQMC, History and Museums Division, 1995).
4. Jones interview.

5. Interview with Col. Robert L. Hayes III, 19 Nov. 2003 (MCHC, Washington, D.C.); Osman interview; Zinni interview.

6. Hayes interview; interview with Lt. Col. James E. Bacchus, 20 Nov. 2003 (MCHC, Washington, D.C.).

7. David Josar, "Marines, Army to Coordinate Humanitarian Aid," *European Stars and Stripes,* 30 March 2003.

8. Bacchus interview; notes on meeting with Col. Keith A. Lawless, 25 Nov. 2003 (Copy in Reynolds Working Papers, MCHC, Washington, D.C.), hereafter Lawless notes. For the MCLC, reach back worked well, validating a twenty-first century model for staffing.

9. Lawless notes.

10. Maj. Gen. H. P. Osman sitrep to Gen. J. P. Abizaid, 7 April 2003 (Copy in Reynolds Working Papers, MCHC, Washington, D.C.), hereafter Osman sitrep.

11. Bacchus interview.

12. Osman sitrep for 24 March 2003.

13. Dan Williams and Philip P. Pan, "U.S. Plans to Create Military Command in Northern Iraq," *Washington Post,* 25 March 2003, p. 20.

14. Lawless notes.

15. Osman interview.

16. Osman sitreps for 12 and 13 April 2003.

17. See interview with Col. John P. Holden (USMC), 9 June 2003 (Naval Historical Center, Washington, D.C.). At the time, Colonel Holden was serving as the deputy chief of staff for plans for the 6th Fleet.

18. Interview with Col. Andrew P. Frick, 12 Sept. 2003 (MCHC, Washington, D.C.).

19. Capt. Arnaldo L. Colon, Editor, "U.S. Marines in North Iraq, A Certain Force," n.d. (filed with 26th MEU ComdC, Jan.–June 2003 [MCHC, Washington, D.C.]).

20. Frick interview. Colon, "A Certain Force," describes the command arrangement in some detail and is generally a very good source like a command chronology narrative. It tracks closely with my other basic source on 26th MEU, the narrative summary in the command chronology, 1 Jan. 2003–30 June 2003, but includes more detail.

21. Interview with 1st Lt. Sunny-James M. Risler, 15 Oct. 2003 (MCHC, Washington, D.C.).

22. Interview with Sgt. Bryan L. Gilstrap, 16 Oct. 2003 (MCHC, Washington, D.C.).

23. Colon, "A Certain Force," reports seven confirmed kills. The *New York Times* reported that on 15 and 16 April there were seventeen Iraqis killed and thirty-nine wounded but does not specifically state that all of these casualties were from firefights at the governate building. The command chronology does not state a precise number, only that "several Iraqis were killed or wounded." 26th MEU(SOC) ComdC, Jan.–June 2003 (MCHC, Washington, D.C.). After the firefight there were allegations that the Marines had overreacted—that is, that their response had not been proportional to the threat. At Colonel Frick's behest, 26th MEU's staff judge advocate, Maj. Ian D. Brasure, conducted an informal investigation to determine if there needed to be a more formal investigation of the allegations. After talking to participants in the firefight, he came to

the conclusion that that would not be necessary. Brasure telephone conversation with author, 17 May 2004. For a general reference with mentions of the incident, the allegations, and the general mood of the city, see David Rohde, "Deadly Unrest Leaves a Town Bitter at U.S.," *New York Times,* 20 April 2003, p. A-1.

24. Colon, "A Certain Force." According to General Osman, who was apparently recording information that had been passed to him: "Col Frick decided to abandon the RCC that had been occupied based on suggestions by several local leaders. Late yesterday, the Marines guarding the RCC spotted several men establishing a machine gun position and carrying an RPG in a building situated about 200 meters from the RCC. In light of the firefight from the previous day and what appeared to be an upcoming fight, it was decided a more secure location was in order." Osman sitrep for 17 April 2003.

25. Frick interview; Holden interview. The Holden interview records the view of the MEU from the 6th Fleet perspective and contains praise for the "remarkable things" that Colonel Frick accomplished with little help and vague guidance. Holden states that the reason for redeploying the MEU after such a short period of time was that CFLCC decided that with the 101st on site, there was no longer any need for the Marines.

26. Osman sitrep for 22 April 2003.

27. The SACEur, General Jones, concluded that Osman's accomplishments were out of all proportion to the size of his unit. Jones interview. The MCLC evokes the utility of the kind of engagement that was practiced so well by officers like General Zinni when he traveled around the CentCom area of operations to establish relationships with local leaders. The military historians Murray and Scales have argued that this is the next level the U.S. military needs to reach. Just as the Marine Corps and its sister services learned how to operate lighter and faster between 1991 and 2003, there is now a need to learn how to be attuned to the cultural contexts in which they operate, refining the ability to find and manipulate "non-kinetic"—social or political—pressure points, which can often eliminate the need for "kinetic," or traditional military, interventions. See generally, Murray and Scales, *Iraq War,* especially chapter 7.

Chapter 10

1. House of Commons, *Lessons of Iraq,* Vol. 1, p. 45. As noted above, this is a great source, full of direct quotations, without the "happy" feel of many British and American lessons-learned reports.

2. McKiernan interview no. 1. See Huelfer interview for evidence of early consideration of this option by CFLCC planners.

3. House of Commons, *Lessons of Iraq,* Vol. 1, p. 44: "It was always planned that the Royal Marines Commandoes would operate in the south." As the British Marine commander, Brig. Jim Dutton, explained: "It was going to be . . . just one commando unit, in conjunction with the SEALs."

4. Ibid., p. 45.

5. R. T. Johnson interview, and interview with Col. Jeremy M. F. Robbins, RM, 16 April 2003 (MCHC, Washington, D.C.); Murray and Scales, *Iraq War*, pp. 135–36. Murray and Scales place the relationship between the British and the Americans in the Gulf in a larger context, discussing developments over the preceding decade. House of Commons, *Lessons of Iraq*, Vol. 1, pp. 32–34, states that at senior levels, British and American officials held increasingly detailed discussions about Iraq from the summer of 2002 onward. It appears there was a continuum, a series of lesser decision points, rather than one or two decisive conferences or agreements. A recent arrival on the bookshelves, John Keegan's *The Iraq War* (New York: Knopf, 2004) is said to contain useful data on the British division. Excerpts from the book on the MEF, however, contain inaccuracies and add little to the literature.

6. "Major General R. V. Brims CBE," www.nato.int/sfor/comssfor/commndsw/t000121a.htm (Copy in Reynolds Working Papers, MCHC, Washington, D.C.).

7. Reynolds journal, 22 April 2003 entry.

8. Copy in Reynolds Working Papers, (MCHC, Washington, D.C.). House of Commons, *Lessons of Iraq*, Vol. 1, p. 195, describes the British "manoeuverist" approach in much the same terms as FMFM 1: "long at the heart of British defense doctrine it is 'one in which shattering the enemy's cohesion and will to fight, rather than his materiel, is paramount.'"

9. See, for examples, G. W. Smith interview no. 2 and Hummer interview.

10. Commander 1(UK) ARMD DIV's Diary, entry for 7 March 2003 (Copy in Reynolds Working Papers, MCHC, Washington, D.C.), hereafter Commander's Diary.

11. Conway interview.

12. House of Commons, *Lessons of Iraq*, Vol. 1, p. 92. The British Ministry of Defence's *Operations in Iraq: First Reflections* (London, 7 July 2003), p. 8, states that the deployment phase was complete by 18 March; that means simply that the force had arrived in theater, not that all parts of the division were ready to cross the line of departure.

13. House of Commons, *Lessons of Iraq*, Vol. 1, p. 93.

14. Ibid., p. 94.

15. Interview with Maj. Gen. Robin V. Brims, 10 May 2003 (MCHC, Washington, D.C.). To be sure, there were one or two instances of friction between British and American officers. See note 50, chapter 3, for an example of such friction.

16. For an excellent discussion of this topic from the British point of view, see House of Commons, *Lessons of Iraq*, Vol. 1, pp. 193–95. This report points out that the distance from being a maneuverist to espousing effects-based planning is not far—they are certainly consistent.

17. See, for example, interview with Capt. Tracey A. Morris, 30 March 2003 (MCHC, Washington, D.C.).

18. Latsko interview; interview with Lt. Col. Edward C. Quinonez, 12 May 2003 (MCHC, Washington, D.C.). See also Ministry of Defence, *Operations in Iraq: Lessons for the Future* (London, 11 December 2003), p. 34: "the implications of

maintaining contact and congruence with US technological and doctrinal advances should continue to be assessed."

19. Reynolds journal, entry for 22 April 2003.
20. Jones interview.
21. Col. Nicholas E. Reynolds, "Brief by Maj Chris Parker," 11 May 2003 (Copy in Reynolds Working Papers, MCHC, Washington, D.C.).
22. Ibid.; Walker interview; Maj. Cary J. Schorsch, "UK ASE Chronology," n.d. (est. 10 May 2003) (Copy in Reynolds Working Papers, MCHC, Washington, D.C.). The value of the Marine contribution is suggested by the House of Commons report on the war, which stated that the British forces needed more practice and training when it came to close air support. House of Commons, *Lessons of Iraq,* Vol. 1., p. 63. To the same effect, see the comments of Capt. Arnold Kiefer of 1st ANGLICO, interview 17 March 2003 (MCHC, Washington, D.C.), who found that the British did not have as much experience with combined arms as did the Marine Corps and tended to view the employment of supporting arms in a sequential way. They did not use and deconflict all of their supporting arms options. Captain Kiefer added the comment that their light infantry skills were otherwise world-class.
23. Commander's Diary, entry for 20 March 2003. The implication was that the Iraqi missiles were fired in retaliation for the U.S. missile strikes against Baghdad the night before.
24. Commander's Diary, entry for 21 March; Ministry of Defence, *Lessons for the Future,* p. 12: "42 Commando's insertion started badly in appalling visibility, made worse by blowing sand and smoke from fires started the previous day. Tragically, the US Ch-46 'Sea Knight' helicopter carrying the headquarters of the Brigade Reconnaissance Force crashed. . . . With the cloud base dropping still further, the insertion was aborted, forcing the Brigade HQ rapidly to identify other aviation assets and plan a new insertion for 42 Commando at dawn, using RAF Chinook and Puma helicopters. Although the landing took place six hours late, onto insecure landing sites, and in some case miles away from those originally intended, all objectives were secured." There was apparently some bad blood over the U.S. Marine Corps' decision to abort, which may explain why the British decided to use their own assets.
25. Ibid., p. 12.
26. Commander's Diary, entry for 22 March 2003.
27. Interview with Col. Thomas D. Waldhauser, 14 April 2003 (MCHC, Washington, D.C.). Waldhauser also noted the MEU's air combat element was detached while the MEU was in Iraq. He would have preferred to keep his own ACE, but apart from that had no complaints about air support. This tracks with Task Force Tarawa's experience; its ACE had also been stripped away when it landed in Kuwait.
28. Ministry of Defence, *Lessons for the Future,* p. 25.
29. Commander's Diary, entry for 23 March 2003.
30. House of Commons, *Lessons of Iraq,* Vol. 1, p. 97.
31. Ibid.
32. Latsko interview.

33. Max Hastings, "The Real Story of How We Won," *Sunday Telegraph* (London), 7 Sept. 2003, p. 4. Murray and Scales, *Iraq War,* pp. 144–53, gives a good overview of the situation in Basrah.

34. Hastings, "The real story."

35. Ibid.; Commander's Diary, entry for 26 March 2003. As General Mattis had demonstrated outside Al Kut, the MEF was very much aware of the legal implications of besieging a city, which both the Marine and the British divisions wanted to avoid.

36. House of Commons, *Lessons of Iraq,* Vol. 1, p. 99.

37. Commander's Diary, entry for 26 March 2003.

38. Interview with Lt. Col. Donald C. Wilson, 22 April 2003 (MCHC, Washington, D.C.), described the working of British intel. See also a comment by Murray and Scales, *Iraq War,* p. 145, to the effect that the British Intelligence Service had established a network in Basrah in the decade after the Gulf War, which if accurate, suggests amazing foresight on the part of the British.

39. Murray and Scales, *Iraq War,* p. 149, gives a good description of this. According to Scales, the regime loyalists were the ones with the cell phones; if you had a cell phone, you could be a target for a British sniper. See also Latsko interview.

40. House of Commons, *Lessons of Iraq,* Vol. 1, p. 98.

41. Commander's Diary, entry for 4 April 2003.

42. Murray and Scales, *Iraq War,* pp. 150–51; Commander's Diary, entry for 5 April 2003. "Chemical Ali" was not in fact captured until the summer. See K. L. Vantran, "CentCom Officials Announce Capture of 'Chemical Ali,'" Armed Forces Information Service, 21 Aug. 2003.

43. Commander's Diary, entry for 6 April 2003. See also I MEF Sitrep 061800ZApr03 to 071759ZApr03 (Copy in Reynolds Working Papers, MCHC, Washington, D.C.).

44. Brims and Latsko interviews. According to Murray and Scales, *Iraq War,* p. 151, "the initial plan of attack was to punch deep into the city and pull back out at night. . . . [But] the operation on this 'terribly long day' was going so successfully that Major General Brims decided to finish off the Iraqis with a final stroke." To similar effect, see Sudarsan Raghavan, "British Take Most of Basra," *MiamiHerald.com,* posted on 6 April 2003, quoting the British liaison officer to the MEF, Maj. Simon Plummer, who stated that what started out as a probe became a four-pronged, final assault when it became clear there was only minimal Iraqi resistance. While both sources are certainly consistent with the British practice of exploiting opportunities, as opposed to "fighting the plan," the firsthand sources suggest a slightly more deliberate, planned approach. As General Brims commented on 10 May, the division had developed a plan and waited for the right opportunity to execute it, as opposed to simply reacting to events. Brims interview.

45. Murray and Scales, *Iraq War,* p. 152.

46. House of Commons, *Lessons of Iraq,* Vol. 1, pp. 149–50.

47. Ibid., p. 62.

48. Ibid., p. 153.

49. Ibid.

50. I MEF Sitrep 061800ZApr03 to 071759ZApr03 (Copy in Reynolds Working Papers, MCHC, Washington, D.C.).
51. House of Commons, *Lessons of Iraq,* Vol. 1, p. 156. This led into a somewhat philosophical discussion of whether the division's actions and the effects desired by the division were really in sync. The point was that the division had won the war, but was anyone on the British side set up to win the peace?

Chapter 11

1. Peter Baker, "Top Officers Fear Wide Civil Unrest; Bloodshed among Iraqis Could Create Challenge for Invading Troops," *Washington Post,* 19 March 2003, p. A-18.
2. Benson, "Brief at Naval War College." Benson was the senior planner at CFCCC. See also Franks, *American Soldier,* pp. 441, 524–26. Franks wrote that he left it to the Pentagon to plan and run postcombat operations and noted that ORHA lacked the resources it needed to do its job. Franks's decision has been criticized. See, for example, Bacevich, "Modern Major General," p. 129.
3. Moran interview. See also G. W. Smith interview no. 2; interview with Brig. Gen. Stephen Hawkins, USA (CG of C/JTF-IV), 14 March 2003 (U.S. Army Center of Military History, Washington, D.C.); and Benson, "Brief at Naval War College."
4. Interview with Lt. Col. Brian K. McCrary, 6 Nov. 2003 (MCHC, Washington, D.C.).
5. G. W. Smith interview no. 2.
6. Peter Baker, "U.S. Forces Will Redeploy into 3 Zones," *Washington Post,* 16 April 2003, p. A-31.
7. Michael R. Gordon and John Kifner, "U.S. Generals Meet in Palace, Sealing Victory," *New York Times,* 17 April 2003.
8. IMEF Sitrep 141800ZApr03 to 151759ZApr03 (Copy in Reynolds Working Papers, MCHC, Washington, D.C.), announcing the upcoming meeting.
9. I MEF ComdC, Jan.–June 2003 (MCHC, Washington, D.C.): I MEF Sequel ("Post Hostility Operations" to I MEF OpOrd 1003V "Basic Order" and "FutOps Command Chronology," Jan.–June 03. I MEF Fires helped to prepare the order; once the need for planning deep fires had passed, both MEF and CFLCC used their skills as planners of "effects-based operations" for planning and assessing Phase IV operations.
10. IMEF Sitrep 111800ZApr03 to 121759ZApr03 (Copy in Reynolds Working Papers, MCHC, Washington, D.C.).
11. Margaret Warner, "A Marine's View," Public Broadcasting System Online News Hour, 26 Sept. 2003. Good sources on the division during this period are 1stMarDiv ComdC, Jan.–June 2003 (MCHC, Washington, D.C.), section 2, chapter 8, and Brig. Gen. John F. Kelly, "Tikrit, South to Babylon," *Marine Corps Gazette,* Feb.–April 2004. (The last is a three-part article.)
12. Max Boot, "Reconstructing Iraq," *Weekly Standard,* 15 Sept. 2003.
13. Interview with Lt. Col. Patrick J. Malay, 23 Aug. 2003 (MCHC, Washington, D.C.).

14. Reynolds journal, entry for 4 May 2003.

15. See, for examples, interviews with 2d Lt. Glen J. Bayliff, 4 May 2003 (MCHC, Washington, D.C.); Lt. Col. Christopher C. Conlin, 24 Aug. 2003 (MCHC, Washington, D.C.); Lt. Col. Andrew Pappas, 20 Aug. 2003 (MCHC, Washington, D.C.); and Maj. Joseph A. Cabell, 28 Aug. 2003 (MCHC, Washington, D.C.). Lieutenant Colonel Conlin, "mayor" of An Najaf, described his experiences in that city, while Lieutenant Colonel Pappas, head of a counter-insurgency task force, expressed considerable frustration at the lack of support from CPA in restoring the infrastructure. Criticism of ORHA and CPA was almost universal among Marines interviewed by field historians. See, for additional examples, interviews with Maj. David P. Holahan, 6 Nov. 2003 (MCHC, Washington, D.C.), and Lt. Col. Robert O. Sinclair, 7 Nov. 2003 (MCHC, Washington, D.C.). Both Lieutenant Colonel Conlin and Major Cabell commented on how useful the Reservists' skills—and temperament—were.

16. For a balanced discussion of this policy, see Peter Slevin, "Wrong Turn at a Postwar Crossroads?" *Washington Post,* 20 Nov. 2003, p. A-1. This was a Pentagon decision, opposed by many in the field, including General Franks. Franks, *American Soldier,* p. 441.

17. IMEF ComdC, Jan.–June 2003 (MCHC, Washington, D.C.), section 2, "FutOps Command Chronology."

18. Pamela Hess, "Raid in Iraq's 'Indian Country,'" United Press International (Wire Service), 5 Aug. 2003. Journalist Max Boot visited the same unit shortly after Ms. Hess. See Boot, "Reconstructing Iraq." Lt. Col. Pappas has described his experiences in a comprehensive interview. Pappas interview.

19. Pappas interview.

20. Interview with Maj. Steven B. Manber, 21 Aug. 2003 (MCHC, Washington, D.C.).

21. Pamela Hess, "General: Iraq Chem-Bio Arms Intel Wrong," United Press International (Wire Service), 30 May 2003.

22. Brig. Gen. John F. Kelly, "Part III: Tikrit, South to Babylon," *Marine Corps Gazette,* April 2004, p. 46.

23. Najaf was the site of a powerful car bomb attack on 29 August. This postponed the turnover, as did a number of issues that the Spanish Brigade raised. The turnover finally occurred in early October. Reflecting his general frustration with the process, one MEF officer cracked that the turnover with the multinational division was like "stuffing cats into a seabag," while another found that many of the foreign soldiers seemed professional and ready to do their job.

24. M. Warner, "Marine's View." To the same effect, see Kelly, "Part III: Tikrit," p. 43: "Our efforts with the local population assisted us in all but eliminating violence by midsummer." Max Boot shared this view. Boot, "Reconstructing Iraq." For the dissenting civilian view, see Neil MacFarquhar, "In Najaf, A Sudden Anti-U.S. Storm," *New York Times,* 21 July 2003: "The lack of Iraqis involved in the reconstruction at all levels, widespread unemployment, and woefully inadequate means of communicating [with U.S. forces] . . . have combined to fuel an ever-higher level of frustration and anger about the American presence." Najaf was in the Marine AO.

25. 1st FSSG ComdC, July–Dec. 2003 (MCHC, Washington, D.C.), section 2, "Current Ops Narrative Summary"; IMEF ComdC, July–Dec. 2003 (MCHC, Washington, D.C.), section 2, "S-3 Operations and Training Narrative Summary"; Sgt. Matthew Miller, "1st FSSG Goes Home," 1 Oct. 2003 (Story ID No. 20031015350, posted on MarineLink).
26. Interview with Brig. Gen. Ronald S. Coleman, 20 April 2004 (MCHC, Washington, D.C.).
27. Ibid.

Chapter 12

1. For basic data on MEF-level staff judge advocates, see I MEF SJA ComdC Jan.–June 2003 (MCHC, Washington, D.C.). See also General Conway's talks on the rules of engagement in chapter 3 above and interviews with Col. William D. Durrett, 11 Feb. 2003 and 9 June 2003 (MCHC, Washington, D.C.).
2. Maj. Gen. James N. Mattis, "Commanding General's Guidance on Law of War," undated (2002?) (Copy in Reynolds Working Papers, MCHC, Washington, D.C.). It is interesting to note that one of the six books on General Mattis's reading list for his subordinate commanders was *Son Thang: An American War Crime,* by Gary Solis, which was about how the 1st Marine Division handled a war crime in Vietnam.
3. Maj. Gen. James N. Mattis, "Memorandum for All Commanders," 20 Dec. 2002 (Copy in Reynolds Working Papers, MCHC, Washington, D.C.); the division staff judge advocate, Lt. Col. John R. Ewers, remembers having "a number of conversations with both General Mattis and General Kelly [the assistant division commander] . . . about law of war . . . and the challenges posed in . . . asymmetric warfare with a foe who was expected to . . . break the rules." Lt. Col. John R. Ewers e-mails to author, 6–7 April 2004 (Copies in Reynolds Working Papers, MCHC, Washington, D.C.).
4. Ibid.; Maj. Joseph Lore e-mails to author, 5 April 2004 (Copies in Reynolds Working Papers, MCHC, Washington, D.C.).
5. Interview with Maj. Peter S. Blake, 15 April 2003 (MCHC, Washington, D.C.).
6. Interview with Col. Randall W. Holm, 31 May 2003 (MCHC, Washington, D.C.).
7. Kuo journal, entry for 29 March 2003.
8. Gidget Fuentes, "Hearing Scrutinizes Reservists' Handling of Prisoners in Iraq," *Marine Corps Times,* Dec. 2003, p. 10.
9. Evan Wright, "The Killer Elite," *Rolling Stone,* 13 June 2003 and 24 July 2003; Peter Maas, "Good Kills," *New York Times Magazine,* 20 April 2003. Wright's articles pull few punches and tell the story of a slice of the war from the E-3 to E-5 perspective. They were subsequently expanded into the book *Generation Kill* (New York: Putnam, 2004), which, while it is well written, has had mixed reviews from Marines.
10. P. J. Kennedy interview.
11. Interview with Col. Joseph F. Dunford, 17 May 2003 (CAT, Studies and Analysis Division, MCCDC).

12. Quoted in interview with Lt. Col. Mark M. Tull, 18 May 2003 (CAT, Studies and Analysis Division, MCCDC).
13. Lt. Col. Clarke R. Lethin, "1st Marine Division and Operation Iraqi Freedom," *Marine Corps Gazette,* Feb. 2004, pp. 20–22.
14. Buhl interview.
15. Reynolds journal, entry for 1 July 2004.
16. Fontenot et al., *On Point,* p. 11.
17. Two excellent sources about the overall lessons-learned process are James Jay Carafano, PhD, "After Iraq: Learning the War's Lessons," *Heritage Foundation Back-grounder,* No. 1664, 3 July 2003, and Col. Mark Cancian, "Learning the Lessons of War," 2004, unpublished article (Copy in Reynolds Working Papers, MCHC, Washington, D.C.). On the Marines in particular, see Lt. Gen. Edward Hanlon Jr., "Leaning Into the 21st Century," *Marine Corps Gazette,* Oct. 2003, pp. 15–17.
18. MCCDC, *OIF Summary Report,* p. 5. For further information, see MCCDC, "Memorandum for the Commandant of the Marine Corps/Battle Assessment Proposal," 19 Jan. 91, and Officer in Charge, MarCent Assessment Team, "Letter of Instruction (Draft)," 3 Dec. 2001 (Copies in Reynolds Working Papers, Washington, D.C.).
19. See Acosta journal, entry for 20 May 2003.
20. Reynolds journal, entry for 29 July 2003; Col. John P. Glasgow Jr. (Ret), "Editorial," *Marine Corps Gazette,* Sept. 2003, p. 2.
21. Glasgow, "Editorial."
22. Thomas E. Ricks, "Ex-Envoy Criticizes Bush's Postwar Policy," *Washington Post,* 5 Sept. 2003, p. A-13; Reynolds journal, entry for 5 Sept. 2003. For a more comprehensive look at lessons learned by General Zinni, see Anthony Zinni, "Ten Mistakes History Will Record about War in Iraq," *Defense Monitor,* Vol. XXXIII, No. 3 (May/June 2004), p. 1.
23. The focus here is on Marine lessons learned. The report of the Joint Forces Command's Joint Center for Lessons Learned highlighted achievements in the joint arena and, except for the issue of fratricide, was generally complimentary about the "jointness" of OIF. See, for example, Vernon Loeb, "Pentagon Credits Success in Iraq War to Joint Operations," *Washington Post,* 3 Oct. 2003, p. A-15.
24. This was not necessarily intended as an argument against all medium- or long-term occupations. See, for example, Gunther interview. With respect to troop strengths, some lessons-learned analysts disagreed with General Mattis's point of view and argued that especially for Phase IV the force had to be much heavier than it had been; the Army chief of staff, Gen. Eric Shinseki, made the famous comment that it would take some four hundred thousand troops to occupy Iraq, and that it would have been better to sacrifice some speed in order to have deployed more force. A slower, heavier force might have gotten the job done better than the fast, light force that conquered Iraq in twenty-one days; the argument, which is generally inconsistent with current Marine thinking about how to fight the MAGTF, is that since the Iraqis were unable to put up much of a fight, it would have been better to proceed more methodically, securing and occupying terrain as the coalition moved forward. This is one of the

general implications of Fontenot et al., *On Point,* and of the 3d ID's after-action report. See, for example, John L. Lumpkin and Dafna Linzer, "Army: Plan for Iraq Flawed," *Hartford Journal,* 28 Nov. 2003, p. A-1. Two thoughtful articles that explore the background to Phase IV in more depth are George Packer, "Letter from Baghdad: War after the War; What Washington Doesn't See in Iraq," *New Yorker,* 24 Nov. 2003, pp. 59–85; Tom Donnelly and Gary Schmitt, "The Right Fight Now," *Washington Post,* 26 Oct. 2003, p. B-1. Packer's article addresses the general topic of postwar reconstructions in the twenty-first century, and concludes that (a) it is lengthy process, (b) it is better when internationalized, and (c) the foundation of success is security. He then goes on to discuss the Pentagon's initial decision not to plan for a long-term occupation. Donnelly and Schmitt highlight the Marines' *Small Wars Manual,* which they say is as good a guide as any to postwar reconstruction. One year after the invasion, the *Foreign Service Journal* (March 2004) printed a number of articles on Phase IV, which did a good job of covering this ground.

Selected Bibliography

Acosta, Jeffrey. "OIF Field History Journal." Unpublished manuscript. MCHC, Washington, D.C. 2003

Allen, Vanessa. "'Great to Have You Aboard' U.S. General Tells Brits," The Press Association (Web-based wire service), 14 March 2003.

Atkinson, Rick. *In the Company of Soldiers.* New York: Henry Holt, 2004.

Atkinson, Rick, Peter Baker, and Thomas E. Ricks. "Confused Start, Decisive End." *Washington Post,* 13 April 2003, p. A-1.

Bacevich, Andrew. "A Modern Major General." *New Left Review,* Sept./Oct. 2004, pp. 123–34.

Baker, Peter. "Arab Volunteers Draw U.S. Scrutiny; Marine Commander Outraged by Willingness to 'Hide Behind Women.'" *Washington Post,* 9 April 2003, p. A-31.

———. "In War, Plans Yield to Improvisation." *Washington Post,* 24 March 2003, p. A-16.

———. "Marines' Orders: Ready, Set, Switch." *Washington Post,* 10 April 2003, p. A-35.

———. "Overtaken by Events, the Battle Plans Are Tossed Aside." *Washington Post,* 21 March 2003, p. A-20.

———. "Tactics Turn Unconventional; Commanders Draw Lessons of Belfast in Countering Attacks." *Washington Post,* 20 March 2003, p. A-23.

———. "Top Officers Fear Wide Civil Unrest; Bloodshed among Iraqis Could Create Challenge for Invading Troops." *Washington Post,* 19 March 2003, p. A-18.

———. "U.S. Forces Will Redeploy into 3 Zones." *Washington Post,* 16 April 2003, p. A-31.

Becerra, Hector, Robert J. Lopez, and Rich Connell. "Report Details 'Friendly Fire' Casualties in Deadly Battle." *Los Angeles Times,* 28 March 2004.

Bennett, Captain Lara A., et al. *No Better Friend, No Worse Enemy.* Camp Pendleton, Cal.: 1st Marine Division, 2004.

Benson, Kevin. "Brief at Naval War College." 25 Aug. 2004. Copy in Reynolds Working Papers, MCHS, Washington, D.C.

Bonadonna, Reed R. "Field Historian Journal." Unpublished manuscript. MCHC, Washington, D.C.

———. "A Short History of Task Force Tarawa," unpublished manuscript in Task Force Tarawa ComdC, January–June 2003. MCHC, Washington, D.C.

Boot, Max. "Reconstructing Iraq." *Weekly Standard,* 15 Sept. 2003.

Branigin, William, and Anthony Shadid. "Authority Melts in Baghdad." *Washington Post,* 9 April 2003, p. A-1.

Brown, Ronald J. *Humanitarian Operations in Northern Iraq, With Marines in Operation Provide Comfort.* Washington, D.C.: USMC, History and Museums Division, 1995.

———. *With Marines in Operation Provide Comfort: Humanitarian Operations in Northern Iraq.* Washington, D.C.: USMC History and Museums Division, 1995.

Carafano, James Jay. "After Iraq: Learning the War's Lessons." *Heritage Foundation Backgrounder,* No. 1664, 3 July 2003.

Catton, Bruce. *Grant Takes Command.* Boston: Little, Brown, 1969.

Clarke, Richard A. *Against All Enemies.* New York: Free Press, 2004.

Coll, Steve. "Hussein Was Sure of Own Survival; Aide Says Confusion Reigned on Eve of War." *Washington Post,* 3 Nov. 2003, p. A-1.

"Colonel Tim: The Making of a Modern Hero." *Independent on Sunday* (London), 25 May 2003, Features Section.

Commanders and Staff of 1st FSSG. "Brute Force Combat Service Support: 1st Force Service Support Group in Operation Iraqi Freedom." *Marine Corps Gazette,* Aug. 2003, p. 37.

Conlin, Christopher C. "What do you do for an encore?" *Marine Corps Gazette,* Sept. 2004, pp. 74–80.

Cooper, Christopher. "How a Marine Lost His Command in the Race to Baghdad." *Wall Street Journal,* 5 April 2004, p. 1.

Cooper, Helene. "U.S. Troops Bypass Cities to Avoid Urban Warfare." *Wall Street Journal,* 28 March 2003.

Cordesman, Anthony H. *The Iraq War: Strategy, Tactics, and Military Lessons.* Washington, D.C.: CSIS, 2003.

Donnelly, Tom, and Gary Schmitt. "The Right Fight Now." *Washington Post,* 26 Oct. 2003, p. B-1.

Ennis, Michael E. "A New Operating Environment." *Marine Corps Gazette,* Aug. 2002, p. 46f.

Field, Maj. Walker M. "Marine Artillery in the Battle of An Nasiriyah." *Marine Corps Gazette,* June 2004, pp. 26–30.

Fontenot, Gregory, E. J. Degen, and David Tohn. *On Point: The United States Army in Operation Iraqi Freedom.* Fort Leavenworth, Kan.: Combat Studies Institute Press, 2004.

Franks, Tommy. *American Soldier.* New York: Regan Books, 2004.

Fuentes, Gidget. "Hearing Scrutinizes Reservists' Handling of Prisoners in Iraq." *Marine Corps Times,* Dec. 2003, p. 10.

Givens, Robert P. *Turning the Vertical Flank.* Maxwell Air Force Base, Ala.: Air University Press, 2002.

Gordon Michael R., and General Bernard E. Trainor. *The Generals' War.* Boston: Little, Brown, 1995.

Gordon, Michael R., and John Kifner. "U.S. Generals Meet in Palace, Sealing Victory." *New York Times,* 17 April 2003.

Grimston, Jack, and John Elliott. "First Picture of Man Who Denounced Tim Collins." *Sunday Times* (London), 25 May 2003, page 1.

Grossman, Elaine M. "To Understand Insurgency in Iraq: Read Something Old, Something New." *Insider,* 2 Dec. 2004.

Hanlon, Edward, Jr. "Leaning Into the 21st Century." *Marine Corps Gazette,* Oct. 2003, pp. 15–17.

Hastings, Max. "The Real Story of How We Won." *Sunday Telegraph* (London), 7 Sept. 2003, p. 4.

Hess, Pamela. "General: Iraq Chem-Bio Arms Intel Wrong." United Press International (Wire Service), 30 May 2003.

———. "Raid in Iraq's 'Indian Country.'" United Press International (Wire Service), 5 Aug. 2003.

Hines, Jay E. "Operation Enduring Freedom." In *21st Century Defense: U.S. Joint Command.* Clearwater, Fla.: Belmont International, 2002.

Hoffman, Frank G. "The U.S. Marine Corps in Review," U.S. Naval Institute *Proceedings,* May 2002, p. 84.

Holtermann, Capt. Jay M. "The 15th Marine Expeditionary Unit's Seizure of Camp Rhino." *Marine Corps Gazette,* June 2002, pp. 41–43.

House of Commons Defence Committee. *Lessons of Iraq,* Vol. 1. London: Stationery Office, 2004.

Jehl, Douglas. "Inspector's Report Says Hussein Expected Guerrilla War." *New York Times,* 8 Oct. 2004, p. A-6.

Josar, David. "Marines, Army to Coordinate Humanitarian Aid." *European Stars and Stripes,* 30 March 2003.

Kelly, John F. "Tikrit, South to Babylon." *Marine Corps Gazette,* February—April 2004.

Koltz, Tony. *Battle Ready.* New York: G. P. Putnam's Sons, 2004.

Lang, Patrick. "Drinking the Kool-Aid." *Middle East Policy,* Summer 2004, pp. 39–60.

Lehnert, Michael R., and Col. John E. Wissler. "Marine Logistics Command, Sustaining Tempo on the 21st Century Battlefield." *Marine Corps Gazette,* Aug. 2003, pp. 30–33.

Livingston, Gary. *An Nasiriyah: The Fight for the Bridges.* Vernon, N.Y.: Caisson Press, 2004.

Loeb, Vernon. "Pentagon Credits Success in Iraq War to Joint Operations." *Washington Post,* 3 Oct. 2003, p. A-15.

Lumpkin, John L., and Dafna Linzer. "Army: Plan for Iraq Flawed." *Hartford Journal,* 28 Nov. 2003, p. A-1.

Maas, Peter. "Good Kills." *New York Times Magazine,* 20 April 2003.

MacFarquhar, Neil. "In Najaf, A Sudden Anti-U.S. Storm." *New York Times,* 21 July 2003.

Mann, Edward C., III, Gary Endersby, and Thomas R. Searle. *Thinking Effects: Effects-Based Methodology for Joint Operations.* Maxwell Air Force Base, Ala.: Air University Press, 2002.

Mann, James. *Rise of the Vulcans: The History of Bush's War Cabinet.* New York: Viking, 2004.

Martin, Paul. "British Tactics in Basra Praised." *Washington Times,* 3 April 2003, p. 1.

Mattis, James N. "The Professional Edge." *Marine Corps Gazette,* Feb. 2004.

Mazzetti, Mark. "Fighting Words: A Marine Commander Readies His Troops for Combat." *U.S. News and World Report* Web Exclusive, 17 March 2003.

———. "Lt. Gen. James Conway, Commander of the 1st Marine Expeditionary Force." *U.S. News and World Report* Web Exclusive, 9 April 2003, p. 1.

McKeldin, Theodore R., III. "OIF Field History Journal." Unpublished manuscript. MCHC, Washington, D.C.

McMaster, H. R. *Dereliction of Duty.* New York: Harper Collins, 1997.

McSweeney, Dan. "Clowns to the Left of Me." U.S. Naval Institute *Proceedings,* Nov. 2003, pp. 46–48.

"Ministry Clears RIR Iraq Hero." *Belfast News Letter,* 2 Sept. 2003, p. 6.

Ministry of Defence (London). *Operations in Iraq: Lessons for the Future.* 11 Dec. 2003.

Murray, Williamson, and Maj. Gen. Robert H. Scales Jr. *The Iraq War.* Cambridge, Mass.: Harvard UP, 2003.

Oliver, Sarah. "Not the Beginning, It's the End: The Words of Lieutenant Colonel Tim Collins." *Mail on Sunday,* 16 March 2003, pp. 6–7.

Packer, George. "Letter from Baghdad: War after the War; What Washington Doesn't See in Iraq." *New Yorker,* 24 Nov. 2003, pp. 59–85.

Pae, Peter. "'Friendly Fire' Still a Problem." *Los Angles Times,* 16 May 2003.

Parker, Nick. "Countdown to Conflict." *The Mirror,* 15 March 2003, pp. 6–7.

Peraino, Kevin. "Low-Key Leader/Lt. Gen. David McKiernan Is the Soft-spoken Soldier with the Hard Job of Commanding U.S. Ground Forces in Iraq." *Newsweek* Web Exclusive, 19 March 2003.

Perry, Tony. "Marine Commander Relieved of Duties." *Los Angeles Times,* 5 April 2003, p. A-15.

Purdum, Todd S. *A Time of Our Choosing: America's War in Iraq.* New York: Henry Holt, 2003.

Quilter, Charles J., II. *With the I Marine Expeditionary Force in Desert Shield and Desert Storm.* Washington, D.C.: USMC, History and Museums Division, 1993.

Raghavan, Sudarsan. "British Take Most of Basra," *MiamiHerald.com,* posted on 6 April 2003.

Reynolds, Col. Nicholas E. "OIF Field History Journal." Unpublished manuscript. MCHC, Washington, D.C.

Ricks, Thomas E. "Ex-Envoy Criticizes Bush's Postwar Policy." *Washington Post,* 5 Sept. 2003, p. A-13.

Saffer, Stu. "Colonel Charlie Quilter, USMC, The Oldest Marine in Iraq." *Laguna Life and People* (Laguna Beach, Cal.), March 2004.

Slevin, Peter. "Wrong Turn at a Postwar Crossroads?" *Washington Post,* 20 Nov. 2003, p. A-1.

"The Smearing of Colonel Tim; The Eve of Battle Speech." *Daily Mail* (London), 22 May 2003, p. 9.

Stearns, LeRoy D. *The 3rd Marine Aircraft Wing in Desert Shield and Desert Storm.* Washington, D.C.: USMC History and Museums Division, 1999.

U.S. Marine Corps. "Expeditionary Maneuver Warfare." *Marine Corps Gazette,* Feb. 2002, pp. A-1 through A-10.

——. *Operation Enduring Freedom Combat Assessment Team Summary Report.* Quantico, Va.: Marine Corps Combat Development Command, 2003.

——. *Planning* (Marine Corps Doctrinal Publication). Washington, D.C.: Department of Navy, 1997.

U.S. Naval Institute. "Interview: Lieutenant General James T. Conway, USMC." U.S. Naval Institute *Proceedings,* November 2003.

Vantran, K. L. "CentCom Officials Announce Capture of 'Chemical Ali.'" Armed Forces Information Service, 21 Aug. 2003.

Vick, Karl, and Daniel Williams. "U.S. Troops Arrive in Kurd Area to Open Front." *Washington Post,* 24 March 2003, p. A-15.

Visconage, M. D. "OIF Field History Journal." Unpublished manuscript. MCHC, Washington, D.C. 2003.

Warner, Margaret. "A Marine's View." Public Broadcasting System Online News Hour, 26 Sept. 2003.

Williams, Dan, and Philip P. Pan. "U.S. Plans to Create Military Command in Northern Iraq." *Washington Post,* 25 March 2003, p. 20.

Woodward, Bob. *Plan of Attack.* New York: Simon and Schuster, 2004.

Wright, Evan. *Generation Kill.* New York: Putnam, 2004.

——. "The Killer Elite." *Rolling Stone,* 13 June 2003 and 24 July 2003.

Zinni, Anthony. "Ten Mistakes History Will Record about War in Iraq." *Defense Monitor,* Vol. XXXIII, No. 3 (May/June 2004), p. 1.

Index

Note: Page numbers followed by the letter *n*, plus a number, refer to endnotes.

About the Author

Col. Nicholas Reynolds joined the Marine Corps in 1975. He served on active duty in the infantry before joining the Reserves, eventually becoming Officer in Charge of Field History. He has written two other histories for the Marine Corps and holds a D.Phil. degree in history from Oxford University.

The Naval Institute Press is the book-publishing arm of the U.S. Naval Institute, a private, nonprofit, membership society for sea service professionals and others who share an interest in naval and maritime affairs. Established in 1873 at the U.S. Naval Academy in Annapolis, Maryland, where its offices remain today, the Naval Institute has members worldwide.

Members of the Naval Institute support the education programs of the society and receive the influential monthly magazine *Proceedings* and discounts on fine nautical prints and on ship and aircraft photos. They also have access to the transcripts of the Institute's Oral History Program and get discounted admission to any of the Institute-sponsored seminars offered around the country.

The Naval Institute also publishes *Naval History* magazine. This colorful bimonthly is filled with entertaining and thought-provoking articles, first-person reminiscences, and dramatic art and photography. Members receive a discount on *Naval History* subscriptions.

The Naval Institute's book-publishing program, begun in 1898 with basic guides to naval practices, has broadened its scope to include books of more general interest. Now the Naval Institute Press publishes about one hundred titles each year, ranging from how-to books on boating and navigation to battle histories, biographies, ship and aircraft guides, and novels. Institute members receive significant discounts on the Press's more than eight hundred books in print.

Full-time students are eligible for special half-price membership rates. Life memberships are also available.

For a free catalog describing Naval Institute Press books currently available, and for further information about subscribing to *Naval History* magazine or about joining the U.S. Naval Institute, please write to:

Customer Service
U.S. Naval Institute
291 Wood Road
Annapolis, MD 21402-5034
Telephone: (800) 233-8764
Fax: (410) 269-7940
Web address: www.navalinstitute.org

visiting the café a few times we noticed an American Master Sergeant watching us from across the room. He seemed quite presentable, with grey hair and bright blue eyes.

"He seems more dignified than those hanging round St Philip's churchyard," Kath observed and I agreed. Eventually he introduced himself. His name was Bill Brock and he was stationed at Honeybourne, dealing with American army pay. He was interested in the Bard's plays and we discussed them, sometimes with a friend of his, Ben, as we waited for our bus, at the pub adjacent to the bus stop. I told them how I'd feigned illness and stayed off school so that I wouldn't have to quote Shakespeare from memory. After seeing 'Twelfth Night' at the Memorial Theatre earlier in the war with a friend I began to appreciate the Bard's work.

The mellow golden sunshine was still with us, softening the ugliness of the black huts and prefabricated camp buildings. Rising to Reveille was still no hardship, although the water at the 'Ritz' seemed colder as each day passed. Washing routine would be a bleak prospect in the depths of winter.

We still sat alone at our table in the mess although Taffy One and her sister always waved to us, and most of the men did too.

We still hadn't made up our minds about the tea but the food was good and plentiful. We were finishing lunch one day when Jack came in to tell us that there was a job to be done on the far side of camp. Olly arrived with the pick-up truck and the three of us piled into the back with our bikes.

"Are we going to that beet field Jack?" I asked.

"Sarge said he was going to let us have a go on the tractor."

Jack laughed, "Not yet, me flowers but you're going to love this job!"

Obviously he wasn't going to reveal anything more, so we would have to be patient. Presently Olly stopped the truck at the door of a Nissen hut which stood behind a hangar. Sarge was waiting and he grinned at us as we climbed out.

"I got just the job for you today, girls."

I had never smelled rotting potatoes before. It was nothing short of... unique. The hut was stacked from floor to ceiling with rotting potatoes. As there had been a bumper crop of potatoes the previous year the seed potatoes had been conveniently forgotten until an administrative officer, secretly known to us as Ginger Elephant, had one day opened the door, sniffed the air and immediately bellowed for the gardeners. So Sarge, anxious to please his superiors as usual had decided to give us the job of sorting out the gooey mess. He told us what he wanted us to do as we stood, almost holding our noses.

"Now then, I want yer to climb up and push them sacks to the floor." Muriel stared at him, "They'll burst all over the place!"

"And haven't you got a ladder?" asked Kath as she looked at the height of the piles.

He muttered, "Sort 'em out and re-sack 'em in clean 'uns. You can climb up easily enough." He indicated a pile of unused sacks in one corner. We exchanged glances and the men retired with the excuse of pressing business elsewhere.

The smell was so diabolical that Kath said, "I think we ought to buy some cigarettes to take the smell away. We can get some at the NAAFI."

Muriel and I agreed somewhat reluctantly as we had never been smokers. On the second day of our incarceration Squadron Leader Goslett arrived, peered in through the haze of cigarette smoke, sniffed delicately and asked,

"How are you getting along, ladies?"

Before we could remove our fag ends from our parched lips he had gone. I was glad that my Woodbine had been lent a little dignity by a carved wooden cigarette holder given to me by one of the Admin. Clerks!

Between puffs I said darkly, "I don't know about you two but I know who I'd like to shut in here."

Kath and Muriel guessed correctly, "Sarge?"

That night in the King's Head we drank cold cider gratefully and told Bob the PI Sergeant about the job we were doing.

"You girls are marvellous!" he said admiringly. "I just hope that Bert Lenner appreciates you!"

We doubted it but were delighted to receive this piece of unsolicited praise.

"I'm beginning to think those three have retired now they've got you ladies," he smiled, "You've done wonders."

Presently another Sergeant arrived and Bob introduced us. He was 'Don' Harrison, in charge of night photography courses. He stared at me in a disconcerting way.

"What's wrong?" I asked, somewhat embarrassed.

"Sorry," he smiled, "I can't get away from work. You're very photogenic, miss; I'd like to take some studies of you."